Web Survey Creator

Reference Guide

© Julian Cole. All rights reserved.
ISBN 978-1-291-16061-1
Third Edition (WSC 2.0)

Table of Contents

SURVEYS ON THE WEB 11
   WHAT IS A WEB SURVEY? 12
      Challenges faced when creating a Web Survey 12
      The rise of Hosted Survey Tools 12
      Is Desktop Survey Design software dead? 12
      Anonymous vs. Non-Anonymous Web Surveys 13
   CONSIDERATIONS WHEN BUILDING WEB SURVEYS 14
      Planning is Key 14
      Ensure you have a purpose! 14
      Don't Be Ambiguous 14
      Keep it Short! 14
      Think about the End Result - Reports 14
   USING WEB SURVEY CREATOR FOR WEB SURVEYS 15
      Opening WSC for the First Time 15
      Activating your Account 17
      Where to get help 17

CREATING OUR FIRST SURVEY 19
   START WITH A PLAN! 20
   CREATING A SURVEY 20
      Adding Pages 21
      Adding our Name Question 22
      Adding our Age Question 24
      Adding our Products Question 25
      Adding our Satisfaction Questions 29
      Adding our Comments Question 30
   PREVIEWING THE SURVEY 31
      Showing a preview to other people 31
   STEP-BY-STEP VIDEO 32
   USING ADVANCED FORMATTING IN YOUR SURVEYS 33
      What are Content Tags? 33
      Where can Content Tags be used? 33
      Listing of Content Tags and their Usage 33
      Example of Content Tag usage 34
   SURVEY THEMES 34
      Components 34
      Structure of Theme 35
      Specific Styles 36
      Question Styles 37
      Other Styles 37
      Percentage Bar and Banner Images 37

SURVEY FLOWS 39
   WHAT ARE SURVEY FLOWS? 40

Example of a needed Flow in the Satisfaction Survey 40
CREATING A SURVEY FLOW IN WEB SURVEY CREATOR 41
   Flow Control Conditions 42
   Conditions with multiple rules 44
   Returning to the Survey Design 44
   Testing the Flow 45
STEP-BY-STEP VIDEO 45

DATA PIPING 47

IMPROVING OUR CUSTOMER SATISFACTION SURVEY 48
SETTING UP DATA PIPING 49
   Step 1: Create an "Access Code" 49
   Step 2: Using an "Access Code" in our Content 49
   Step 3: Test the Data Pipe 50
STEP-BY-STEP VIDEO 51
QUESTION DATA PIPING REFERENCE 52
   An Example of more complex Data Piping – Matrix Questions 52
   Standards Used in this Reference Guide 53
   Data Grids (e.g. Matrix Questions) 54
   Numeric Grids 54
   Date Time Questions 54
   Demographic Address 55
   Demographic Email 55
   Demographic Name 55
   Demographic Phone 55
   Drop Down List 56
   Multiple Selection List 56
   Single Line Text 56
   Multiple Line Text 56
   Numeric 56
   Ranking 57
   Single Selection List 57
   Slider 57
   Star Rating 57
DISTRIBUTION TAGS – CREATING AND PIPING 58
PIPING INTO POST-RESPONSE EMAILS 59
   Email Content 60

SURVEY DISTRIBUTION 61

WHEN TO USE ANONYMOUS SURVEYS 62
   Creating Survey with an Anonymous Distribution 62
VIEWING A DISTRIBUTION 62
   Starting and Stopping a Survey Accepting Responses 63
   Opening the Survey or Distributing the Survey Link 64
   Placing a Survey Link on a Web Site 65
   Embedding a Survey into another Site 65
   Using a QRCode on Mobile Devices 65
   Sharing the Survey on Facebook or Twitter 66
   What happens when a Respondent clicks a link? 66
EDITING A DISTRIBUTION 66
   Setting up a Custom Link 68
   Tracking IP addresses 68

Starting, stopping and Restarting Surveys 68
Dealing with Anonymity 69
Survey Completion Settings 70
Survey Password 71
Survey Embedding Options 71
CREATING A RESPONDENT DISTRIBUTION 71
ADDING RESPONDENTS TO A DISTRIBUTION 73
Import Method #1: New Respondents from Text or File 73
Import Method #2: Update Existing Respondents from Text or File 75
Import Method #3: Import Respondents from another Survey 77
Import Method #4: From an Address Book 78
IMPORTING RESPONSE DATA 81
SENDING AN INVITATION 83

SURVEY REPORTS **85**
WHAT IS A "REPORT"? 86
Opening the Statistics Overview 86
Navigation in the Overview Portal 86
Working with Overview Charts 86
CREATING AN EXTERNAL WEB PORTAL 87
What is a Web Portal? 87
Creating a Web Portal 88
CONTROLLING ACCESS TO WEB PORTALS 94
Creating Multiple Portals 94
Closing a Portal 94
WEB SURVEY CREATOR REPORTS & EXPORTS 95
Responses Export 97
Choices & Comments 97
SPSS Export 98
SurveyCraft Export 99
Using Previously Created Reports 99

CREATING MARKET RESEARCH SURVEYS **101**
CHALLENGES FACING MARKET RESEARCH PROFESSIONALS DOING WEB SURVEYS 102
Creating complex Web Surveys efficiently 102
Avoiding the Software "tax" 102
Need for high quality, unbiased responses 102
Need for a balanced group of Respondents 102
Keeping up with the move to mobile 103
Integration with other software packages 103
DEALING WITH BIAS 103
Choice Randomization 104
Matrix Randomization 108
Page Randomization 109
Tips for Page Randomization 109
A/B Testing 110

QUOTA MANAGEMENT **113**
WHY USE QUOTAS? 114
The "More is Better" Rule 114
The "Balance is Better" Rule 114
HOW CAN QUOTAS BE MANAGED? 115

    Early Survey Termination 115
  SETTING QUOTA RULES 115
    Dealing with Tough Quotas 116
    Quota Overflow 116
  TIPS FOR QUOTA MANAGEMENT 117
    Adding quotas after a survey has commenced 117
    Testing whether someone fails the quotas in multiple places within a survey 118
  QUOTA MANAGEMENT EXAMPLE 119
    Makeup of Respondents Required 119
  PREPARING OUR SURVEY 119
    Gender/Age/Location Questions 119
    Quota Fail Terminate Page 121
  CREATING OUR QUOTAS 121
    Using the Quota Builder 121
    Creating the Location Quotas 124
  ADDING QUOTA FAIL TERMINATE PAGE LOGIC 125
  MANUAL ADJUSTMENT OF QUOTAS 127
    Adding a Single Quota 127
    Editing a Quota 128
    Editing Multiple Quotas at once 128
  TRACKING QUOTAS 129
    Current Status of Quotas 129
    Response Counts 130
    Individual Question Statistics 130

MOBILE SURVEYS 131

  MOBILE VS. DESKTOP 132
    The humble P.C. is far from dead 132
    Mobile doesn't have to mean basic 132
  LAYOUT MANAGEMENT 133
    Text Entry 134
    Question "Morphing" 134
  KEEPING THE "SEXY" IN YOUR SURVEYS 135
    Gotta have Video! 135
    Touch-enabled Sliders 135
    Drag 'n' Drop 136
  GOING MOBILE: WORKING SMARTER, NOT HARDER 136
  AN EXAMPLE SURVEY 136
    Making a WSC survey mobile-capable 137
    Targeting Specific Platforms 138

MIXED MODE SURVEYS 141

  WELCOME TO CATI! 142
  SETTING UP YOUR CATI PROCESS – THE BASICS 142
    Overview of Key Aspects of CATI Survey Setup 143
  CATI RESPONDENTS 145
    Types of Respondent Data 145
    Importing Respondent Data – An Example 147
  CHANGING SYSTEM-WIDE CATI SETTINGS 152
    Setting up CATI Users 152

  Setting User Filters *155*
  Setting Time Zone Rules *157*
  Setting up CATI Stations *159*
  Setting up CATI Statuses *159*
 Setting up Interviewer Screen Viewing 164
  Installing Screen Viewer Software on a Workstation *165*
  Setting up a Workstation for Screen Viewing *169*
  Viewing a Workstation through WSC *170*
 The CATI Interviewer Module 172
  Key Features of the Interviewer Module *172*
 The Mixed-Mode Workflow 178
  A Basic CATI Workflow *179*
  Making an Appointment *182*
  Sending a Link to a Survey via Email *184*
 How does CATI find the "Next Contact"? 186
  Getting the pool of "Valid" Respondents to Call *186*
  Ordering the pool of "Valid" Respondents *188*
 Mixed Mode Appendix: Listing of Time Zone Codes 189

RESEARCH PANEL INTEGRATION 203

 Overview of Research Panels 204
 Using a Research Panel 205
  Setting a respondent's unique code *205*
  Passing back the Survey Result *206*
 Panel Example: SurveyVillage 207
  Completes *207*
  Screen Outs *207*
  Quota Outs *207*
 Integration of Web Surveys with Contact Profiler 209
  What is Contact Profiler? *209*
  Why use Integration? *209*
  Who can use Integration? *209*
  Web Survey Integration Overview *209*
  Integration Checklist *209*
  Overview of the Integration Process *211*
  Hey, what just happened? *214*
 Integrating with Contact Profiler Screeners 215
  What are Respondent Screeners? *215*
  Screeners in Contact Profiler *216*
  The Contact Profiler Workflow *216*
  How WSC fits in the standard Workflow *216*
  Screener Integration: Step-by-Step *217*

PRODUCT TESTING 221

 The Problem with Product Testing 222
 Using Surveys to do Product Tests 222
  Base list of Products *222*
  Questions for Each Product *222*
  Advanced Survey Functionality *223*
  Page Looping *223*
  Flow Control *223*
  Data Piping *224*

    Choice Linking *224*
  PRODUCT TESTING EXAMPLE 225
    Our Products *225*
    Product Questions *225*
    Setting up the Product Test *225*
  CREATING OUR EXAMPLE 226
    Our Initial Question *226*
    Looping Source Pages *227*
    Product Questions *227*
    Data Piping the Brand Name *227*
    Data Piping the Models for a Brand *228*
    Flow Control *230*
    Choice Linking *233*
    Building the Page Loops *235*
    Page Looping - What just happened?! *237*
    What do I do with all these pages? *238*
    Page Looping DOs and DON'Ts *239*

INTRODUCTION TO SCRIPTING 241

  WHAT IS SCRIPTING? 242
    To Script or not to Script? *242*
  AN INTRODUCTION TO JAVASCRIPT 243
    JavaScript is the most popular *243*
    JavaScript works Everywhere *244*
    JavaScript can react to Events *244*
  JAVASCRIPT BASICS 244
    The <script> tag *244*
    JavaScript is Case Sensitive *244*
    JavaScript Code Essentials *245*
  ADDING SCRIPTING IN WSC 251
    WSC Scripting Objects *251*
    How to Use a Question in Scripting *252*
    How to add Scripting to a Survey *252*

SCRIPTING #101: DEALING WITH DATA 255

  WORKING WITH DATA IN SCRIPTING 256
    Rule #1: Script for each Question Type *256*
    Rule #2: Data Location effects Script syntax *257*
    Getting Data for Questions on the Current Page *257*
    Getting Data for Questions on a Previous Page *257*
  READING AND WRITING DATA – THE BASICS 258
    Writing Data to a Text Question *258*
    Reading Data from a Text Question *260*
  DATA SCRIPTING FOR OTHER QUESTION TYPES 261
    Choice Questions *262*
    How do Multi-Select Choice Questions Work? *264*
    Numeric Questions *265*
    Matrix Questions *265*

SCRIPTING #101: VALIDATION OF RESPONSES 267

  WHAT DOES VALIDATION DO? 268
    Validation Example *268*

  Validations Available without Scripting *269*
 Validation using Scripting 270
  Why is scripted validation needed? *270*
  How Does Scripted Validation Work? *270*
  Scripted Validation Logic *270*
  What the Respondent Sees *271*
 Scripted Validation Example 271
  Preparing for our Validation Script *272*
  Writing the Script: Step-by-step *273*
  Putting it all together: The Final Script *275*

SCRIPTING #101: TWEAKING THE INTERFACE 277

 Overview of Interface "Tweaking" 278
 Creating Content Using Scripting 278
  Using a Content Container *278*
  Modifying Existing Content *279*
 Dealing with UI Events 281
  What Events can be Hooked into? *281*
  How can Events be Used? *282*
 UI Event Example 285
  Drop-down List with "Other" *285*

SCRIPTING #101: ORDERING OF PAGES & CHOICES 287

 Page Ordering in the Designer 288
  Basic Page Order *288*
  Randomization of Pages *288*
  Another way to randomize - A/B Testing *289*
  Page Ordering through Scripting *290*
  Our Example: Ordering Pages based on Gender *292*
  Page Ordering in a Nutshell *295*
 Ordering Choices 296
  Standard Ordering of Choices *296*
  Setting up for Scripted Choice Ordering *296*
 Example: Scripted Choice Ordering 297
  Choice Questions *297*
  Single Range Matrix *301*
  Dual Range Matrix *304*

SCRIPTING REFERENCE 305

 Scripting Objects 306
  args *306*
 Function Reference 310
 Additional Objects 324
  SurveyQuestion *324*
  SurveyChoice *326*
  SurveyChoiceTag *326*
  SurveyRow *327*
  SurveyHierarchicalListItem *327*
  SurveyRowTag *327*
  SurveyQuota *327*
  SurveyDistribution *328*

Surveys on the Web

Web Surveys are an efficient means of collecting information from a large number of respondents very quickly.

The proliferation of advanced internet-capable devices makes it easier than ever before to design engaging surveys that can provide you with quality data.

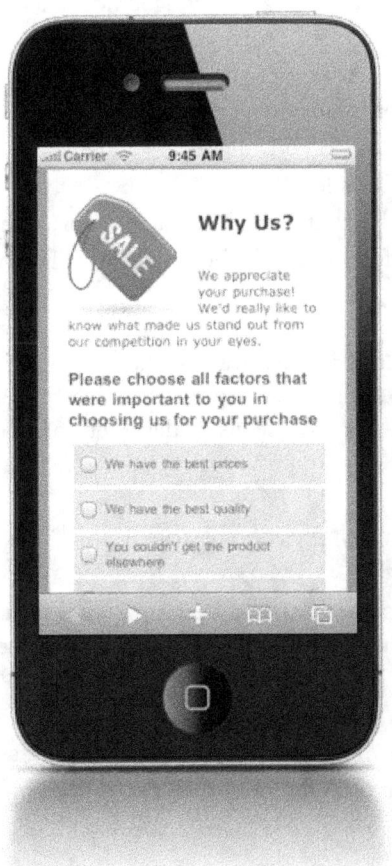

What is a Web Survey?

A Web Survey can be described simply as a set of questions - sometimes only a single question, though this is normally described as a "poll" - that are displayed in a logical manner to be answered by respondents through a Web Browser.

The goal of a Web Survey is to collect data efficiently. By using the Web, a large number of people can be reached quickly and cheaply.

Challenges faced when creating a Web Survey

There is a certain level of underlying complexity associated with Web Surveys. Key challenges that must be dealt with when creating a Web Survey are:

- The survey content needs be appealing and easy to read
- Input fields need to be easy to complete
- All data entered needs to be stored
- Reports need to be generated
- Other issues, such as sending of invitation Emails, need to be dealt with

Perhaps one of the biggest challenges that has arisen quite recently is the fact that the methods used for participating in Web Surveys has changed as in the last few years the "Web" has moved from PCs to mobile devices like tablets and smartphones. This adds another level of complexity to managing "Content".

The rise of Hosted Survey Tools

Clearly the issues that must be resolved to get a Web Survey up and running can only be dealt with by using an application that helps you create a Web Survey. While both Desktop and Web-based applications have been around for a while, the industry is fast moving almost exclusively to Web-based (or "hosted") survey tools.

- Hosted tools have a number of advantages over desktop-based competitors:
- They can be accessed from any Web-browser
- There is no software to be installed
- Data-storage, and all related activities such as backups, are handled for you
- Access is usually provided for a monthly fee (rather than having to make a large up-front payment)

One of the biggest factors that has lead to the growth of hosted tools is the level of advancement we have seen in Web browser capabilities over the last few years. Leading hosted survey tools have leveraged these advances to produce tools that have easy-to-use visual designers, and other features that were formerly only found on desktop products.

Is Desktop Survey Design software dead?

There are still some specific circumstances when a desktop survey design tool may be more appropriate than a hosted tool. These circumstances generally only apply to large corporates and government departments:

- Web browsing is locked down making use of hosted products impractical
- Very old browsers are being used that do not support the technologies needed to run a hosted tool

- Data must be stored internally - not on a hosted site - based on internal organization rules.

Under these circumstances, a Desktop based survey tool such as our **Professional Quest** software can be used to create your surveys.

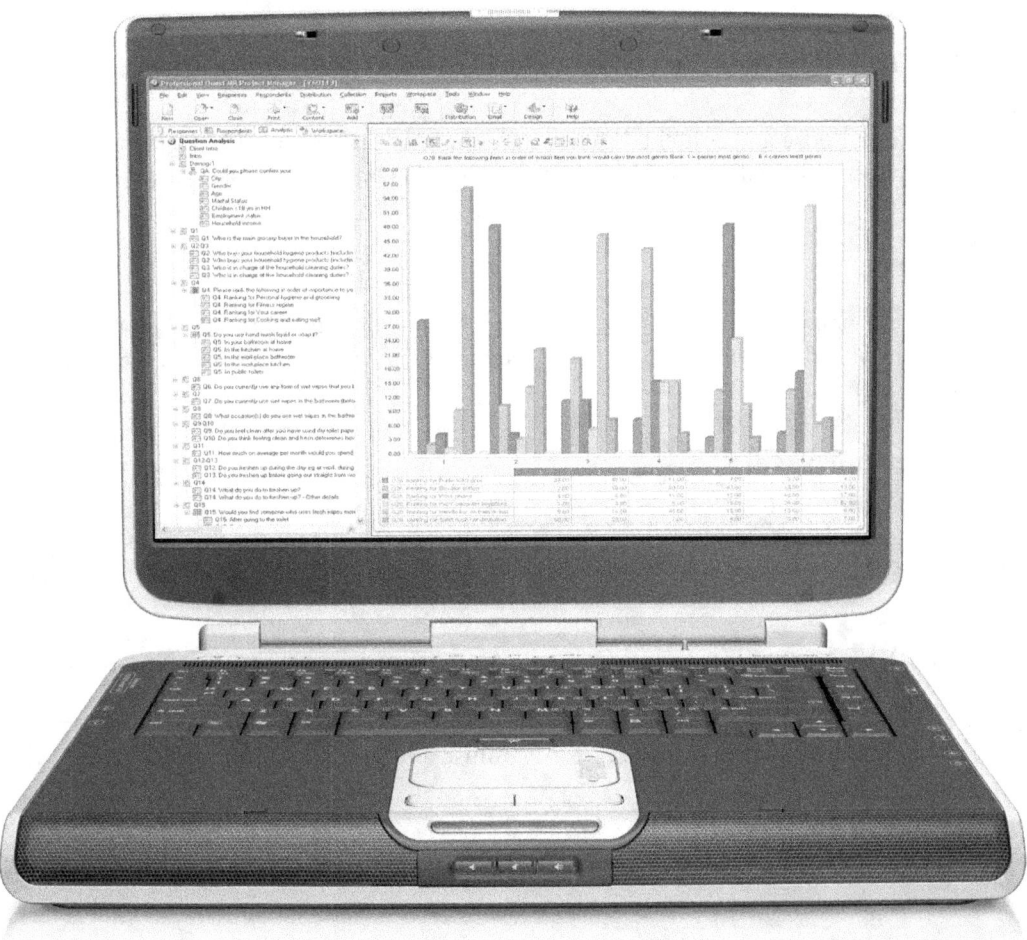

Visit http://www.professionalquest.com for further information.

Anonymous vs. Non-Anonymous Web Surveys

There are two general types of respondents for Web surveys:

Anonymous Respondents	Non-Anonymous Respondents
Respondents click on a general link to complete a survey, and they are not identified in any way	Respondents are sent an Email with their own personal link. Their response can be directly linked back to them

For a majority of surveys, anonymity is actually desired. An anonymous respondent is often more likely to provide an honest answer. For example, if you are running an **Employee Engagement Survey**, employees are likely to be more honest if they feel their opinions can not be tracked back to them.

On the other hand, there are times when knowing who the respondent is will be beneficial. For example, if you are running a Customer Survey, it would be useful to know which of your customers are unhappy. Unlike employees, they would be happy to be identified so that their issues are addressed.

Considerations when building Web Surveys

Surveys can vary widely in purpose and content, but there are some common principles that apply to all Web Surveys. The key things you need to consider when creating a Web Survey are as follows:

Planning is Key

Any survey, no matter how simple, will benefit from planning. A badly designed survey will not receive a decent level of response, nor will it provide the results you are after (since you probably don't even know what results you really want).

Ensure you have a purpose!

While this seems obvious, many surveys have been created that are simply "fishing expeditions". They are longer than they need to be, and will receive a worse response rate because people prefer shorter surveys.

Don't Be Ambiguous

If you ask a question, you want to make sure that the answer you get is not affected by how the question is phrased. It is particularly bad when the answers offered confuse a respondent. For example:

> How often do you catch a train?
> - Never
> - Rarely
> - Infrequently
> - Often

What is the difference between *rarely* and *infrequently*? These are ambiguous values, and should be avoided.

Keep it Short!

No one likes to complete a long survey - the shorter your survey is, the more completed responses you will receive. The longer people spend completing a survey, the less care they will take with their answers (they will lose interest) so more is definitely not better.

Think about the End Result - Reports

When planning a survey, it is easy to lose sight of the ultimate goal - high quality, meaningful reports. Make sure when you are planning that you have thought of what reports you want, and how you want to filter and cross-tabulate them. You can't filter based on a question you never asked!

Using Web Survey Creator for Web Surveys

Creating a Web Survey can only be achieved by using the right tool for the job. While there are many options open to you, few if any provide a solution with the features of our Web Survey Creator (WSC) product. The remainder of this book will focus on creating Web Surveys using Web Survey Creator.

Opening WSC for the First Time

Web Survey Creator can be accessed from the following Web address using any modern browser:

http://www.websurveycreator.com

The first time you visit the site, you will need to set yourself up as a registered user. You can do this by clicking on the Signup menu at the top of the screen.

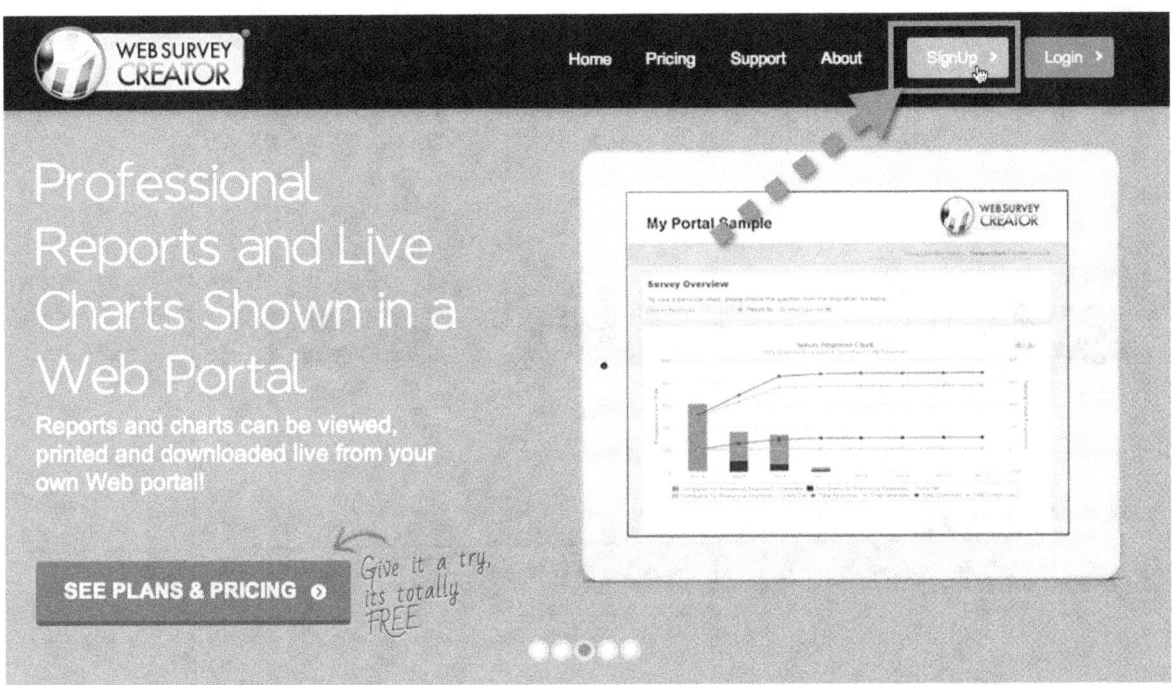

You must choose which version of the software you wish to purchase. If you are not ready to purchase the software yet, you can choose the Basic Edition, which is free.

Click on the **Signup Now** button to begin the signup process.

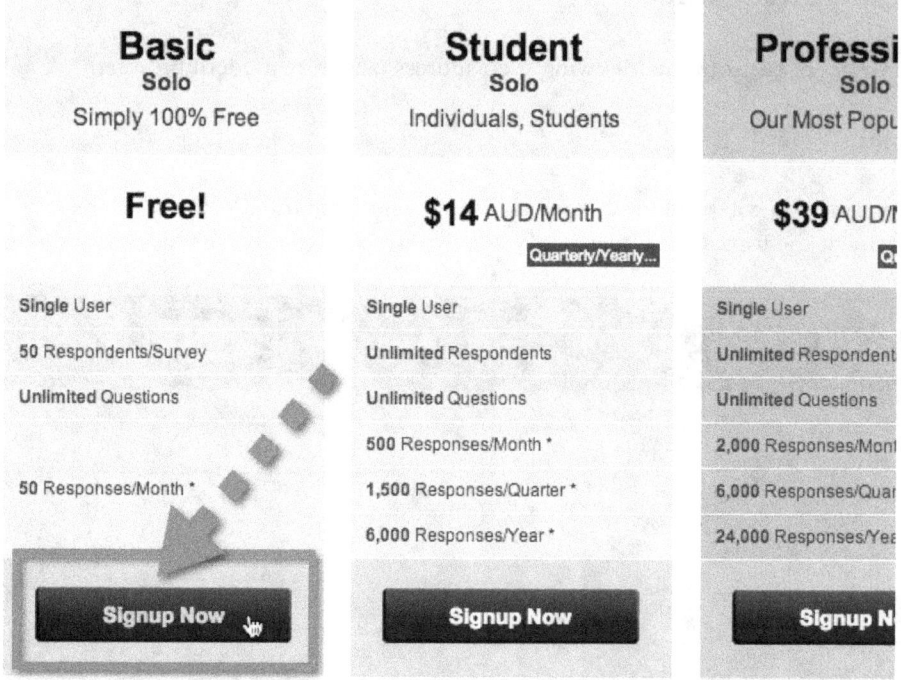

Fill in your details, and press the **Create Account** button.

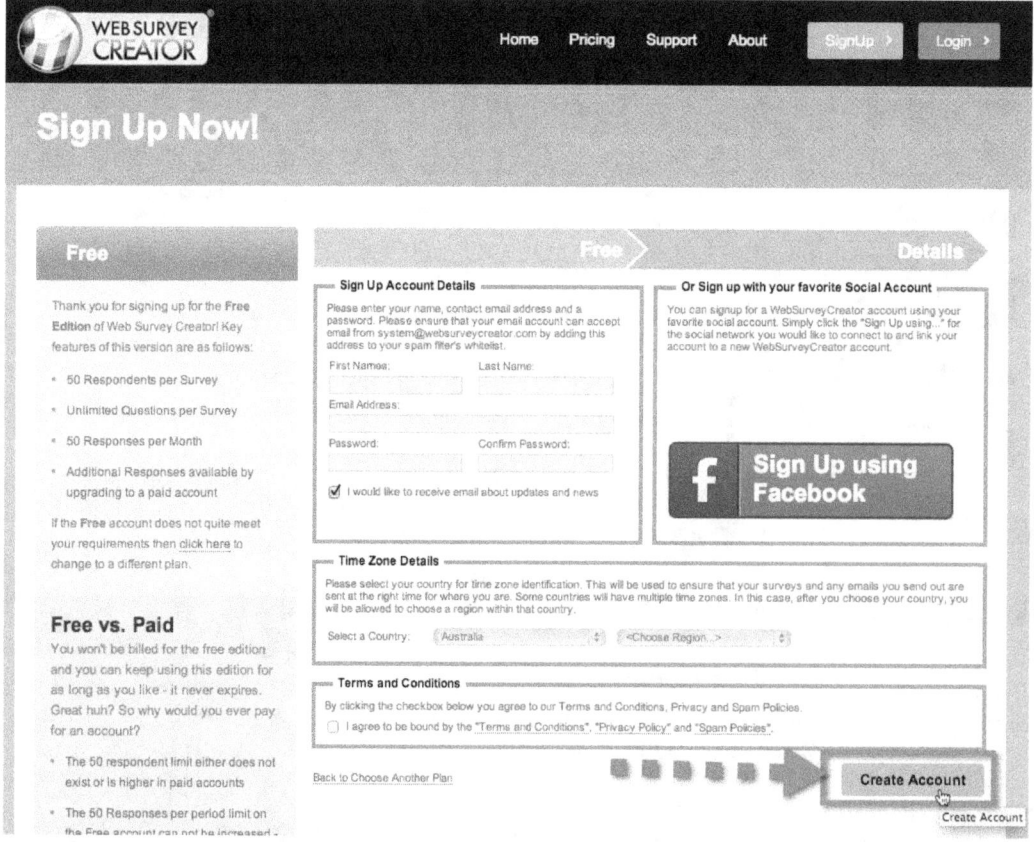

You can optionally sign in using your Facebook credentials. This will mean that you won't need to learn yet another login – your Facebook login is all you need to get into your account. If you have Facebook open on your computer, when you go to Web Survey Creator, it won't even need to ask you for your login details at all – it will know who you are and go straight to your surveys.

Activating your Account

You will be sent an Email to activate your account. This is to ensure you entered your email address correctly, and you can access that Email account. For ease of use, the system gives you 7 day's grace to activate your account, so you can use it immediately without waiting for the activation Email.

An unactivated account will have a warning at the top of the screen until activation occurs.

Where to get help

On-line Help

Online assistance can be found from the Support menu at the top of the page.

From within the Support area, you can:

1. See a listing of any questions you have previously asked, together with their status, and any answers given (you must be logged in to get to this tab)
2. Select a Help Topic to view
3. Go to the Support Request Form to enter a support request

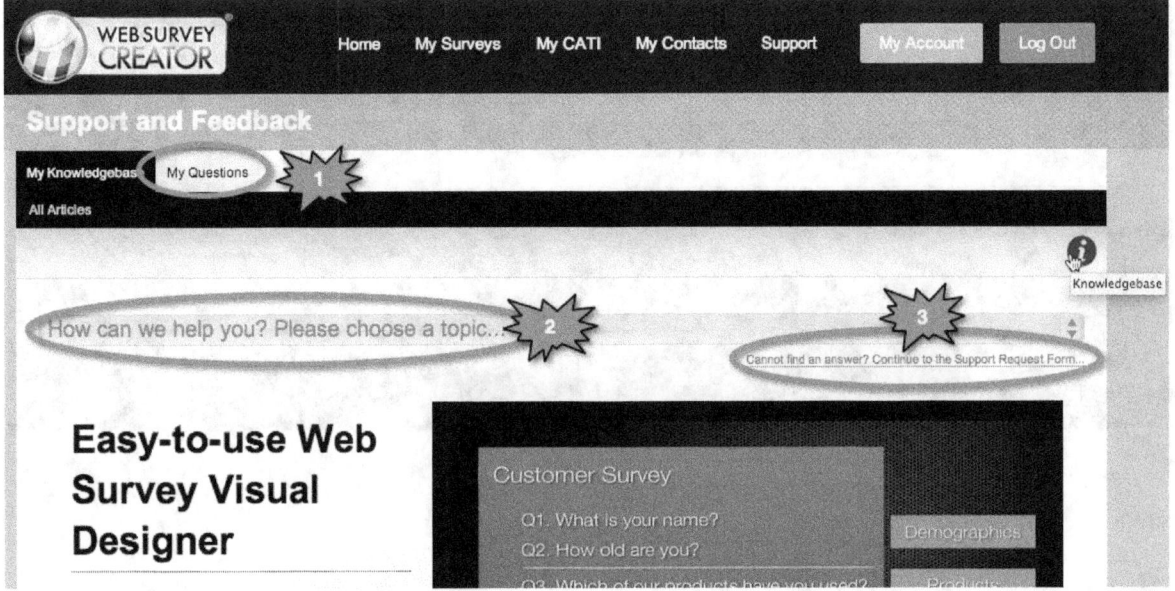

Surveys on the Web   17

Tutorials

Step-by-step tutorials are available on key areas of the software. These tutorials can be accessed by pressing the Information button on the toolbar from wherever you are in the software.

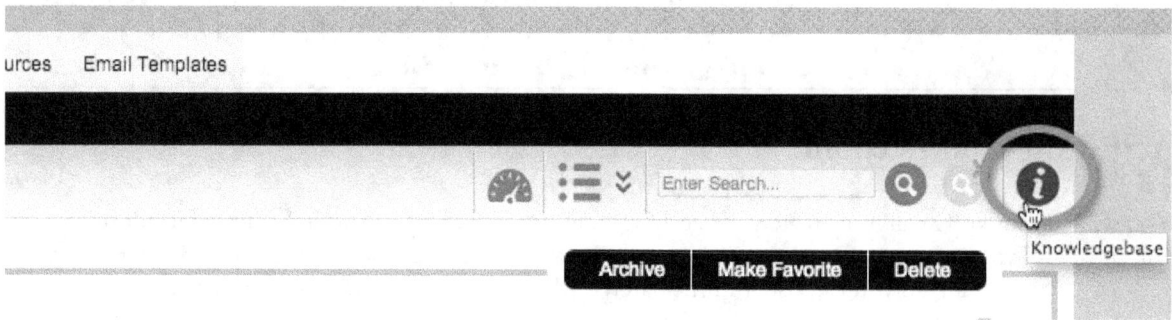

The tutorials cover key areas of the software, including areas covered in this manual.

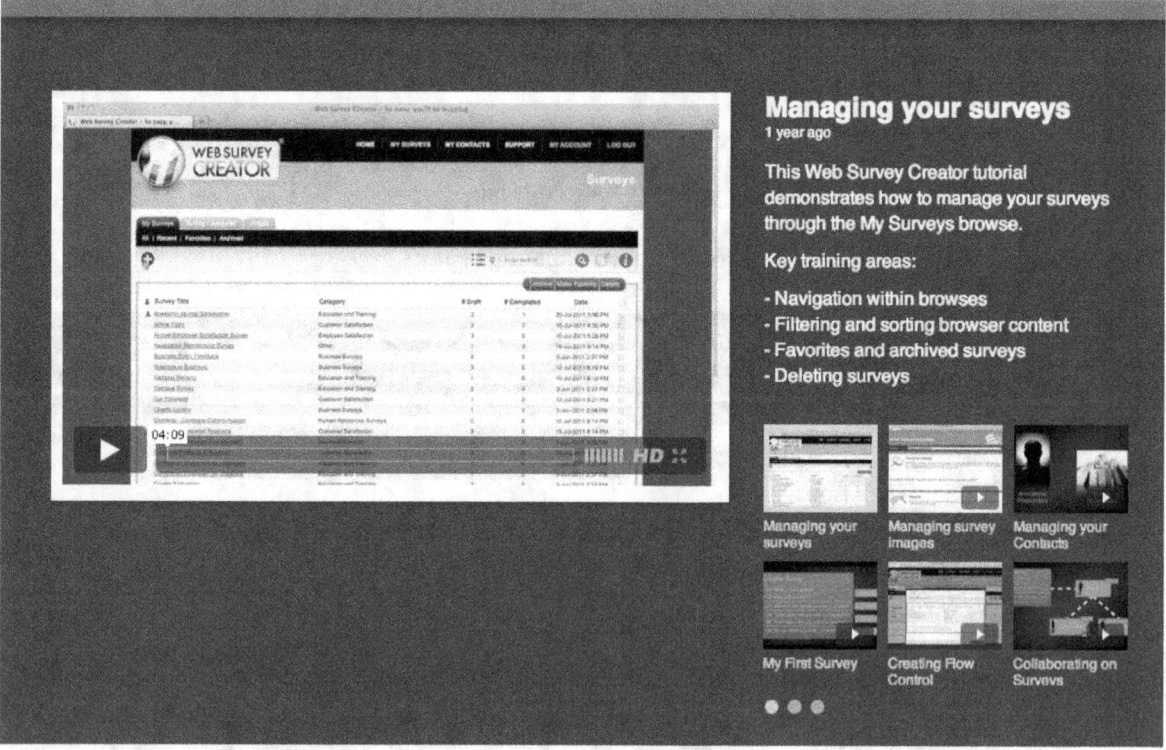

Creating our first Survey

In this chapter, we will create our first survey using Web Survey Creator.

There are many different ways a survey can be created. This is the time to get into good habits and really start to use the power of the product.

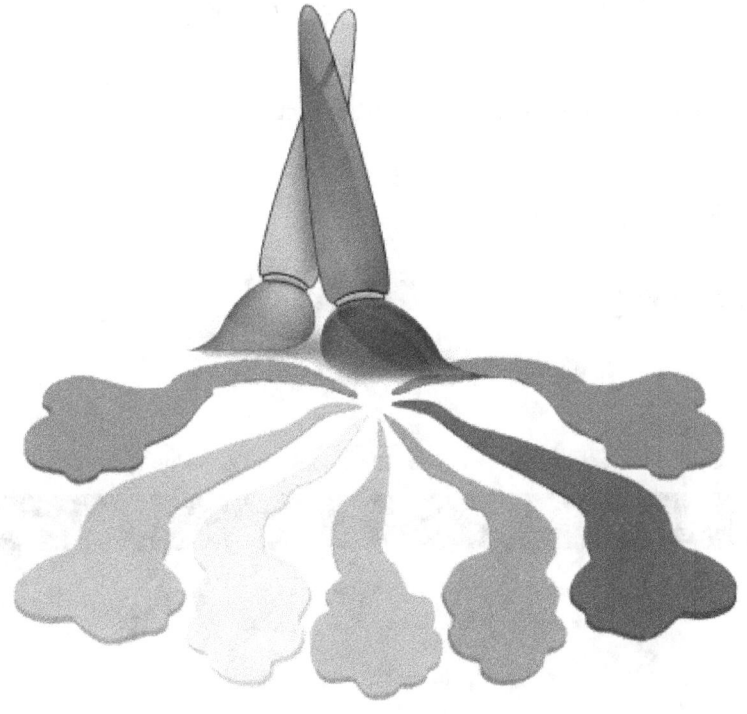

Start with a Plan!

The key to any good survey design is planning. The approach you take to creating your survey will affect the quality of the end result.

Our first survey is going to be a Customer Satisfaction Survey with the following content:

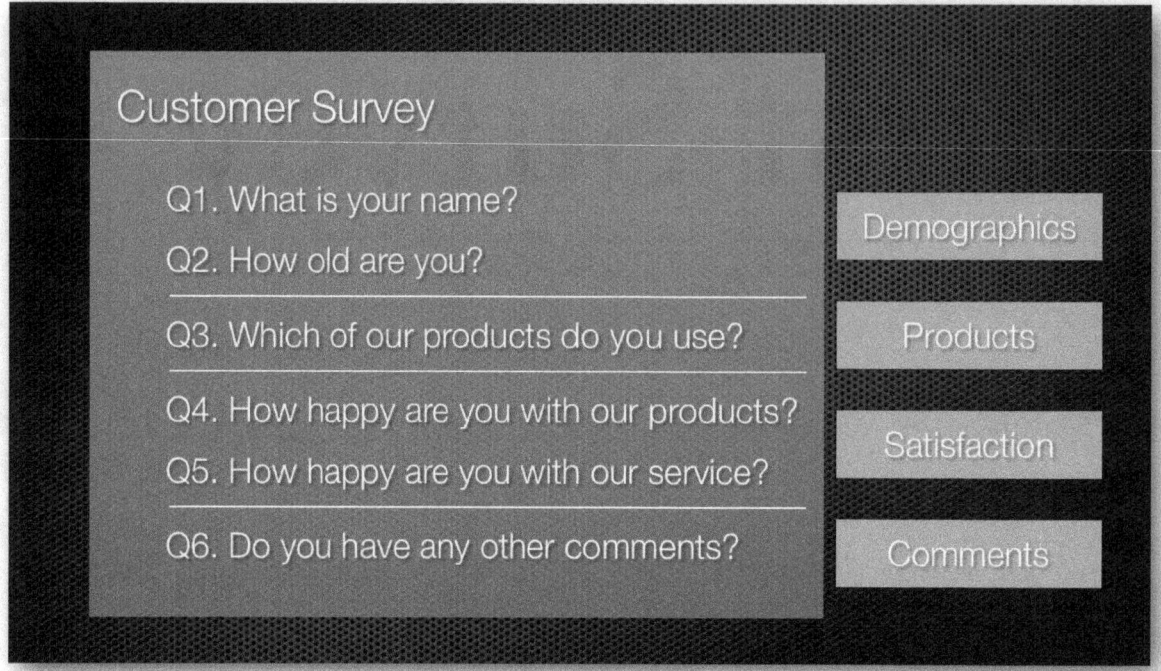

These questions naturally fall into a number of areas - Demographics, Products, Satisfaction and Comments.

While we could place all the questions in a single page, particularly for such a short survey, best practice is to separate similar questions onto different pages.

We will create each page, as we need it.

Creating A Survey

To create a new survey, we press the **Plus** button on the **My Surveys** Tab.

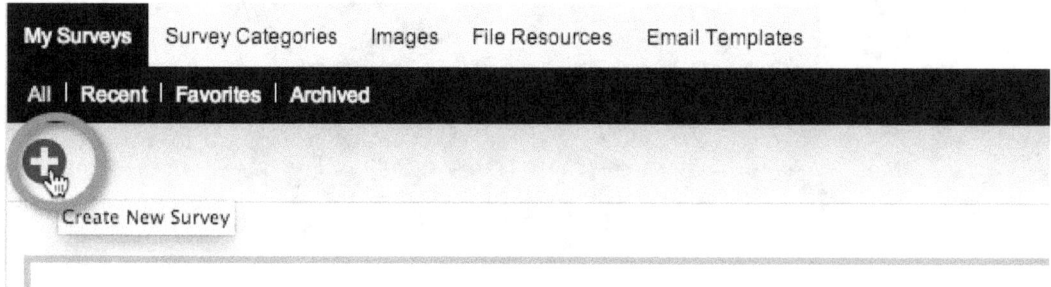

There are some choices we need to make:

1. Do we want to create a survey from scratch, or use a previous survey or a survey template as a starting point?
2. What do we want to name our survey?
3. What theme, category and language do we want to use?
4. What survey response type do we want (anonymous, with respondent list etc.)?

In our case, we are going to build the survey from scratch, we're going to call it **Annual Customer Satisfaction Survey** and we will place this survey in the **Customer Satisfaction** category.

Theme and language can remain at the default settings, and we are creating the survey as an anonymous survey (which is also the default setting).

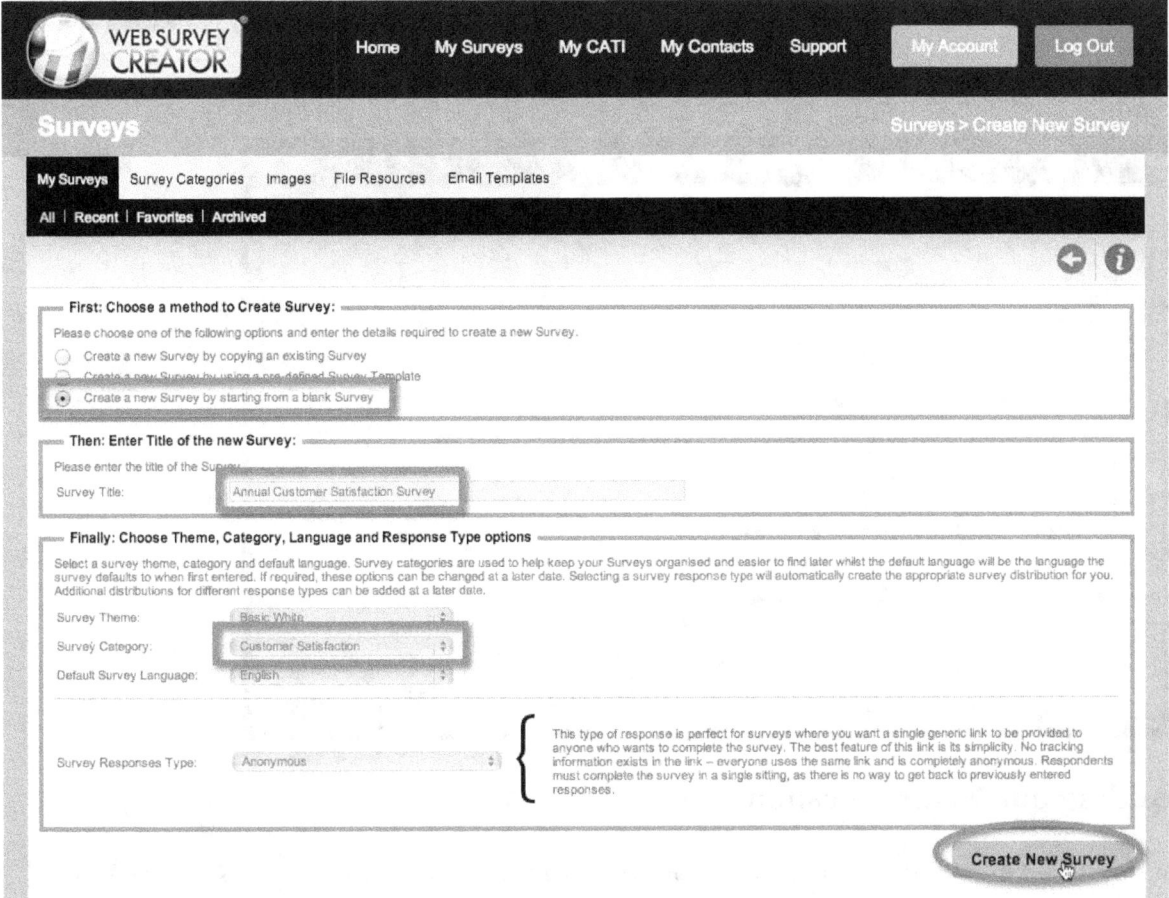

When we save our survey details, we are immediately taken into the **Content Designer** for the survey.

Adding Pages

Based upon our prior planning we know we will need 4 pages.

Our first page is created for us when the survey is created.

Pages are automatically named for us – this page is called **Page 1**. While this doesn't need to be changed, it is easy to change the name to **Demographics**.

We click the **Edit** button to enter our new page name.

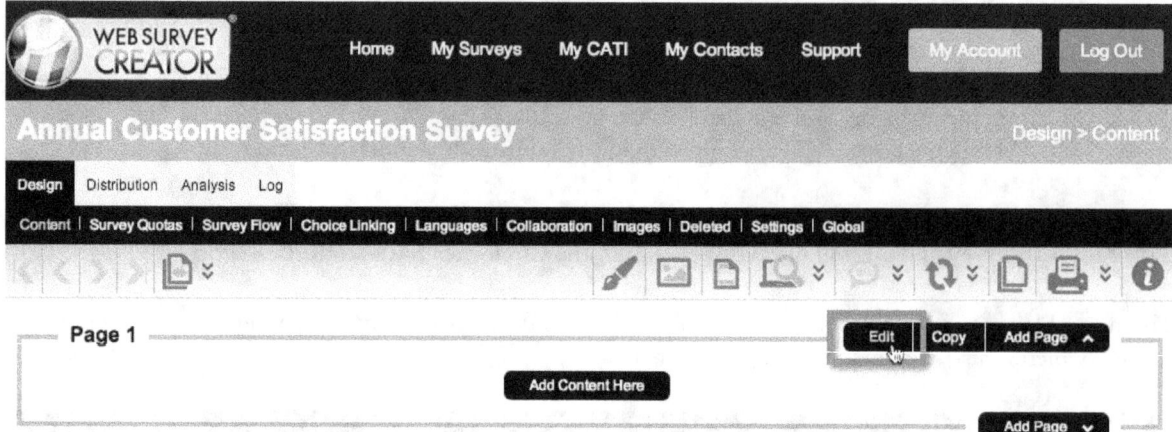

Once we change the name of the page, we can press the **Save Page** button.

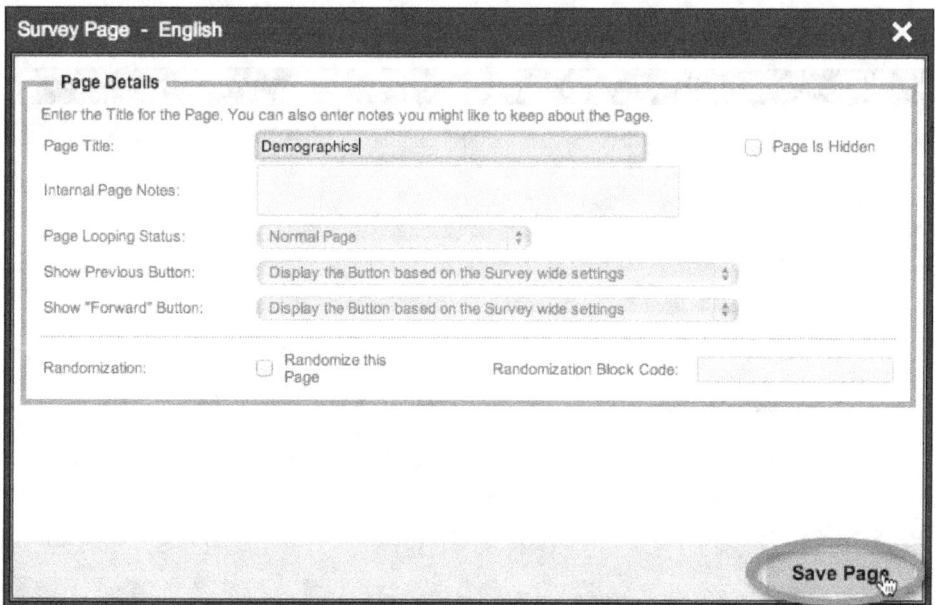

Adding our Name Question

We now need to start adding our questions, one at a time. Questions are added by pressing the **Add Content Here** button, and then choosing **Name** from the **Demographic Question** menu.

Whenever adding any content to a survey, we always start by choosing the type of content we want to add.

> WSC has a number of specialized question types for certain common questions like "Name". If we need to ask a respondent's name, rather than using a text question, we can use a specific demographics question.

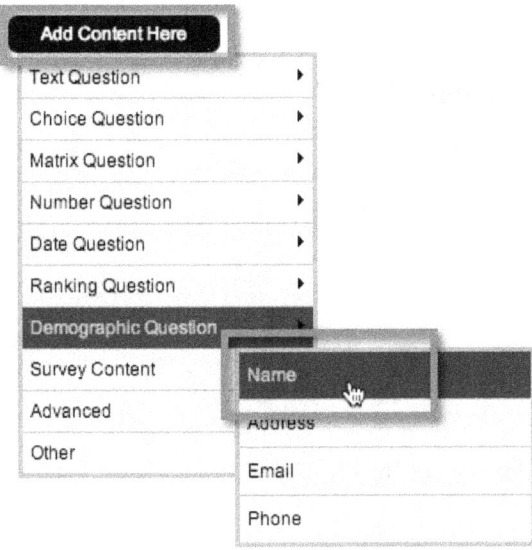

When we select the **Demographic Question** type and choose **Name**, we see specific formatting that can be selected for this type of question.

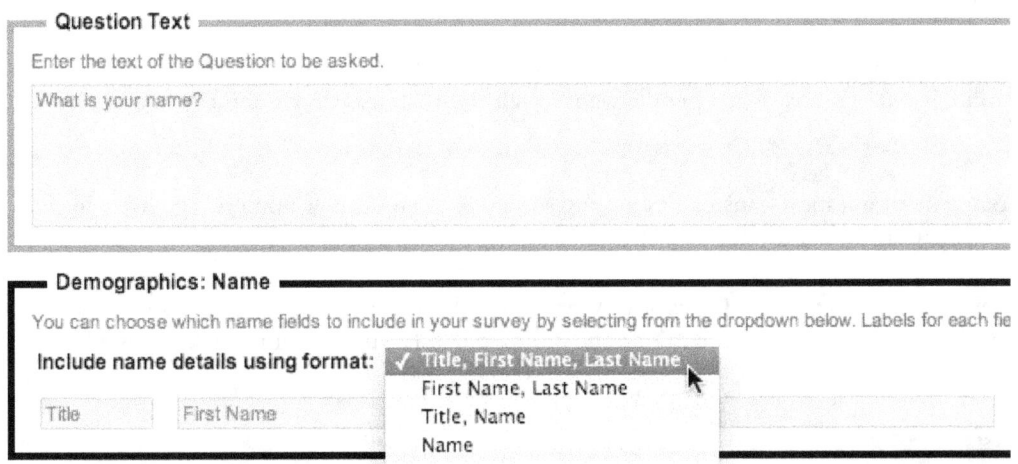

We'll make this question mandatory, and save it by clicking **Save Content**.

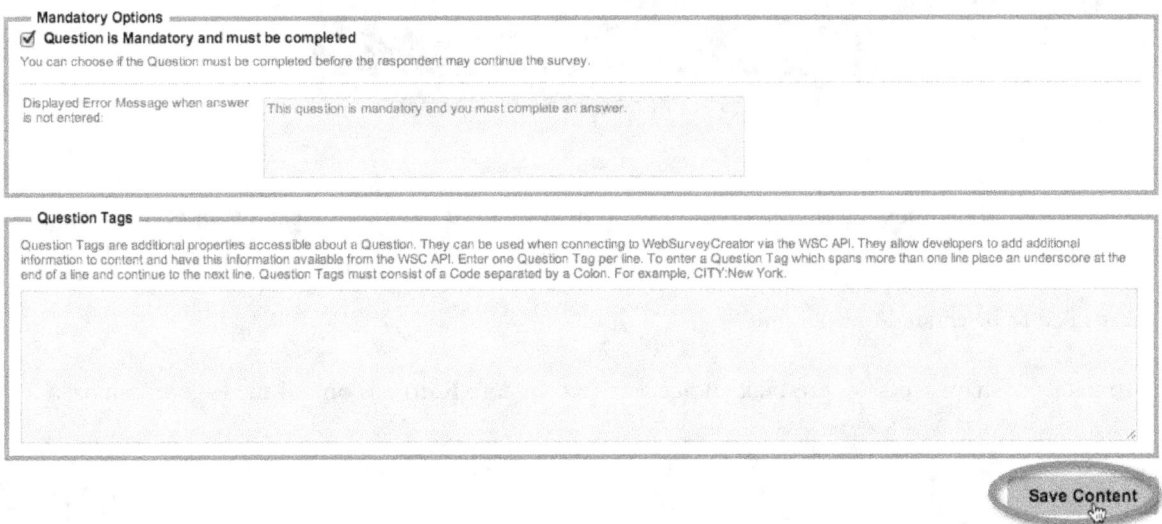

The question is shown in the Content Designer in the same layout as it will appear in the survey.

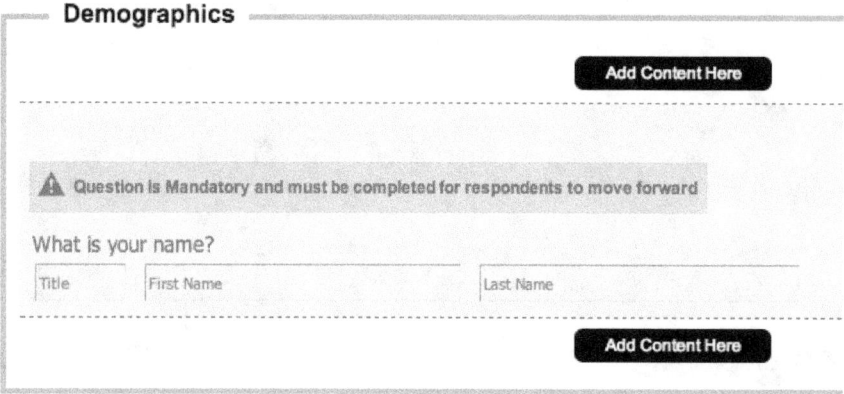

Notice how much better the question now looks compared to a single text question. We are now going to get well-formatted names entered into our survey.

Adding our Age Question

Let's move onto the Age question. We want to add it after the name question, so we click on the **Add Content Here** button below the name question.

We need to choose content type again. Age is often set up incorrectly as a number. While asking for your exact age is technically correct, how many people want to tell you that, and do we actually need to know the exact age?

We use a different type of question – instead of getting someone to enter their numeric age, we will give them a range of age groups to choose from.

This means we need to select a **Choice Question**. We want to show the choices as buttons on the screen, and of course someone can only be in one age group, so we'll select "Multiple Choice, Radio Buttons (Choose Only 1)".

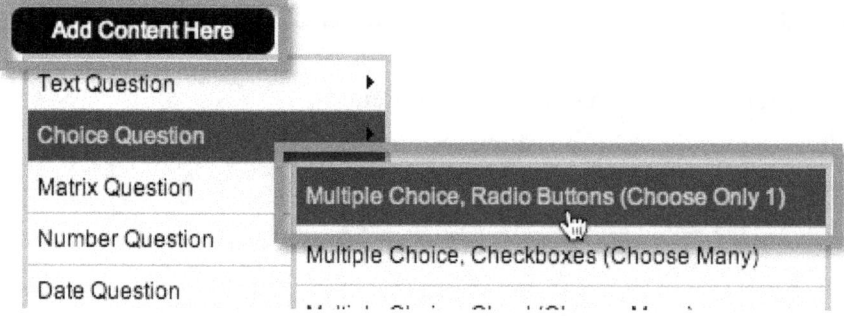

We enter the question text "How old are you?" and then we need to enter the **selection choices** for the question.

These need to be entered one per line.

Fortunately we have access to pre-built choice lists, and an **Age Range** is one of the lists we can use.

24 Creating our first Survey

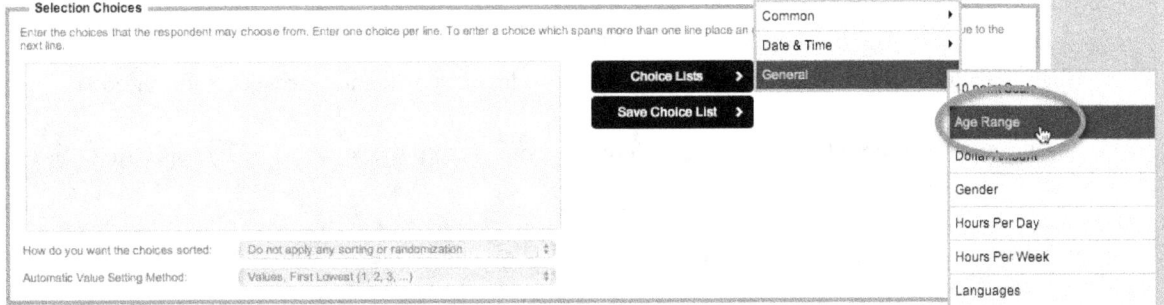

This list looks good, but we'll extend the ranges shown with one additional range for 65 to 74 year olds.

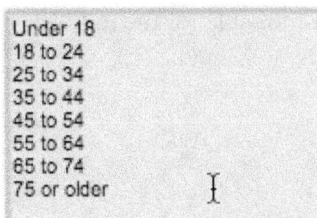

We won't make this question mandatory, because people may not wish to tell me their age. We can therefore simply save the content.

Adding our Products Question

Adding the products question is very similar to adding the age question, but with a few differences.

We want to place it on the second page of the survey.

We can add a page from the toolbar, or by simply clicking *Add New Page Here* on the bottom of our first page.

By default it is called Page 2, but as before, we can edit this.

We will change this page's name to "Products".

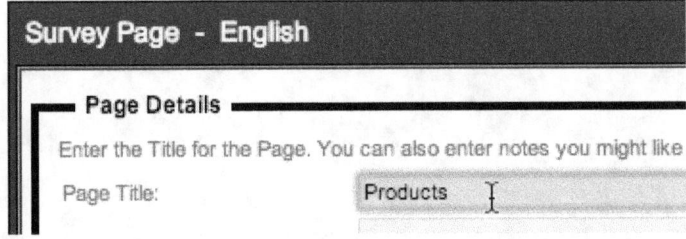

Creating our first Survey 25

Our company produces electronic goods, so the list of products we will show are electronics goods.

Of course our customers could buy multiple different products from us, so we MUST ensure that this is a "choose many" question type.

The importance of picking the correct type of choice question can be clearly seen in this example.

> The #1 error in survey design is choosing the wrong type of choice question. Always ask yourself, "Does it make sense that I can pick more than one choice?"

In our example, being able to select multiple products makes sense, but it is impossible for me to be in multiple age groups.

We add the question using the steps we have already learnt:

1. Click **Add Content Here**
2. From the drop-down menu, choose **Choice Question -> Multiple Choice, Checkboxes (Choose Many)**
3. Enter our question "Which of our products have you used?"
4. Enter the choices:

```
Television
Projector
Washing Machine
Refrigerator
Hi Fi System
```

Let's also add two additional options:

1. "Other" for any of the minor products we sell that are not in the list; and
2. "I have never bought a product from you" to ensure people who never bought from us have a valid option to pick.

The **Selection Choices** will therefore look as follows:

```
Television
Projector
Washing Machine
Refrigerator
Hi Fi System
Other
I have never bought a product from you
```

After we save this question, we can see a respondent can choose multiple answers.

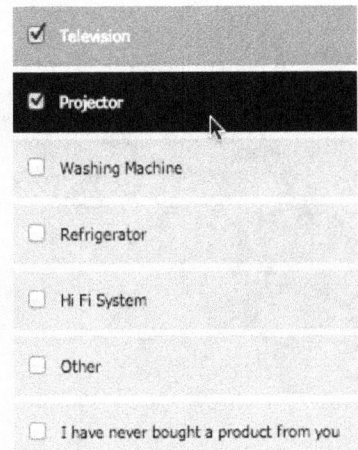

We can make a couple of modifications to these values to enhance the user experience. Let's edit this question.

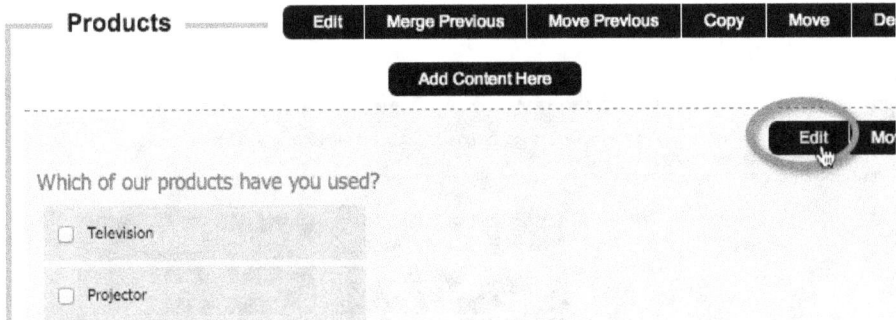

We'll edit the "Other" choice.

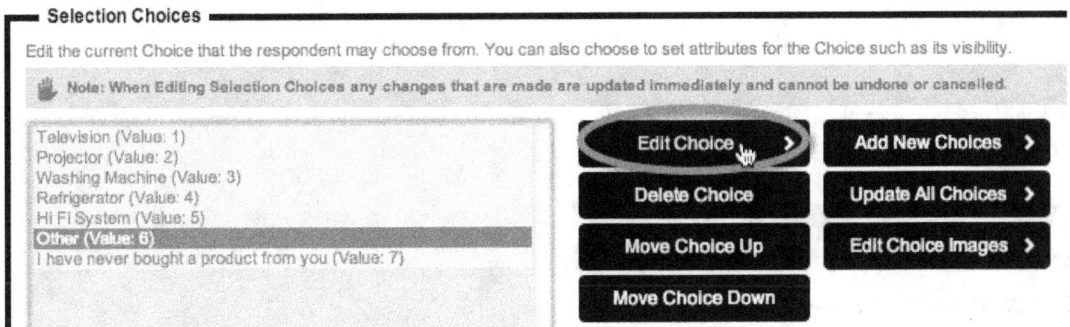

We will indicate that it is an "Other, please specify" option.

Creating our first Survey   27

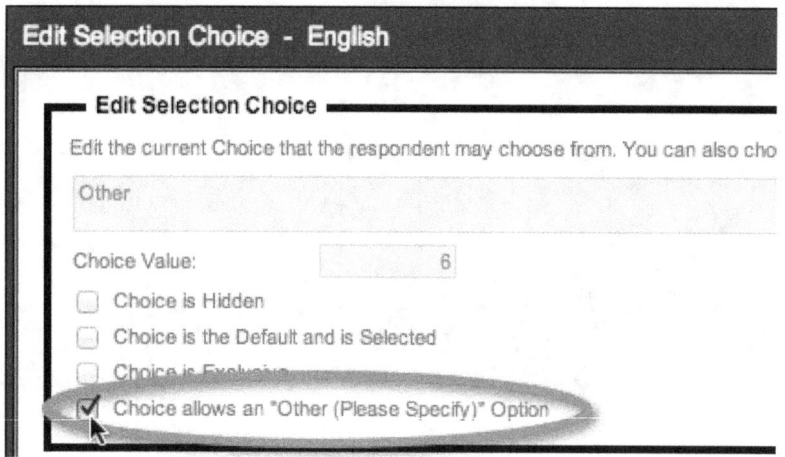

We save this change by clicking the **Save Choice** button.

We will also edit the "Never bought" choice.

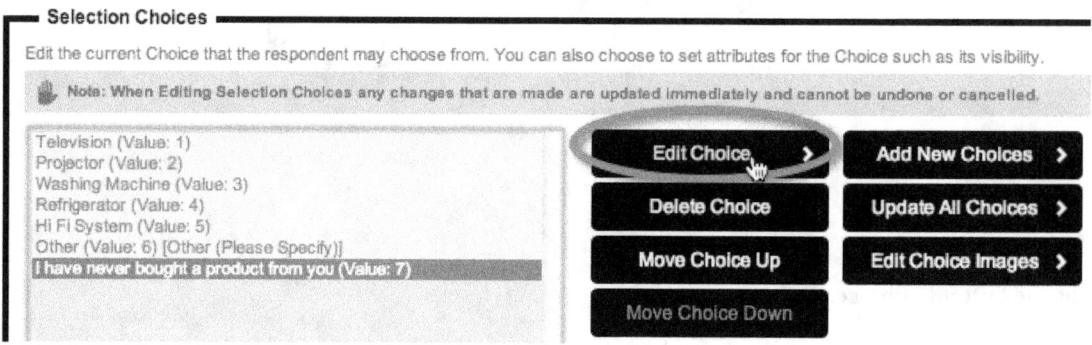

We will make this choice exclusive. This means whenever this option is checked, all other options will be unchecked automatically.

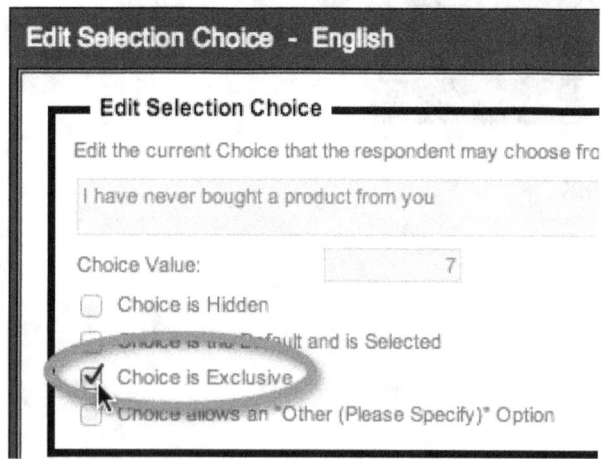

These values will now have specific behaviors based upon these new settings.

Adding our Satisfaction Questions

We will add a third page to our survey, and then add our questions about happiness:

- How happy are you with our products?
- How happy are you with our service?

These questions could of course be created as two Choice questions. Respondents could choose one of the following happiness choices.

- Very Happy
- Slightly Happy
- Undecided
- Slightly Unhappy
- Very Unhappy

However, this is another situation where with a little thought we can greatly improve the look and functionality of our survey. Both these questions have the same list of choices, so we can put them together in a **Matrix Question** Type.

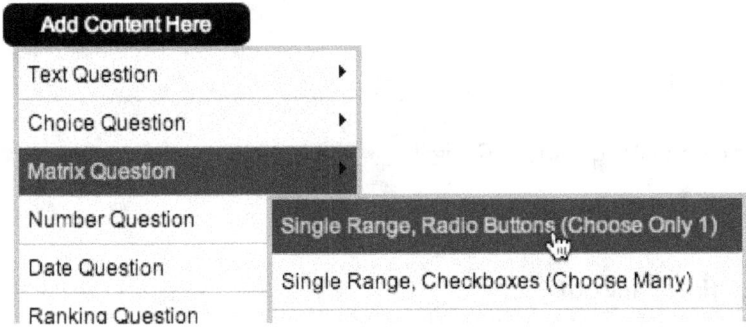

The question can be changed to "How happy are you with…"

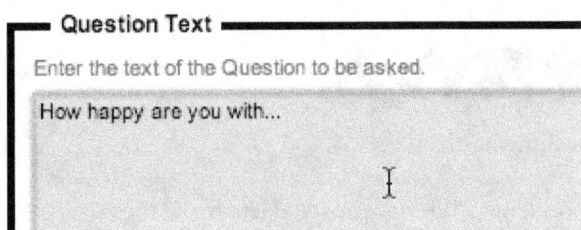

We can enter the choices for the matrix, just like the choices are entered for standard choice questions.

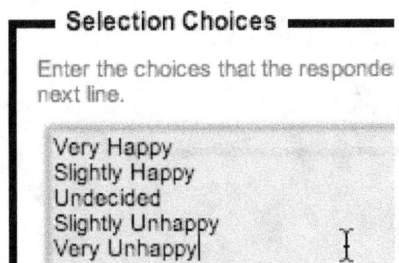

Creating our first Survey 29

"Our Products" and "Our Services" can then be added as rows.

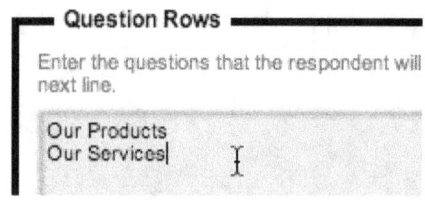

After we save the question, we can see in the designer how the matrix is a compact way of showing these two questions.

Adding our Comments Question

The last question we want to add is our comments question. We will:

1. Add our **Comments Page**
2. Click **Add Content Here**
3. Choose **Text Question -> Multiple Lines of Text**

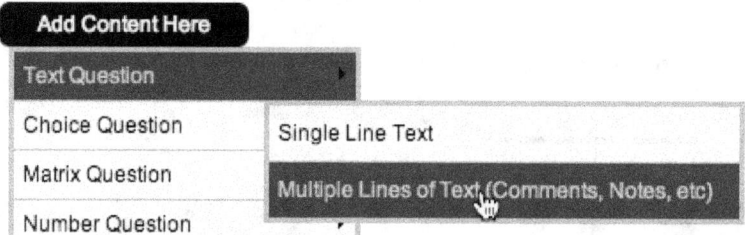

4. Enter our question "Do you have any other comments?"

5. We will also add some formatting to give respondents a bit more space – lets make the comments go across the page, and show 5 lines for them to enter their comments.

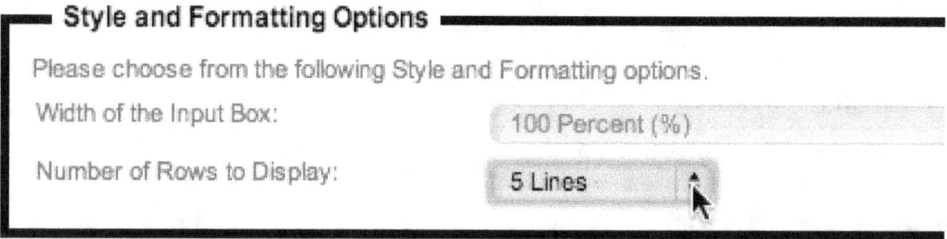

Fantastic! – Our survey is done.

Previewing the Survey

To see how the survey looks, we can preview it by selecting the **Quick Preview** option.

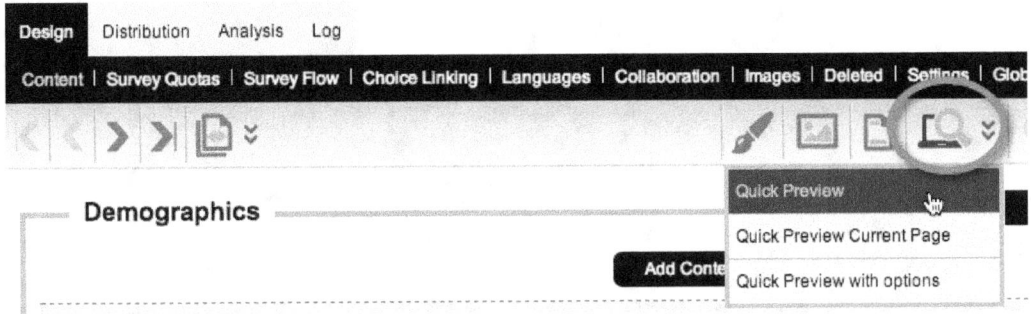

Previewing is particularly useful for testing logic like mandatory questions, and the exclusive and other settings we added to our product list question.

Showing a preview to other people

If you need to show the preview to someone else, they don't need to have a login for Web Survey Creator. All you need to do is select **Quick Preview with options**.

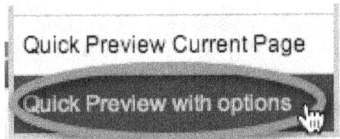

One of the options is to **Share Preview with Others**.

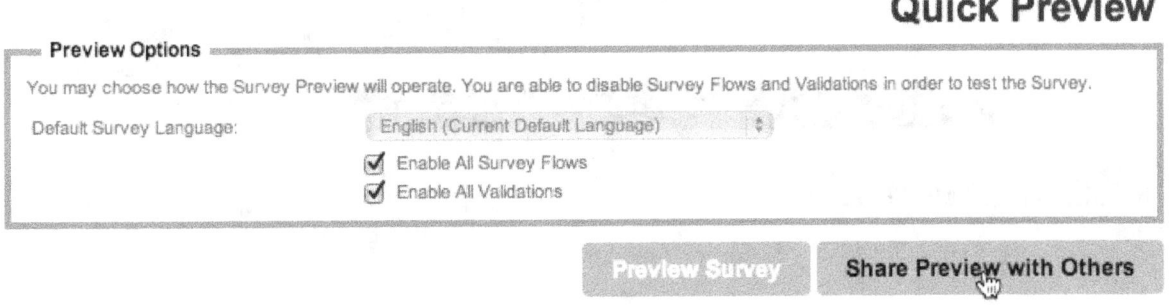

Multiple Email addresses can be entered (one per line) and a link to the preview will be sent to each of them.

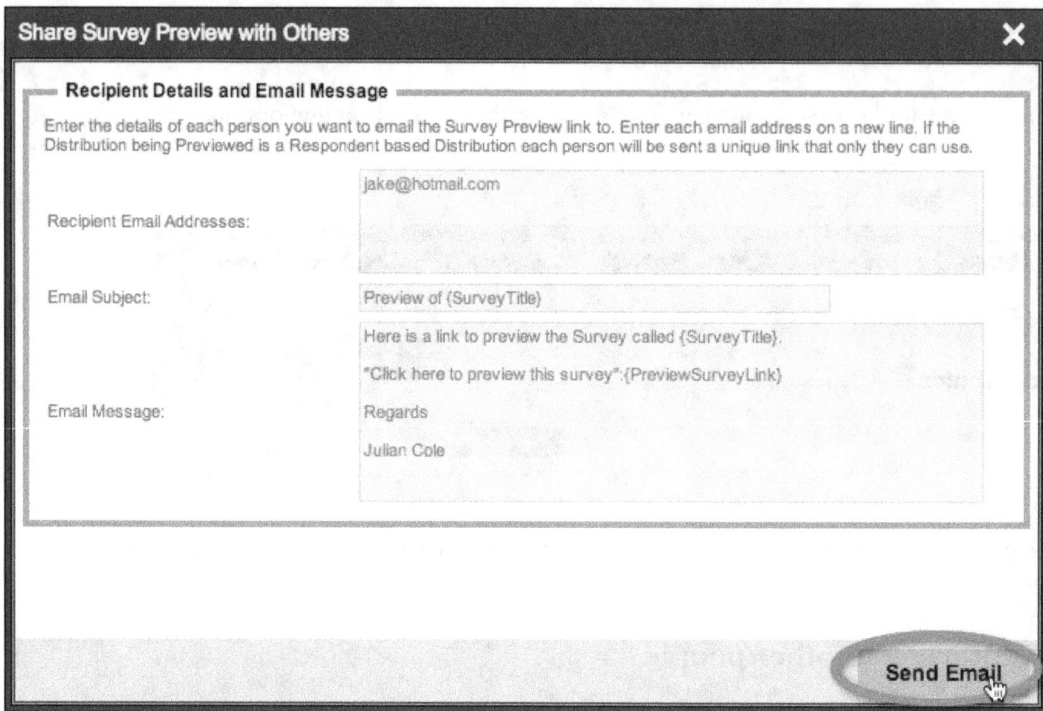

Step-by-step Video

If you would like to see how this first survey has been built, you can view it in our step-by-step video. You can access this video online by pressing the **Knowledgebase** button on the toolbar while working on survey content.

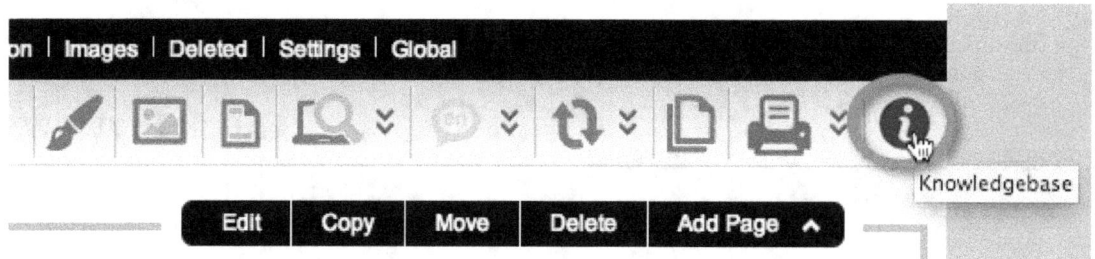

The video is called **My First Survey**.

Using advanced formatting in your Surveys

Formatting can be added to surveys through the use of **Content Tags**

What are Content Tags?

Content Tags are simply a means of incorporating standard HTML functionality in survey content, without exposing the full range of HTML to a survey designer (doing the later would open the system to all sorts of security and layout issues).

Where can Content Tags be used?

Content Tags can be used anywhere you use standard text content in your surveys. This includes:

- Text Content blocks
- Question Text
- Choice Text

Most of the time, straight text will suffice in these areas, but Content Tags can be useful if you want to:

- Place emphasis on part of the content
- Add small help text below your question
- Add Bullet Points
- Use color in your text
- Place an image in some text content

Listing of Content Tags and their Usage

Tag Combination	Description	Usage
<h1></h1>	H1	<h1>My Heading</h1>
<h2></h2>	H2	<h2>My Sub Heading</h2>
<b></b>	Bold	<b>This is bold</b> but this isn't
<strong></strong>	Bold	<strong>This is bold</strong> but this isn't
<u></u>	Underline	<u>This is underlined</u> but this isn't
<i></i>	Italic	<i>This is italicized</i> but this isn't
<ol><li></li></ol> <ol type:style><li></li></ol>	Ordered Lists - with Css Ordered List Style e.g upper-roman	<ol><li>One</li><li>Two</li></ol>
<ul><li></li></ul> <ul type:style><li></li></ul>	Ordered Lists - with Css Unordered List Style e.g square	<ul><li>Banana</li><li>Apple</li></ul>
<nobold></nobold>	No Bold - Turns of Bold where the current style is Bold	This is in Bold <nobold>but this is not</nobold> but this is again.
<small></small>	Equivalent to font-size:small	<small>This is small</small> but this isn't
<webhelptext></webhelptext>	Equivalent to font-size:x-small; font-style:italic	<webhelptext>This is small and italicized</webhelptext>
<link:mailto:emailaddress>Text</link> <link:mailto:emailaddress|nostyle>Text</link>	Link for Email Address - with no style	<link:mailto:fred@me.com>Mail to Fred</link>
<link:url>Text</link> <link:url|nostyle>Text</link>	Link from http or https based URL - with no style	<link:http://www.me.com>Click to Go To Me</link>

Tag Combination	Description	Usage
<image:url> <image:url|tooltip>	Image from http or https based URL - jpeg/gif/png - with Tooltip	<image: http://www.me.com/cat.jpg>
<image:filename> <image:filename|tooltip>	Image from Person's File - jpeg/gif/png - with Tooltip	<image: cloud.jpg>
<font:text>	Font using CSS Font Style	<font: italic bold 22px courier>Text</font>
<color:#hex>	Color using HEX Name	<color:#334455>Text</color>
<color:name>	Color using Font Name	<color:Red>Text</color>
<colour:#hex>	Color using HEX Name (English Spelling)	<colour:#334455>Text</colour>
<colour:name>	Color using Font Name (English Spelling)	<colour:Red>Text</colour>

Example of Content Tag usage

A simple example of using content tags would be to change the text of the products question as follows:

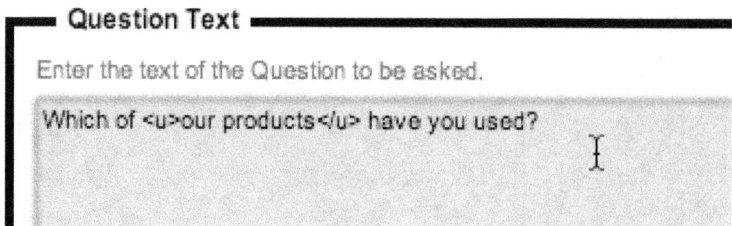

The result of this would be to highlight the words "Our Products" through an underline.

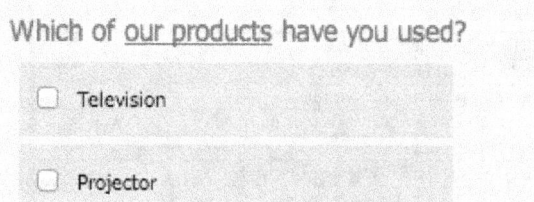

Survey Themes

Let's now take a look, in general terms, how some of the theme structures in WSC work and what sort of capabilities are available for designing themes.

Components

Each theme in WSC consists of a number of components that work together to allow the survey to be rendered in a consistent manner.

The key elements are standard html styles (css) and images. There are three (3) styles sheets that are available.

1. Standard
2. Tablet
3. Mobile

Each style sheet essentially contains the same series of classes and is only included in the page for the device that it is appropriate for. That is, a desktop PC will receive the Standard style sheet whereas an iPad will receive the Tablet style sheet.

When attached to a simple survey the "White" Theme will look similar to this:

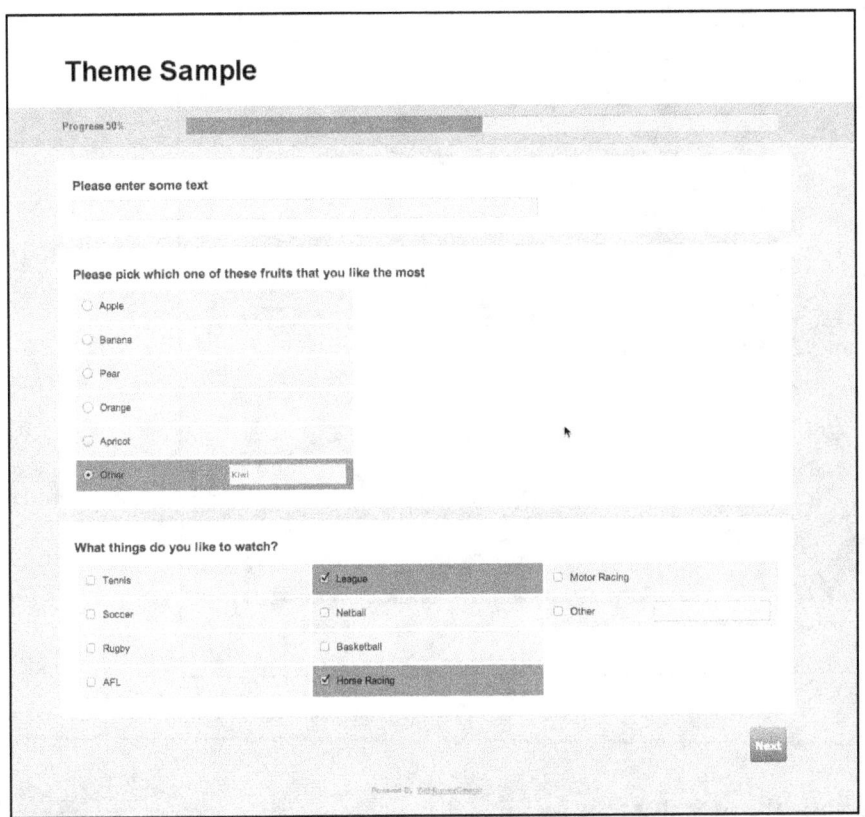

Structure of Theme

The structure of this survey is straightforward. It consists of the following pieces:

1. Banner Zone
2. Percentage Zone
3. Question 1
4. Question 2
5. Question 3
6. Next Button
7. Powered By Zone

You will notice that each of the questions is split into a separate visual region separating it from other questions. Further the choice questions have specific styles for selection of individual choices. They also have styles for highlighting (hovering) over individual choices.

The same survey with a simplified theme (using background colours to highlight CSS regions) is shown here. In this example the banner image and percentage bar image have been removed

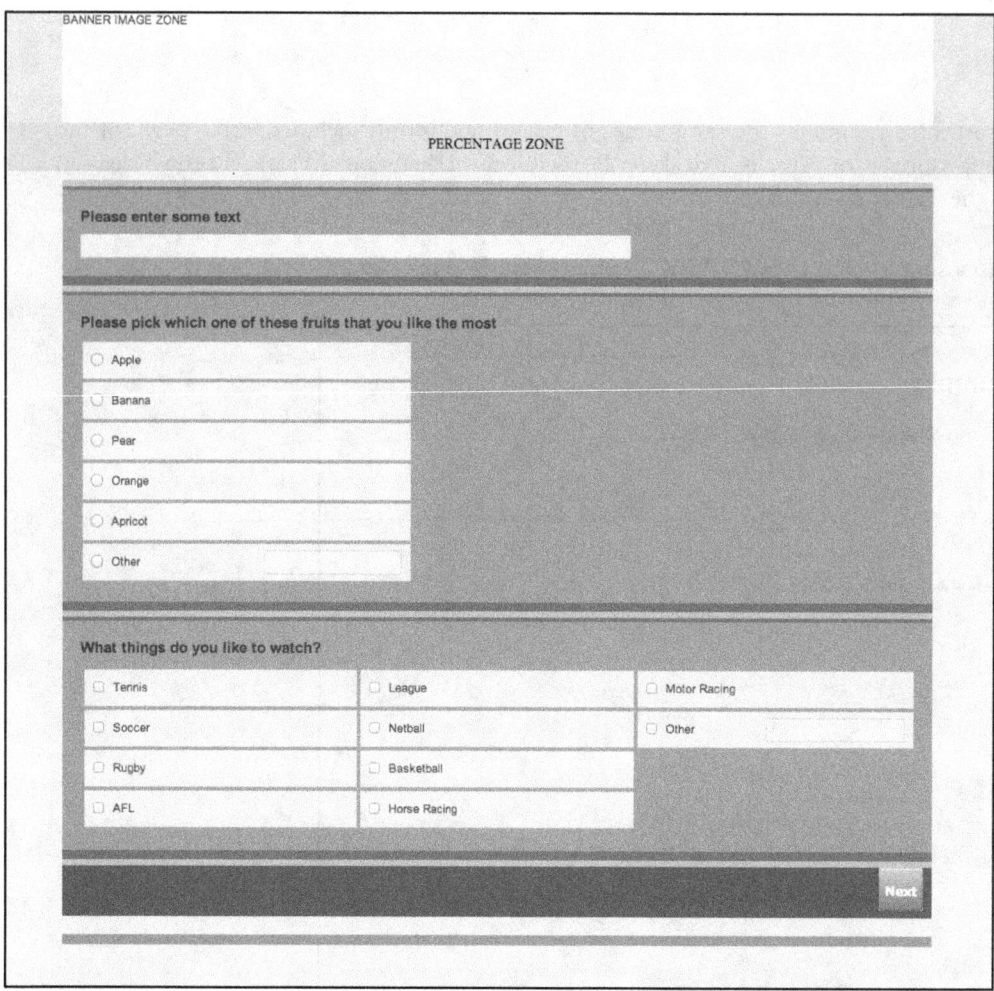

Specific Styles

There are specific styles for each of the areas that have colour in the sample image. In addition there are a number of nested styles so that very complex control over these regions can be rendered.

For example for a specific question there are a number of DIVS with attached styles that nest.

```
<body class="wsc_body">
    <div id="SurveyPanel">
        <div class="wsc_background">
            <div class="wsc_mainbody">
                <div class="wsc_mainbodyzone">
                    <div class="wsc_surveyzone">
                        <div class="wsc_pagezone">
                            <div class="wsc_question-zone">
```

This structure allows quite complex styles to be created.

Question Styles

At the point of the question there are additional styles that are available.

For example, take a look at this question:

Please enter some text

It consists of styles for the label text (wsc_labeltext) and styles for the input control (wsc_textfield).

The style wsc_textfield actually consists of a large number of related styles that are used to manage hovered, focussed, disabled and normal states that can occur through the use of the control.

Similar styles are used for other types of standard input controls such as checkbox and radio buttons that are used in choice based questions.

More complex questions may also have other styles that may be altered.

Other Styles

Other areas of the rendered survey page will use other styles. For example, take a look at this control:

It is actually made up of at least three (3) styles that work co-operatively to show the button.

Percentage Bar and Banner Images

In areas such as the percentage bar and banner there are a number of images that are used to build a percentage bar or banner image on the fly. These images are used as the basis for the construction of the completed image and are layered together with text (if required) to build the complete image.

When adjusting styles in WSC for these areas it may be required to alter the images – perhaps giving them a shorter height or shorter width depending on the needs

Survey Flows

All but the most basic Web Surveys require some form of branching or page skipping. This is known in Web Survey Creator as "Flow Control".

In this chapter, we will look at how to add flow control to your surveys.

What are Survey Flows?

The best way to understand flows is to look at an example. We will use the **Customer Satisfaction Survey** we created in the previous Chapter.

The basic structure of that survey is as follows:

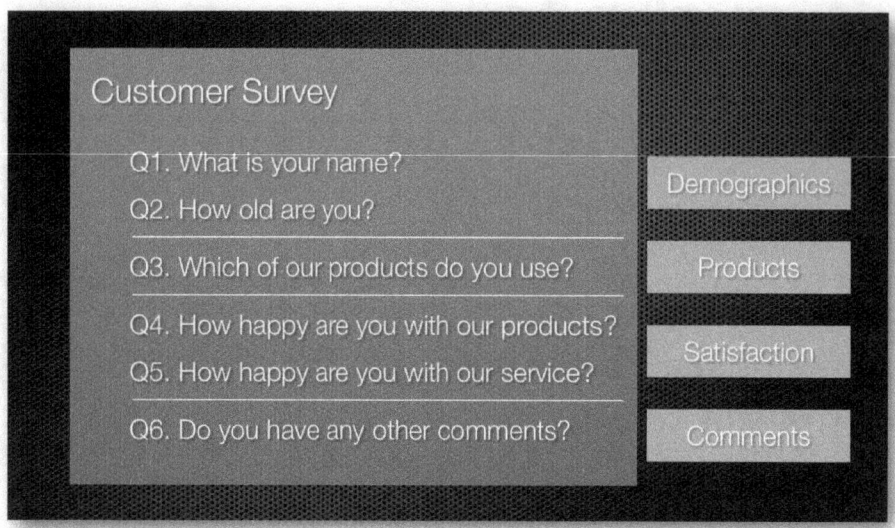

We broke this survey into a number of pages – Demographics, Product, Satisfaction and Comments. In this survey, a respondent currently answers the questions on each page, one page at a time.

An example of a survey flow is skipping the satisfaction page and jumping from the products page to the comments page.

Example of a needed Flow in the Satisfaction Survey

In our survey the products question includes a choice that indicates the respondent has never bought a product from our company. If they have never bought a product, it makes sense that they will not be able to answer any questions about our products and service. We will therefore skip those questions, and go straight to the comments question.

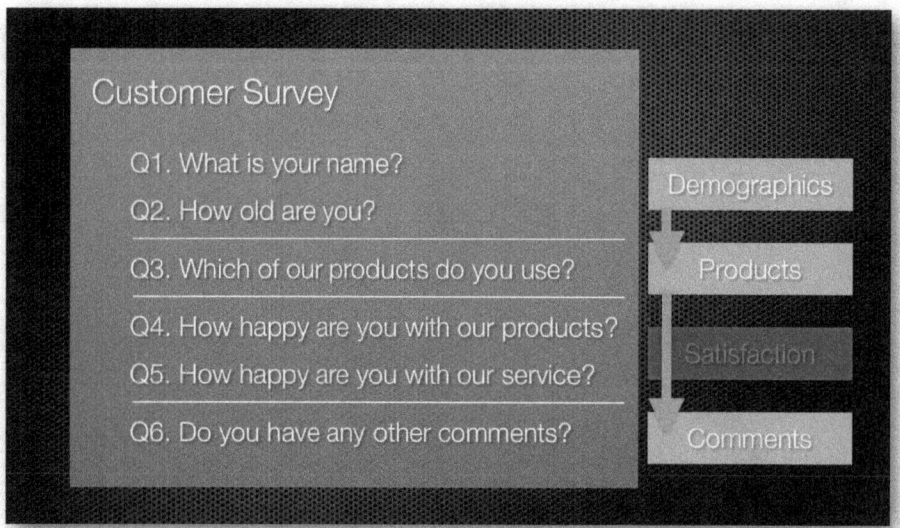

Creating a Survey Flow in Web Survey Creator

Let's open our Customer Satisfaction Survey in Web Survey Creator, and go to the second page to have a look at the product question.

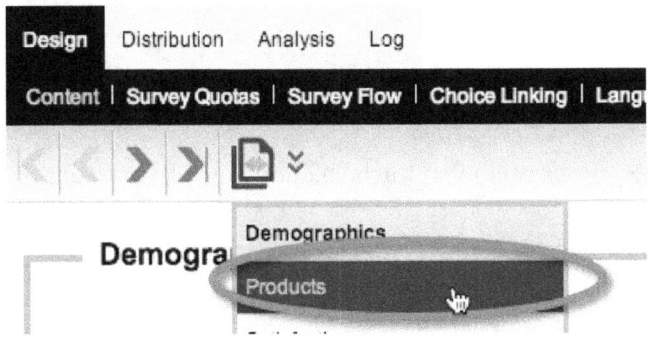

We can see that there is a Choice called "I have never bought a product from you".

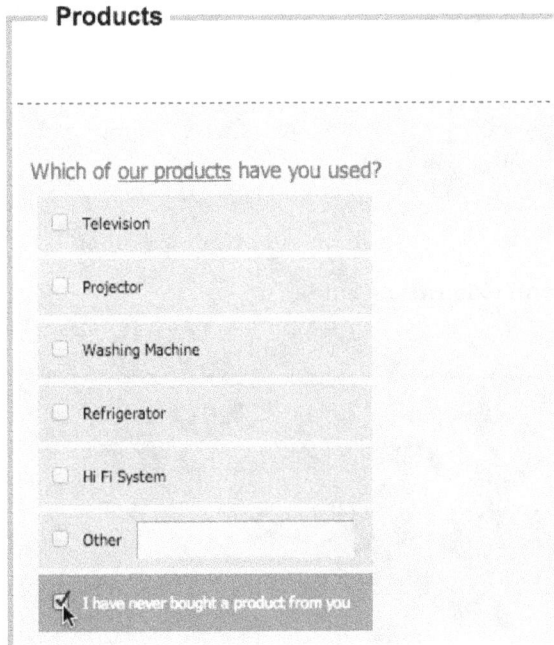

This will be the choice that, if chosen, should hide the third page in our survey.

To add flow control to our survey, we click on **Survey Flow** from under the **Design** tab.

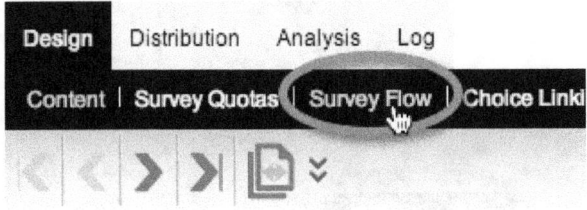

There are currently no flows set up in this survey.

We click the **Add** toolbar button to add a new flow.

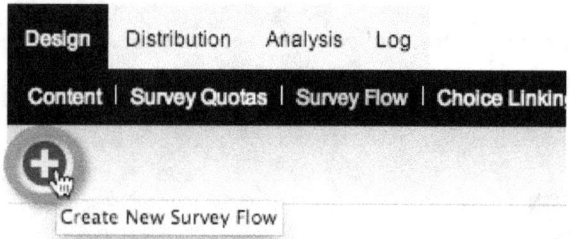

The first step in setting up a flow is to choose the page or pages that will be hidden by the flow. In our example, we want to hide the satisfaction page.

Note that the **Survey Flow Title** is automatically updated for us.

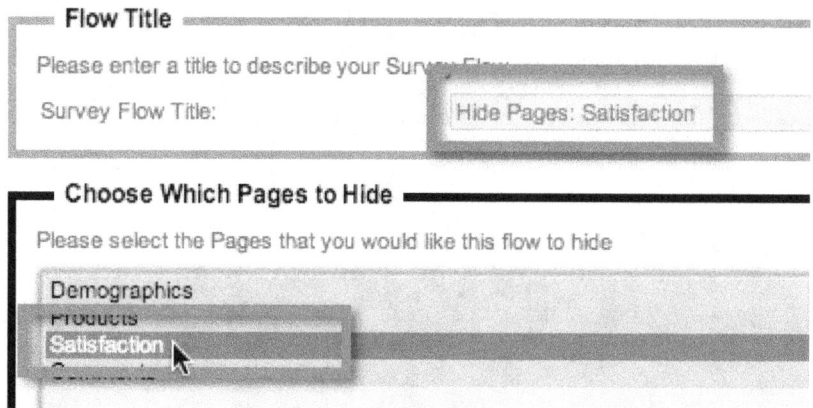

We save the flow by pressing the **Save & Continue to Add Conditions** button.

Flow Control Conditions

There are two parts to any flow:

1. Choosing the Pages we want to hide
2. Setting the Conditions that when passed will hide the page

We have already set up the first part of our flow - now we need to set our conditions.

42   Survey Flows

Note that only questions that appear before the page we want to hide are selectable in our conditions.

We want to choose the question "Which of our products do you use?"

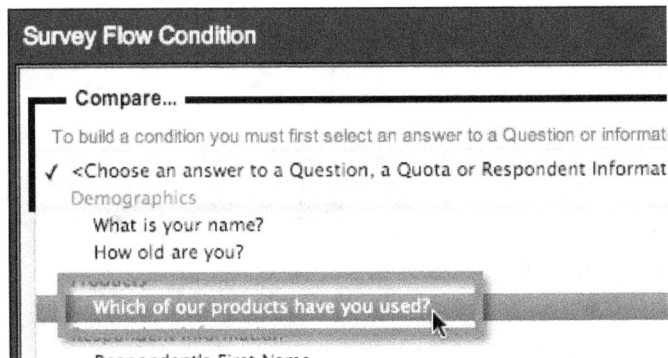

Based upon the Choices within this question, we are shown the condition types and choice values we can use in our condition.

We want to hide the page if the answer to this question is equal to "I do not use any products".

If this question is flagged as non-mandatory, it would be possible for a respondent to not choose any answer. We will assume an unanswered question is the equivalent of saying that they don't have any of our products.

Therefore, we want to indicate that the condition is still met if the question is not answered.

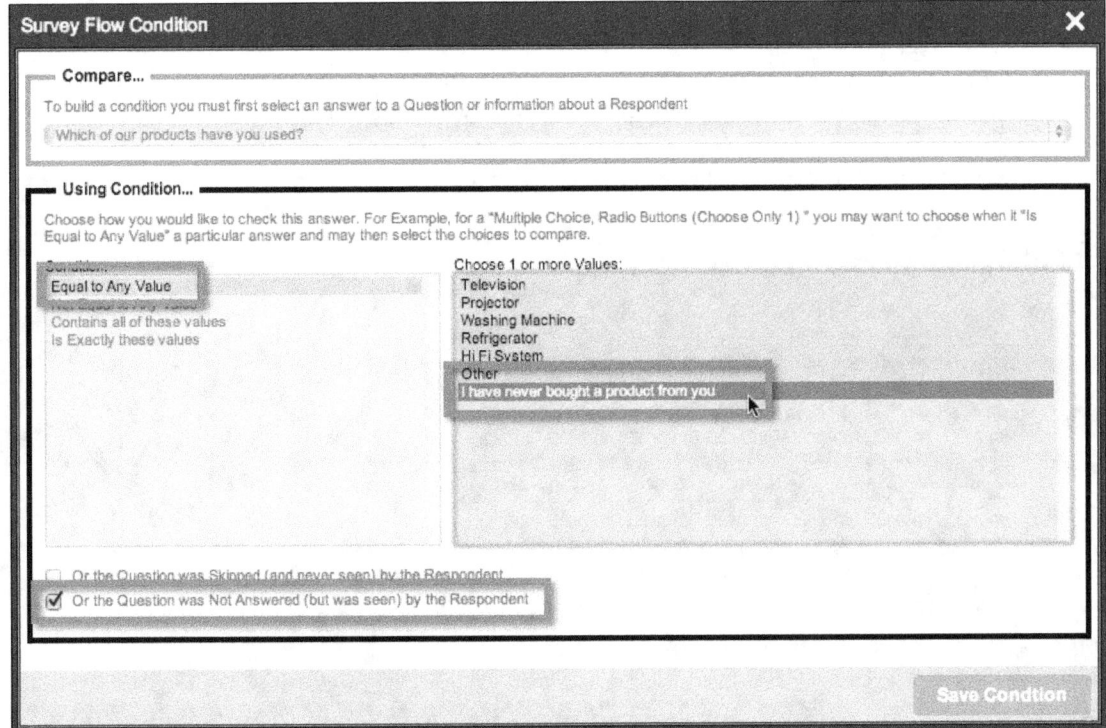

We can save the condition by pressing the **Save Condition** button.

That's all we need to do for our example.

Survey Flows 43

Conditions with multiple rules

Once we have entered our condition, the survey flow editor looks as follows:

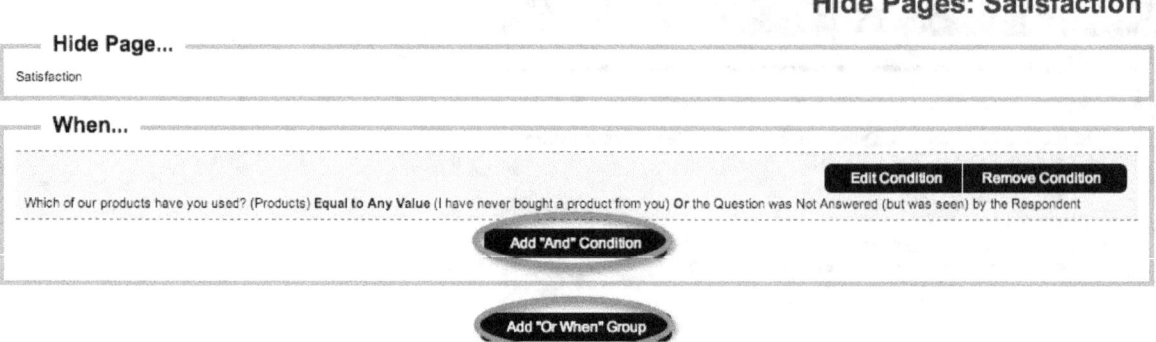

As you can see, "and" and "or" conditions can both be added to create a more complex condition if needed in the future.

Returning to the Survey Design

We can click **Content** under the **Design** tab to jump back to our Survey content.

If we go through the pages of the design, we can see that the flow is flagged in two places:

On the question used in the flow as show here:

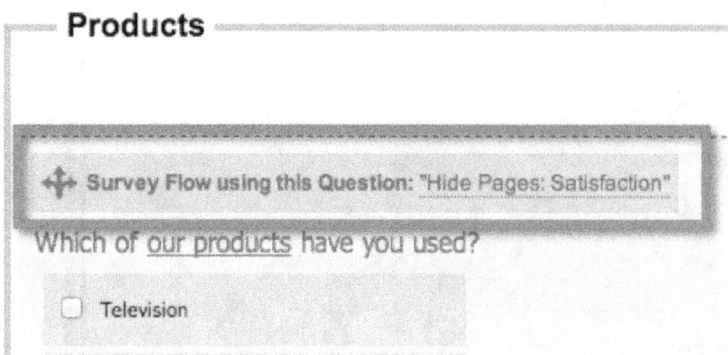

And on the page that will be hidden by the flow shown here:

This makes it easy to see where flows are being used, and a quick way to jump to the flow itself should we need to change it.

Testing the Flow

We need to preview our survey to check if the flow is working.

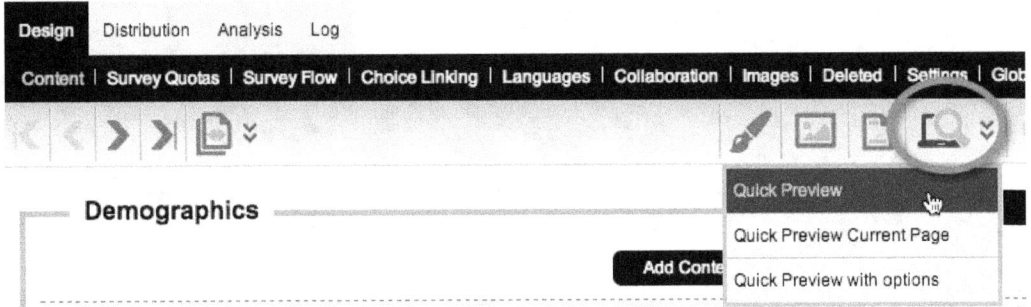

To confirm the flow is working, we can try the following test:

> *Let's assume we use a refrigerator.*
>
> Since we use one of the company's products, the questions about our level of satisfaction are shown.
>
> *Now, let's go back and say we do not use any products.*

Great – our flow is working as we intended.

Step-by-step Video

If you would like to see how this flow has been built, you can view it in our step-by-step video. You can access this video online by pressing the **Knowledgebase** button on the toolbar while working on flows.

The video is called **Creating Flow Control**.

Data Piping

Data Piping allows you to pass respondent and response information into survey content.

This makes it possible to personalize the survey, or customize survey content based upon an individual respondent's answers.

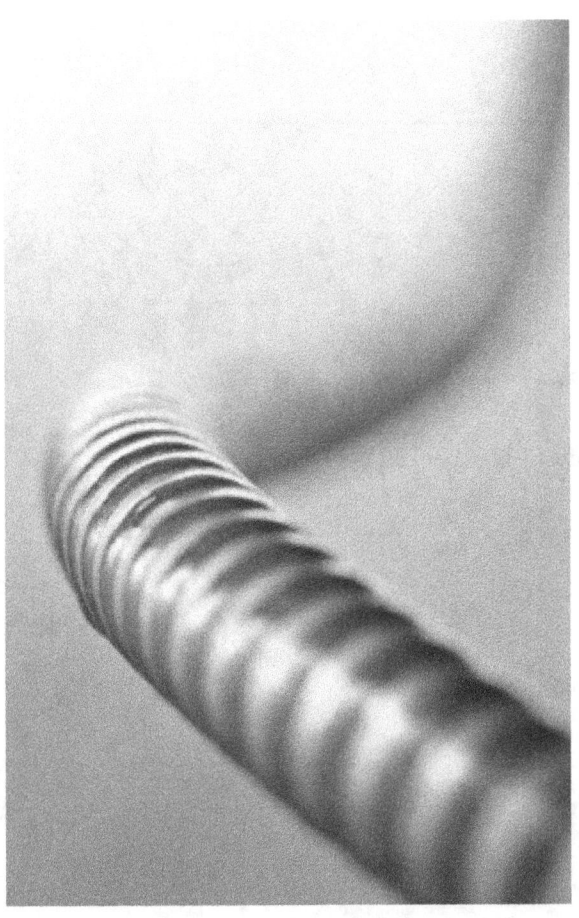

Improving our Customer Satisfaction Survey

The best way to understand data piping is to look at an example. We will use our *Customer Satisfaction Survey* for this example.

We already have the following question in this survey:

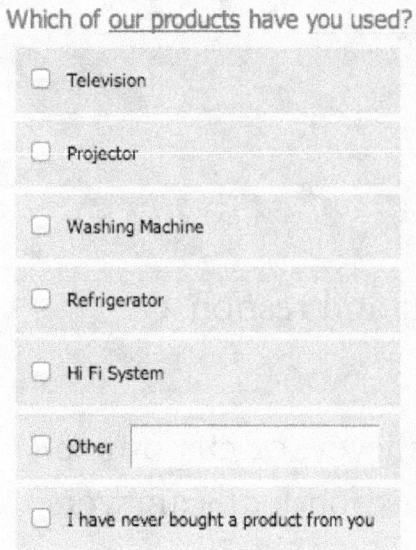

If a respondent chooses one or more products, they are asked how they rate our products and services:

At the moment, the question is very generic:

How happy are you with...

Using **Data Piping** we can have a much more specific question that reminds the respondent what they entered.

Setting up Data Piping

Step 1: Create an "Access Code"

Data Piping can use any question that has been set up with an **Access Code** as the source of the data piping data. We want to use the products question as the source of the data piping data. We can click the **Edit** button to edit this question:

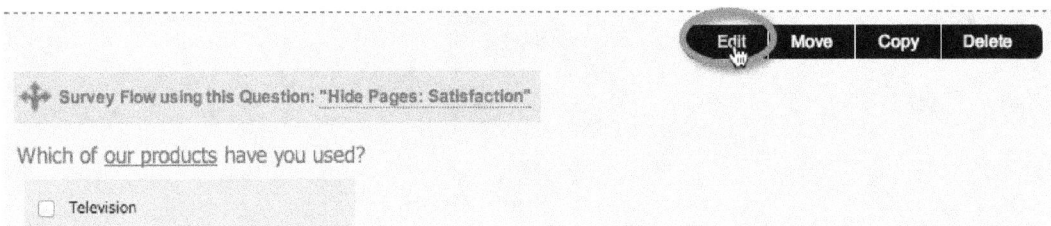

The Access Code can be entered for the Question. We can enter any alphanumeric characters for this code:

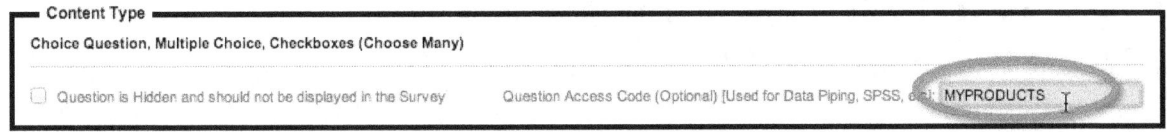

We have called it *MYPRODUCTS*. Now we can save the question, and it is ready to be used.

The code we are using for this question is shown in the designer.

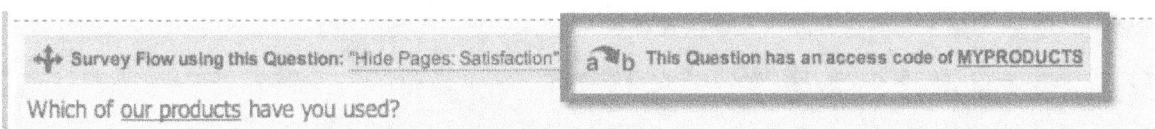

Step 2: Using an "Access Code" in our Content

Now that we have set up our Access Code, using it in the survey content is as simple as entering the code as part of our survey text.

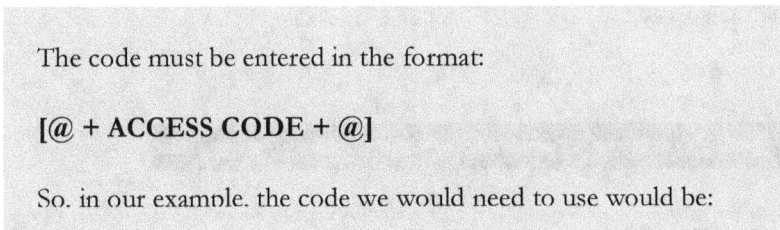

The code must be entered in the format:

[@ + ACCESS CODE + @]

So, in our example, the code we would need to use would be:

Survey Distribution 49

We will edit our satisfaction matrix to add this code:

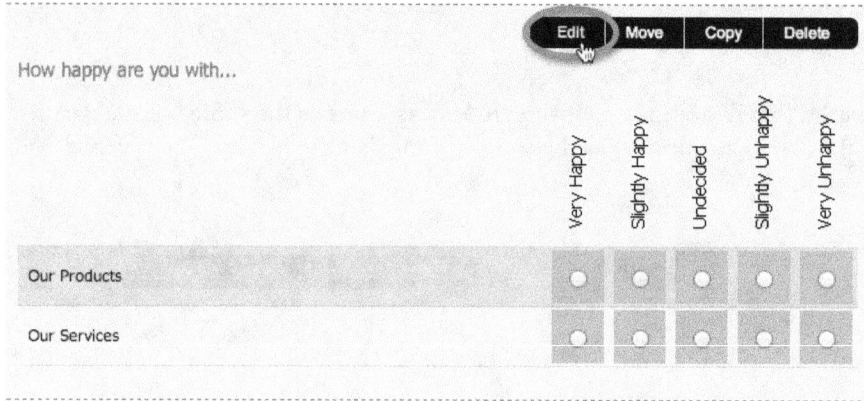

We will change the question text so that it refers to the products the respondent purchased:

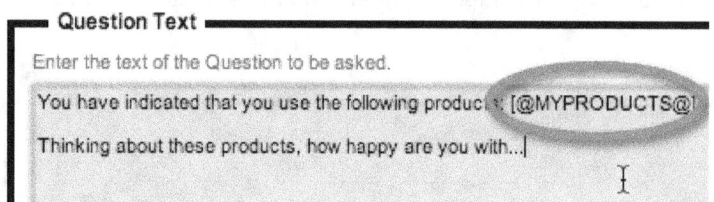

Note how the code is entered just like any other piece of question text.

In the designer, the question will now look as follows:

> You have indicated that you use the following products: [@MYPRODUCTS@]
>
> Thinking about these products, how happy are you with...

The designer does not deal with responses directly, and therefore can only show the code itself. To test this data pipe, we need to preview the survey.

Step 3: Test the Data Pipe

We can test a data pipe by previewing the survey.

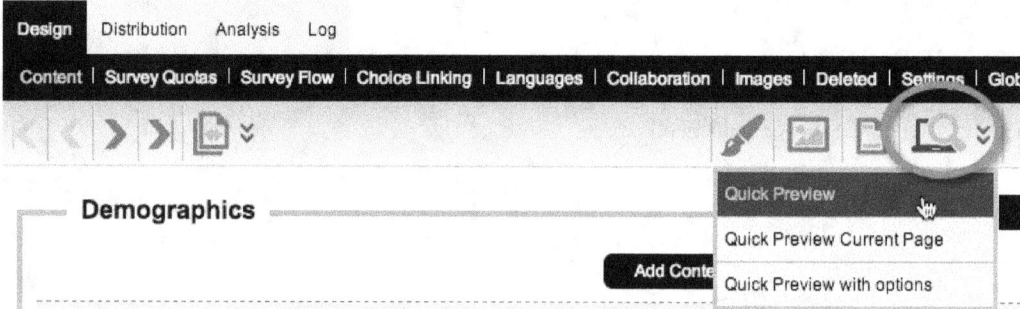

To test, we will say that we have used a Refrigerator and a Kettle (which is entered as an "other" item).

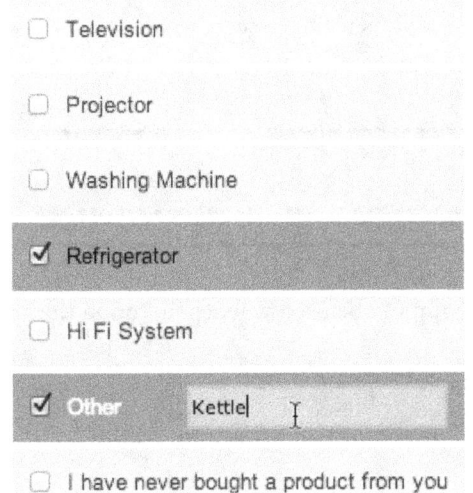

When we go to the next page in the preview, we see the data piping in action:

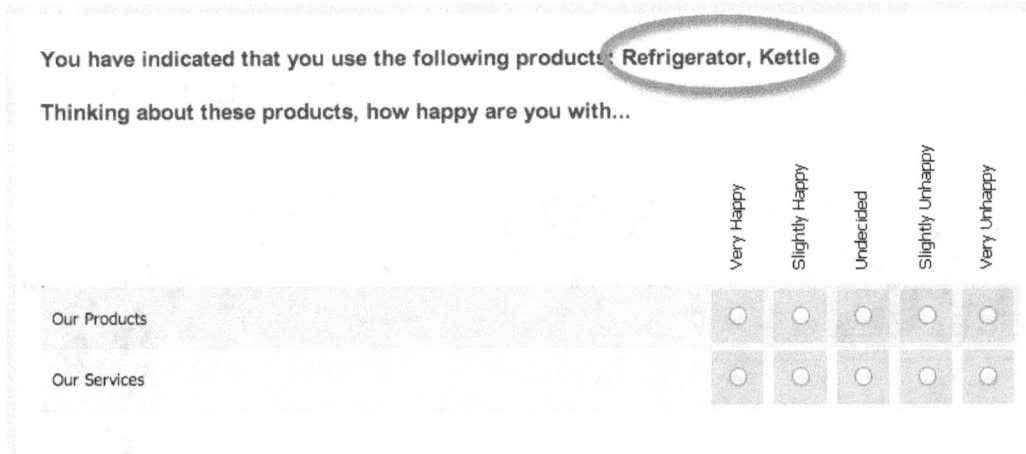

Step-by-step Video

If you would like to see more examples of creating data piping, you can view it in our step-by-step video. You can access this video online by pressing the **Knowledgebase** button on the toolbar.

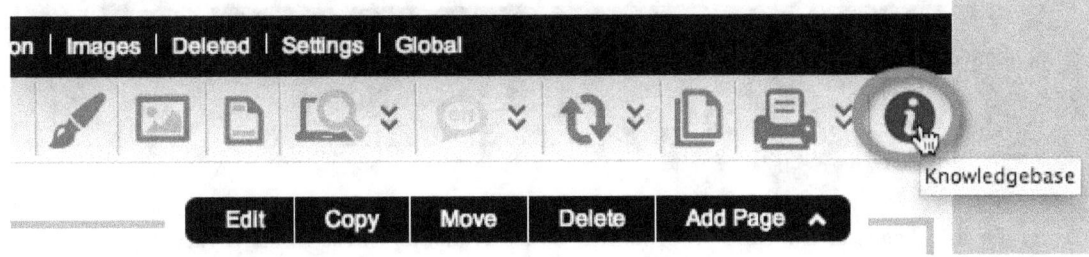

The video is called **Data Piping**.

Question Data Piping Reference

Data Piping is straightforward from a **Source Question** perspective - as we have seen, you simply add a code to the question.

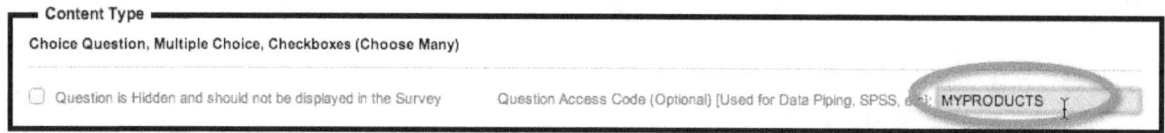

When it comes to using that data piping code, however, the way it must be used will depend upon the type of question we are referring to.

In the example above, the usage is simple:

[@MYPRODUCTS@] will return a list of products

An Example of more complex Data Piping – Matrix Questions

A matrix question has both rows and columns, so entering a single textual code will not suffice because it doesn't tell me exactly which data I am looking for.

The tutorial video in the previous section explains how we must refer to both the grid and the row we are looking for:

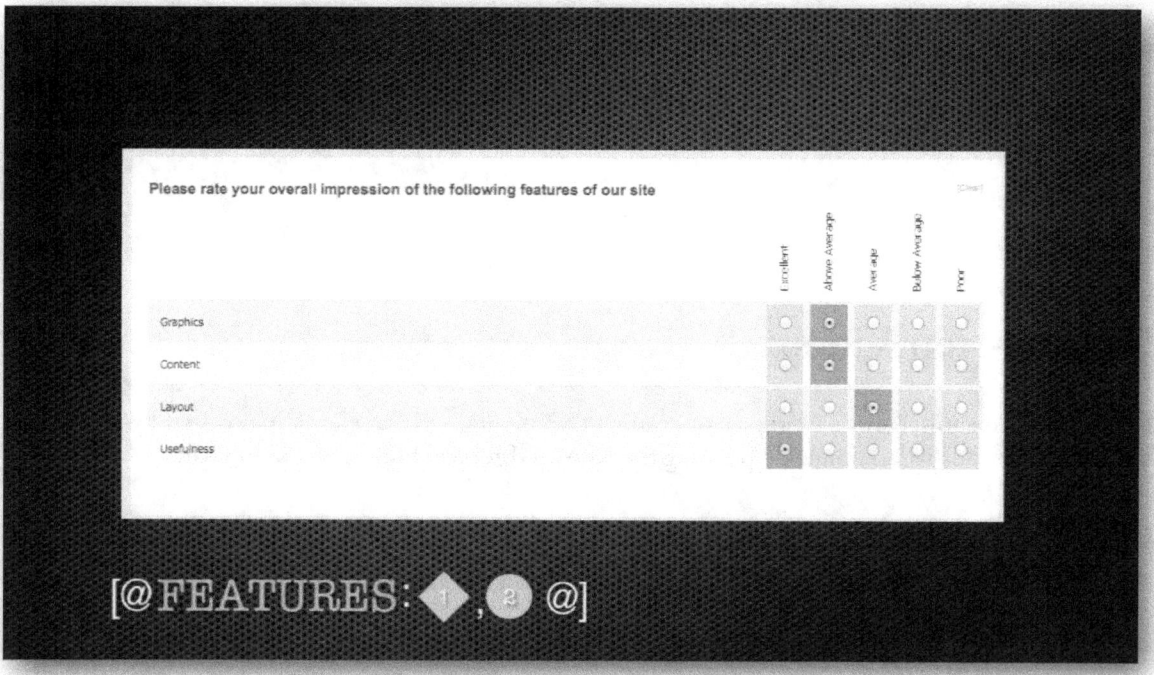

The tutorial video also discusses the various formatting codes available. These can also vary depending upon the type of question.

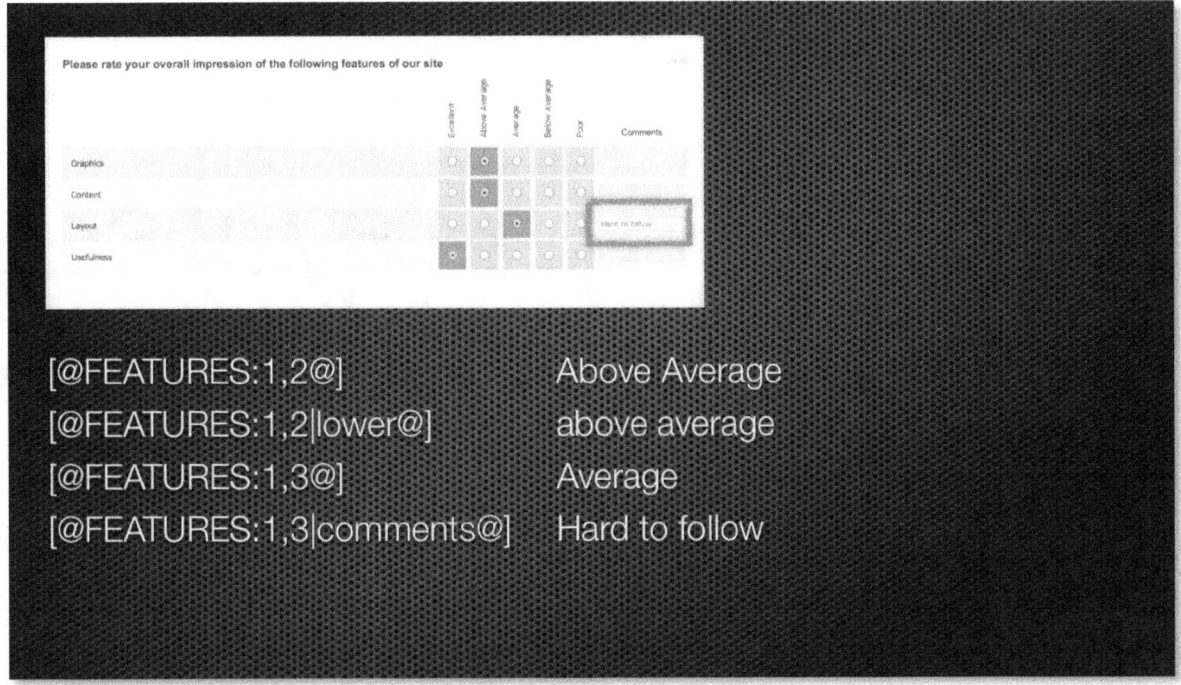

[@FEATURES:1,2@]	Above Average
[@FEATURES:1,2|lower@]	above average
[@FEATURES:1,3@]	Average
[@FEATURES:1,3|comments@]	Hard to follow

Clearly, different question types need to be dealt with in different ways. This Data Piping Reference takes you through these different question types.

Standards Used in this Reference Guide

When looking at a particular data piping code, the structure of the code is as follows (spaces are only shown for ease of readability):

`[@ QQQQQ: subcode | format @] where:`

| QQQQQ | is the code that has been entered on the source question |

#hidden# may be included to hide any data pipe. The format for a hidden code would therefore be:

`[@ QQQQQ: subcode | format #hidden# @]`

Data Grids (e.g. Matrix Questions)

Questions that take the form of "Data Grids" have a couple of elements which makes describing the data you are after a little trickier than other questions:

- Rows
- Columns
- One or more grids
- Additional data (e.g. comments on every row, tag data on choices)

The valid content for a Data Pipe code for these types of question is as follows:

subcode	x,y where x = GRID and y = ROW
format	tag:TAGNAME where TAGNAME is the code of the TAG
	upper lower comments

Examples

`[@FEATURES: 1,2@]`

`[@FEATURES: 1,2|lower@]`

`[@FEATURES: 1,2|comments@]`

`[@FEATURES: 1,2|tag:MOREINFO@]`

Numeric Grids

Questions that take the form of "Numeric Grids" need to have the following items referenced:

- The Grid (which will always be 1)
- Rows
- Columns

The valid content for a Data Pipe code for these types of question is as follows:

Subcode	x,y,z where x = GRID and y = ROW

Examples

Get the value from row 3, column 2 of a numeric grid:

`[@NUMGRID: 1,3,2@]`

Date Time Questions

Nil - all based on format of date time field

Demographic Address

subcode	fulladdress / address (default) addressline / address city state postalcode / zipcode / postcode / zip country
format	lower upper singleline

Examples

`[@ADDRESS: fulladdress@]`

`[@ADDRESS: city|upper@]`

`[@ADDRESS: fulladdress|singleline@]`

`[@FEATURES: 1,2|tag:MOREINFO@]`

Demographic Email

subcode	*None*
format	lower upper

Examples

`[@EMAIL|lower@]`

Demographic Name

subcode	fullname (default) firstname lastname / surname title
format	lower upper

Examples

`[@NAME: fullname@]`

`[@NAME: lastname|upper@]`

Demographic Phone

subcode	*None*
format	lower upper

Examples

`[@PHONE|lower@]`

Drop Down List

subcode	*None*
format	lower upper a,b,c,..,Z values for each choice

Examples

`[@MYDROPDOWN|lower@]`

`[@MYDROPDOWN|Alt2;Alt2;Alt3;@]`

Note: The second example explains that if the first value is selected, show the text "Alt1" rather than the actual text in the list etc.

Multiple Selection List

subcode	x where x = CHOICE
format	lower upper a,b,c,..,Z values for each choice tag:TAGNAME where TAGNAME is the code of the TAG

Examples

`[@MYLIST|lower@]`

`[@MYLIST|Alt2;Alt2;Alt3;@]`

`[@MYLIST:1|tag:MYDATA@]`

Single Line Text

subcode	*None*
format	lower upper

Examples

`[@SLTEXT|lower@]`

Multiple Line Text

subcode	*None*
format	lower upper

Examples

`[@MLTEXT|lower@]`

Numeric

Nil - based on format

Ranking

subcode	None
format	lower upper a,b,c,..,Z values for each choice tag:TAGNAME where TAGNAME is the code of the TAG

Examples

[@MYRANK|lower@]

[@MYRANK|Alt2;Alt2;Alt3;@]

[@MYRANK|tag:MYDATA@]

Single Selection List

subcode	None
format	lower upper a,b,c,..,Z values for each choice tag:TAGNAME where TAGNAME is the code of the TAG

Examples

[@MYSSL|lower@]

[@MYSSL|Alt2;Alt2;Alt3;@]

[@MYSSL|tag:MYDATA@]

Slider

Nil - shown as number

Star Rating

Nil - shown as number

Distribution Tags – Creating and Piping

There are times when you want to get data into your survey, with different data for different distributions. Taking distribution data and getting it into a survey is very straightforward:

1. Go to the distribution methods for your survey by clicking on **Methods** under the **Distribution tab**.

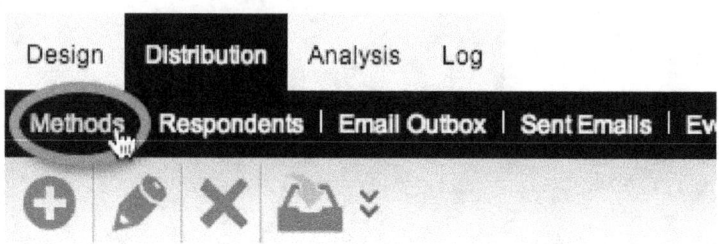

2. Click on the **Edit Distribution** button on the toolbar.

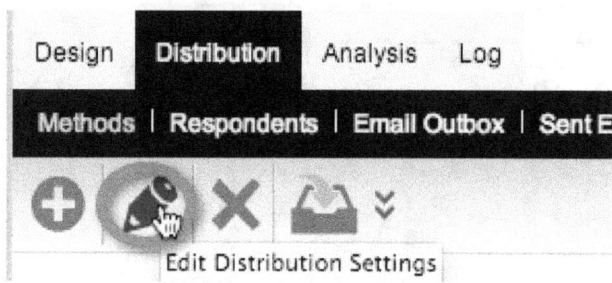

3. Enter tags and values into the distribution.

4. Use the tags in the survey.

The city in this distribution is [@DISTRIBUTIONTAG:CITY@]

The city in this distribution is New York

Piping into Post-Response Emails

Emails can be sent at the end of a response through the "Event API". Examples of workflows that can be created through the Email sending "Event API" include:

1. Sending an Email to all respondents at the conclusion of a survey indicating their response has been successfully submitted
2. Sending an Email to a company service manager if a respondent indicates a certain level of unhappiness with the service they have received

Setting up an Email can be achieved through the following steps:

1. Choose the **Event API** from the **Distribution tab**

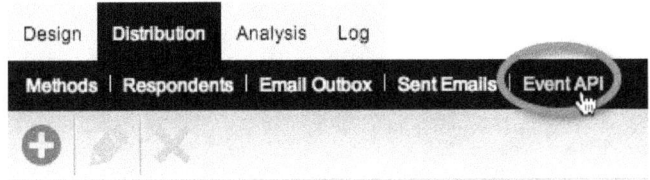

2. Click **Create Event** on the toolbar

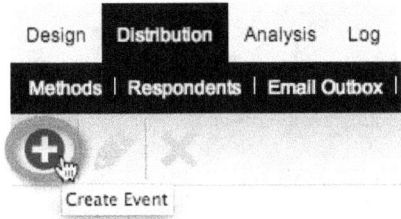

3. Choose the **Send Email** event

Survey Distribution 59

4. Set up the details for the Event

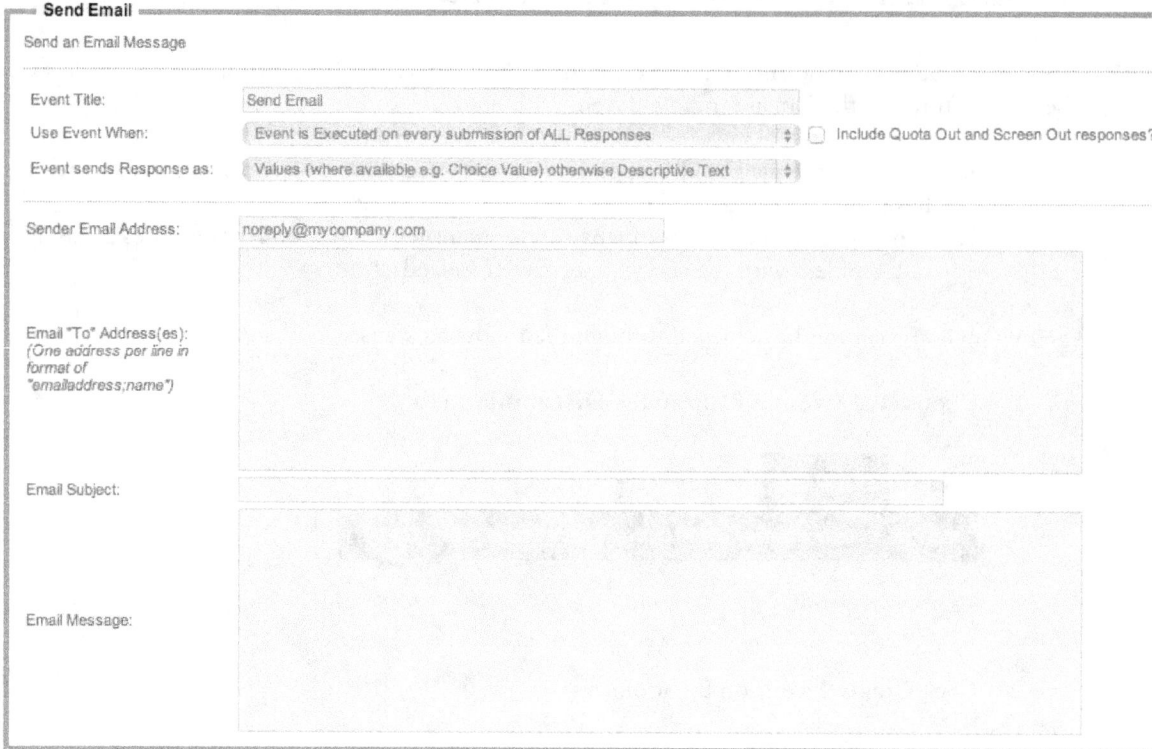

Email Content

When an Email is sent, sometimes all that is needed is some generic text. Often, however, there needs to be information in the Email that comes from the survey data or the respondent. The way to get information into the Email is to use data piping symbols. All parts of the Email can be piped – who the Email is sent to, the Email subject and the Email message content.

Possible system data piping codes are:

_USERNAME
_PASSWORD
_TOKEN
_RECALLCODE
_SUBMITTEDDATE
_EDITEDDATE
_COMPLETETYPE
_LANGUAGE
_TOTALTIME
_RESPONDENTCODE
_RESPONDENTFIRSTNAME
_RESPONDENTLASTNAME
_RESPONDENTEMAILADDRESS

In addition to this, standard question access codes can be used. All codes can be used with the standard data piping format of:

[@ + ACCESS CODE + @].

Survey Distribution

Once you have set your survey up, the next step is collecting responses. To collect responses, you need to distribute your survey.

This chapter describes how you can distribute anonymous surveys, and surveys to known respondents, using Web Survey Creator.

When to use Anonymous Surveys

Anonymous distribution is often the best way to send a survey under the following circumstances:

- In situations where people are often more willing to answer questions honestly if their responses cannot be directly attributed to them (for example, an employee survey)
- You may not know who your respondents are until they actually answer the survey (for example, a survey link on your Web site for visitors to click on)

Creating Survey with an Anonymous Distribution

Each survey you create in Web Survey Creator can be sent anonymously with literally no work needed to set up the distribution. The default type of distribution that is set up when a new survey is created in Web Survey Creator is an anonymous distribution.

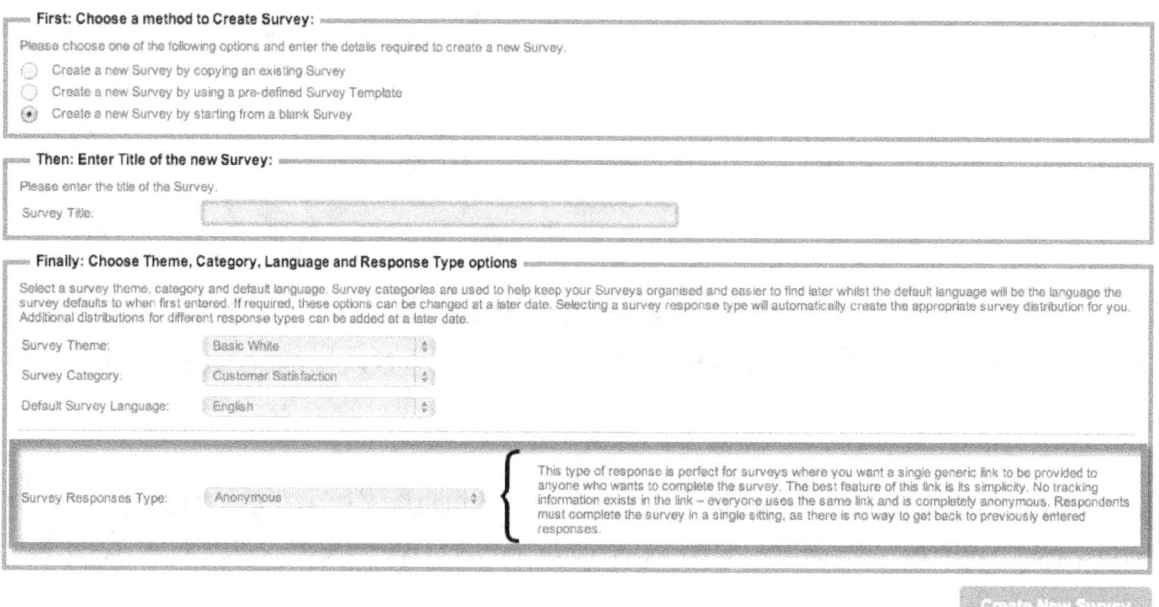

Viewing a Distribution

We can view distributions for a survey under Methods on the **Distribution** tab.

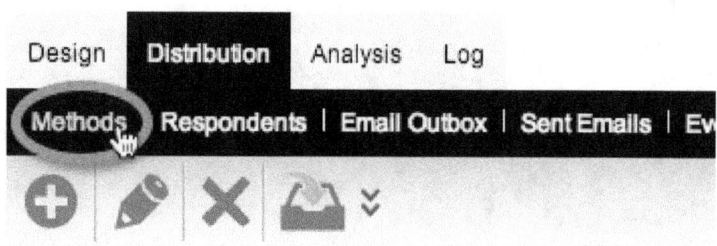

On this view, there are a number of buttons available to perform the most common actions for the distribution, without actually editing the distribution.

Starting and Stopping a Survey Accepting Responses

All versions of Web Survey Creator except the on-premise version (which has an option to not accept responses by default) will immediately allow responses to be accepted into the distribution that is created with the Survey.

You can easily tell whether a distribution is currently accepting responses – it will look as follows:

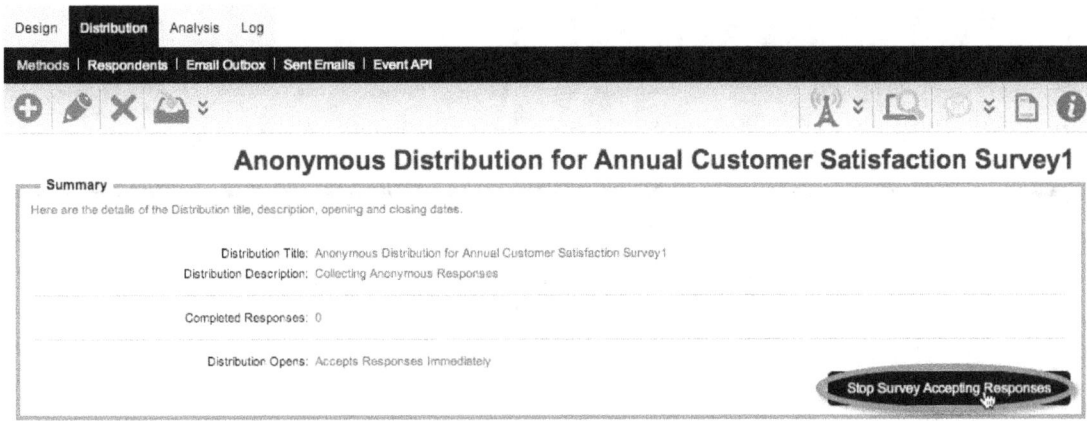

To stop accepting responses, we can click the **Stop Survey Accepting Responses**.

A distribution that is not accepting responses will be missing the button above. In fact, it will be missing all buttons on the view:

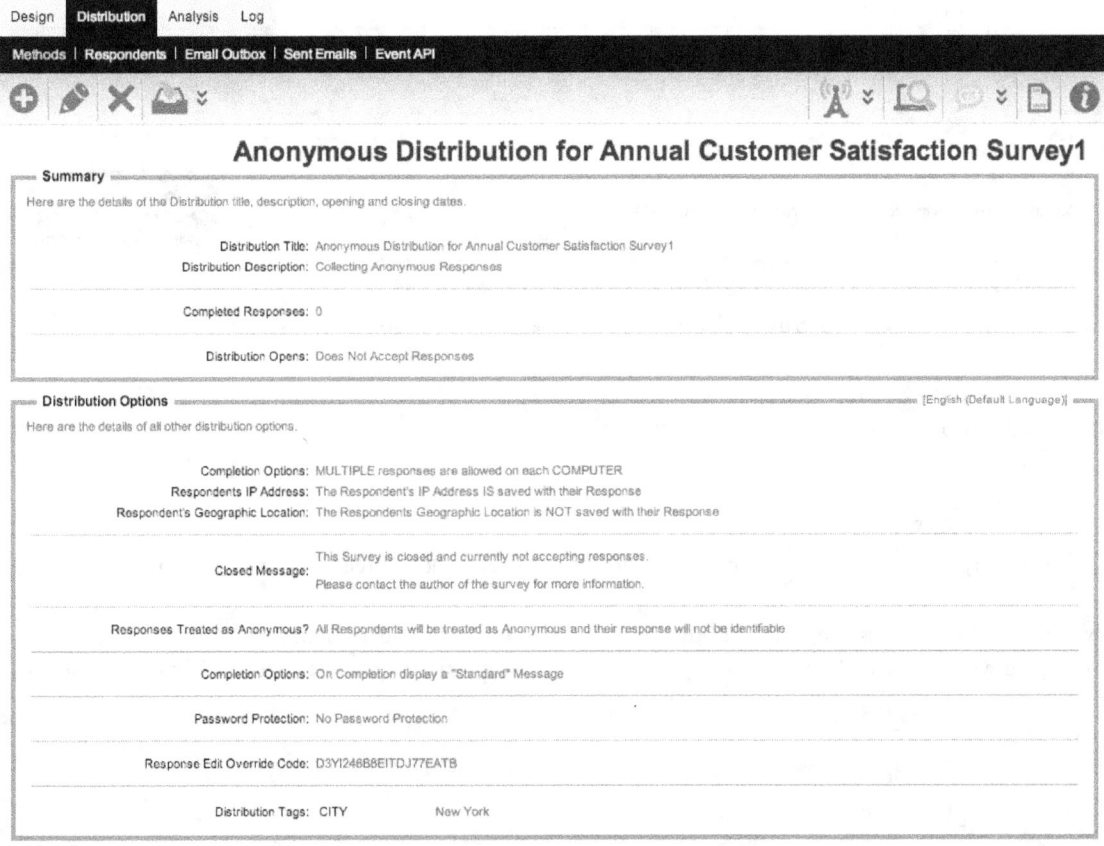

To start a distribution that was previously stopped, you need to:

1. Edit the distribution method.

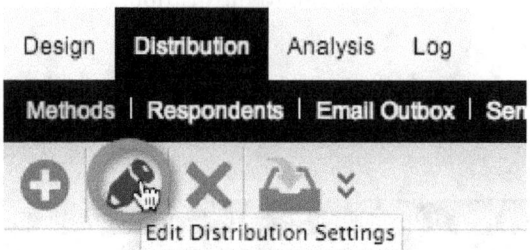

2. Choose the open the distribution immediately, or at a particular time/date.

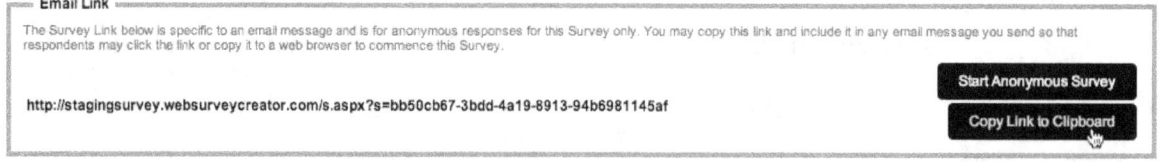

3. Save the distribution.

Opening the Survey or Distributing the Survey Link

Assuming our distribution is accepting responses, there will be a link available to open the survey.

We can click **Start Anonymous Survey** to open the survey in a new browser window

To distribute our survey to respondents, we can simply copy the survey link by pressing the **Copy Link To Clipboard** button. Once we have copied the link, we can:

1. Paste it into an Email
2. Use it on our Web site
3. Or do anything else we would normally do with a Web link to give people access to that link.

While we could also use this method to copy a link and paste it into social media sites such as Facebook and twitter, we would normally use the specific link sharing capabilities for these sites (discussed below).

Placing a Survey Link on a Web Site

A link in Email will look like a standard URL. If you want to place a link on a Web site, we may want the link to look more like a button. We can do this by copying the link under Web Page Link.

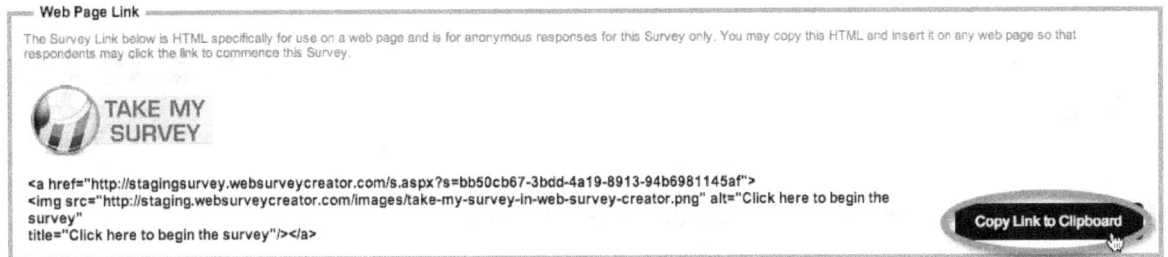

Embedding a Survey into another Site

There may be times when you want the survey to appear to be part of another site. In these cases the survey is "embedded" into the page by using particular HTML code. This can be copied and used in your page by clicking **Copy Script to Clipboard**.

Using a QRCode on Mobile Devices

QR is short for Quick Response. A cell phone can read these images quickly. They are used to take a piece of information from a transitory media and put it in to your cell phone. The reason why they are more useful than a standard barcode is that they can store (and digitally present) much more data, including URL links, geo coordinates, and text. The other key feature of QR Codes is that instead of requiring a chunky hand-held scanner to scan them, many modern cell phones can scan them.

To use the QRCode we can copy the image from our browser.

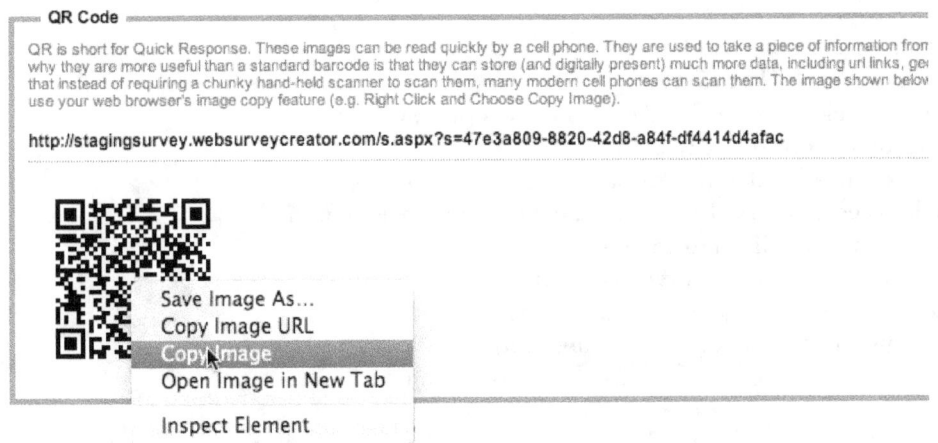

Survey Distribution 65

Sharing the Survey on Facebook or Twitter

There are two buttons – **Share Survey Link on Facebook** and **Tweet Survey Link** that will post our survey link directly to these sites.

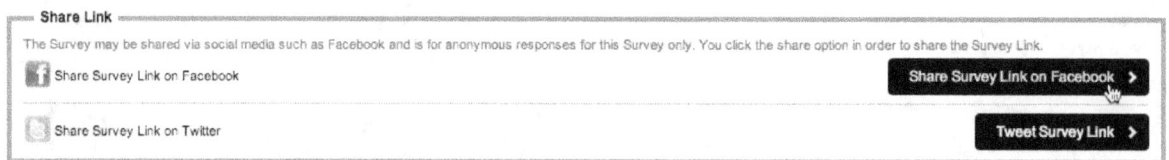

What happens when a Respondent clicks a link?

Regardless of which method of distributing links is used, the survey will always show in a similar manner. So we need to consider what happens when a respondent clicks on the link. Obviously they will be taken to the survey, but there are a number of variations on how the survey will manage their response.

These options can be changed when we edit the survey distribution.

Editing a Distribution

The anonymous distribution that is created automatically for us is set up with the most commonly used settings, but these settings can of course be changed to meet our exact requirements.

To delve into the settings for the distribution, we need to actually edit the distribution by pressing the **Edit** button on the toolbar.

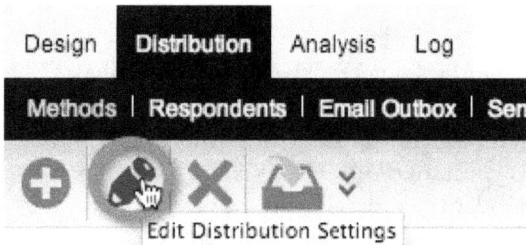

The **Distribution Edit** window allows us to configure everything about the distribution, including:

1. Whether we want to use a **custom link**
2. Whether we want to **track IP Addresses**
3. When the survey should be opened and closed to **accept responses**
4. Whether to include an **Introductory Page**
5. Whether **cookies** can be used to manage access to the survey
6. Whether individual **computers should be restricted** to a single response
7. Whether respondents can **edit their responses**
8. What should be displayed when a **survey is complete**
9. Whether a **password** needs to be used to access the survey
10. What settings to use for the survey if it is **embedded**
11. What **tags** to include on the distribution for use in the survey

The full distribution edit window is shown here:

Distribution Title

Please enter the title and description for this Distribution Method. The description can be used to give details about the Method for later reference.

Distribution Title: Anonymous Distribution for Annual Customer Satisfi

Distribution Description: Collecting Anonymous Responses

Custom Link: http://stagingsurvey.websurveycreator.com/s/

Respondent Geographic Location:
- [✓] Save the Respondents IP address with their Response
- No Location Request
- [✓] Show "Powered By WebSurveyCreator" on Surveys

When will this distribution be allowed to accept responses? [English (Default Language)]

You can choose when this distribution will accept responses and when it will stop accepting response. You can choose dates and times and/or when a certain number of responses have been completed. You can also enter a message respondents will see when the survey is not accepting responses.

- ( ) Does Not Accept Responses
- (•) Accepts Responses Immediately
- ( ) Accepts Responses from a Date and Time

- [ ] Should close on a specific Date and Time
- [ ] Should close when a Response Count is reached

Closed Message: This Survey is closed and currently not accepting responses. Please contact the author of the survey for more information.

Do you want to show an "Introduction Page" at the beginning of the Survey? [English (Default Language)]

You can optionally include an Instructions Page at the beginning of your survey. This can be used to provide the respondent with details about how to complete the survey or other information such as deadlines.

- [ ] Yes, I want to show an Introduction Page at beginning of the Survey

Are you happy to use COOKIES to control access to the survey?

COOKIES will allow us to control whom has started a survey and what their response was. However cookies are not shared between different browser types (e.g. between Chrome and Internet Explorer), some jurisdictions may restrict or prohibit cookie use and some respondents may have cookies disabled. You will need to determine from your respondent makeup whether you can use cookies or not. When cookies are not used multiple responses will be allowed from a single computer.

- [✓] Yes, I want to allow the use COOKIES to control access to the survey

How many responses will be allowed to be entered from a single computer?

You can restrict the number of responses that will be entered from each computer - that is, from a single Web Browser as cookies are not shared between different web browser types (e.g. between Chrome and Internet Explorer).

- ( ) Only one response per computer
- (•) Multiple responses may be entered per computer

When Respondents return to the Survey what should they be allowed to do?

You can control what a Respondent will be allowed to do each time they return to the same Survey. If any of the options listed are selected the respondent will be provided with a "Come-back-Later" Code to allow them to re-enter their response.

- [ ] Respondents can leave the survey and return later to complete an uncompleted response
- [ ] Respondent may return to the survey and edit an already completed response

What should happen when the Survey Completes? [English (Default Language)]

You can choose what experience the Respondent will have when they finish the Survey. If no options are selected a "Standard" message will be displayed on completion of a response.

- [ ] Display a "Thank you" Message
- [ ] Redirect them to a Web Page

Do you want to password protect this distribution? [English (Default Language)]

You can control whether Respondents must enter a password to access the Survey

- (•) No Password Protection required
- ( ) One Password that all Respondents must enter

Survey Embedding Options

You can choose to embed an anonymous Survey into your own web site. If you wish to embed your Survey into your own website set the following parameters for the display of the Survey. You are able to set the Width and Height of the Frame that the Survey will reside in. You can also choose how the Survey will be displayed. Selection of the display method will be useful when a small Width Frame is selected. You can also choose if you wish the Banner to be displayed and whether Scroll Bars should be displayed for Surveys that are longer or wider than the Frame Width and Height.

Width of Frame: 100% [350-1200 (for Measurements in Pixels) or 20% to 100% (for Measurements in %)]
Height of Frame: 500 [350 - 1200 (for Measurements in Pixels)]

Display Mode: Use Tablet Display of Survey for Display of Embedded Survey
Banner Display: Show Banner (Title, Logo) on Survey
Scroll Bar Display: Show Scrollbars on Surveys that are Wider or Longer than Frame Width and Height

Distribution Tags

Edit the Distribution Tags. Enter one Distribution Tag per line. To enter a Distribution Tag which spans more than one line place an underscore at the end of a line and continue to the next line. Distribution Tags must consist of a Code separated by a Colon. For example, CITY:New York.

Distribution Tags: CITY:New York

Let's look at the key settings that you can change from this **Edit** window.

Setting up a Custom Link

In addition to the title and description, we also have an option to provide a custom link for the survey – this can be thought of as a more "human readable" link than the automatically generated survey link.

Custom Link: http://stagingsurvey.websurveycreator.com/s/ custsat

Examples of an automatically generated link could look something like this.

http://stagingsurvey.websurveycreator.com/s.aspx?s=47e3a809-8820-42d8-a84f-df4414d4afac

The custom link, however, could look something like this.

http://stagingsurvey.websurveycreator.com/s/custsat

As we can see, they are much more readable.

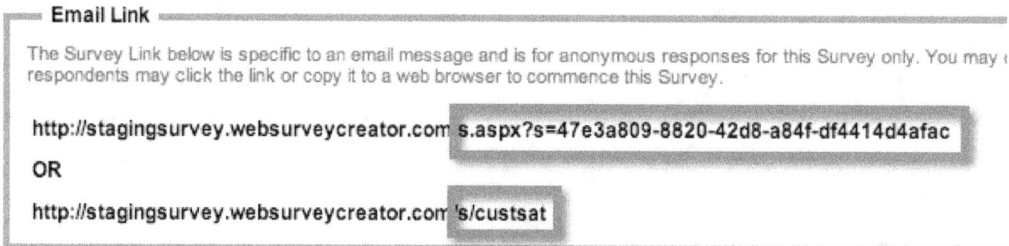

Tracking IP addresses

Every survey completed by a respondent is tagged with the address of their computer on the Internet, referred to as an IP Address. While this doesn't identify a person specifically (and therefore doesn't stop them from being anonymous), it does provide some information such as the general location of the person. For example, we can usually work out which city in the world a person is from using their IP Address.

While it is not recommended, we can uncheck the **Save IP Address** check box on the distribution if we want so even less is known about a respondent.

Starting, stopping and Restarting Surveys

The next group of settings relates to whether the survey is open to accept responses. Pressing the **Stop Survey Accepting Responses** button, like we did earlier in this chapter, was just an expedient way to change the settings we see here without having to edit the distribution directly. Because we had clicked the button to stop accepting responses we can see here that responses will not be accepted.

We are now editing the distribution, so we have a lot more options to choose from, including:

- Re-opening the survey to accept responses
- Choosing when the survey closes based on either a time and date, or a number of responses
- Setting the text for the closed survey message

When will this distribution be allowed to accept responses?

You can choose when this distribution will accept responses and when it will stop accepting response. You can choose dates and tir completed. You can also enter a message respondents will see when the survey is not accepting responses.

○ Does Not Accept Responses   ● Accepts Responses Immediately   ○ Accepts Responses from a Date and Time

☐ Should close on a specific Date and Time
☐ Should close when a Response Count is reached

Closed Message: This Survey is closed and currently not accepting responses.
Please contact the author of the survey for more information.

Dealing with Anonymity

One of the biggest issues with having an anonymous survey is that the survey IS anonymous. This makes it hard to deal with issues such as:

- Stopping people from entering multiple responses
- Allowing people to come back into a partially complete response and complete it
- Allowing people to edit their previously completed response
- Ensuring only the people we want have access to the survey

The distribution has a number of options to manage such issues.

If we want to stop duplicate responses from a single computer, we need to leave cookies enabled on our survey, and select **Only one response per computer**. This will hinder a person's ability to enter two responses to the survey from their computer.

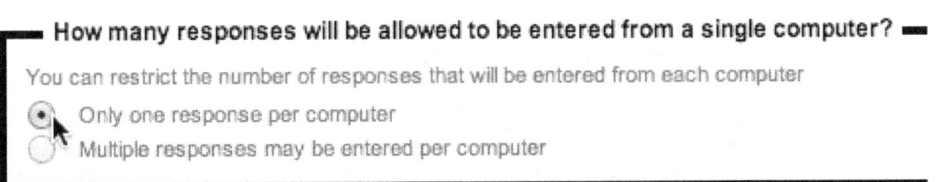

If we want people to be able to either complete a partial response, or edit a previously entered complete response, we check the appropriate check boxes under the **Return to Survey** settings.

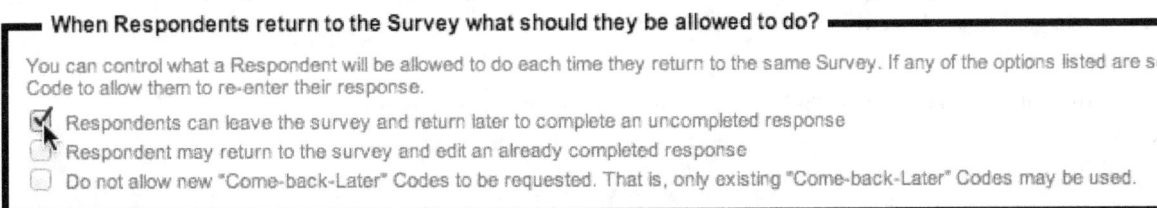

If we want respondents to be able to return, a "Come back Later Code" will be generated for them when they first start the survey.

Here is an example of how the survey would look to a respondent when we use this code. All the descriptive text is fully configurable in the distribution.

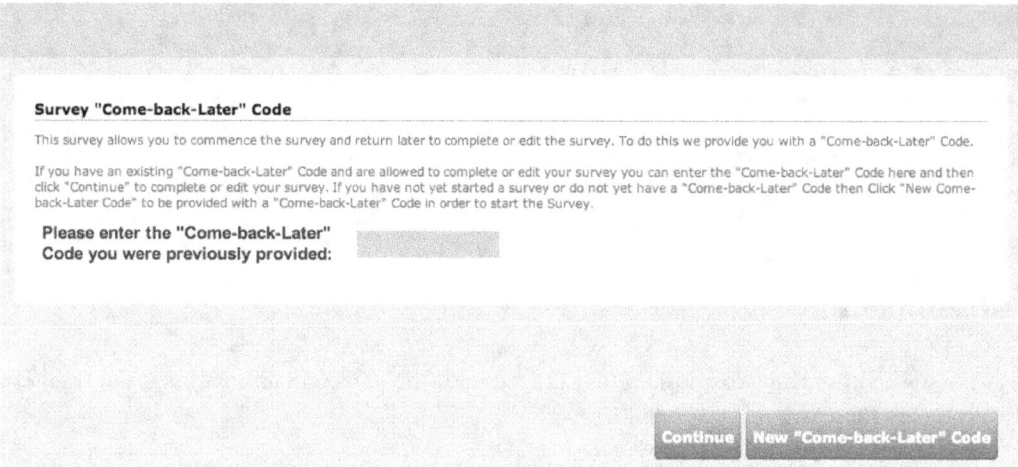

- A returning respondent enters a code they previously wrote down and presses the **Continue** button to proceed into the survey and complete or edit their previous response.
- New Respondents don't have a code – they simply press the **New Come Back Later Code** button to begin the survey.

Before the survey commences, they will then be given their own **Come back later code** which can be used if they need to re-enter the survey and edit their response at a later stage.

Survey Completion Settings

We can choose what a Respondent will see when the survey completes. Usually this will simply be a thank you message, but we have the option to also redirect to another Web page.

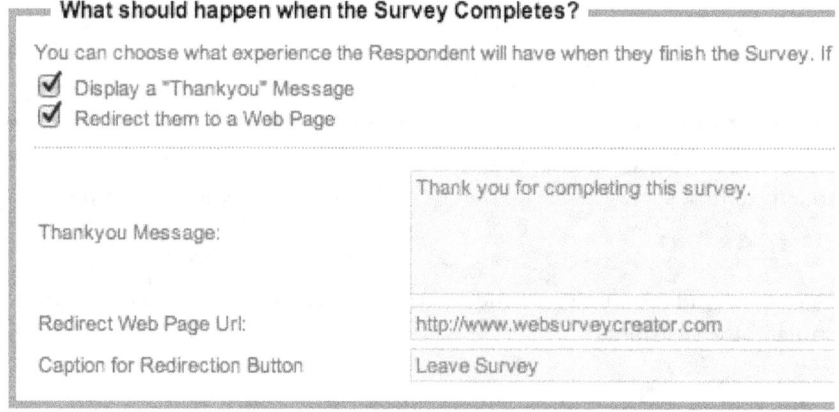

Survey Password

We can indicate whether or not we want to require a password for entry into the survey. Enforcing a password means that unauthorized people who stumble across the survey link will not be able to complete the survey, because they will not be able to start the survey without the password that we have only provided to authorized people.

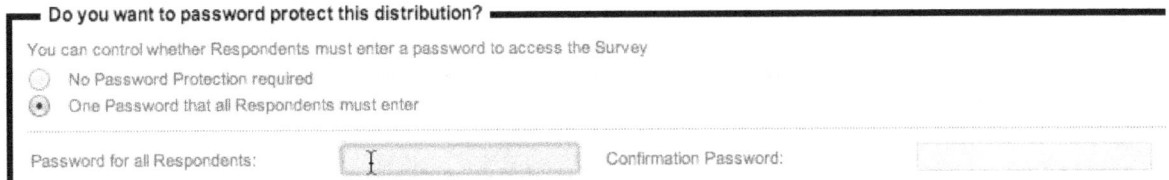

Survey Embedding Options

If you intend to embed the survey in another page, you need to set up how the embedded survey will operate. For example if you have a small area to embed the survey, you may choose to use a mobile phone version of the survey, and limit its width to 320px wide.

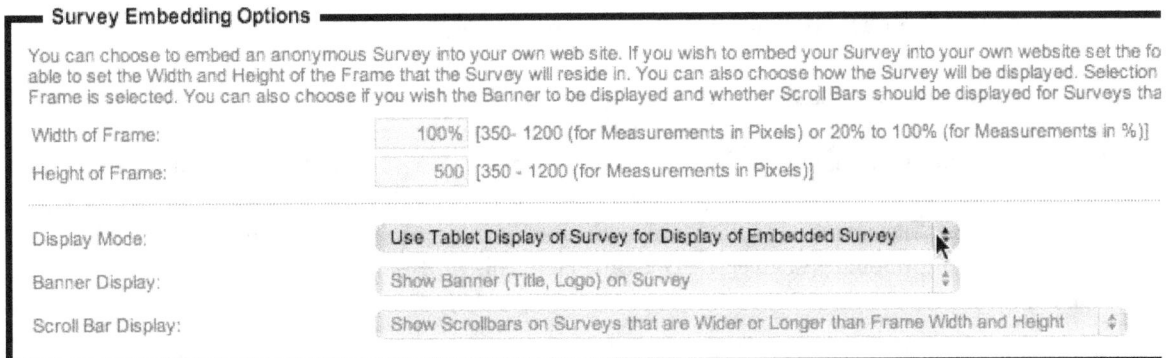

Creating a Respondent Distribution

We have seen how an Anonymous Distribution is created when we create a new survey in Web Survey Creator. If, however, we don't want anonymous respondents, we need to create a new distribution, known as a **Respondent Distribution**.

We click the **Create New Distribution Method** button from the distribution methods toolbar.

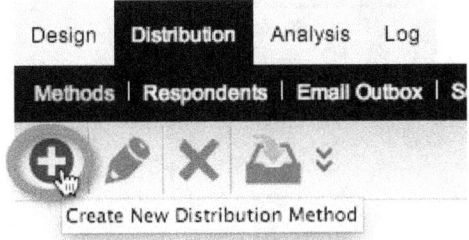

The type of distribution we want to create will use a list of respondents, so we would choose **You create Respondents here and have us send out emails for you**.

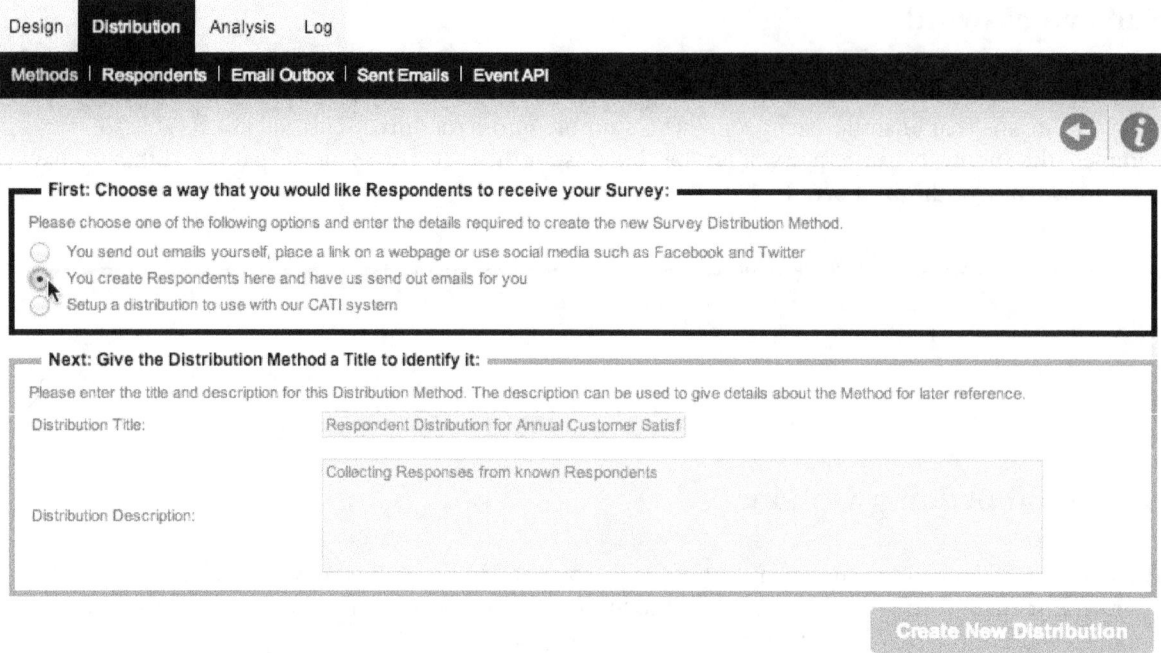

We click the **Create New Distribution button** to create our distribution.

To see what options we can change on the distribution, see the previous section in this chapter called "Creating Survey with an Anonymous Distribution" (the options are exactly the same as for anonymous distributions). For this section, we will assume that the default settings are sufficient for our use.

Unlike an anonymous distribution, you will notice that a link can't just be copied and used for this type of distribution - each respondent will receive a personal link. This is made clear when viewing the distribution:

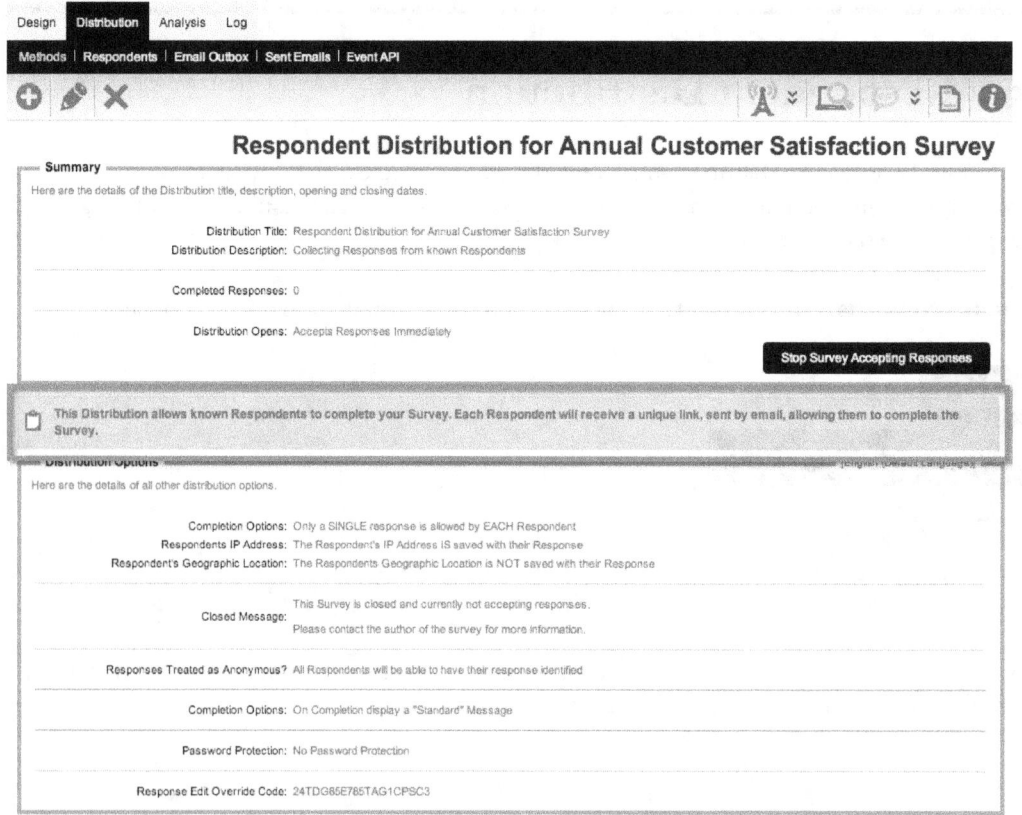

72   Survey Distribution

Adding Respondents to a Distribution

Once the distribution is set up, we need to add respondents to it. This is the list of people we will be emailing with an invitation to the survey.

We set up these people under **Respondents** on the **Distribution** tab.

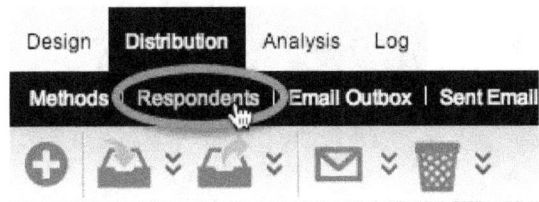

There are four methods to load respondents:

1. Import NEW Respondents from Text/File
2. Update EXISTING Respondents from Text/File
3. Import Respondents from another survey
4. Import Respondents from your Address books

We will look at each of these methods in turn.

Import Method #1: New Respondents from Text or File

The most common way to add respondents into a distribution is to import a list of new respondents into the distribution. The steps to do this are as follows:

1. Click on **Import NEW Respondents from Text/File** from the Import Respondent toolbar button

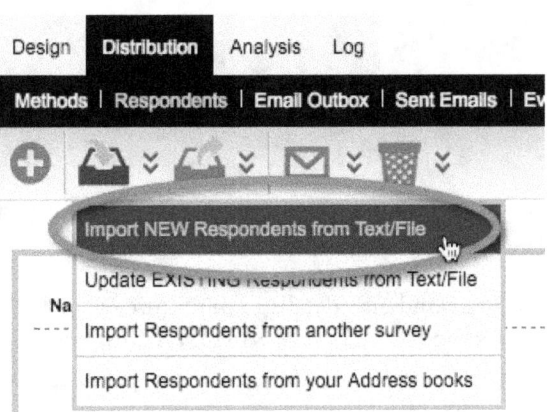

Survey Distribution 73

2. The import window will be shown. A distribution to import into must be selected, and the respondents to import must either be pasted in as text, or uploaded from an Excel file. If a text import will be performed, and a starting format is needed, click **Insert Template** to create sample data in the text field that can be used as the basis.

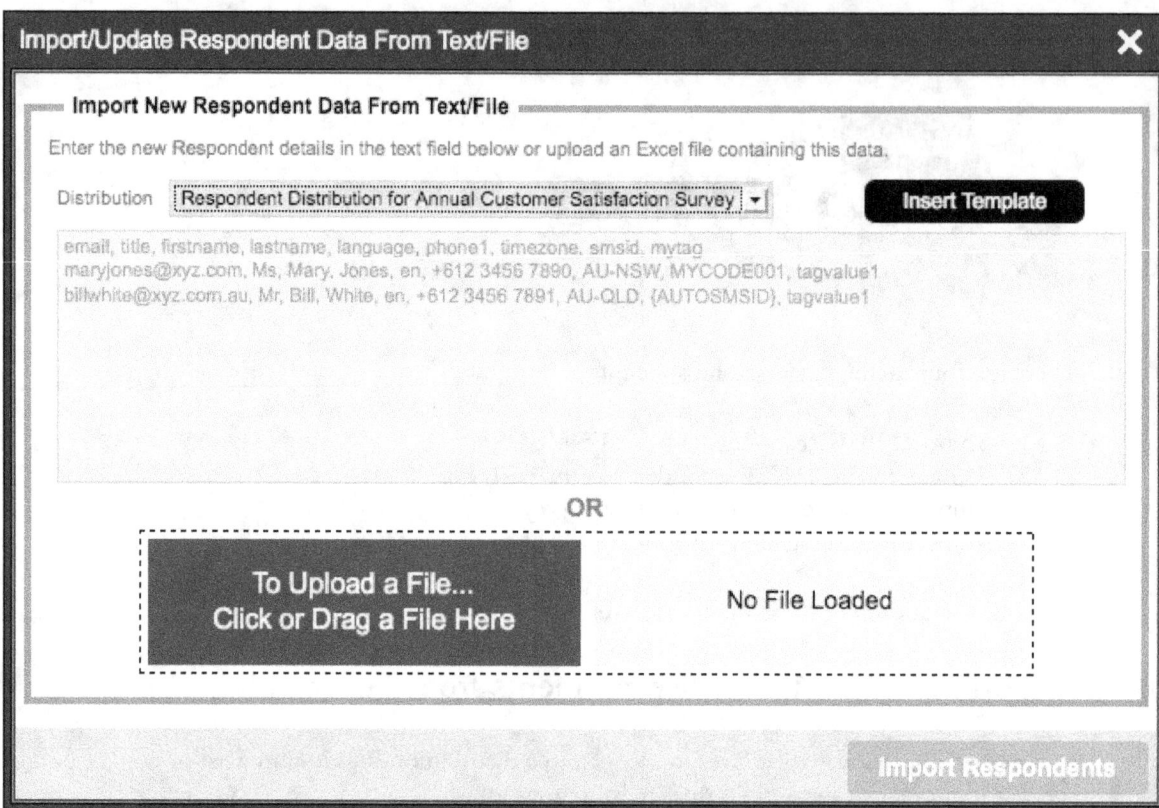

3. Click the Import Respondents button to perform the import.

What is SMS ID, and why would we use it?

SMSID is the "Sample Management System Identifier" and is effectively an external identifier for a respondent. It has two main uses:

1. If respondents are being imported from another system or list that has a unique ID for each respondent, the SMSID can be used to store that external ID – thus providing a way to refer back to the original system or list.
2. As a unique identifier that makes updating a respondent's details in the future easy (this will be looked at in more detail in the next import method – "Update EXISTING Respondents from Text/File")

If the import data does not have anything that could be used as SMSID, but you would like unique IDs attached to each respondent, **{AUTOSMSID}** can be put in for each respondent, and the system will generate an ID for you.

What format does the import use?

The format of the import follows uses the following rules:

1. The first row of the import (the first line if importing by text, or first row if using an Excel import) lists the data that the subsequent rows will include. This includes a pre-defined list of standard fields (email, title, firstname etc.), together with response and respondent tag data.

2. Each subsequent line/row in the import file contains the data for each field

If an Excel file is used for the import, it just needs to use rows and columns instead of the lines and comma delimiters used for a text import. Here is the same import data, shown as a text import, and in Excel:

```
email, title, firstname, lastname, language, phone1, timezone, smsid, mytag
maryjones@xyz.com, Ms, Mary, Jones, en, +612 3456 7890, AU-NSW, MYCODE001, tagvalue1
billwhite@xyz.com.au, Mr, Bill, White, en, +612 3456 7891, AU-QLD, {AUTOSMSID}, tagvalue1
```

	A	B	C	D	E	F	G	H	I
1	email	title	firstname	lastname	language	phone1	timezone	smsid	mytag
2	maryjones@xyz.com	Ms	Mary	Jones	en	+612 3456 7890	AU-NSW	MYCODE001	tagvalue1
3	billwhite@xyz.com.au	Mr	Bill	White	en	+612 3456 7891	AU-QLD	{AUTOSMSID}	tagvalue1
4									

How do I pre-populate a response for the imported respondent?

The import automatically knows that you are trying to import response data when the code you use in the import file matches the access code used in a question. For example, if a survey has a gender question with the Access Code "GENDER" the import data could look as follows (gender data has been highlighted to make it easy to see):

```
email, title, firstname, lastname, language, phone1, timezone, GENDER
maryjones@xyz.com, Ms, Mary, Jones, en, +612 3456 7890, AU-NSW, 1
billwhite@xyz.com.au, Mr, Bill, White, en, +612 3456 7891, AU-QLD, 2
```

To pre-populate a question, it <u>must</u> be given an access ID. If the question is a choice questions, the choices must all be given unique values, because the import uses values to set the correct choices in the data

Any import data that uses a code that does not match an access code is assumed to be a respondent tag, and is added directly to the respondent.

For more information on importing question data, see the related topic later in this chapter.

Import Method #2: Update Existing Respondents from Text or File

Creating new respondents and updating existing respondents have been split so that they are distinct processes. The most important question to be asked for an update is:

How can I find the right respondent to update?

WSC allows two methods to identify a respondent:

1. Using the SMSID (if it exists)
2. Using the internal respondent identifier

The SMSID is the best choice if it exists, because it is an ID you can set yourself, and easily see on a respondent. If you do not have an SMSID, you will need to get the internal respondent identifiers by exporting the respondents first (the export can include this identifier in the respondent data).

The steps to do a respondent update are as follows:

1. Click on **Update EXISTING Respondents from Text/File** from the Import Respondent toolbar button

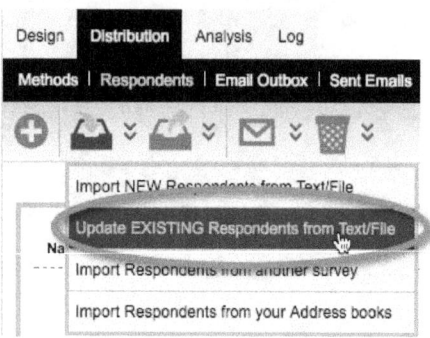

2. The import window will be shown. A distribution to import into must be selected, and the respondents to import must either be pasted in as text, or uploaded from an Excel file. If a text import will be performed, and a starting format is needed, click **Insert Template** to create sample data in the text field that can be used as the basis.

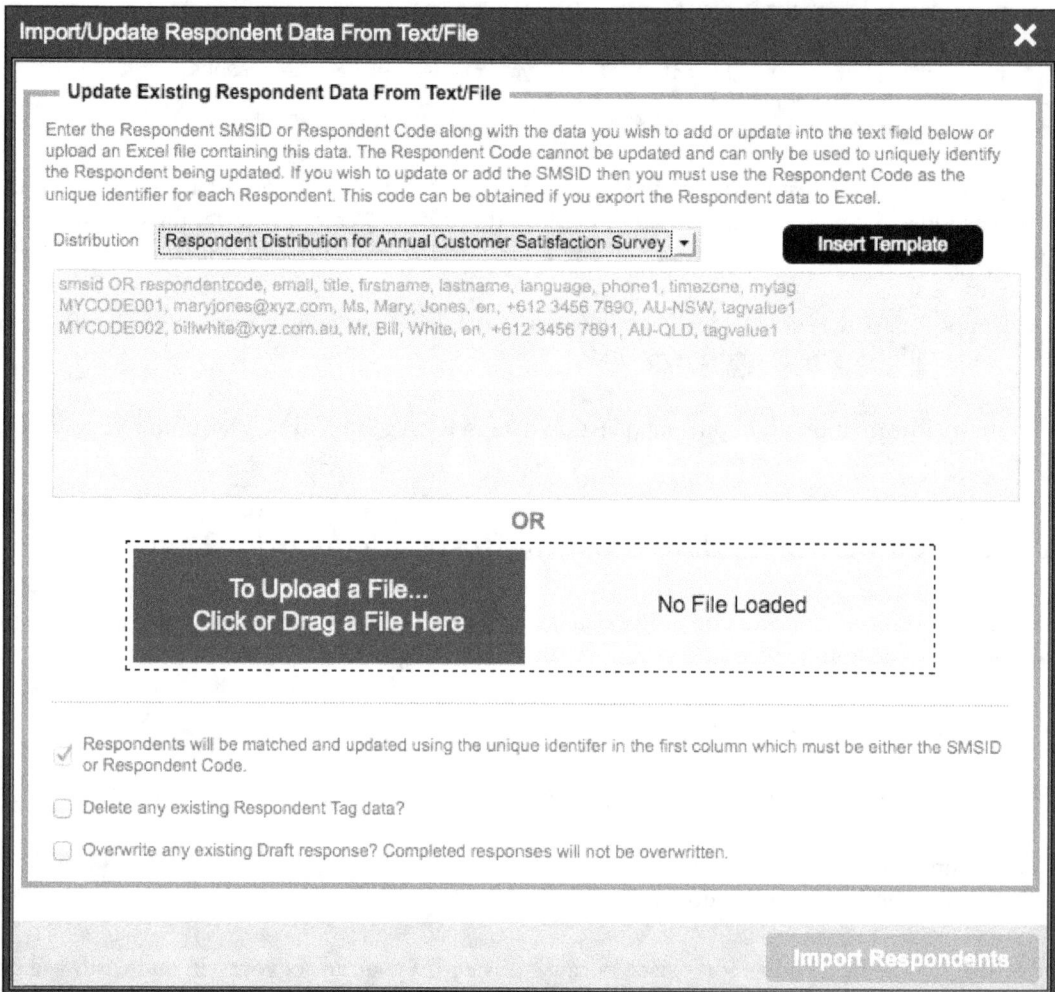

3. Click the Import Respondents button to perform the import.

How does the update format differ from an import?

Here is an example of a valid update format:

```
smsid, email, title, firstname, lastname, language, phone1, timezone, mytag
MYCODE001, maryjones@xyz.com, Ms, Mary, Jones, en, +612 3456 7890, AU-NSW, tagvalue1
MYCODE002, billwhite@xyz.com.au, Mr, Bill, White, en, +612 3456 7891, AU-QLD, tagvalue1
```

The key difference from an import of a new respondent is that it must have an SMSID or Respondent ID as the first column of data. This will be used to find a unique respondent in the distribution to update.

If response data is included in the update, it will only be placed into draft responses, and only if the checkbox "Overwrite any existing Draft response?" is checked. Data in completed responses is never updated.

NOTE: If draft responses are updated, the previous draft will be removed and replaced with the new data (i.e. Old data will be lost), so all data needed in the draft must be included in the update.

Import Method #3: Import Respondents from another Survey

Importing respondents from another server allows respondents to easily be used on multiple surveys. The steps to do this are as follows:

1. Click on **Import Respondents from another survey** from the Import Respondent toolbar button

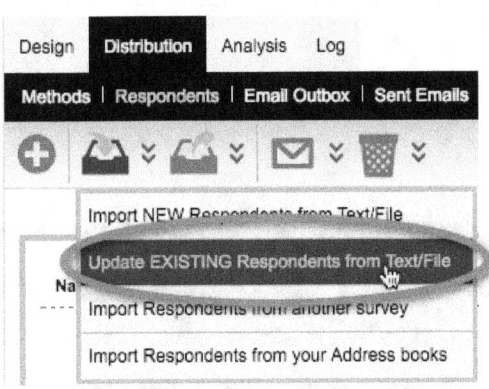

2. The import window will be shown. Choose the survey, distribution and respondent status of the respondents to copy.

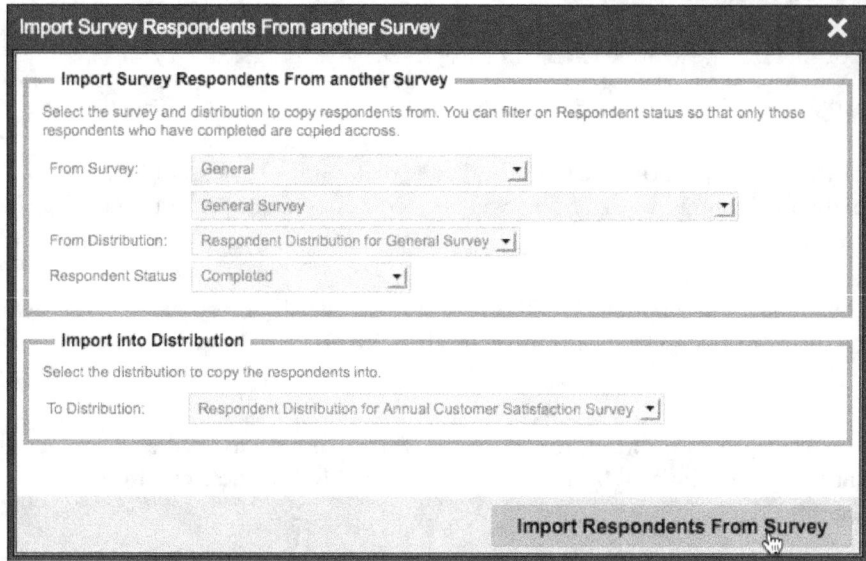

3. Click the Import Respondents From Survey button to perform the import.

Import Method #4: From an Address Book

Setting up an Address Book

Respondents can either be created directly in a respondent distribution as discussed above, or they can be created in an **Address Book** for later use in a respondent distribution. If you wish to use an address book, the address book would need to have been set up, and respondents imported into it. This section explains what needs to be done to create an Address Book and import respondents into this Address Book for later use.

A summary of the steps to create this Address Book is as follows:

1. Click on the My Contacts menu

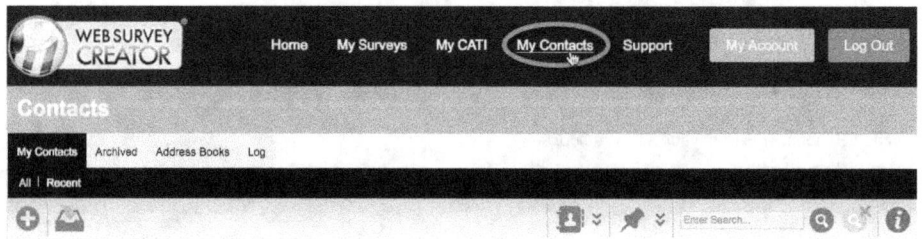

2. Click on the Address Books tab

3. Click the Create New Address Book button on the toolbar

4. Name the Address Book and click the Save Address Book button

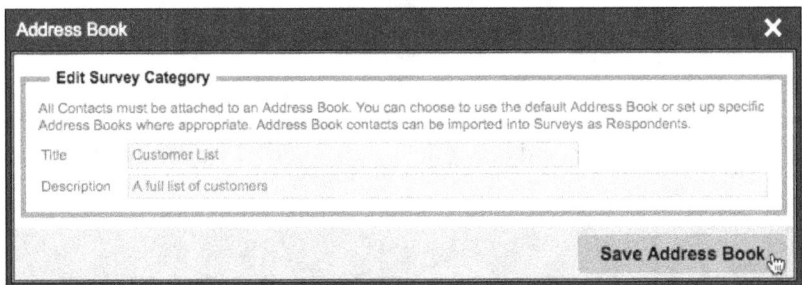

5. Return to the My Contacts tab, and click Create Contacts from Text List on the toolbar

6. Choose the Address Book we have just created, and paste in the details of the customers in the format requested in the import page.

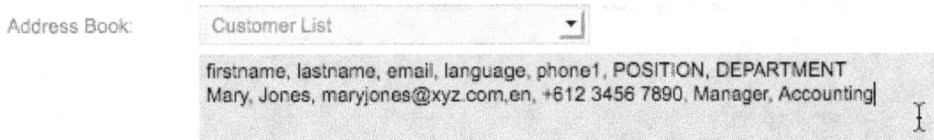

The contacts will be imported into the Address Book for use in one or more surveys

Creating a respondent from a text list is demonstrated in more detail in the video tutorial on **Managing Contacts** that can be found by clicking on the **Knowledgebase** button on the toolbar.

Depending upon the size of the import, it could take some time. A message is shown at the top of the screen until the import has been completed. We can press the update status link to refresh the status of this message. Once the message is gone, we know that the import is complete.

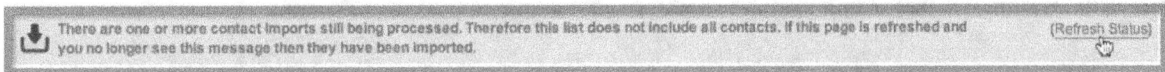

Survey Distribution 79

Importing from an Address Book

We've just created an Address Book with our contacts in it. We now want to use these people in the Customer address book as our respondents.

We need to go to **Respondents** under the **Distribution** tab.

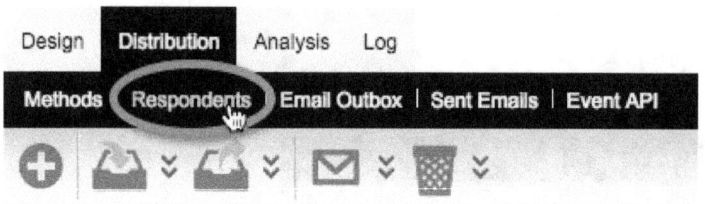

We click on the **Import** button on the toolbar, and select the third option - **Import Respondents from your Address books**.

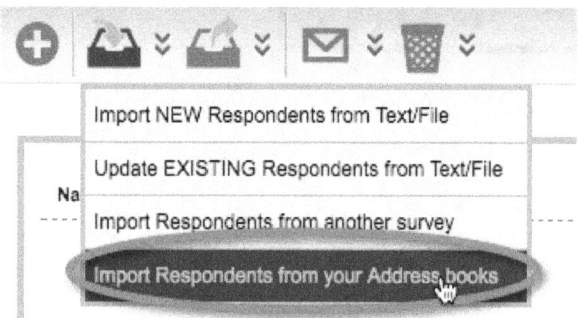

Let's choose our Customer List address book, and then press the **Import Respondents from Contacts** button. Note that you can only

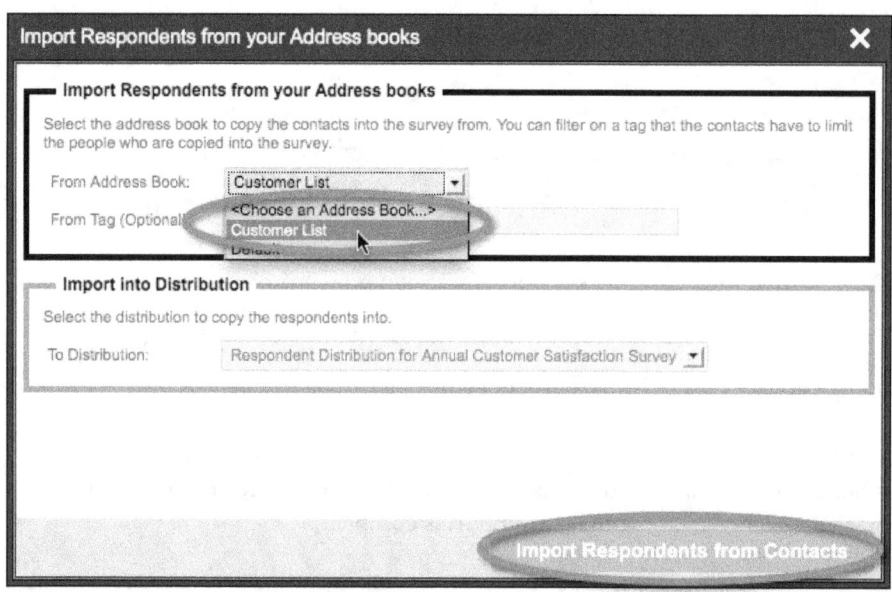

The import processing message will again be shown until the import is complete:

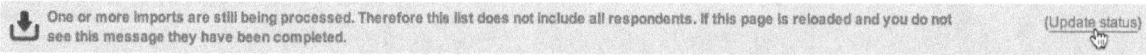

Importing Response Data

As discussed briefly in import method #1 above, it is possible to import response data along with respondent data. The example import format was as follows:

```
email, title, firstname, lastname, language, phone1, timezone, GENDER
maryjones@xyz.com, Ms, Mary, Jones, en, +612 3456 7890, AU-NSW, 1
billwhite@xyz.com.au, Mr, Bill, White, en, +612 3456 7891, AU-QLD, 2
```

In this example, there is a choice question with the code "GENDER" and the values 1 and 2 for the male and female choices. Each additional question you wish to import data for can be added on to each row of data, and all questions are supported in the import.

How can I work out the correct format for my import file?

Some question types are quite complex – matrix questions have rows and columns for example – so the format for data in the import file needs to be set up correctly to support these types. The easiest way to see the formatting for all the different question types in a particular survey is to create an export file with the formatting set up. To do this, create a **Response Export** report with the **Response Import Format** heading format.

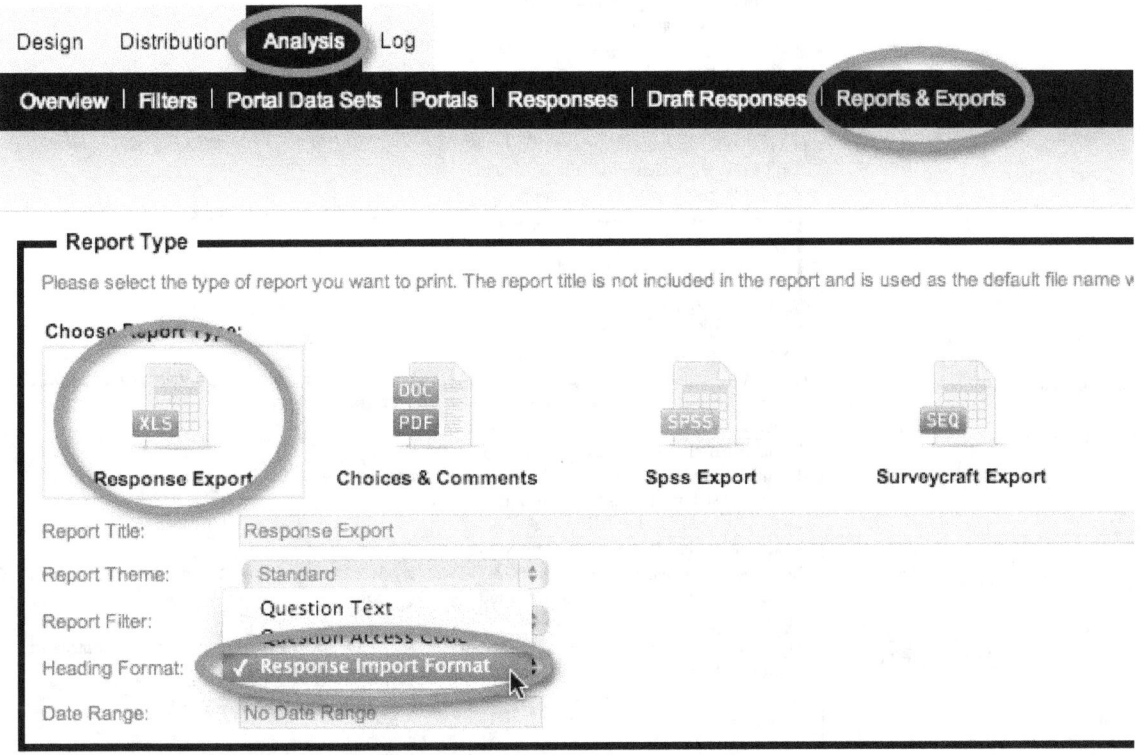

There are two key aspects of the format to look at:

1. How the header is formatted to explain what question is being referred to
2. How the data is formatted to correctly load the data

An example of a spreadsheet in a valid import format is shown below:

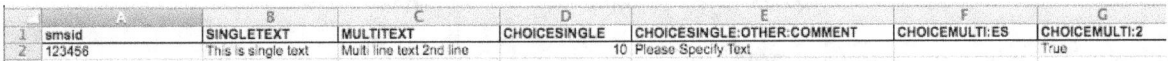

Row 1 is the header format, and Row 2 is the data being loaded.

Import Formats by Question Type

The formatting needed for each major question type is shown in the following table:

Question Type	Details	Example
Text	Same format is used for single and multi-line text questions	...,`mysingletext`,... ...,`My Text`,...
Numeric	Simple number format for import data	...,`mynumeric`,... ...,`1000`,...
Date or Date & Time	The date and time must be entered in a structured yyyy.MM.dd.hh.mm.ss format. If time is not required, enter as 00.00.00	...,`mydatetime`,... ...,`2014.01.06.14.00.00`,...
Star	Simple number format for import data	...,`mystar`,... ...,`1`,...
Slider	Simple number format for import data	...,`myslider`,... ...,`50`,...
Choice – Single Selection	Ensure each choice has a unique value – data is the value of the choice chosen.	...,`mychoice`,... ...,`3`,...
Choice – Multi-Selection *(Choice Cloud question also uses this format)*	Choices must have unique values. Import file has one column per choice, with "True" shown in the selected choices.	...,`mymchoice:1, mymchoice:2`,... ...,`True, ,`...
"Other" item in choice questions	Every choice in a choice question can have an optional "Other specify" text item.	...,`mymchoice:1,mymchoice:1:Comment`,... ...,`True,My other specify text`,...
Choice – drop-down	Similar to a single choice question	...,`mydropdown`,... ...,`3`,...
Hierarchical	Even though these questions use show as multiple individual dropdowns to enhance speed, one complete answer is a single choice. Ensure all choices have a unique value.	...,`myhierarchical`,... ...,`3`,...
Single Selection Matrix	In addition to the matrix question being given a code, each row in the matrix must also be given a code so that the particular row can be referred to in the import *Question Row Tags: CODE:FRONTDESK*	...,`mymatrix:frontdesk`,... ...,`3`,...
Multi Selection matrix	Row codes are used, and every value for each row is shown as a separate column. A "True" in a column indicates that the choice was chosen.	...,`mymatrix:pool:1, mymatrix:pool:2`... ...,`,True`,...
Single Selection Dual Matrix	A dual matrix has two grids, and therefore the import file must reference whether the first or second grid is being imported into.	...,`mydualmatrix:1:frontdesk`,... ...,`3`,...
Multi Selection Dual Matrix	A dual matrix has two grids, and therefore the import file must reference whether the first or second grid is being imported into.	...,`mydtrix:1:pool:1, mydtrix:1:pool:2`... ...,`,True`,...
Comments field on Matrix Questions	Every row in a matrix question can have a comments field.	...,`mytrix:pool,mytrix:pool:Comment`,... ...,`3,My comment text`,...
Constant Sum	Filling in the numbers for each row of a constant sum requires the row code to be used.	...,`mycs:workhrs,mycs:playhrs`,... ...,`12,20`,...
Numeric Grid	Both the row and the column need to be referenced in a numeric grid.	...,`myng:workhrs:1,myng:workhrs:2`,... ...,`10,18`,...
Ranking Question	Each choice to be ranked must be referred to in a separate column. The rank position (as a number) is the data that must be shown.	...,`myr:1,myr:2,myr:3,myr:4,myr:5`,... ...,`1,3,,2,4`,...
Demographics	Demographics question use the code of the question. For multi-part questions (like name), specific secondary codes are used as follows: NAME: xx:Title, xx:First, xx:Last ADDRESS: xx:Street, xx:City, xx:State, xx:Postcode	...,`name:first,name:last,address:city`,... ...,`Bob,Smith,Sydney`,...

Sending an Invitation

OK, we now have our list of respondents. The next step is to send an invitation to these respondents to complete the survey.

We can send emails directly from the **Email** button on the toolbar.

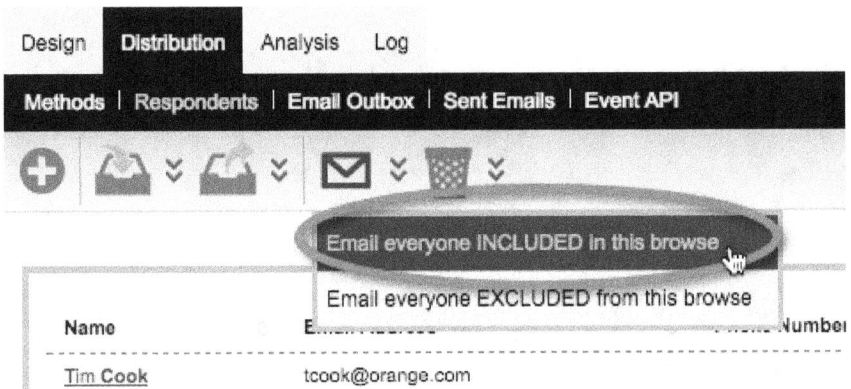

We create a new Email by pressing the Plus button on the toolbar.

There are three things we need to deal with when creating an Email:

- Who the Email will be sent to
- Who the Email will appear to be from
- When the Email will be sent
- What the content of the Email will be

Who to send to and when to send are pretty straightforward – we want to send to all respondents the respondents in the browse, and we want to send the Email immediately.

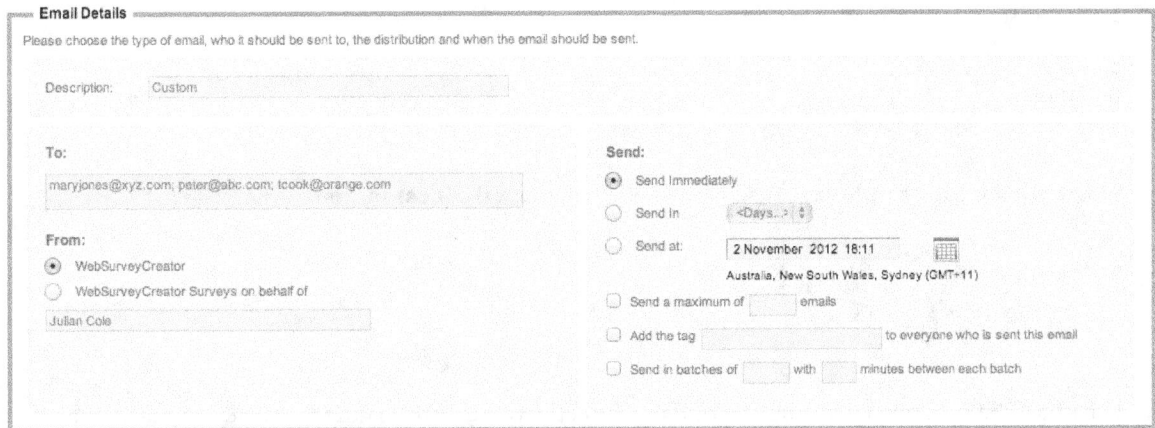

The easiest way to start our Email content is to load from a standard template.

Survey Distribution   83

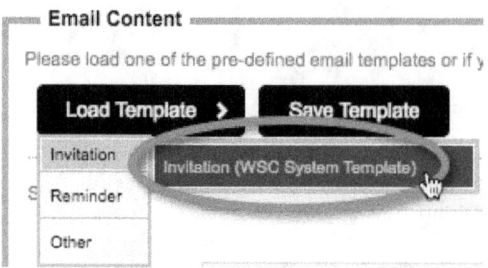

We can enter whatever we like for our Email content, but there are a couple of key things that need to be included.

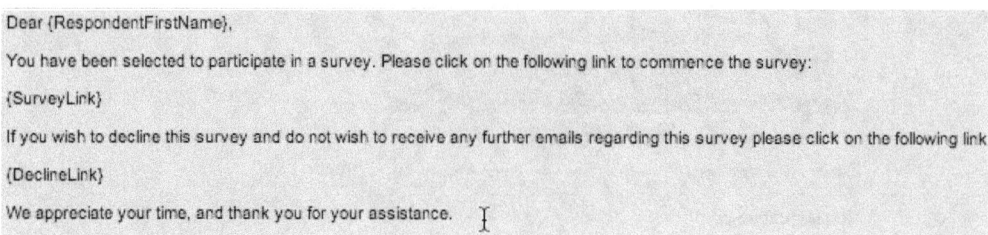

The Email must include a link to our survey, and it must include a **Decline Link** that allows a person to indicate they do not wish to include any more Emails. This second link is a requirement to meet anti-SPAM regulations.

Other content that may be entered includes the respondent's name. The available data that can be included can be chosen from the **Integration Symbol** drop-down.

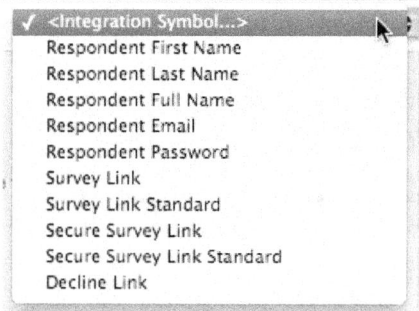

To ensure we are happy with the Email format, we can press the **Test** button.

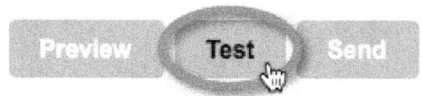

An Email will be sent for one of the respondents directly to our Email address, so we can check the Email link works, and the content looks good in our Email system.

Once we are happy with the Email, we can press the **Send** button.

We have now distributed our survey!

Survey Reports

Reporting is the main objective of any survey process. The types of reports you want to produce may vary from survey to survey, and will also depend on your audience.

Senior management will often just want a quick overview of results. Researchers, however, will want a detailed extract of raw responses in a format they can use in a statistical analysis program.

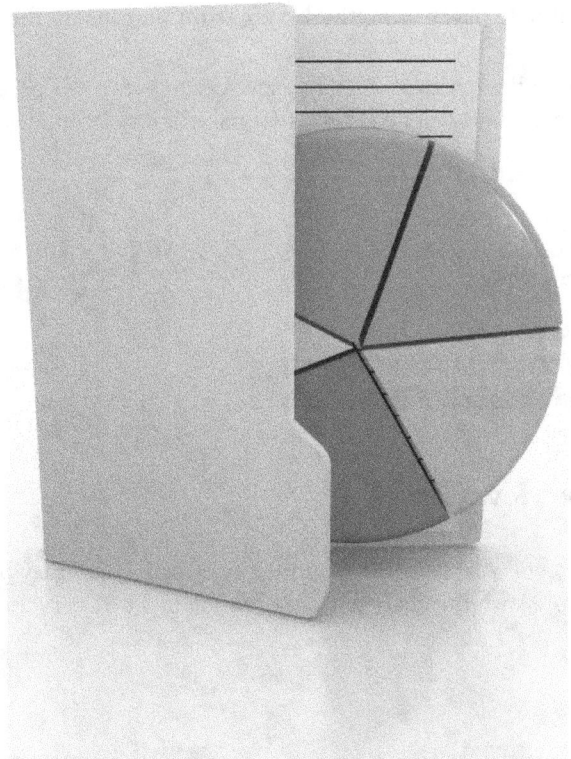

What is a "Report"?

When we are talking about a "report" the first thing that jumps to mind is some sort of paper document with charts and figures on it. While this definitely is a "report", there are all sorts of other variations we need to consider:

1. An **Online Statistics Portal** that provides real-time results through a browser
2. A native report produced in a word processor, such as Microsoft Word
3. A native export to a spreadsheet program such as Microsoft Excel
4. A native export to a statistics program such as SPSS

One of the biggest issues with Web Portals can be the time it takes to set them up. Fortunately, Web Survey Creator provides a **Statistics Overview Portal** that requires no setup at all.

Opening the Statistics Overview

The Statistics Overview Portal is accessible from *Overview* under the *Analysis tab*.

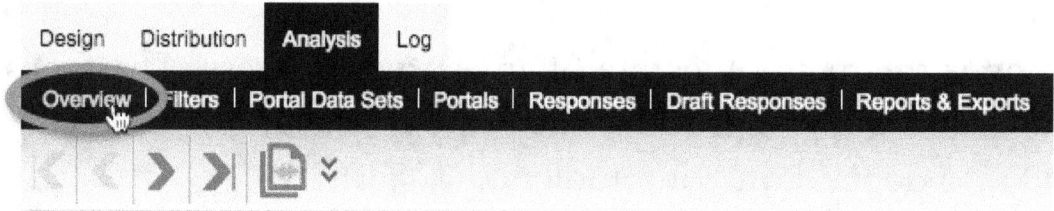

The content of the portal will depend upon the questions asked, and the version of WSC being used.

Navigation in the Overview Portal

The Overview Portal shows:

- A front page with general survey statistics
- Question pages - with each page matching a page in the survey design

We can navigate between these pages using the **Navigation** buttons on the toolbar.

The **Select Page** button on the toolbar is also a quick way to get to the page we want. We simply click on the page we want to go to, and we will be shown that page in the Overview.

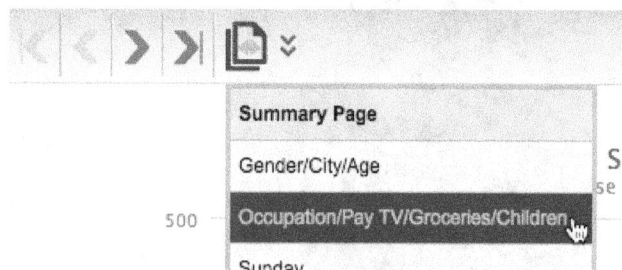

Working with Overview Charts

The beauty of the Overview is that it works without any effort. There may be times, however when you want to do something more with the chart than just look at it. The overview chart interface allows you to:

Refresh Chart Data - the overview is very fast, even when large amounts of data exist, because it pre-calculates the data, and updates it regularly (rather than calculating every time you go to the chart). Pressing the *Refresh button* will perform an immediate refresh.

Edit Chart Settings - headings, pre- and post- text can all be changed for a particular chart. This is great for adding explanatory text for a chart.

Embed Chart – the live chart can be embedded into another Web page by taking the embedding code and placing it in the page.

Download/Print Chart - if we want to quickly add the chart to a report, we can click the **Print** button or the **Download** button for the chart.

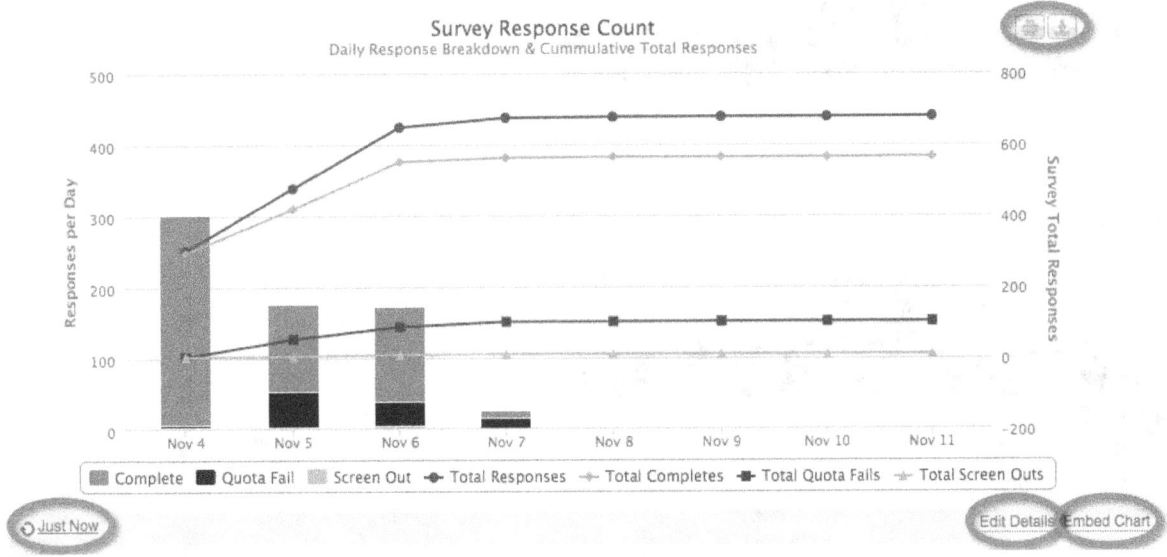

Creating an External Web Portal

The Statistics Overview is great for showing the statistics for a survey, but has limitations:

- Only WSC users have access to the overview - external stakeholders have no access
- All questions and statistics are shown - you can't exclude certain questions for example

What is needed is a way to view the parts of the Overview you want to view, and to allow this view to be accessible to people outside of WSC users.

What is a Web Portal?

From the perspective of WSC, a **Web Portal** can be thought of as a "view" of some or all of the content available in the Statistics Overview.

A Web Portal differs from the Statistics Overview in the following ways:

- A Web Portal is accessible to people who are not users of WSC
- The Web Portal theme and layout borrow from the theme and layout you have used for your Web Survey.

The content in the Statistics Overview is fixed, whereas Web Portal content is configurable:

- A "Home Page" for instructions and other details can appear at the front of the portal
- You choose which survey overview charts to show - some, all or none
- You choose which survey question stats to show - some, all or none
- Only one chart is shown on screen at once (isn't tied to the page structure of the survey)

For market research users, a **table of quotas** can optionally be shown as a portal item.

Creating a Web Portal

Web Portals are created from **Portals** under the **Analysis** tab.

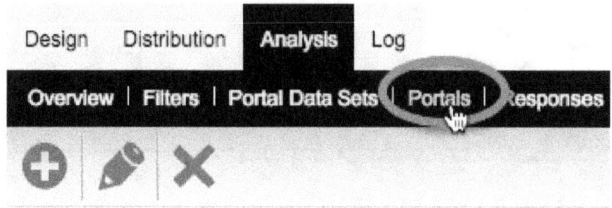

To add a new portal, we click the **Create Portal** button on the toolbar.

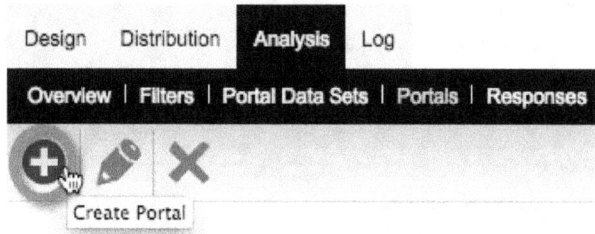

When we create our Web Portal, the settings we can change relate to what we want to include in the portal.

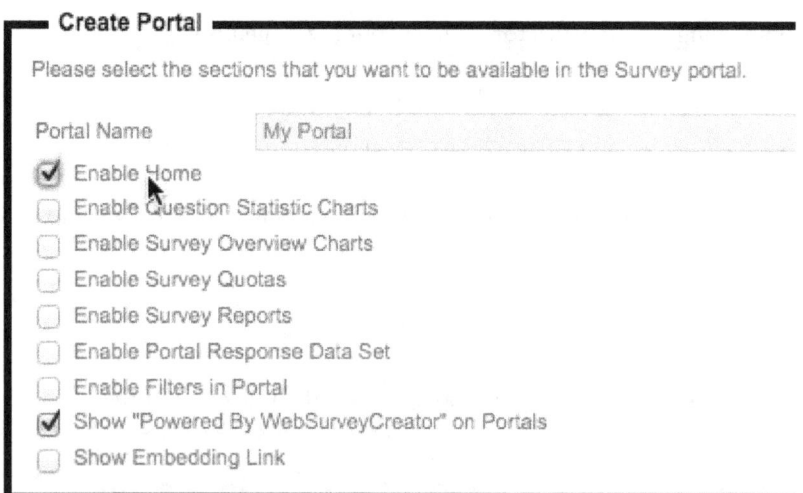

Let's look at each piece of content we can include.

88 Survey Reports

Home Page

To include a **Home Page**, we must ensure it is included in the content we are showing by checking the **Enable Home** checkbox.

The content that can be entered is straight text, however with the right **Content Tags** you can do a lot of clever things. For example, the following content:

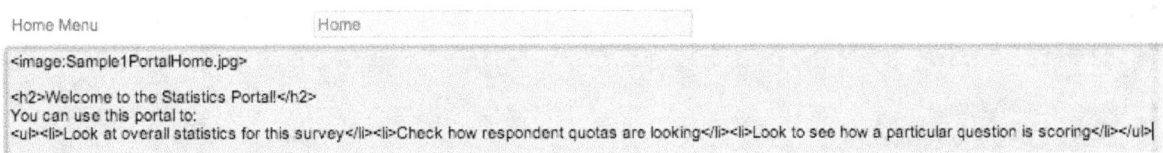

Includes a number of things to assist with formatting – in particular it includes an image. It creates the following result:

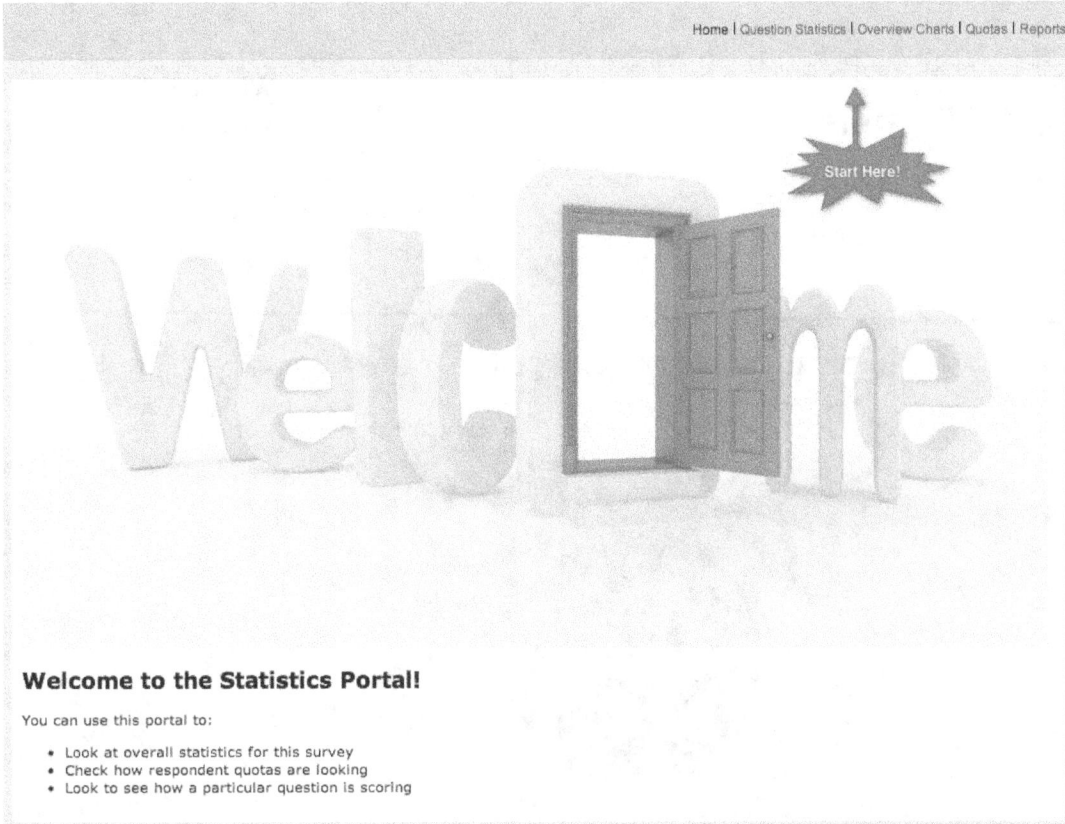

Question Statistics

To include **Question Statistic Charts,** we must ensure it is included in the content we are showing by checking the **Enable Question Statistics Charts** checkbox.

The settings that can be changed are shown below.

Survey Reports   89

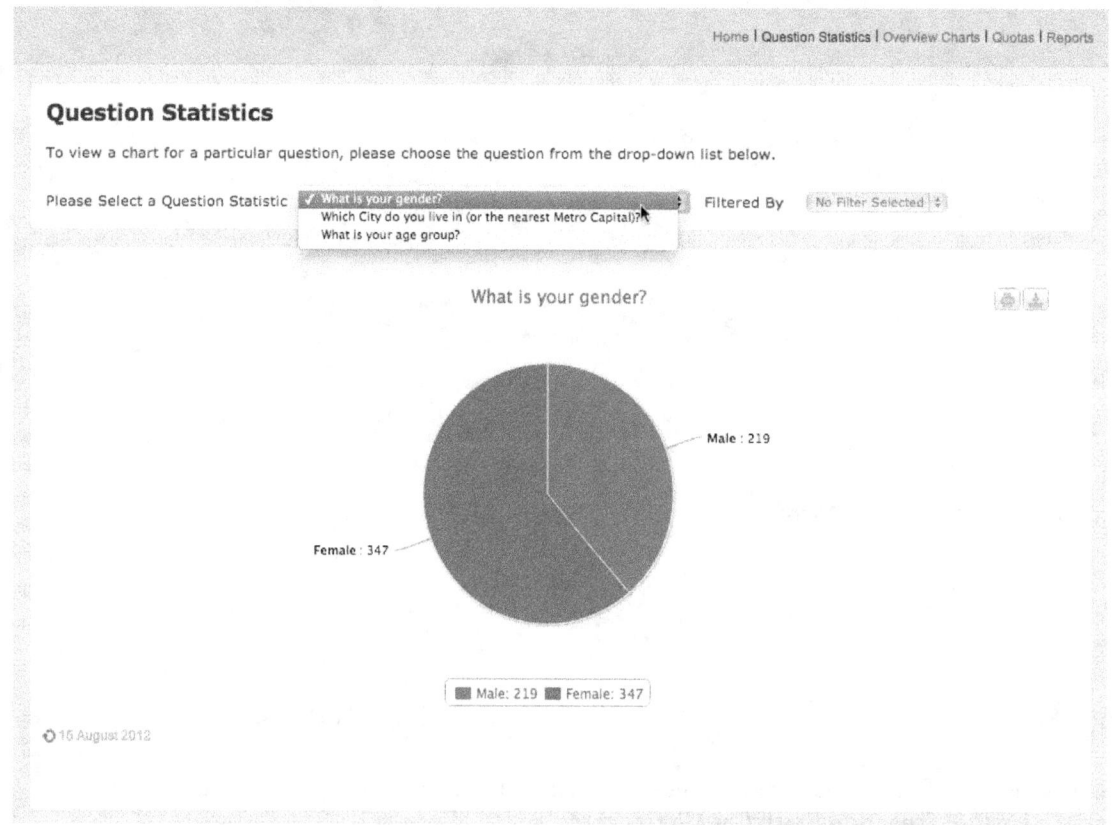

Note that we can decide not to show all questions. We have therefore only selected the ones we want to show (gender, city and age).

The resulting portal page for Question Statistics looks as follows:

My Portal Sample

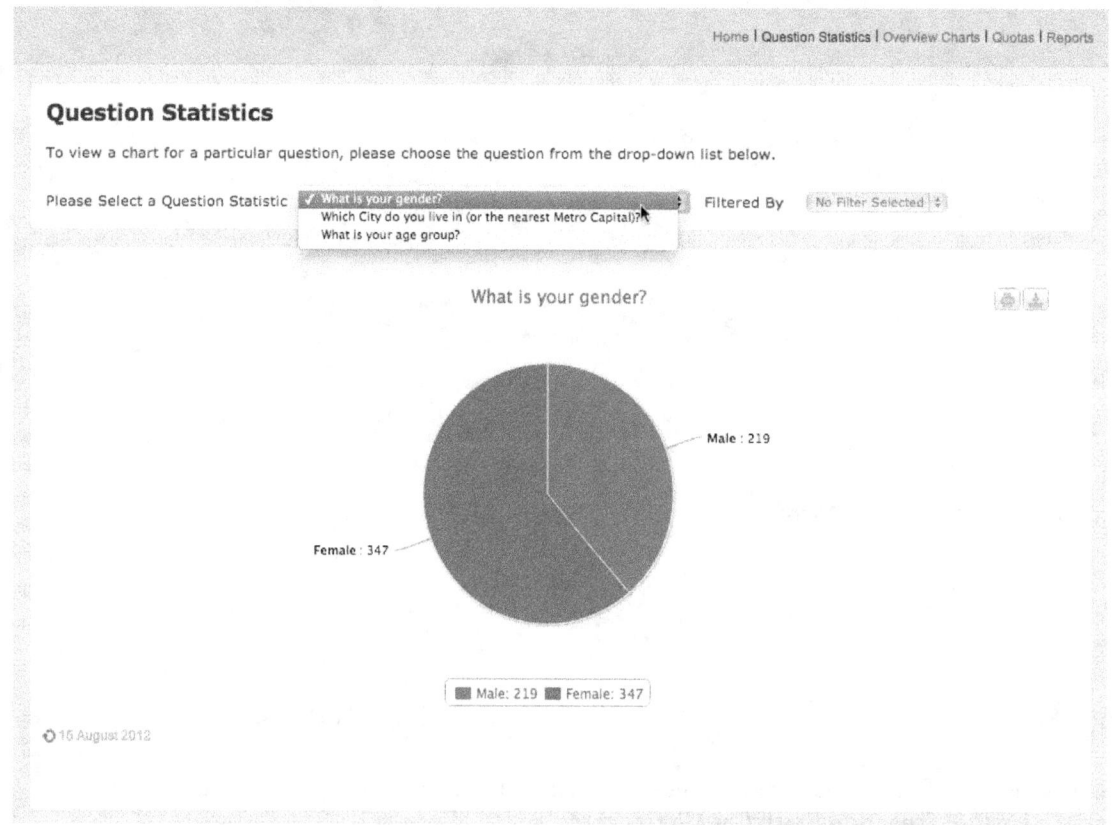

90   Survey Reports

Survey Overview Charts

To include **Survey Overview Charts**, we must ensure it is included in the content we are showing by checking the **Enable Survey Overview Charts** checkbox.

The settings that can be entered are very similar to the statistics questions. The settings we have chosen for our portal are shown here:

Note that we have decided to show all overview charts.

The resulting portal page for Overview Charts looks as follows:

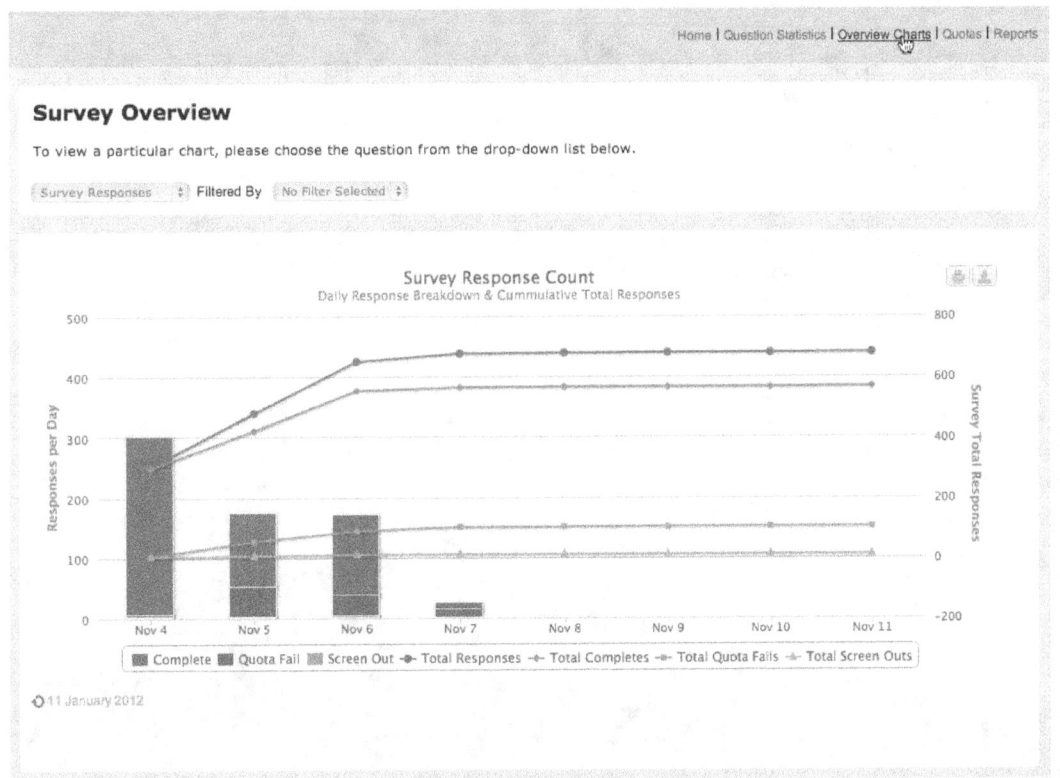

Survey Quotas

To include **Survey Quotas**, we must ensure it is included in the content we are showing by checking the **Enable Survey Quotas**.

Quotas can only be created in the Market Research editions of Web Survey Creator. If you are using a lower license this option will not be available.

Nothing really needs to be set up for Quotas, just some basic details:

Survey Quotas

The Quota section allows you to display up to date Survey Quotas in a tabular view wi

Quotas Menu	Quotas
Quota Totals Text:	Total
Quota Limit:	1000

```
<h2>Survey Quotas</h2>
The current status of all survey quotas are shown in the table below.
```

The chart that is shown will be based upon the survey quotas that have been set up. Note that the setup of quotas is discussed in a future chapter.

My Portal Sample

Home | Question Statistics | Overview Charts | Quotas | Reports

Survey Quotas

The current status of all survey quotas are shown in the table below.

Quota Title	Limit	In Quota	Remaining	Draft
City - Adelaide	51	51	-	8
City - Brisbane (inc Gold Coast)	103 (17)	118	2	14
City - Melbourne	152 (28)	185	-	27
City - Perth	62	50	12	2
City - Sydney	157	162	-	20
Female, 16-24	33 (7)	36	4	6
Female, 25-29	36 (19)	53	2	7
Female, 30-39	48 (27)	76	-	8
Female, 40-49	43 (22)	67	-	8
Female, 50-54	25 (15)	33	7	2
Female, 55-64	37 (13)	48	2	11
Female, 65+	46	34	12	3
Male, 16-24	34	23	11	-
Male, 25-29	36	25	11	4
Male, 30-39	47 (13)	60	-	6
Male, 40-49	41 (20)	46	15	6
Male, 50-54	25	18	7	4
Male, 55-64	36	22	14	4
Male, 65+	38	25	13	2

Survey Reports

To include **Survey Reports**, we must ensure it is included in the content we are showing by checking the **Enable Survey Reports** checkbox.

When setting up the reports, we can choose which reports we want to show.

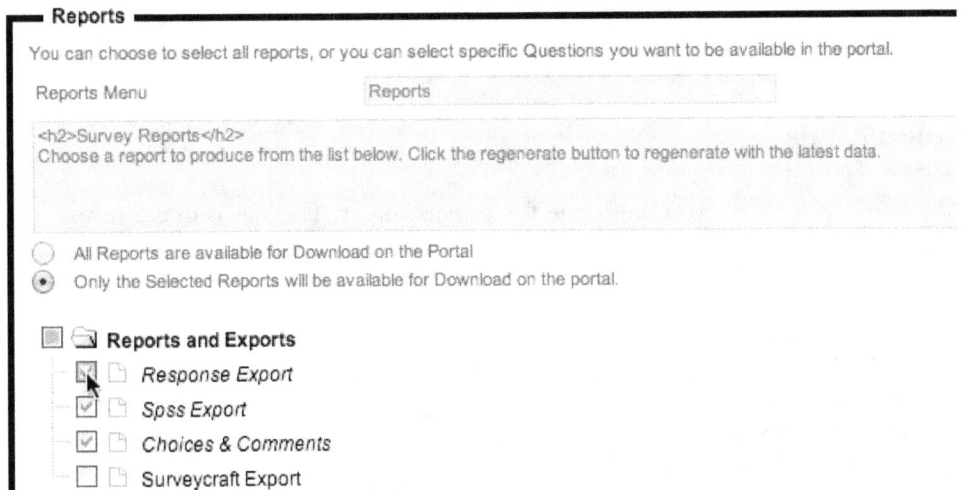

When we create a new report in WSC, the settings are stored so that the report can be reproduced. The reports shown for selection in the portal settings screen are the reports that were previously created. We will see how to create reports in the next section of this chapter.

The portal for reports will look as follows:

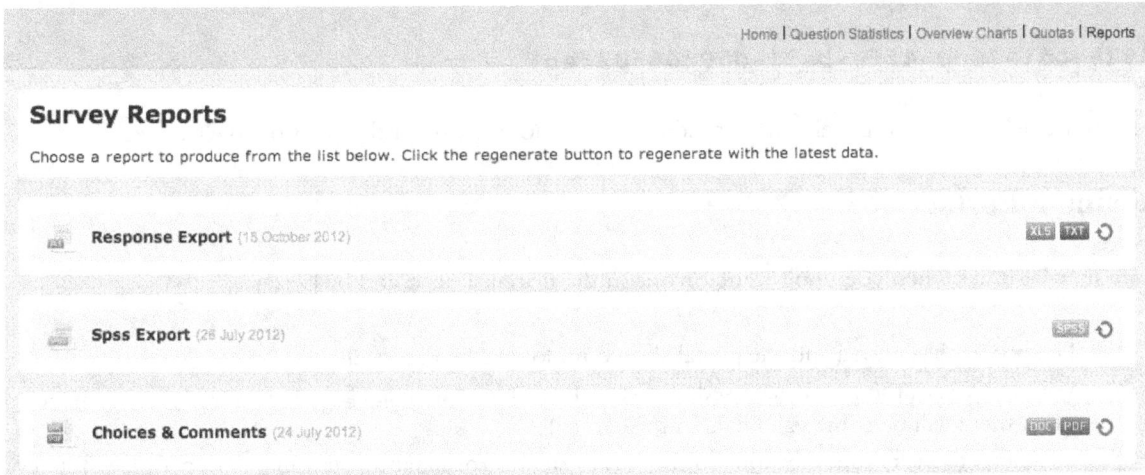

Survey Reports   93

Controlling access to Web Portals

Web Portals can contain a wealth of information. This is great if you are authorized to see that information, but could be a problem if you are not supposed to see it.

Rather than protect Portals with a complex user system, Web Survey Creator takes a different approach, which could be described as *"Create the Right Portal for the Right Person"*.

So, how does this work?

Creating Multiple Portals

There is no limit to the number of portals you can create for a single survey. The idea is to create an additional portal for each type of person who needs access to it. An example would be:

Who	What they want	What they Get
Your Manager	Wants to know if we are getting enough responses...	Overview stats only
Researcher	Wants to get the raw responses for their stats package	Reports only
Your Client	Wants to know everything (like all clients)	Full Portal

Each portal you create has a unique link generated for it that can not be guessed, and therefore is secure as long as you only send it to the people who need it. For example, a portal link could be:

http://portal.websurveycreator.com/p.aspx?p=4528e4df-75cc-4ffe-ba31-d59cd6602f4b&lang=en&t=h

The portal is identified with the identifier:

`4528e4df-75cc-4ffe-ba31-d59cd6602f4b`

Every portal is given a completely different identifier, so no one except the right people can get in.

Closing a Portal

There may be times when you don't want anyone in the portal. This could be because:

- The project has ended and the portal should no longer be accessed
- You don't want the portal accessed until a certain time/date (e.g.. give a client access on day 3, when there will be some valid data in the survey)
- You need to make modifications to the survey or the portal, and you don't want people using it

The **Portal Open Settings** allow you to:

1. Open the portal (the default state)
2. Close the portal
3. Open at a specific time/date
4. Close at a specific time/date

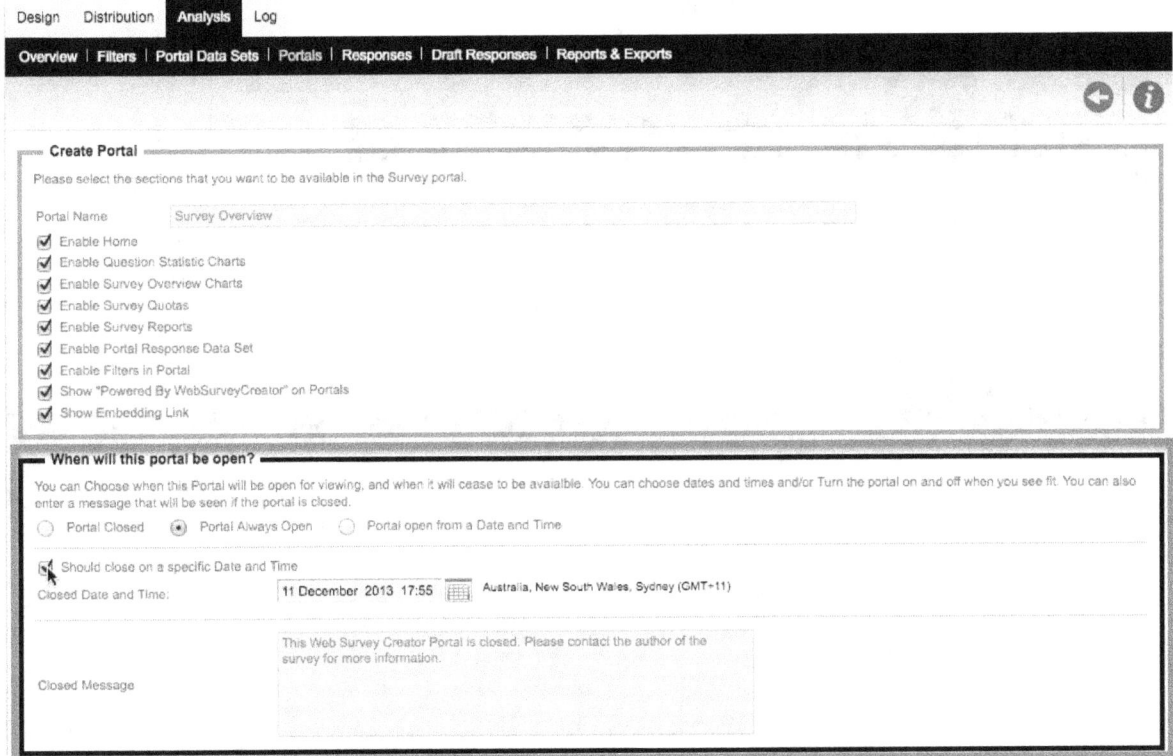

Web Survey Creator Reports & Exports

Web Survey Creator produces a number of different report types:

Report	Details
Responses Export	An export of responses to an Excel spreadsheet
Choices & Comments	A Word document that contains the two main questions we want quick information on - choice questions and comments
SPSS Export	An export of the survey data as a native .sav file that can be opened in SPSS for further analysis
SurveyCraft Export	An export of survey data that can be imported into the SurveyCraft MR analysis tool

All reports are created in a similar way, and with a consistent interface. The steps to creating any report are:

Go to **Reports & Exports** on the **Analysis** tab.

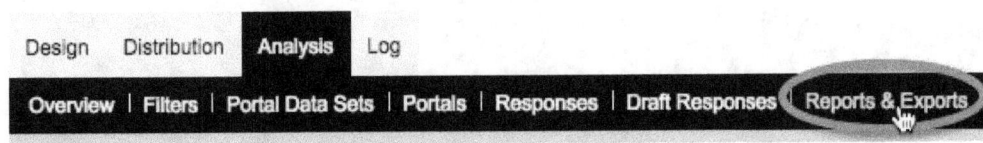

Survey Reports

Click the **Create Report** button on the toolbar

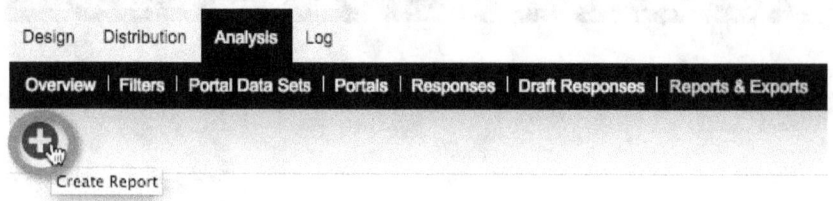

Choose the report type, and enter the details for the report

Responses Export

A responses export is the perfect way to extract the raw responses of a survey, together with summary statistics. The export is in Microsoft Excel format, making it easy for most people to open without any specialized software. This report can be extracted in a format that is most appropriate to your version of Excel (or even can be exported as a text file).

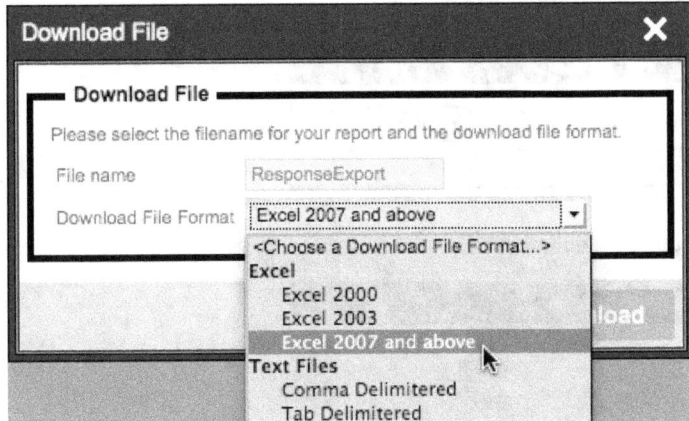

This report goes across multiple worksheets, providing:

1. Raw Response Data
2. Summary Statistics
3. Comments

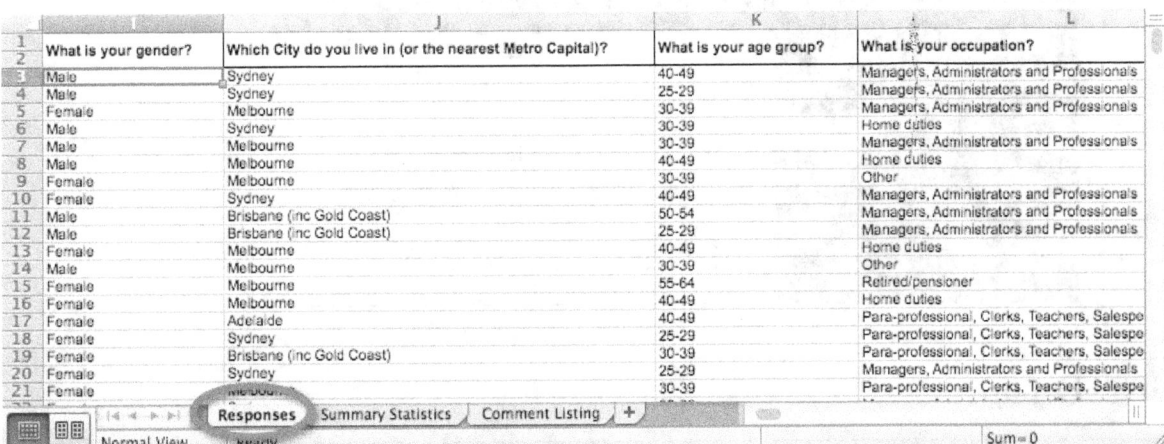

Choices & Comments

The Choices & Comments report can be generated as either a Word document or a PDF file.

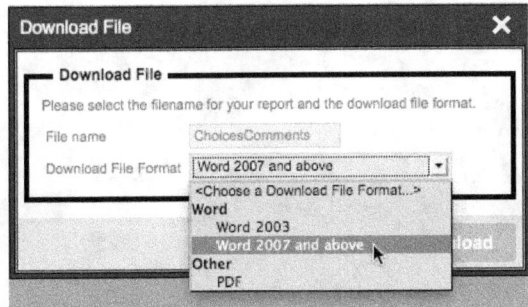

In both cases, the report follows a simple structure that provides an easy-to-read summary of the current survey statistics and comments that have been entered.

Choices & Comments

What is your gender?

	Count	Percentage	
Male	219	38.69%	
Female	347	61.31%	
	566		

Which City do you live in (or the nearest Metro Capital)?

	Count	Percentage	
Sydney	162	28.62%	
Melbourne	185	32.69%	
Brisbane (inc Gold Coast)	118	20.85%	
Adelaide	51	09.01%	
Perth	50	08.83%	
None of the above	0	00.00%	
	566		

What is your age group?

	Count	Percentage	
16-24	59	10.42%	
25-29	78	13.78%	
30-39	136	24.03%	
40-49	113	19.96%	
50-54	51	09.01%	
55-64	70	12.37%	
65+	59	10.42%	
	566		

SPSS Export

The SPSS Export creates a file that the SPSS statistical package can load natively. All aspects of the data, including choice labels, are brought into SPSS.

The file can be saved locally for opening in SPSS.

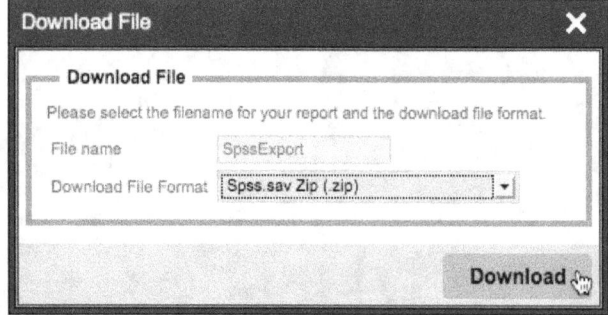

SurveyCraft Export

SurveyCraft is a product used by Market Research companies. Importing data into SurveyCraft requires two files:

`.txt`	A text file with a listing of all the questions
`.seq`	A file with all the survey data

Web Survey Creator makes these files easy to download in a single compressed file (.zip).

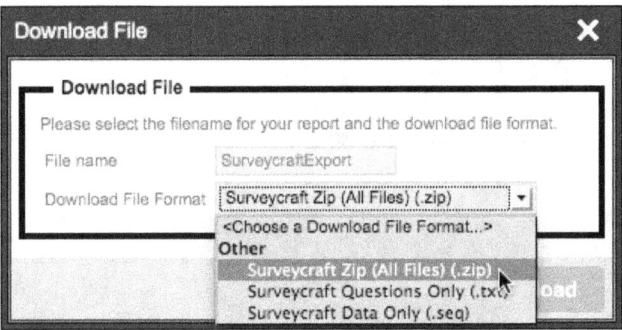

Using Previously Created Reports

Every report you create can be easily reprinted from the **Reports Browse**.

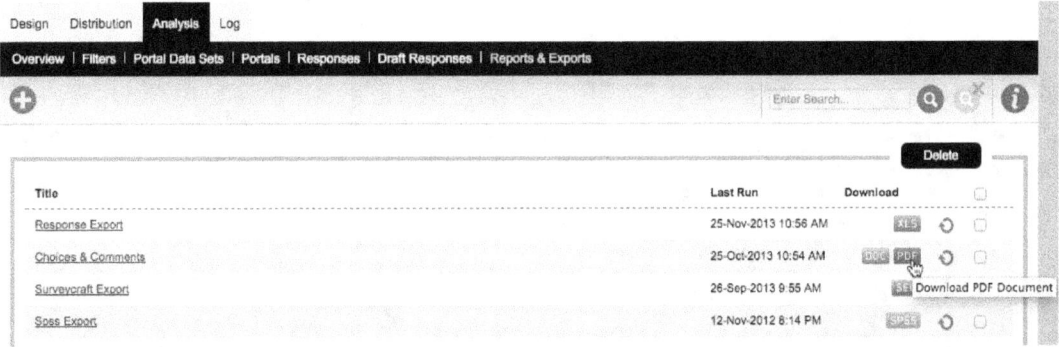

All reports are immediately available for download without regenerating the data. For example, we can grab the **Choices & Comments** report in Word format by clicking on the **DOC** icon for the report.

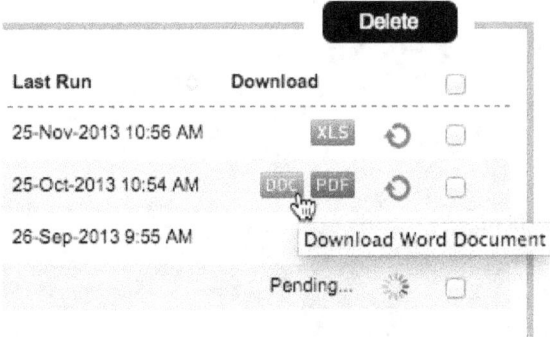

Survey Reports 99

If we want a report with the latest data, we can click the **Refresh** icon.

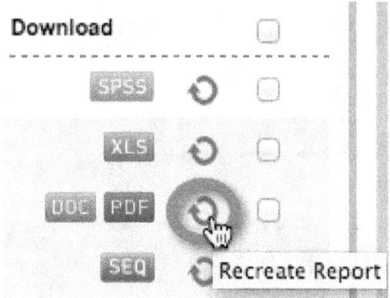

The report will indicate that it is regenerating.

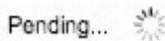

Once the report has been recreated, you can click on the **DOC** icon again to download this newly generated report.

Creating Market Research Surveys

Market Research Surveys are similar to any other Web Survey, except that they need more advanced capabilities to deal with things such as ensuring you have a balanced sample, and minimizing bias within the Survey Data.

Correctly managing these surveys requires a powerful Web Survey tool specifically designed to handle these advanced capabilities.

Challenges facing Market Research Professionals doing Web Surveys

Market Research professionals are faced with a rapidly changing landscape for Web Surveys where clients are expecting surveys that are more engaging, and that can be completed on a large array of devices.

Creating complex Web Surveys efficiently

As complexity has increased, Web Survey software tools have had to meet the challenges faced in efficient ways to ensure that the creation of MR surveys is still within the capabilities of non-technical users.

Web Surveys are now expected to:

- Support "flashy" interfaces that engage respondents
- Allow advanced functionality like drag and drop for responses, rather than more traditional choice questions and grids
- Provide complex validation based upon multiple rules
- Manage respondent quotas so that a representative group of respondents can be found
- Provide real-time results to stakeholders through interactive online portals

It is important for MR professionals to be able to meet all these needs without excessive increases in their time - after all, regardless of anything else clients always want things cheaper as well!

Avoiding the Software "tax"

There are a number of players in the Market Research arena - many of them quite large. They are used to dealing with the big end of town where upfront costs *and* per response costs of $1 or more are the norm.

This software "tax" hurts your bottom line every time you try and do something. It makes good sense to try and find a system that works well, and has unlimited responses, or low per-response costs.

Need for high quality, unbiased responses

Collection of accurate, high quality data is the most critical goal for any market research survey. As researchers, we are constantly fighting against:

- Apathetic & lazy respondents e.g. no care in answering, speedsters rushing to the reward
- Mis-aligned respondent goals e.g. some just want the biggest reward for their response
- Inappropriate respondents e.g. the wrong person completing a response
- Fatigued respondents e.g. a survey is too long to maintain respondent interest

While completely eradicating these problems is a tall order, there are a number of things that can be done to minimize their occurrence.

The next section explains the features of a Market Research Survey that can be used to minimize bias.

Need for a balanced group of Respondents

It is often important to ensure that your respondents match a broad section of the community. Failure to do so could lead to results that appear to be valid, but are in fact seriously affected by the people that have been responding.

An extreme example of this would be asking the following question:

> *Which of the following did you play with when you were a child?*
>
> - Toy Trucks
> - Barbie Dolls
> - Make-up

This question has a substantial gender bias, and is likely to produce wildly different responses depending upon the gender of the respondent.

Quota management is used for balancing respondents to a survey - this is the subject of our next section.

Keeping up with the move to mobile

One of the biggest changes in recent years is the move to surveys that are responded to on mobile devices. In less than two years, allowing respondents to complete their surveys on their mobile phone or tablet has gone from a "nice to have" to a "must have".

Often, the best place to catch a respondent is on their phone. They may not be willing to sit at their computer and answer a survey because there are things they would prefer to be doing, but if they are on a bus or train, or just sitting around, a survey on their mobile might even be a welcome distraction.

No survey package can be considered in this market unless one of it's key features is high quality mobile survey delivery.

Integration with other software packages

A survey is often the middle of a complete process. For example, the process may start with an invitation sent out from a Panel Management tool, and may end with an export to a statistics package. It is important that the Web Survey tool chosen can support this sort of integration.

Dealing with Bias

In many ways, Market Research Surveys are just like any other survey. You need to ask questions, and get responses to those questions. As discussed in the previous section, there are specific problems that must be dealt with when performing market research that require added functionality beyond a basic survey tool.

We will have a look at some of the fundamental functionality needed for market research in this chapter. We will demonstrate this functionality in Web Survey Creator.

You cannot "convince" a respondent to be unbiased. What surveys have to do is balance the effect of bias so that it is effectively "cancelled out" when looking at the data as a whole.

Randomization simply refers to "shuffling" survey content so that it will appear in a different order for different respondents. This will give content an equal chance of being considered by a respondent, and spreads the effect of:

1. Questions and choices earlier in a survey being given more consideration (before a respondent's attention drifts)
2. Less care and thought being taken by a respondent the longer a survey continues (as they become fatigued with the whole process)

Choice Randomization

A choice question with randomized choices will "mix up" the choices differently for each respondent. When randomized, the same question may appear as follows:

Which of the following brands have you heard of?

☐ BMW   ☐ HONDA   ☐ Ferrari   ☐ Mercedes-Benz

Which of the following brands have you heard of?

☐ HONDA   ☐ BMW   ☐ Ferrari   ☐ Mercedes-Benz

Which of the following brands have you heard of?

☐ Mercedes-Benz   ☐ HONDA   ☐ Ferrari   ☐ BMW

Pegging Choices

There are some situations when you don't want to randomize every single item in the list.

What fruits do you like?

☐ Apple

☐ Pear

☐ Orange

☐ Other _____

☐ Don't like fruit

If we randomize this question, it could look as follows:

104   Creating Market Research Surveys

What fruits do you like?

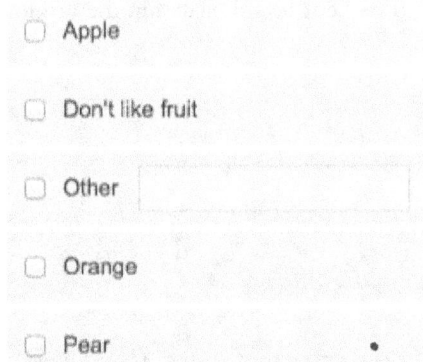

This doesn't really work - having the choices "other" and "don't like fruit" in the middle of the list is confusing, and off-putting (particularly since the "don't like fruit" option is exclusive and disables the other values).

What fruits do you like?

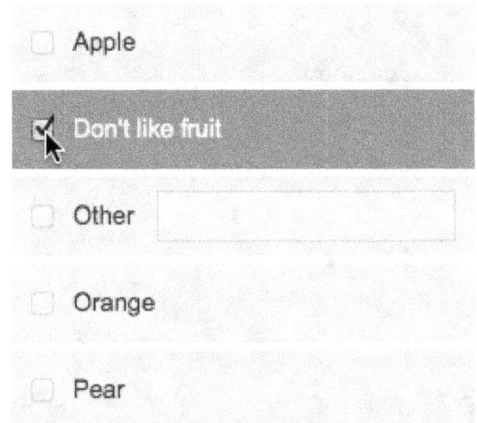

Fortunately, Web Survey Creator has a simple solution to the problem - individual values can be "pegged".

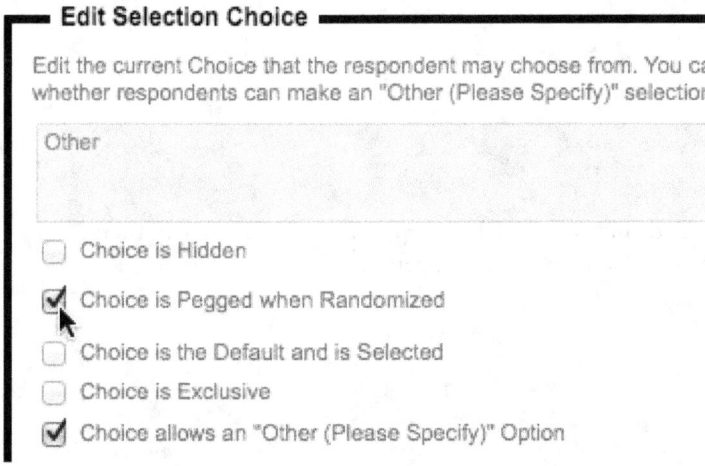

Pegged choices will not change their position - other choices are randomized around them.

Creating Market Research Surveys 105

Grouping Related Choices

Another issue with randomization is where you want some choices to be kept together within the random choice list. These would be related choices, such as:

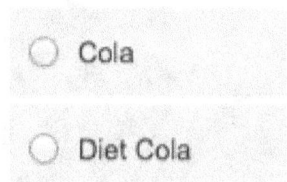

Even when randomizing all choices, you may want to keep the Cola drinks together so that Cola lovers can easily choose between diet and non-diet variants. What we ant to avoid, is a question that looks something like this when randomized:

What is your favorite drink?

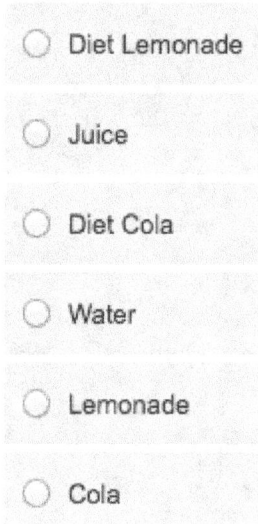

In Web Survey Creator, consecutive choices can be kept together by using the same *Block Code* for the choices.

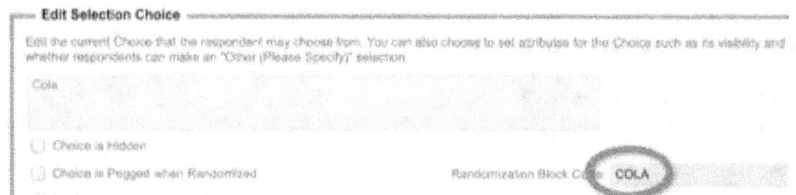

If we use a block code "COLA" for the Cola drinks, and "LEM" for the Lemonade, we can then randomize the choices and the related drinks will always be kept together.

An example of how the question might look is as follows:

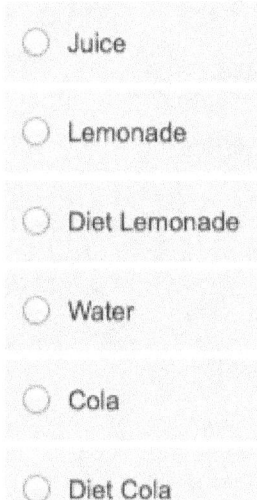

What is your favorite drink?

○ Juice

○ Lemonade

○ Diet Lemonade

○ Water

○ Cola

○ Diet Cola

Randomizing Consistently

It sounds strange, but "consistent randomization" can be important in a survey. For example, if you are asking multiple questions about a series of products, you may want the products to be randomized *in the same way* for every question. This is consistent randomization.

Web Survey Creator allows you to pick consistent randomization as one of the options when you turn randomization on.

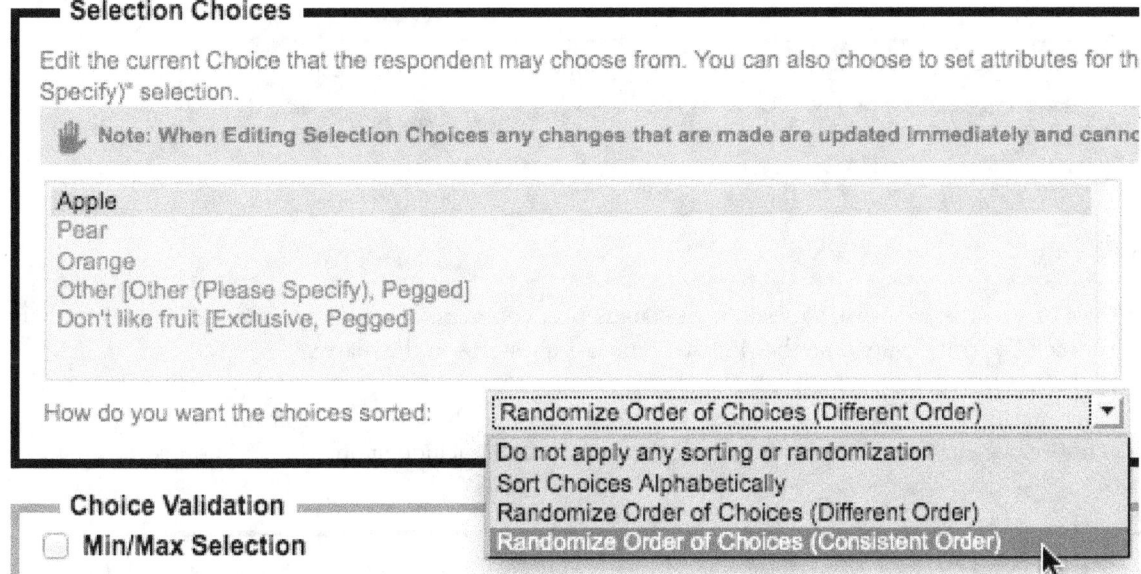

Creating Market Research Surveys   107

Matrix Randomization

Rows and columns in a matrix can be randomized in exactly the same way as choices.

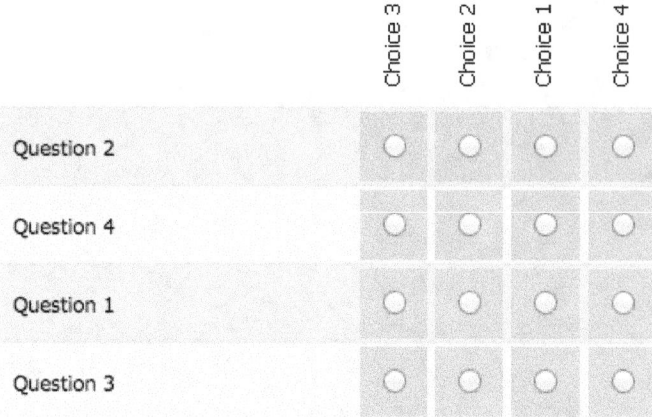

Matrix Columns

Columns in a matrix are exactly the same as choices in a choice question, and randomization is the same.

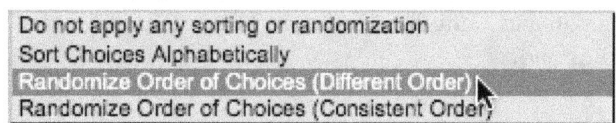

Columns can be pegged and grouped as well.

Matrix Rows

The rows of a matrix are usually questions or statements. You may wish to randomize their order so that people aren't "over it" every time they hit the same last questions in the matrix.

The randomization options are the same as for choices, though the way you peg a row is slightly different - you choose pegging from a drop-down list of options (which include hiding the question completely).

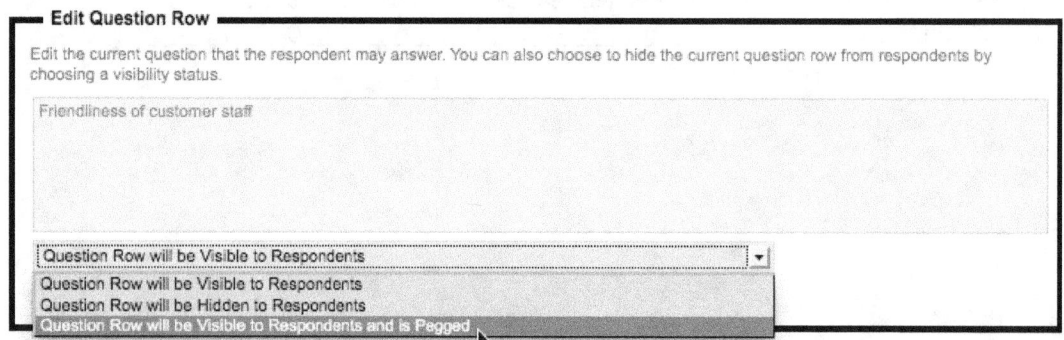

Page Randomization

Page randomization provides the most dramatic way of randomizing survey content. You can change the order of consecutive pages in the survey randomly for each respondent using this capability.

To use page randomization, you need to:

1. Edit the first page you want to randomize

2. Check the randomization check box

   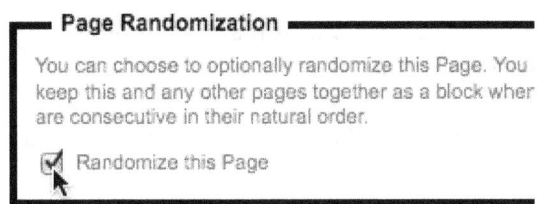

   If you want to group pages together in the random order, enter an optional Block Code

3. Save the page
4. Repeat for each subsequent page you wish to randomize.

Tips for Page Randomization

Page randomization can have a big effect on the flow of your survey, and therefore is the most "destructive" method of randomization if you get it wrong. It is therefore important to be careful when implementing this type of randomization.

We have a couple of tips to ensure you get the most from page randomization.

Tip 1: Ensure your Random pages are consecutive

The system will randomize all pages that are consecutive and flagged as random. You can not have a non-random page in the middle of a series of random pages and expect the random pages to mix - you will end up with two groups of random pages - either side of the non-random page.

Tip 2: Don't create impossible logic!

Whenever you randomize a page, you get an explicit warning:

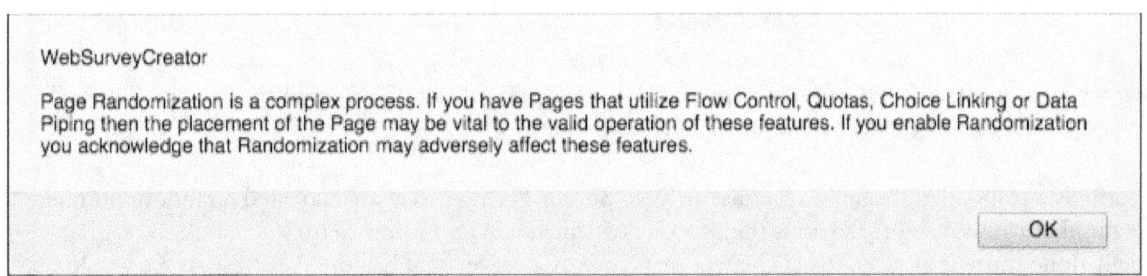

Creating Market Research Surveys

It is up to you to ensure you don't create a situation where the page order created through randomization. Consider the following example:

> **Page 1**
>
> Do you smoke?
>
> **Page 2** (Hide for people who don't smoke)
>
> Are you looking to quit smoking?

We could randomize these pages, but it would be a very bad idea. One of the random orders of pages would ask whether you want to quit smoking, even before we know whether you smoke.

Flow control will not work in this instance, because a page that is hidden by flow control appears before the question used in the flow control is even asked...

Tip 3: Test Thoroughly

Random pages are unpredictable by definition. It is important to enter test responses multiple times so you can try many variations of the page orders.

A/B Testing

Users of A/B testing will distribute multiple samples of a test to see which single variable is most effective in increasing a response rate or other desired outcome. The test, in order to be effective, must reach an audience of a sufficient size that there is a reasonable chance of detecting a meaningful difference between the control and other tactics.

Web surveys are a great candidate to use A/B testing, since gaining access to a large audience is relatively easy. A simple example of an A/B test is shown below.

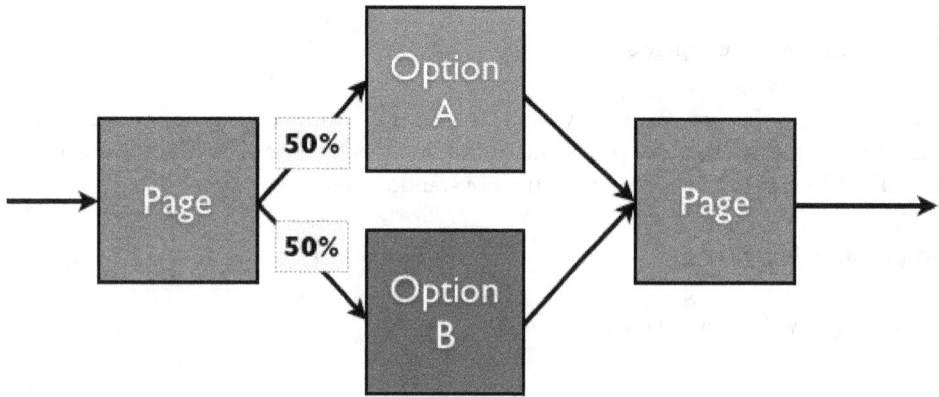

What we want is 50% of respondents to go to the page Option A, and 50% to go to the page Option B. Achieving this result is another example of randomization.

As soon as a respondent begins a response in Web Survey Creator, they are allocated a random number. This number can be used for various things - one of which is A/B testing. Setting up an A/B test is actually done through flow control. The true structure of a survey that has the A/B test above would be:

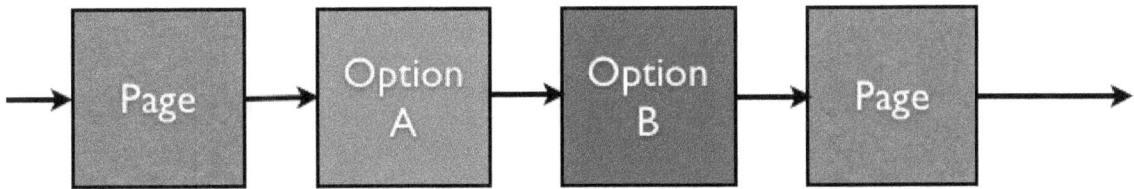

The create our A/B test, we want to hide the Option A page 50% of the time, and hide the Option B page 50% of the time.

Hiding the option A page would require the following flow:

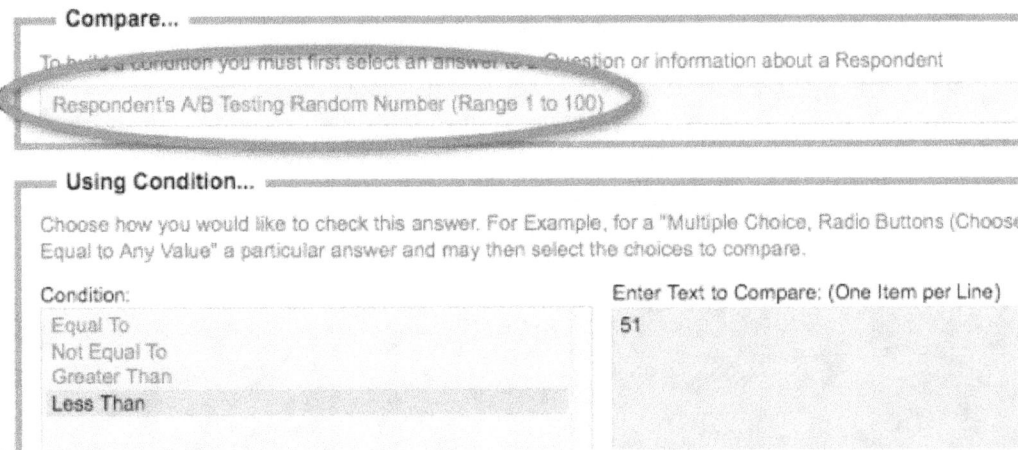

We use the **A/B testing Random Number** for the Respondent (which is always a number between 1 and 100) to do the flow. We want to hide the Option A page if the number is less than 51 (i.e. the number is between 1 and 50).

The hiding of the option B page would be the opposite test - hide the page when the A/B testing Random Number is greater than 50 (i.e. the number is between 51 and 100).

Of course this methodology wouldn't just apply to a two page test - you could have up to 100 options that are randomly chosen between, since the AB testing Random Number is equal to 1 of a possible 100 values.

Quota Management

Quota management is a key element of most market research surveys.

By controlling the quotas for a survey, you can ensure you get a balanced sample, and minimize your costs for panel respondents by ensuring you only pay for the people you actually need.

Why use Quotas?

The "More is Better" Rule

Many surveys work on the principle "the more respondents, the better" and therefore place no limits on how many people may answer the survey.

An example of such a survey would be a customer survey - you want as many customers as possible to complete the survey, and you don't want to place any limitations on this.

The reason why this rule works for these surveys is that each respondent's "voice" is as important as any other respondent. In our example, every respondent is a "customer", and their views are equally important.

The "Balance is Better" Rule

Let's consider a different example - let's say we have a survey about what people like and dislike about a fast food brand. This may seem to be another perfect candidate to apply the "more is better" rule. This would be a mistake, and here's why:

As a general rule, men prefer (and eat more) fast food than women

Younger men are likely to eat more fast food than older men (once their cholesterol and age catch up with them and they need to be more careful)

Middle-aged women and anybody over 60 are more likely to respond to a survey than people under 25 (who think Email is archaic, and surveys are a waste of their time)

OK, so what would this all mean if respondents are left to their own devices?

People who like fast food the least would make up a disproportionate number of survey responses - women and older men. Extrapolating this to say something about the community as a whole is meaningless. Young people who love fast food won't be represented sufficiently to provide a balance.

The answer is to provide a balanced group of respondents, by only taking a set number of people from various sections of society. Once you have enough answers from middle aged women, you simply don't need any more. You need to go out and find a sufficient number of young males!

A "Quota" can be based on anything you like, but commonly is based upon:

- Age
- Gender
- Location

If you take these three things into account when considering your respondents, you can make the respondent makeup mimic the makeup of society, and therefore provide a more accurate view of society's views.

How can Quotas be managed?

Early Survey Termination

You can not control who will click through to your survey, and when they will do it. This means that an unbalanced sample of people is likely to start the survey.

> The goal of a quota management system is to stop respondents you don't want at the earliest possible point.

Being terminated in a survey will be at least mildly annoying to someone who has taken the time to complete the survey. The last thing you want to do is inflame the situation by making them answer a lot of questions before they are terminated.

Best practice when creating Web Survey for Market Research is to have a survey with the following structure:

All questions to determine whether a respondent is suitable for the survey are asked in the first few pages of the survey

Terminate Pages for "Screen-Outs" (people who you are not interested in) and "Quota-Outs" (people you are interested in, but you want to limit the numbers) appear next.

Flow control is used to skip appropriate people over the terminate pages. Everyone else hits one of the terminate pages, and the survey is over.

Terminate pages are simply pages that end the survey - they don't have a **Next** button like other pages - they simply have a **Submit** button.

Setting Quota Rules

Quota management all comes down to using a set of rules to determine whether someone should be completing a survey. Each quota basically deals with 2 things:

1. Who are we looking for? (e.g. Males, 18-25)
2. How many of them do we want as respondents in our survey?

Web Survey Creator keeps track of the rules that have been created, and the number of people who have met each quota, in its Quota Management System.

Quota Title	Limit	In Quota	Remaining
City - Adelaide	51	51	-
City - Brisbane (inc Gold Coast)	100 (20)	118	2
City - Melbourne	152 (28)	185	-
City - Perth	62	50	12
City - Sydney	157	162	-
Female, 16-24	33 (7)	36	4
Female, 25-29	36 (19)	53	2
Female, 30-39	48 (27)	76	-
Female, 40-49	43 (22)	67	-
Female, 50-54	25 (15)	33	7
Female, 55-64	37 (13)	48	2
Female, 65+	46	34	12
Male, 16-24	34	23	11
Male, 25-29	36	25	11
Male, 30-39	47 (13)	60	-
Male, 40-49	41 (20)	46	15
Male, 50-54	25	18	7
Male, 55-64	36	22	14
Male, 65+	38	25	13

Dealing with Tough Quotas

There are often particular quotas that are harder to fill than others. A particular survey may be considered worthless if all quotas are not filled, so this can be a serious issue.

If we consider our previous example, we can see where the harder quotas are:

Quota Title	Limit	In Quota	Remaining
City - Adelaide	51	51	-
City - Brisbane (inc Gold Coast)	100 (20)	118	2
City - Melbourne	152 (28)	185	-
City - Perth	62	50	12
City - Sydney	157	162	-

We can see that while there are plenty of people in most of the other location quotas, we are still looking for 12 people from Perth.

> Tough quotas are normally dealt with by "opening up" a survey until we get enough of the quota. This means going over quota in other areas so that we can at least get to the minimum level needed for the hard quota.

Opening up a survey is a very rough technique that has to be manually handled.

Fortunately, Web Survey Creator provides two features that make this process a whole lot easier and more controlled - quota overflow, and priority quotas.

Quota Overflow

In the event original quota numbers have to be modified, an "overflow" figure can be entered rather than changing the original figure - making it a lot easier to see what changes we have made.

Quota Title	Limit	In Quota	Remaining
City - Adelaide	51	51	-
City - Brisbane (inc Gold Coast)	100 (20)	118	2
City - Melbourne	152 (28)	185	-
City - Perth	62	50	12
City - Sydney	157	162	-

In our example, Brisbane has an overflow of 20 respondents (on top of the original quota of 100) and Melbourne has an overflow of 28 respondents (on top of the original quota of 152).

"Priority" Quotas

Quotas in Web Survey Creator work as follows:

As soon as all questions relating to quotas are completed, the system allocates every quota that a respondent meets to them. For example, a respondent may have the following quotas attached to him:

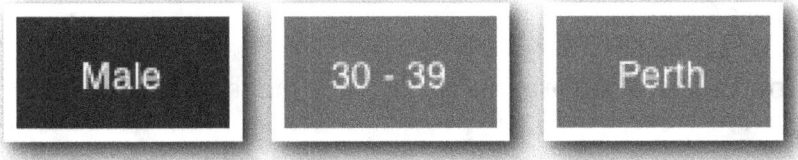

Based on our example, we already have too many male 30-39 respondents:

Male, 30-39   47 (13)   60

Therefore this respondent would fail quota - *even though we really need people from Perth* - because letting them through would mean we end up with too many 30-39 year old men.

> There are times when having one quota go over target is less of a problem than not getting enough of another quota.

If we wanted to make sure we let someone from Perth through, we could set our Perth quota as a "priority" quota. This tells the system to allow anyone from Perth through as a respondent, even if their other quotas are full. As soon as Perth is full, the priority quota will no longer be in effect.

Priority quotas make it very easy to focus on your hard-to-get people. They need to be used cautiously, however, as they will lead to other quotas being over-subscribed.

Tips for Quota Management

Adding quotas after a survey has commenced

The best advice that can be given about adding quotas after a survey has commenced (and responses have been received) is to avoid doing it! The main reasons to try and avoid the late inclusion of quotas are:

You will have completed responses from people who were never tested against your new quotas (since quotas are calculated as a person enters their survey response).

You risk making mistakes like inclusion of questions in quotas that appear after the quota out page (therefore making the quota out page logic invalid).

If you do add or change a quota after a survey has commenced, Web Survey Creator does help you play "catch-up" with existing responses - you can generate the correct quotas for existing responses by clicking the *Re-calculate Quotas* toolbar button under the *Survey Quotas* menu.

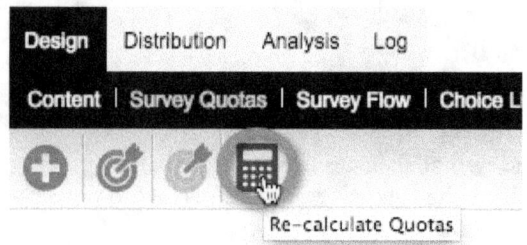

Testing whether someone fails the quotas in multiple places within a survey

There is nothing worse than a respondent almost getting to the end of a survey, and suddenly they are kicked out because their quota is full. Web Survey Creator avoids this situation by calculating quotas as early in the survey as possible, and from that point on there is a simple rule:

Once you're in, you're in!

What this means is if at the time the quotas were calculated there was still room for a respondent, they will be allowed to complete the survey. This may lead to a slight over-run of numbers for certain quotas if there are a number of people in that quota who finish around the same time.

A person doesn't raise the number in a quota until they have submitted their completed response, so the quota out won't be triggered until the needed number of people have completed their response.

There may be times when this default behavior will cause too much of an over-run, or add unnecessary cost to a job. For example:

A survey may be really long, so a lot of people could be in the middle of the survey (beyond the quota test) when their quota is finally filled.

A significant number get past the quota test, and then leave their response in draft, to be completed later. No matter when they come back (even long after their quota is filled) they will be allowed to complete their response and add to the number in their quota.

So, how do we test for quotas more than once in a survey? Fortunately Web Survey Creator makes it simple.

If you add more than one **Quota Fail Terminate** Page to your survey, quotas will be retested prior to the second and subsequent terminate pages.

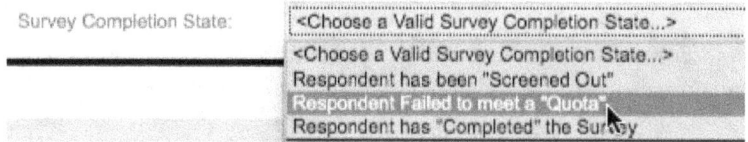

What this means is you can choose when a re-check occurs (if at all). If you don't care about annoying a respondent who has spent their time completing the answers to the survey, you could even have an additional quota fail page right near the end of the survey.

Quota Management Example

Our example survey will be for a fictitious Fast Food chain - Worldburger. They have recently introduced a new "healthier choices" menu that adds healthier options to their menu, and they want to see whether people are aware of the change, and what they think of the change.

Makeup of Respondents Required

In order to get a good cross-section of respondents, they have requested the following gender makeup for responses:

	16-24	25-29	30-39	40-49	50-54	55-64	65+
Female	33	36	48	43	25	37	46
Male	34	36	47	41	25	36	38

This will provide a good spread of ages, and a slight skew towards women (who are the primary focus of the "healthier choices" campaign).

An additional requirement is to have a geographical spread of respondents that roughly represents the proportional number of people in various cities who visit Worldburger stores in any given week.

Sydney	Melbourne	Brisbane	Perth	Adelaide
157	152	103	62	51

Both of these requirements add to a total of 525 people. They are not *interlocking quotas*, so it doesn't matter what the gender/age makeup is for each geographical location.

Preparing Our Survey

Gender/Age/Location Questions

Quotas are calculated based on responses entered into a survey. For our survey, we therefore need to ask about a person's gender, age and location.

For a detailed explanation about adding questions, see our basic survey guide. For the purposes of this example, we will just look at the completed questions.

On our first page, we will ask for the respondent's gender:

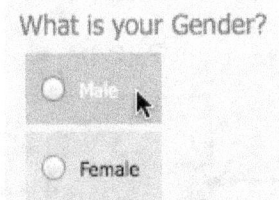

On the second page, we will ask for the respondent's age:

On the third page, we will ask where the respondent lives:

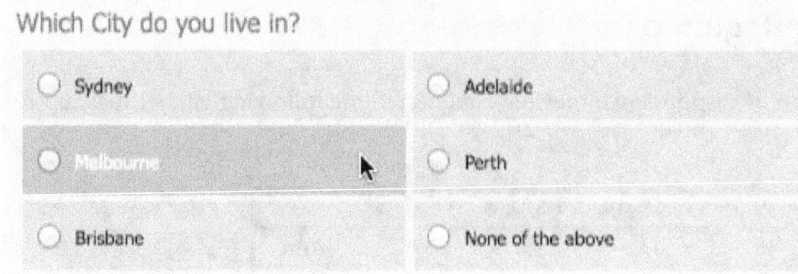

We now have a survey with the following structure:

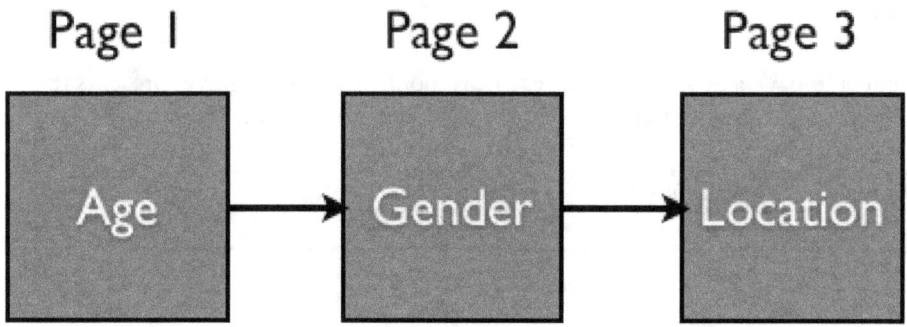

Once a respondent has answered these three questions, we will know whether or not they fit a quota.

If a respondent doesn't fit into a quota, we need to end the survey for them.

The fourth page in the survey will therefore be a **Quota Fail Terminate** Page. If a respondent does not fit into quotas, they will see this page. If they do fit into a quota, this page will be hidden and they will move onto page 5.

This logic is explained in the following diagram:

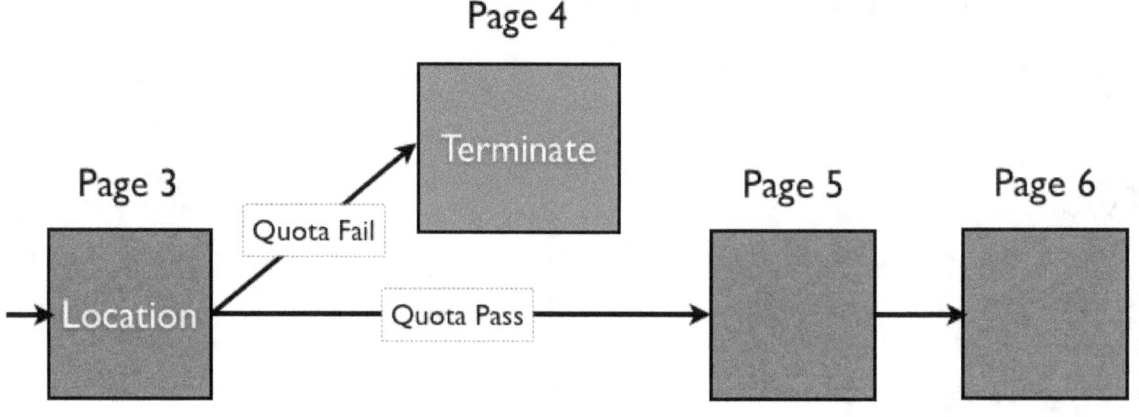

Quota Fail Terminate Page

We need to create the **Quota Fail Terminate** Page. This is simply a matter of creating a page in the survey, then:

1. Clicking the *Edit button* to edit the page details

2. Changing the type of page to indicate that it is a terminate page.

    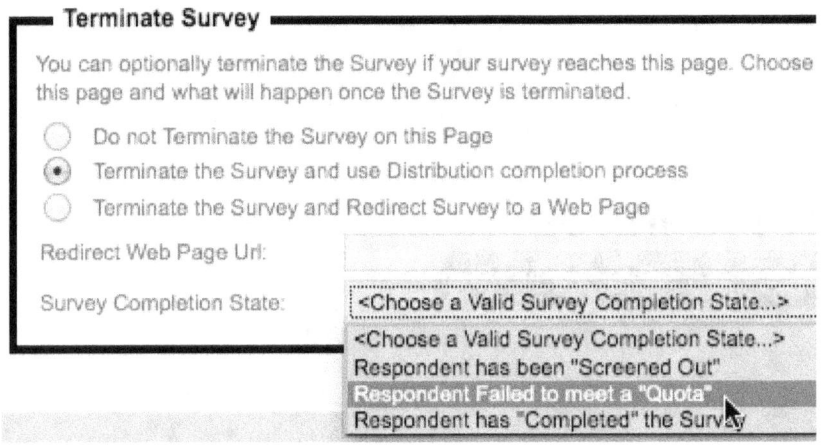

A terminate page is different to a normal page because:

- It has a submit button, <u>not</u> a next button on it. This means it will be the last page seen by the respondent in the survey.
- It has the ability to redirect to a specific location - which is very important when integrating with external respondent panels (a point we will discuss more fully in a future chapter).

Creating Our Quotas

So far we have the questions that are used in our quota, and we have a terminate page. What we are lacking is a calculation of the quotas, and a survey flow to properly handle the showing or hiding of the terminate page. Let's look at these issues in turn.

Using the Quota Builder

We have to set up quite a few quotas in this survey. In fact, we have to set up:

2 Genders x 7 Age Ranges = 14 Gender/Age Quotas *and* 5 Location Quotas

That's a total of 19 Quotas.

While setting each quota up manually can be done, fortunately Web Survey Creator has a **Quota Builder** that does most of the work for us. It let's us create related quotas in a single process.

Creating the Gender/Age Quotas

Let's create the gender and age quotas first. The steps for creating these quotas are as follows:

1. Click on the **Survey Quotas** menu under the **Design** tab

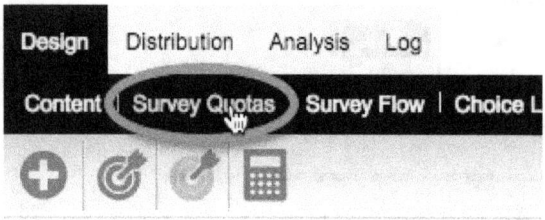

2. Choose the **Quota Builder** from the toolbar

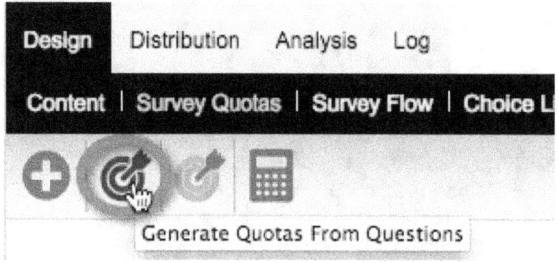

3. Choose **Gender** as the first question we want to use in our quotas

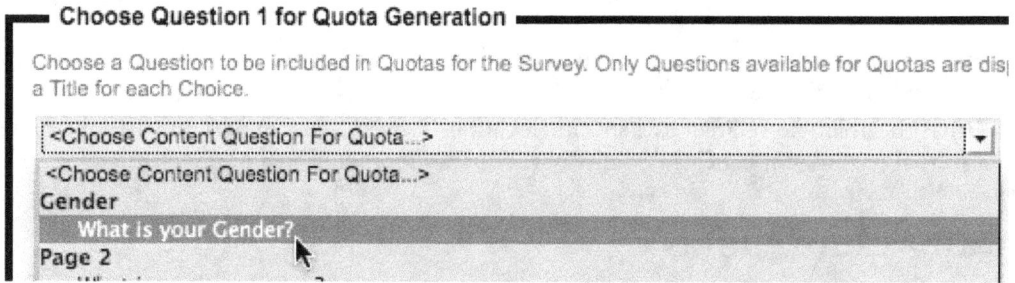

4. Choose both of the values for this question to indicate that they will both be used in the quota (note that we can optionally change how they will be described in the quota)

5. Choose **Age Group** as the second question we want to use in our quotas

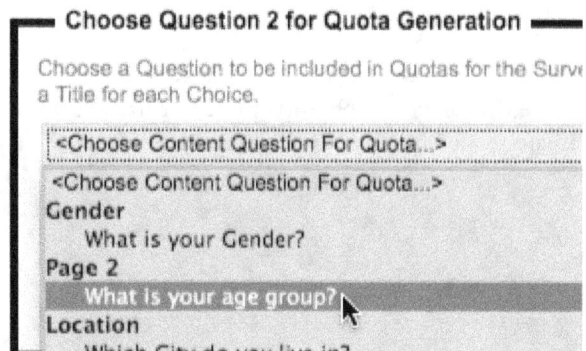

6. Again, choose all values. We can do this quickly by pressing the **Toggle Selection** link

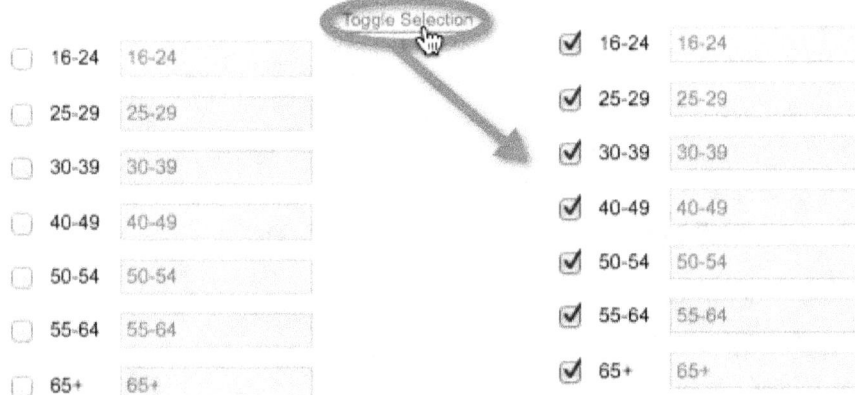

7. Press the **Set Quota Limits** button

8. All combinations of the choices selected will be presented ready for quota numbers to be entered

#	Title	Quota Access Code	Limit
1	Male, 16-24	MALE16-24	0
2	Male, 25-29	MALE25-29	0
3	Male, 30-39	MALE30-39	0
4	Male, 40-49	MALE40-49	0
5	Male, 50-54	MALE50-54	0
6	Male, 55-64	MALE55-64	0
7	Male, 65+	MALE65	0
8	Female, 16-24	FEMALE16-24	0
9	Female, 25-29	FEMALE25-29	0
10	Female, 30-39	FEMALE30-39	0
11	Female, 40-49	FEMALE40-49	0
12	Female, 50-54	FEMALE50-54	0
13	Female, 55-64	FEMALE55-64	0
14	Female, 65+	FEMALE65	0

9. Enter the quota numbers as per the original request from Worldburger

#	Title	Quota Access Code	Limit
1	Male, 16-24	MALE16-24	34
2	Male, 25-29	MALE25-29	36
3	Male, 30-39	MALE30-39	47

10. Press the **Save Quotas** button

The Quotas will all be shown under **Survey Quotas** on the **Design** tab.

Quota Title	Code	Limit	In Quota	Remaining
Female, 16-24	FEMALE16-24	33	-	33
Female, 25-29	FEMALE25-29	36	-	36
Female, 30-39	FEMALE30-39	48	-	48
Female, 40-49	FEMALE40-49	43	-	43
Female, 50-54	FEMALE50-54	25	-	25
Female, 55-64	FEMALE55-64	37	-	37
Female, 65+	FEMALE65	46	-	46
Male, 16-24	MALE16-24	34	-	34
Male, 25-29	MALE25-29	36	-	36
Male, 30-39	MALE30-39	47	-	47
Male, 40-49	MALE40-49	41	-	41
Male, 50-54	MALE50-54	25	-	25
Male, 55-64	MALE55-64	36	-	36
Male, 65+	MALE65	38	-	38

Creating the Location Quotas

The location quotas can be created in the same way as the gender/age quotas - in fact, they are even easier to create, since all the quotas are only based on a single question - *City lived in*.

We need to choose all values except "None of the above", which would be inappropriate as a quota.

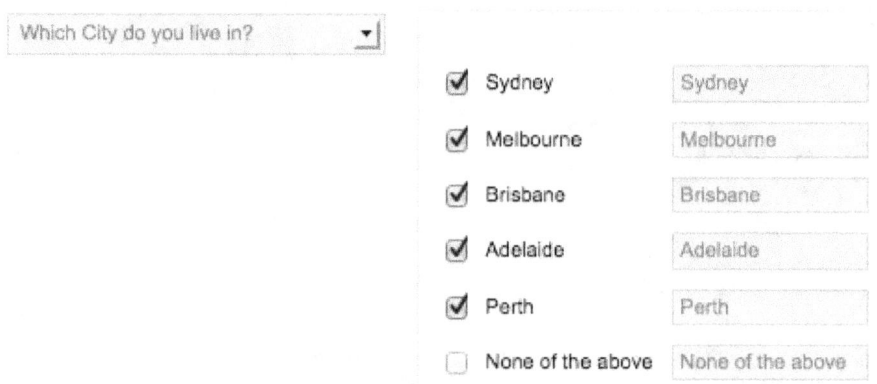

Quotas are shown alphabetically in the Quotas Browse - but we want the cities to appear together. We can do this by changing the descriptors for the cities before saving.

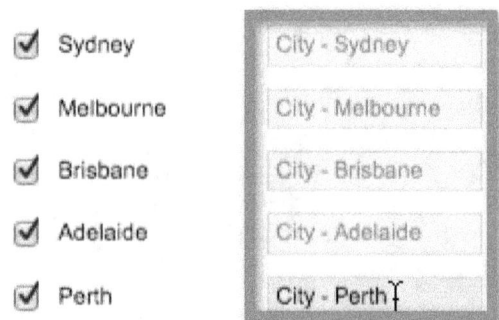

Once the location quotas are added, they will also be shown at the top of the **Survey Quotas Browse** (because they are first in the alphabetical order).

Quota Title	Code	Limit	In Quota	Remaining
City - Adelaide	ADELAIDE	51	-	51
City - Brisbane	BRISBANE	103	-	103
City - Melbourne	MELBOURNE	152	-	152
City - Perth	PERTH	62	-	62
City - Sydney	SYDNEY	157	-	157
Female, 16-24	FEMALE16-24	33	-	33
Female, 25-29	FEMALE25-29	36	-	36

Adding Quota Fail Terminate Page logic

We have already created our quota terminate - there's just one problem!

> If survey flow logic is not added to hide a terminate page, the page will always be shown - and every respondent will be terminated!

Now that we have our quotas set up, we can correctly hide the terminate page (since the hide rule will be directly related to whether a respondent can fit in the quotas).

The steps for creating our terminate page logic are as follows:

1. Click on **Survey Flow** under the **Design** tab.

2. Add a **New Flow**

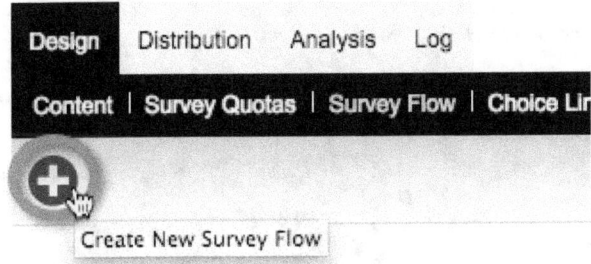

Quota Management 125

3. Choose to hide the terminate page

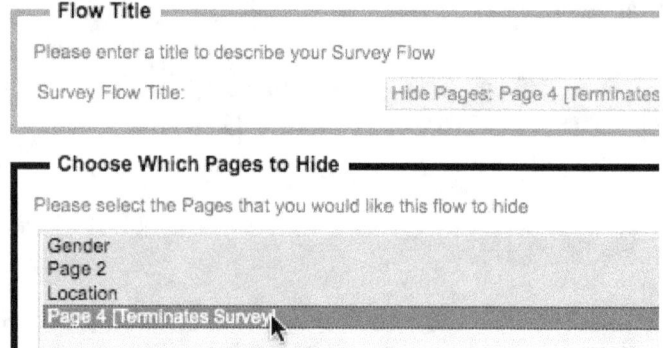

4. Click the **Save & Continue to Add Conditions** button

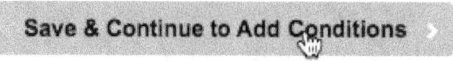

5. Click **Add Condition**

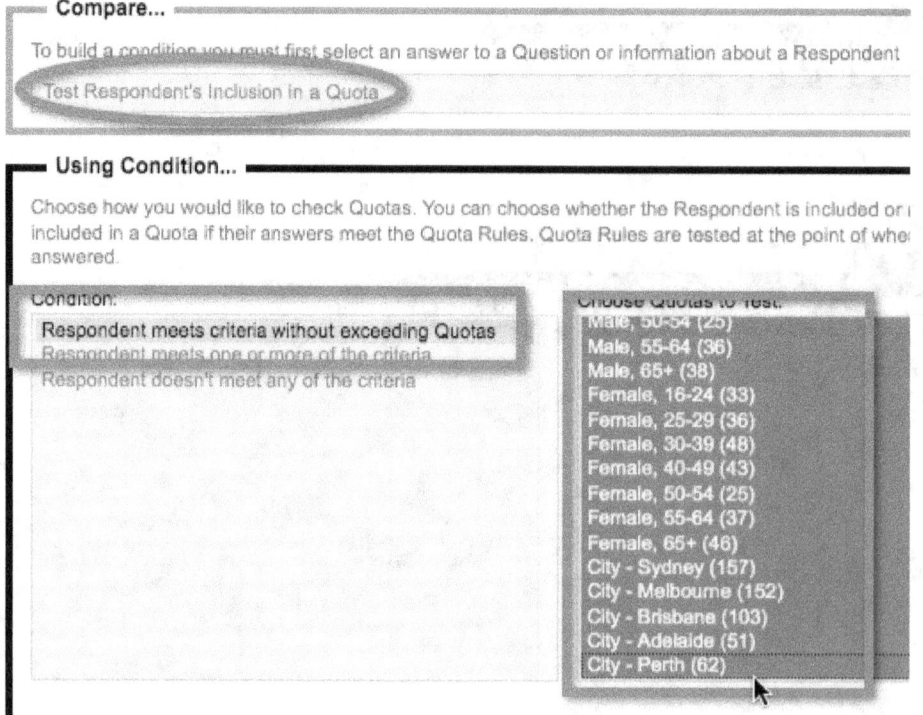

6. Choose to **test all the quotas**, as shown below

7. Click **Save Condition**

The terminate page will now only be shown under the following conditions:

1. The respondent matches at least one of the quotas
2. All of the quotas attached to the respondent still have room (the only exception to this rule is if **Priority Quotas** exist, as discussed in the previous section).

Manual Adjustment of Quotas

If you need to add or edit single quotas, you can do this through the Quota Management System.

Adding a Single Quota

To add a single Quota, click on the *Create Quota* toolbar button.

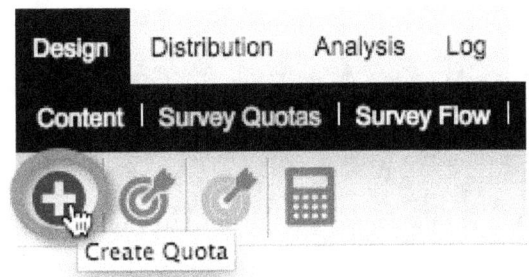

All details for the quota need to be entered, including a title for the quota.

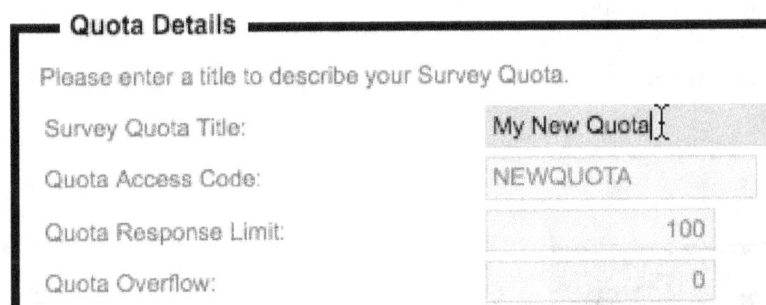

The Quota Rules can be added one at a time, in a similar way to flow control.

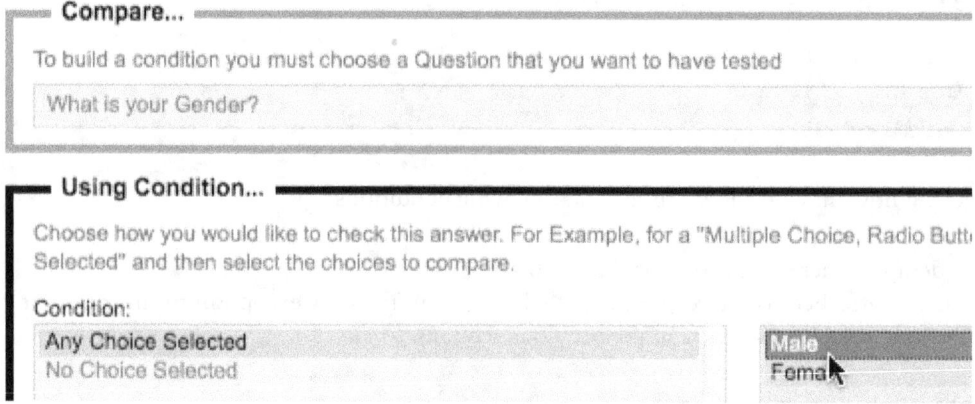

Editing a Quota

Editing a Quota is simply a matter of clicking on the Quota Title in the Quota Browse.

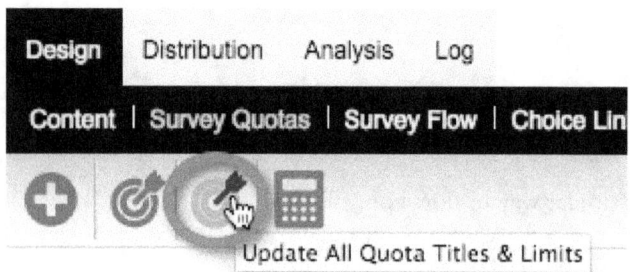

Editing Multiple Quotas at once

If you need to modify quotas, quite often it's going to be one the following details that needs to be changed:

- How many people you are looking for in the quota
- How much of an overflow you will allow
- The access code or description for the quota

Web Survey Creator makes it easy to modify these details *en masse* by clicking on the **Update All** toolbar button under **Survey Quotas**.

Titles, access codes, limits and overflow amounts can all be adjusted from a single screen.

Tracking Quotas

Quotas can be easily tracked under **Survey Quotas**, as we have already seen. This works well if you have set up the survey, and you are a Web Survey Creator user, but what if you are an outsider - like a client?

Let's assume that the management at Worldburger wants to keep an eye on the progress of the survey. Fortunately there is a way for them to do this in WSC - through a *Web Portal*.

A Web Portal can show a number of things including:

Current Status of Quotas

All quotas are listed, together with the number of respondents who are currently "In Quota" and how many are still needed.

My Portal Sample

Home | Question Statistics | Overview Charts | Quotas | Reports

Survey Quotas

The current status of all survey quotas are shown in the table below.

Quota Title	Limit	In Quota	Remaining	Draft
City - Adelaide	51	51	-	8
City - Brisbane (inc Gold Coast)	103 (17)	118	2	14
City - Melbourne	152 (28)	185	-	27
City - Perth	62	50	12	2
City - Sydney	157	162	-	20
Female, 16-24	33 (7)	36	4	6

Quota Management

Response Counts

A daily count of responses is shown, together with a cumulative total - broken down by type (quota outs etc.)

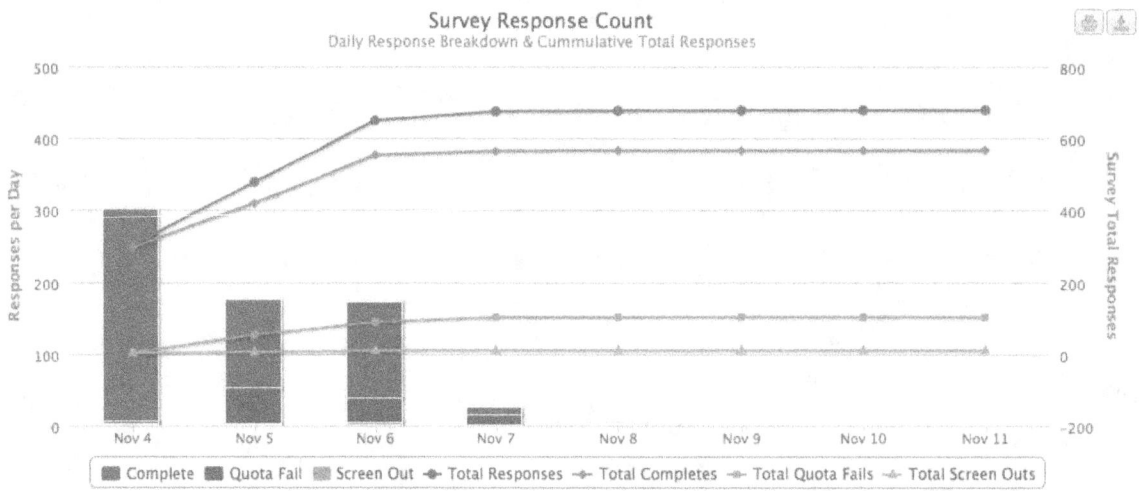

Individual Question Statistics

Current counts for responses to each of the questions in the survey.

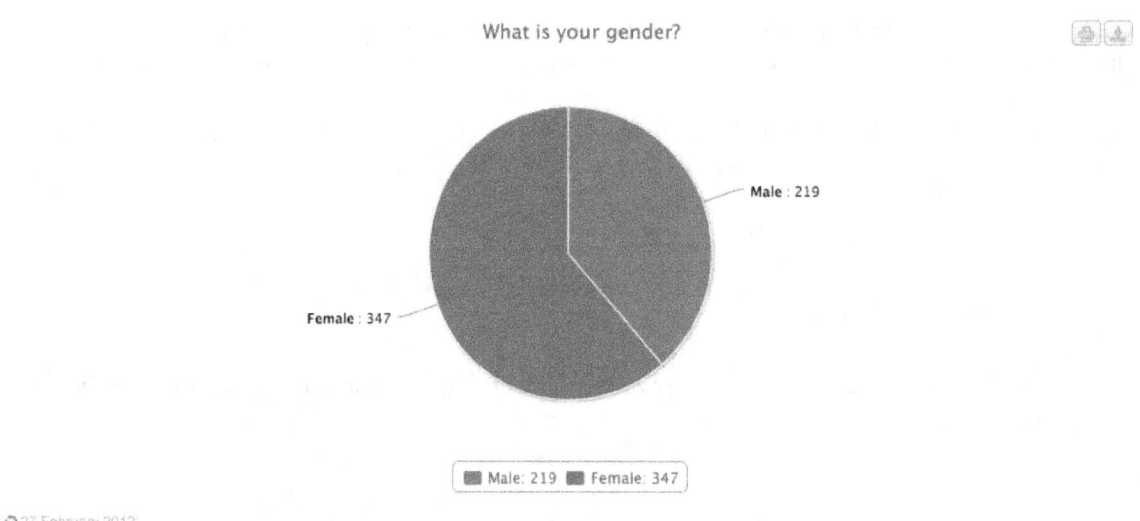

Mobile Surveys

The world of Surveys is currently changing at a pace not seen since the original shift to the Web. Having a Web Survey is no longer enough - your surveys now need to be accessible on mobile devices.

"Smart phones" are your window into higher response rates, and more satisfied respondents.

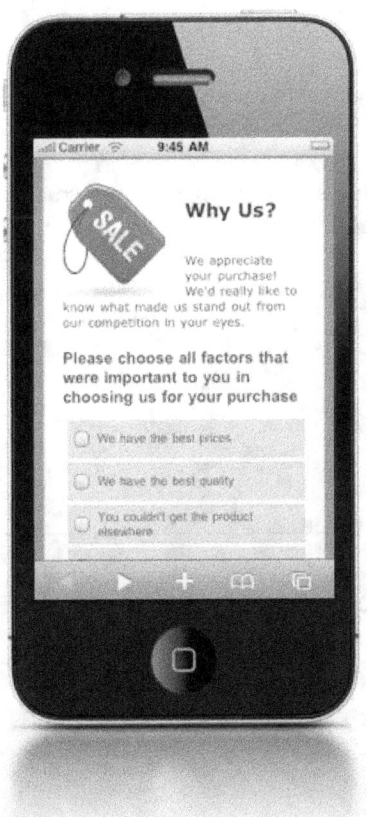

Mobile vs. Desktop

The expectations that respondents now have when it comes to Web Surveys are quite easy to quantify. Unfortunately they are not so easy to meet, since many of the expectations are not easy to achieve.

Expectation	Problem
Survey completion on a mobile device or a desktop computer - not just one	Many survey solutions have full-featured "desktop" and cut-down "mobile" versions. Choose one or other when setting up (not both).
"Sexy" surveys	"Sexy" usually equals flash-based desktop questions. Not mobile compatible.
If using a mobile device, survey is still full-featured	Usually formatting and functionality on mobile devices is cut down

The existence of mobile devices with true Web browser capabilities is a relatively new phenomenon (some suggest it began with the iPhone in 2007) and many of the gaps between expectations and the reality of Web Surveys on mobile devices is simply a result of large, established software packages still trying to "catch up" with the expectation.

Going "half-way" with cut-down mobile-specific survey tools misses the point - people have "cool" mobile devices and expect the things they do on those devices to be "cool" as well.

> There is an added benefit to getting to people via their mobile phone or tablet - the sorts of people who use these devices are often the younger demographic that are so hard to get any response out of.

The humble P.C. is far from dead...

Regardless of how much people like using their mobile devices, there is still an important place for desktop (and laptop) computers. It is therefore critical that a Web Survey continues to work well in a standard PC environment. There are a number of benefits to this environment that will never be eradicated by the onslaught of mobile devices:

1. Large amounts of text are easier to enter on a full-sized keyboard
2. Virtually every household has a PC (and can share it, unlike personal mobile devices) for completion of surveys
3. A significant percentage of respondents do not have or want smart mobile devices
4. Older generations often feel more comfortable using a PC, since that is what they are used to

Mobile doesn't have to mean basic

With use of the right technologies, there is only really one limitation that you have to work around on a mobile device...

> Mobile devices have less screen real estate than desktops. The interface provided must take this into account.

Layout Management

Images need to be resized, and wide layouts changed to fit a mobile screen.

Advanced text question types - like demographics - look best using a form-style layout on a desktop. Again, on a mobile device, the layout needs to be modified.

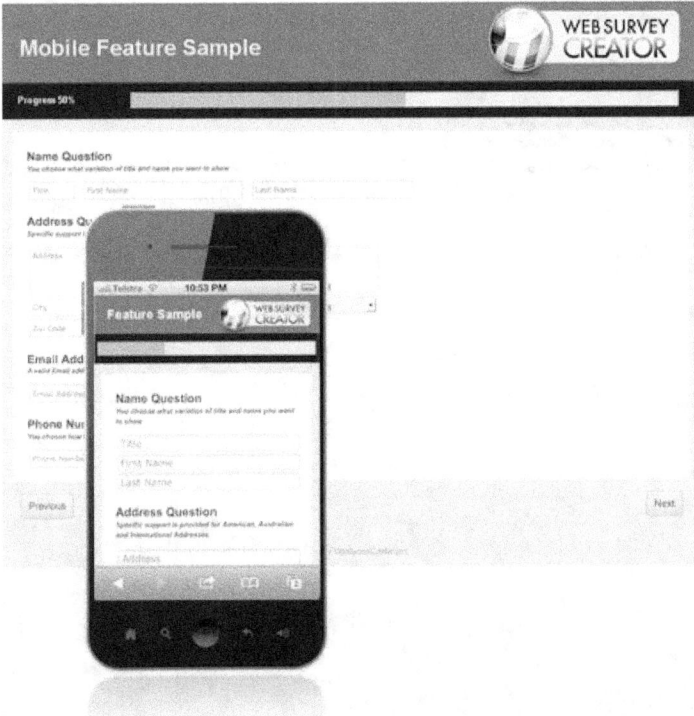

Text Entry

On a desktop, text entry is easy - the keyboard in the primary input device. On a mobile, text fields not only need to be formatted for the screen - they also need to work with the input system on the device.

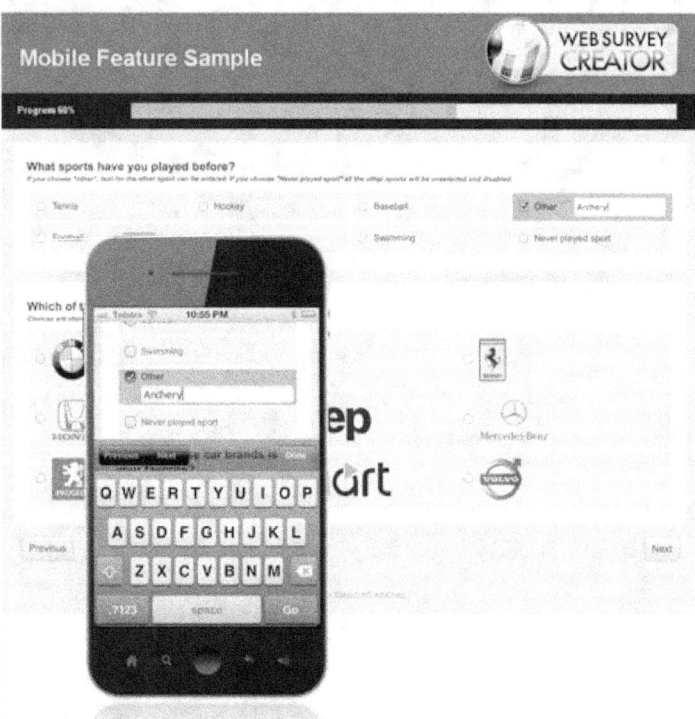

Question "Morphing"

Some question types simply cannot be used on a mobile because the screen size simply doesn't allow for a useable experience. An example is a matrix question, which requires the full width of the screen to be able to be entered on a desktop.

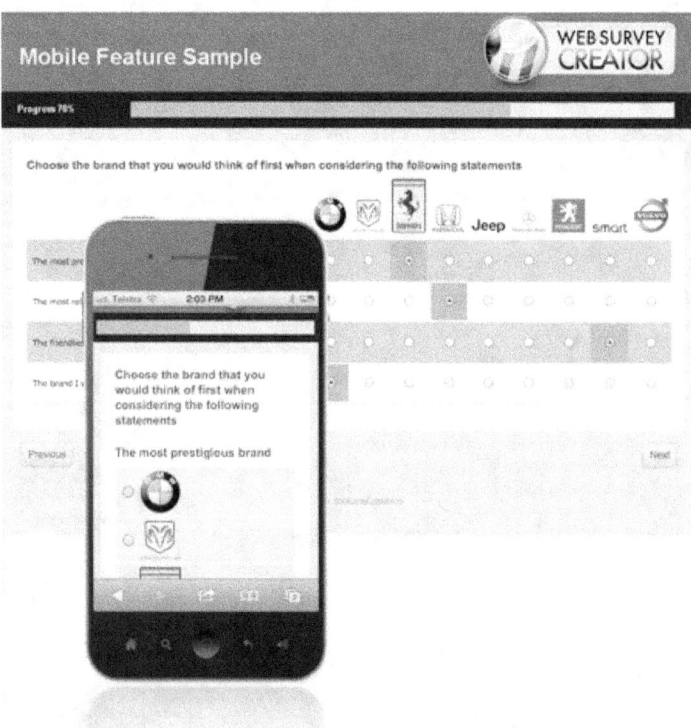

Keeping the "Sexy" in your Surveys

One of the biggest issues faced when supporting mobile devices is to avoid losing all the "sexy" capabilities that respondents have become used to.

Gotta have Video!

Many market research surveys use video as a way to show product material such as advertisements.

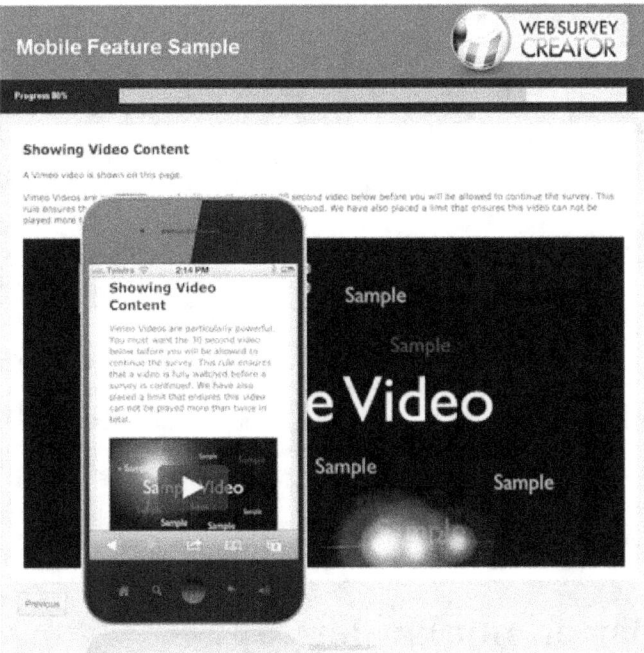

Touch-enabled Sliders

Sliders are used more and more in surveys. It's important to have the same capability on mobile devices - including advanced implementations like the component breakdown slider question below.

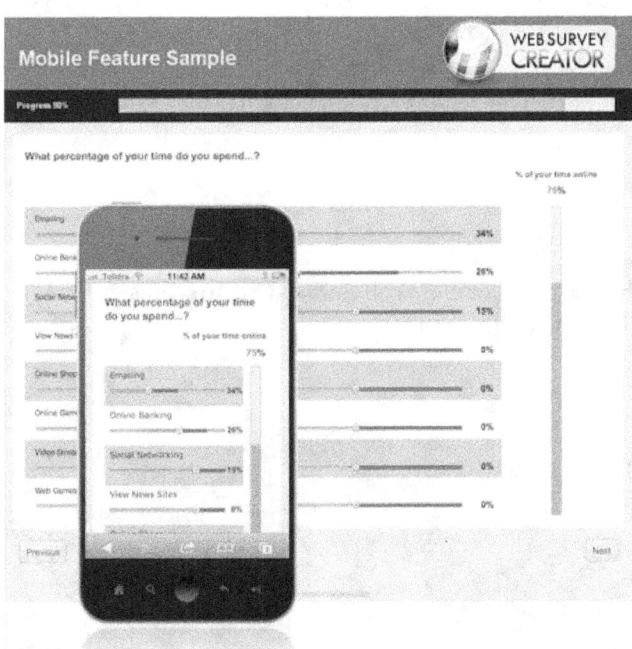

Drag 'n' Drop

Mobile users love their touch-screen smartphones. Drag 'n' drop needs to be available on the phone to mimic dragging operations on the desktop version of survey questions.

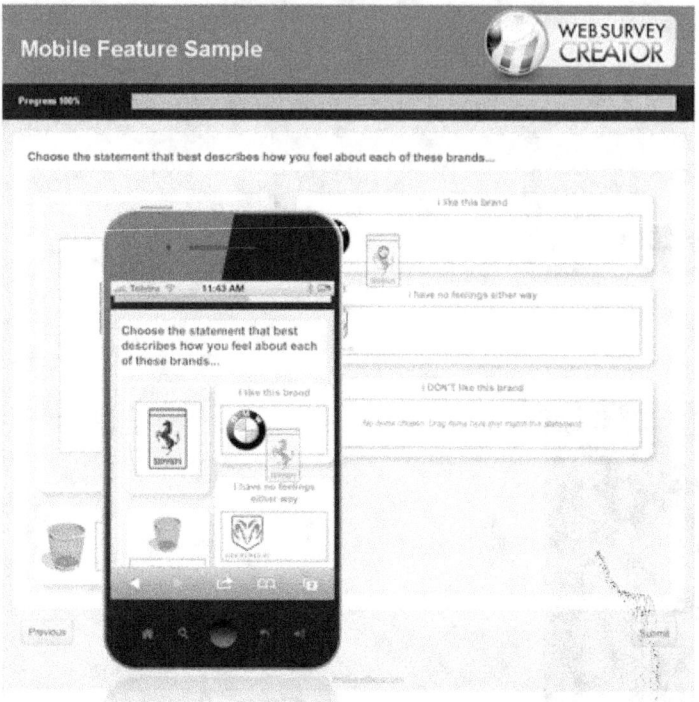

Going Mobile: Working smarter, not harder

If you want to create Web Surveys that support both mobile and desktop respondents, you need to adhere to some rules when looking for a Web Survey design tool:

1. Never use flash-based questions. They immediately exclude mobile users
2. Avoid solutions that split mobile and desktop survey design into separate modules - you'll be doing twice the work, and possibly have incompatibilities due to limitations in the mobile version
3. Avoid survey solutions for desktop respondents that have mobile capabilities "tacked on". Mobile is too important to be an afterthought.
4. Avoid overly basic mobile survey capabilities - you'll be able to get to mobile users, but not with the kind of survey you need to create.

An Example Survey

The example we will be reviewing in this section has been created in Web Survey Creator. Images of mobile survey capabilities in the previous section came from this example.

To see the full example, visit the WSC sample online:

http://www.websurveycreator.com/c/survey-sample-3.aspx

Making a WSC survey mobile-capable

A survey can tell what browser - and therefore what type of device - it is being run on. Web Survey Creator uses this information to determine how a survey will be displayed.

What do you need to do to make a WSC survey work on a mobile device?

NOTHING

Any survey created in Web Survey Creator will work on a mobile device - they whole basis of the system is you design a survey once and it can be used everywhere.

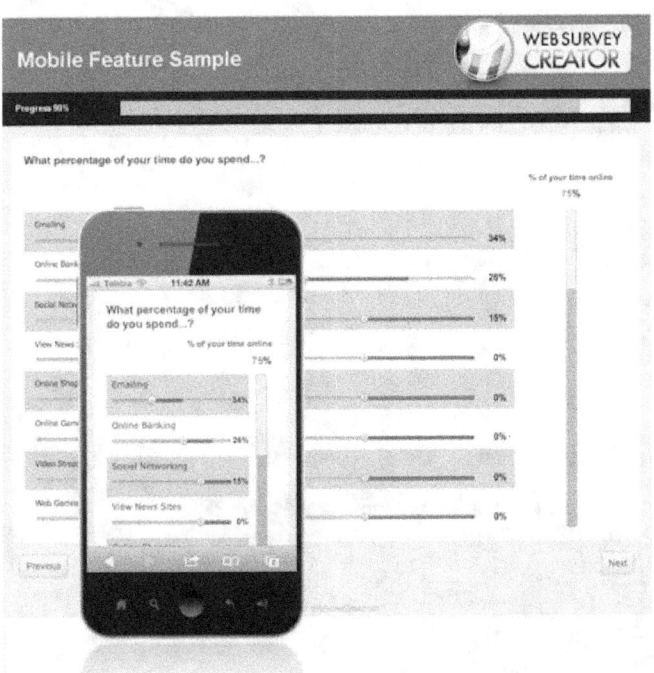

Targeting Specific Platforms

While Web Survey Creator will manage surveys on a mobile device automatically, there may be times when you actively want to do something different for respondents who answer on a mobile as opposed to people who answer on a PC (or on a tablet for that matter).

Whenever Web Survey Creator shows a survey to a respondent, it determines which of the following types of device is being used to view the survey:

PC	Computer running a full PC operating system such as Microsoft Windows or Mac OSX. These are the types of machines that have traditionally been used to complete surveys.
Tablet	Mobile devices that have moderately sized (7"+) touch-screens, and are generally referred to as "tablets" (e.g. iPad, Samsung Galaxy Tab)
Mobile	Mobile devices with relatively small screens (<5") that are generally referred to as "Smartphones".

Web Survey Creator can determine the type of device from the browser that is running on the device. Knowing which device is being used can open opportunities to change the behavior of the survey for different devices.

Device Targeting through Flow Control

Our Mobile Survey Sample doesn't have a single introduction page - it has three. It has one for each type of device.

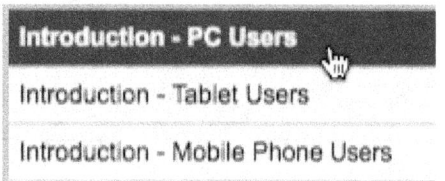

While multiple introduction pages is certainly not mandatory - since WSC will render a single page correctly on all three styles of device - it does give some flexibility in survey design. It allows the designer of the survey:

To show different introduction text based upon the type of device being used.

1. PC

    Welcome to the Mobile Survey Demonstration!

    OK, so you're not running this survey on a mobile phone or a tablet at the moment, are you?

    That's fine - this demonstrates exactly how surveys created in Web Survey Creator work. Three distinct types of device are supported automatically when a survey is rendered - PCs, Tablets and Mobile Phones.

2. Tablet

    Welcome to the Mobile Survey Demonstration!

    Cool - it looks like you are running this survey on a Tablet. It will work pretty much like a survey on a PC, except that the sizing will suit a tablet, and the touch interface is supported for all questions.

3. Mobile

Welcome to the Mobile Survey Demonstration!

Cool - it looks like you are running this survey on a Mobile Phone.

All questions can be answered on your phone, but they will be formatted to suit the size of screen.

You can proactively limit content based upon the device. In our example survey, the introduction for mobile phones is shorter and does not contain any images - taking into account the fact that the survey is likely to be done on a 3G network.

Setting up Flow Control

To set up the introduction pages in the sample, we did the following:

1. We created three pages - one for each of the devices we wanted to target

2. We then created three survey flow rules - one rule each for the introduction pages. The rules tested the type of device that way being used to view the survey

   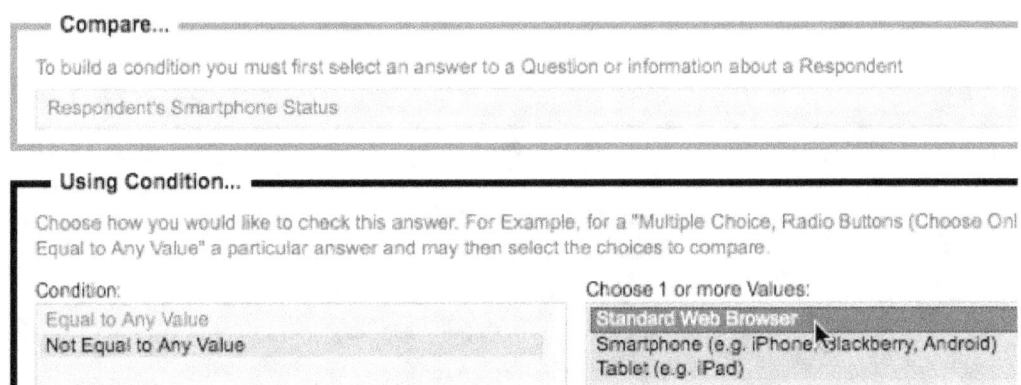

Mobile Surveys   139

Mixed Mode Surveys

Computer-assisted telephone interviewing (CATI) existed long before the rise of Web-based surveys (CAWI). Even as the use of Web surveys has risen rapidly, it has become clear that the future of interviewing would be a mix of CATI and CAWI - often referred to as "mixed mode".

Web Survey Creator has a CATI module that adds CATI capabilities to be used for CATI-only jobs, or in association with Web-based surveys ("mixed mode" jobs).

Welcome to CATI!

Web Survey Creator with CATI has been developed to directly target what we perceive to be the key challenges facing companies engaged in CATI:

- Continued use of aging technology to perform CATI
- Paying expensive software licensing & maintaining expensive infrastructure
- Lack of flexibility - software is tied to the desktop in the office linked to an internal server

Gone are the days when a CATI business could be run efficiently with office-bound computers running desktop software. Web Survey Creator supports modern Web standards, and can be used from any Web browser - either in your office, or from a remote location. You can expand or contract your team at a moment's notice.

Our hosted version of Web Survey Creator takes care of everything for you - Managers, Team Leaders and Interviewers can simply log in from a Web browser. This is great for small to medium firms who want to be freed from the management of their CATI software and hardware infrastructure.

Larger organizations who are used to having more control over their infrastructure, and would like to self-host Web Survey Creator, can do so using our On-Premise version. Features of this version include:

- Unlimited CATI Interviewers, Team Leaders & Managers
- Unlimited Interviews & Web Surveys
- Custom Domains
- Dedicated Server & Database

How you run your CATI operation is up to you:

- Run everything in your office in a traditional CATI call center
- Run a mixture of office and off-site interviewers
- Completely decentralize - our CATI management tools ensure you still have your "finger on the pulse" of your CATI processes without the office overheads

In this chapter we will look at how the WSC CATI module can be set up to be used on its own, or as part of a mixed mode survey process.

Setting up your CATI Process – The Basics

Setting up a CATI process in WSC is very straightforward and will be very familiar to users who have already created Web surveys in the product. It is beneficial to understand the similarities and differences between CATI jobs and Web Survey jobs.

Similarities	Differences
The same survey design is used for both	CATI jobs MUST have respondents, and they must at a minimum have a telephone number.
The general logic and flow is the same – flow control, data piping, scripting etc.	A custom introduction is read out prior to conducting the survey. This is never seen in the Web version of the survey.
Quotas are set up once, and work in the same way for both Web and CATI survey responses.	"Interviewers" are a specific type of user who have access to the CATI module only.

Overview of Key Aspects of CATI Survey Setup

The key steps for setting up a CATI process in Web Survey Creator are as follows:

1. Create a new survey, and set the survey responses type to "CATI Responses"

2. Choose which of the global settings for Call statuses, Email templates and Time zones to copy into the new survey.

   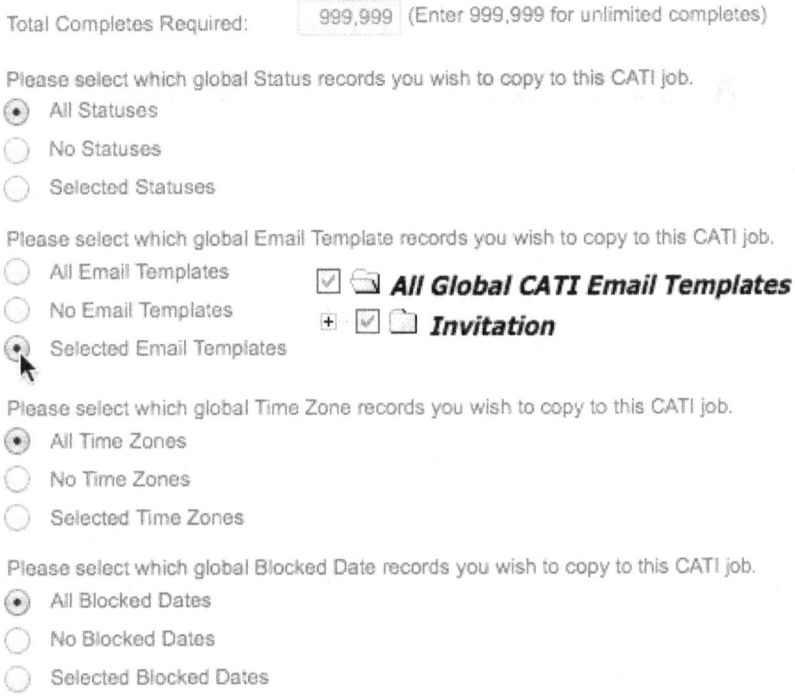

3. Create the survey content (this content will be used for both the CATI and the CAWI surveys)

   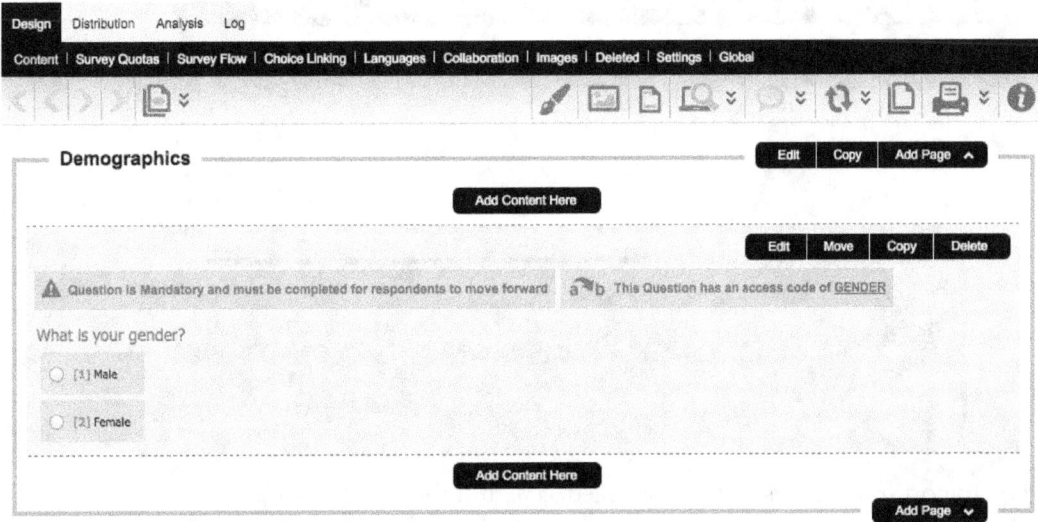

Research Panel Integration 143

> When creating survey content, consider details that are important for a properly constructed CATI survey:
>
> 1. Use codes on questions that you want to import data into (for example, if you have gender data in the respondent import data, ensure the gender question has a code so that imported data will be connected to that question)
> 2. Set up CATI specific content using <cationly> and <catinever> tags in survey content.

4. Set up the Survey Quotas. CATI and CAWI will share these quotas. For CATI quotas are very important, because calls will be served up based upon how full quotas are (the more empty the quota, the more likely someone who meets that quota will be chosen as the next person to call)

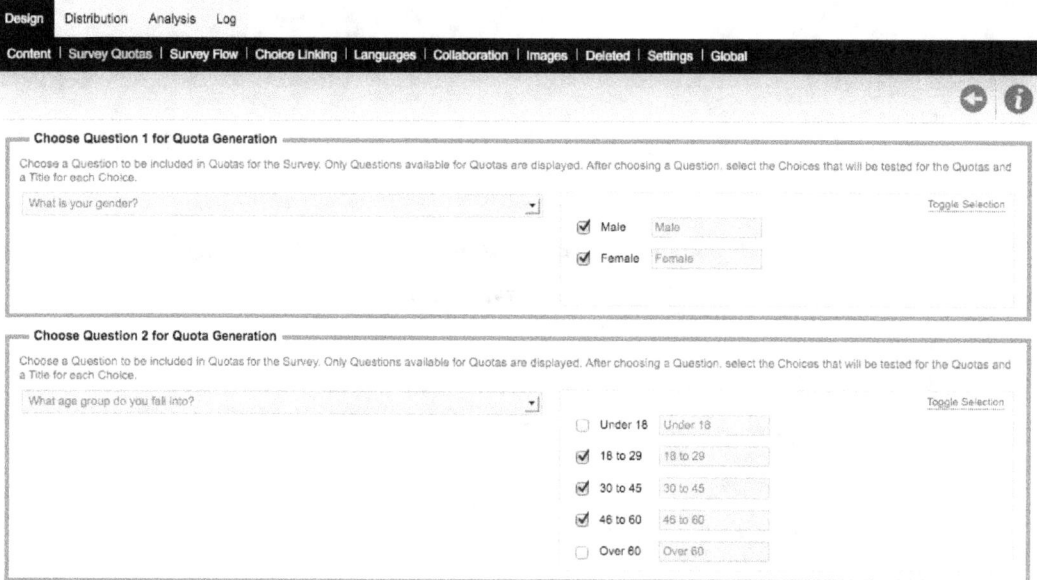

5. Set up survey flows, including flows for terminate pages

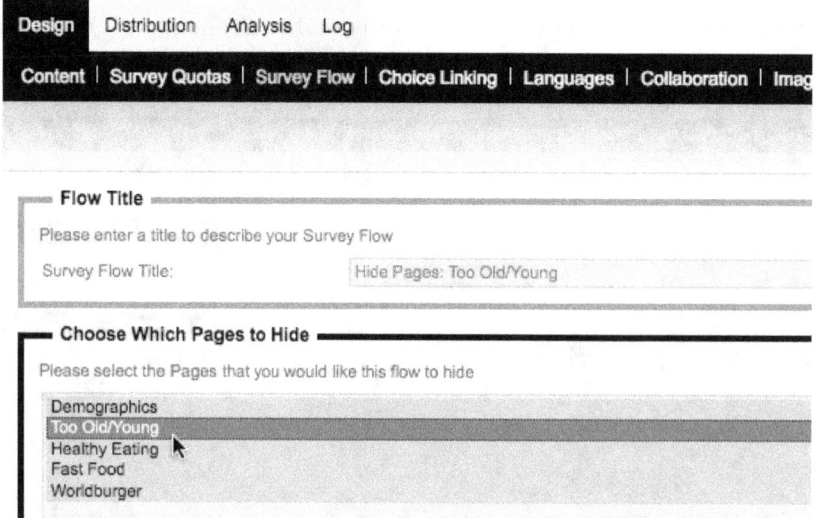

6. Import respondents that will be called as part of the CATI process

144 Research Panel Integration

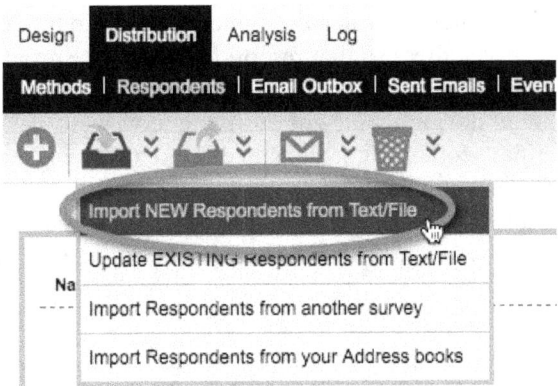

7. If the additional import detail includes data that is used in quotas, you can pre-calculate quotas for all your respondents.

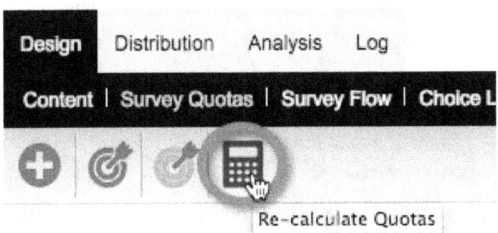

Once these details have been set up, this CATI project is ready to use. A well set up project with good respondent data will have quotas and respondent tags (with non-survey data that may be of use to you) all attached to respondents. For example, a respondent could look something like the following:

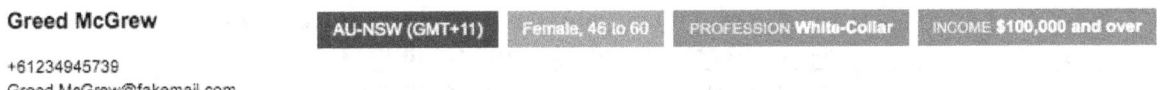

CATI Respondents

Much of the setup that CATI needs has already been discussed in this manual, since CATI surveys are set up exactly the same as Web Surveys. In particular survey design, terminate pages, quotas and survey flow work in exactly the same way for both types of data collection.

Respondents are a little different. Respondents can be used for both CATI and CAWI so again there are many similarities to what we already know for Web Surveys. To get the full benefit of respondents in CATI, however, it is worth looking at "best practices" when setting up and using respondents.

Types of Respondent Data

The key types of respondent data used in a CATI project are as follows:

Telephone number	A single telephone number is the minimal amount of information needed for CATI. Without a telephone number, a call can't be made. The respondent system supports up to 2 telephone numbers, referred to as "phone1" and "phone2" in the import.
Name (incl. Title)	Name is good to have to identify respondents. Would only be excluded if you are calling a series of numbers with no idea who they belong to. Title would normally be blank, but for certain respondents – like doctors – title would be important.

Email Address	While not needed if you intend to call all respondents, "mixed mode" surveys require an Email address so that respondents can be Emailed a link to the survey for completion.
Time zone	If all respondents are in the same time zone as the interviewers, this is not needed (respondent time zones will be defaulted to the user's time zone as part of the import if it is not in the import data). Time zones on respondents are used for appointment times and other time-based rules (like when respondents may be called). Time zones are entered as codes, for example: AU-NSW AU-QLD AU-WA
Language	Usually there is a single language spoken by both the interviewers and the respondents, and therefore language is unnecessary. If multiple languages are being used however, a code for the language spoken by the respondent can be entered. Examples of language codes are: en jp
SMSID	This is a sample management ID. It is provided for people who what to add respondents with an ID that is used by an external system. Generally not needed to be used.
Survey Data	An example of this would be answering a question in the survey about gender by importing the data for each respondent. **Importing data that is relevant for quotas makes it possible for the system to more efficiently serve up the most appropriate respondents to call based on current quota completion levels. Respondents can also be filtered based upon quotas in the CATI system.**
Respondent Tags	Data that you want to track on a respondent, but is not related to a survey question, can be stored in respondent tags. Respondent tags have the format TAG: VALUE. Examples of respondent tags are: PROFESSION: White-Collar INCOME: $30,000-$49,999 Respondents can be filtered based upon tags, and tags are shown directly on respondents in the CATI system: Greed McGrew AU-NSW (GMT+11) Female, 46 to 60 PROFESSION White-Collar INCOME $100,000 and over +61234945739 Greed.McGrew@fakemail.com

> Every respondent needs to include one or more of the following (ie. they can't all be blank) - Email address, Phone 1 or SMSID.
>
> All respondents must be able to be uniquely identified in the system. This identification is based on a combination of Email address, Phone 1 or SMSID, together with the respondent's name.
>
> Therefore, the same phone number can appear more than once, as long as there is something else that uniquely identifies the respondents that have the duplicate phone number. For example, you could import Joe Bloggs and Mary Bloggs, both of whom share their home phone number.

Importing Respondent Data – An Example

The process to import respondents into WSC is very straightforward *if* you set up your data correctly. An example of such data is shown in the spreadsheet below.

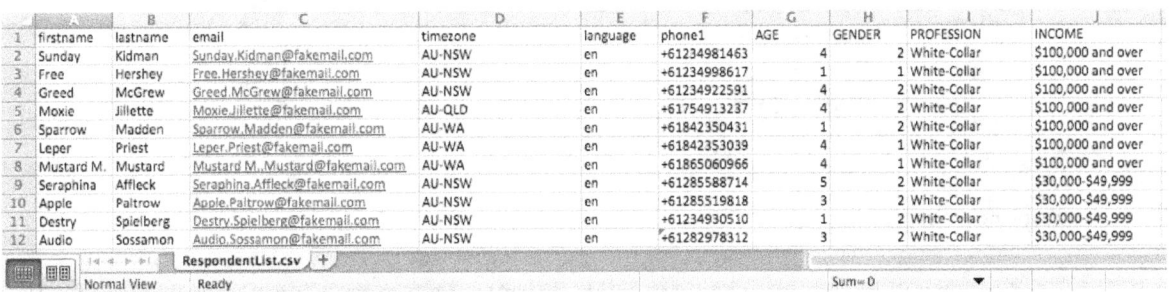

Using Valid Heading Labels

This spreadsheet has valid heading labels in the first row. The first row **MUST** be used for headings – the import uses these headings to determine what data is included in the import.

Columns can be set up in any order, as long as they are properly labeled, and as long as either **email** or **phone1** fields are included (for CATI projects, **phone1** is mandatory). Valid standard labels are:

- Email
- title
- firstname
- lastname
- language
- phone1
- phone2
- timezone
- smsid

In addition to these standard labels, additional labels can be added for survey data and respondent tags.

To add survey data:

1. Set up a question in the survey with a question access code

    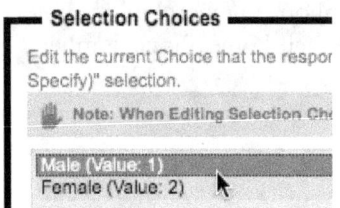

2. If the question is a choice question, ensure choices have values attached

    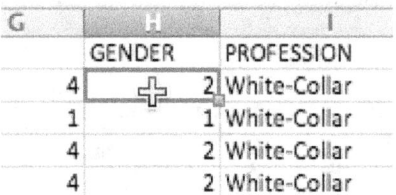

3. In the import file, use the Access Code for the column heading, and place the data in the column

    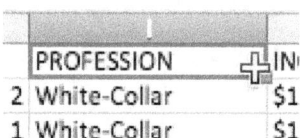

To add a respondent tag:

1. Use a heading in the import file that is NOT the same as any Access Code. This will become the respondent tag code.

PROFESSION	IN
2 White-Collar	$1
1 White-Collar	$1

2. Enter items in the column that represent the values for the tag – note that all data entered will be stored in the system simply as a text field.

    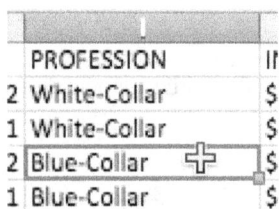

Preparing the data for Import

Data can be imported in one of two formats:

1. Comma delimited text (useful when you have a basic text file with your respondent details in it)
2. As an Excel file (the most common method, since most lists of people are already in this format)

Importing Respondents from a Text File

If we had our example data in a text format, it would look as follows:

```
firstname,lastname,email,timezone,language,phone1,AGE,GENDER,PROFESSION,INCOME
Sunday,Kidman,Sunday.Kidman@fakemail.com,AU-NSW,en,+61234949503,4,2,White-Collar,"$100,000 and over"
Free,Hershey,Free.Hershey@fakemail.com,AU-NSW,en,+61234913444,1,1,White-Collar,"$100,000 and over"
```

> **Important Tip**
>
> Commas are used for separating values, so if you have actual data that includes a comma – like **100,000 and over** – the data needs to be placed on quotation marks to ensure it is imported correctly (i.e. "100,000 and over").

To import respondents from a text file into Web Survey Creator:

1. Select **Respondents** from the **Distribution tab**

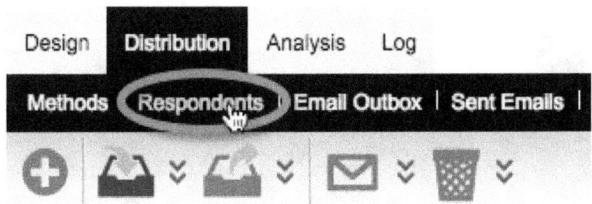

2. Choose **Import NEW Respondents from Text/File** from the **Import Respondents** toolbar

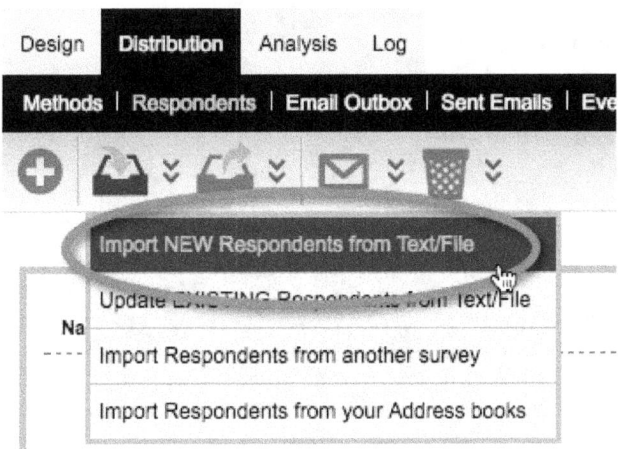

3. Paste in the text data

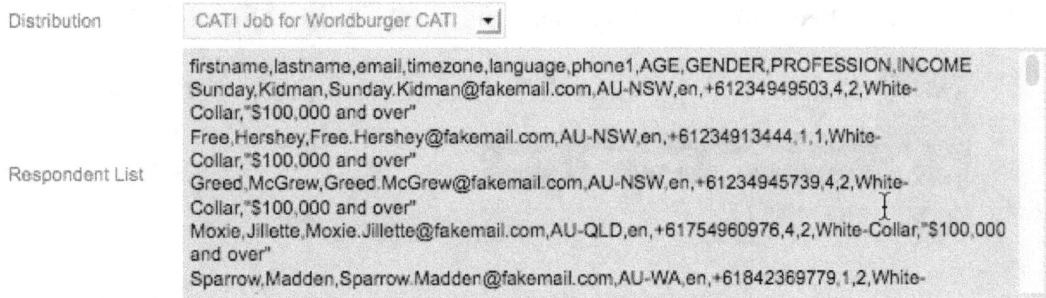

Research Panel Integration 149

4. Press the **Import Respondents** button to import the respondents

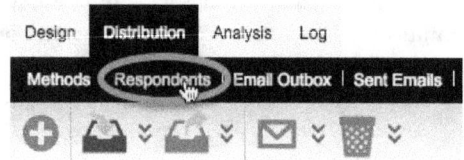

Importing Respondents from an Excel File

To import respondents from a text file into Web Survey Creator:

1. Select **Respondents** from the **Distribution tab**

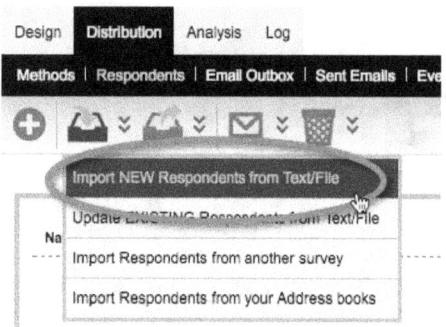

2. Choose **Import NEW Respondents from Text/File** from the **Import Respondents** toolbar

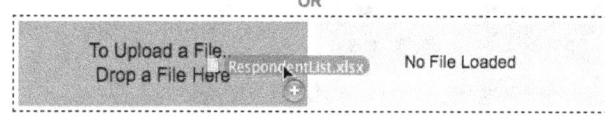

3. Drag the file onto the upload control

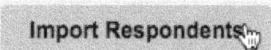

4. Press the **Import Respondents** button to import the respondents

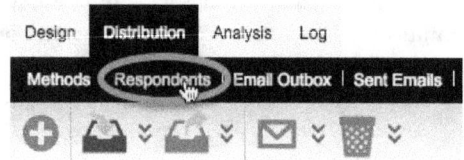

Calculating Quotas

If survey data is imported, and that data is used in quotas, the quotas need to be recalculated to update them for the new data:

1. Choose the **Recalculate Quotas** toolbar button under **Survey Quotas**

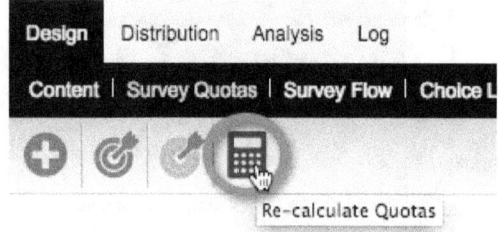

2. Click **Toggle Selection** to choose all quotas to process

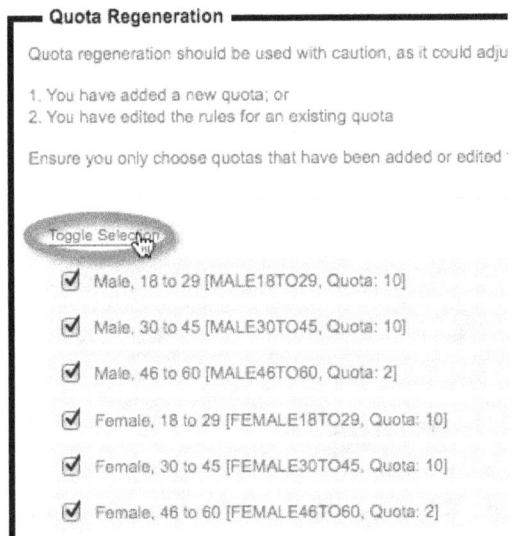

3. Click **Re-calculate Quotas** button to recalculate the quotas.

4. Looking at the "Draft" responses that appear under the quotas after recalculation is complete can show what the results of the quota calculations were. Here we see that there appear to be 4 Females that are 18 to 29 available for us to call:

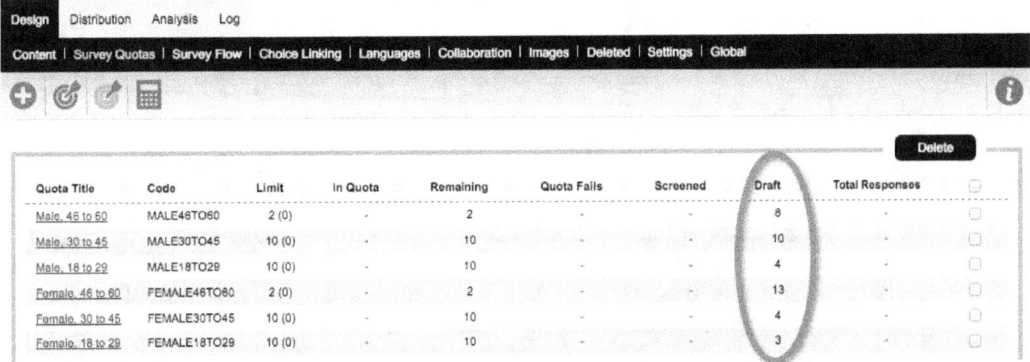

5. The "overall total" of respondents that need to be found for the CATI survey is set when a new CATI job is set up. This number will be shown in the Quota statistics for the job in the CATI module.

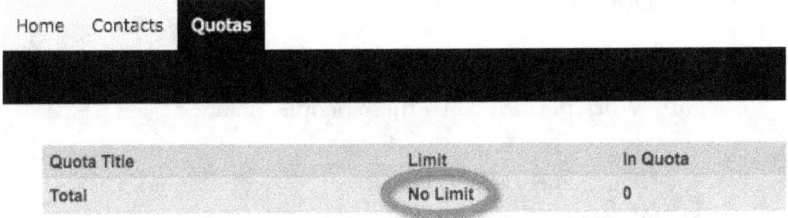

If this number needs to be changed after the survey has been created (for example, after quotas have been added or changed), we need to edit the CATI distribution directly, and enter a **Close Response Count**. While this is not a mandatory step during the creation of quotas, it is something that may need to be changed from time to time.

Research Panel Integration 151

Changing System-wide CATI Settings

The CATI system in Web Survey Creator can be used "out-of-the-box" without having to worry about basic settings. There are, however, a number of settings that can be changed at a system-wide level for CATI if needed. All these changes can be performed by CATI administrators from the **My CATI** top menu (which is visible only to CATI Administrators).

Setting up CATI Users

There are two distinct types of user access in Web Survey Creator:

Content Designers & Managers	Anyone who has access to the main Web Survey Creator application falls into this category. This refers to all access *other* than CATI related access in the system. Some of the key work performed by content designers includes: • Create survey content • Setup survey rules (flows, data piping etc.) • Create distributions • Create respondent lists • Distribute Web Surveys
CATI Administrators & Interviewers	Anyone who has anything to do with the CATI process falls into this category. Work performed by these people includes: • Management of CATI settings through the MY CATI menu • Access to the CATI Web application • Interviewing through the CATI Web application • Management of interviewers in the CATI Web application

The exact access an individual would have within these two categories is set on their user record. The creating and editing of user records can be performed from the **User Management** tab under the **MY CATI** menu.

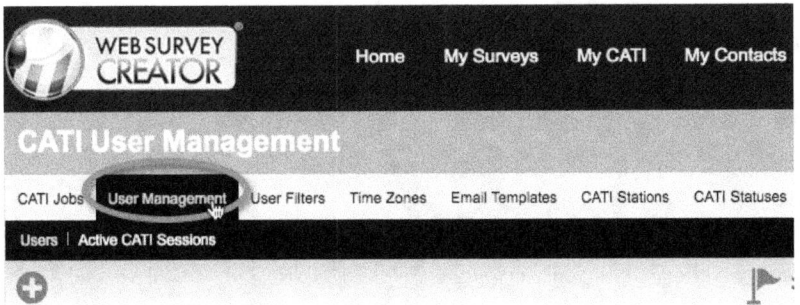

Adding a User

A user can be added by pressing the **New User** toolbar button.

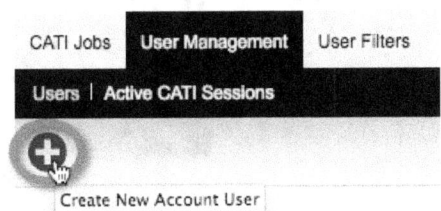

The user details that can be entered are as follows:

Name & Email	Basic user details that identify them. The Email address will be used as the user login.
User Role	Defines the level of access a user has to both the WSC main application (for survey design etc.) and to the CATI Web application (for interviewing respondents etc.)
Time zone	Knowing the time zone of the users is important when CATI is being used, because key information like when an appointment to call back a person should be made must consider the time zones of both the caller (ie. the user) and the respondent.

What if a user does not have an Email address?

As a general rule, all users need an Email address. There is one circumstance, however when an Email address is not available or needed – for casual or transient CATI staff that need to be able to log into the CATI system, but they have no company or other Email address. For these people, there is a "Has No Email Address" option when setting them up.

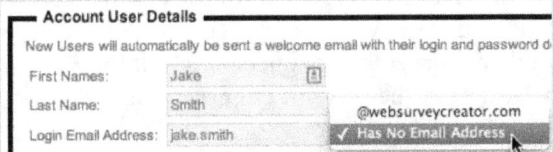

These people can <u>only</u> be given a CATI role (i.e. Their content role is set to "No Survey Access"), and log in with their user name (e.g. "jake.smith") rather than a full Email address.

Research Panel Integration   153

The **User Add** window looks as follows:

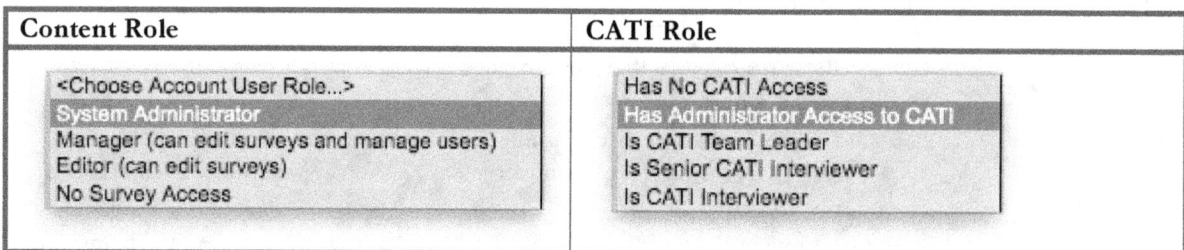

The levels available for the user roles are as follows:

Content Role	CATI Role
<Choose Account User Role...> **System Administrator** Manager (can edit surveys and manage users) Editor (can edit surveys) No Survey Access	Has No CATI Access **Has Administrator Access to CATI** Is CATI Team Leader Is Senior CATI Interviewer Is CATI Interviewer

Any mixture of roles can be chosen for a particular user. Examples of roles that could be set up are:

For an Administrator	**System Administrator** and **Has Administrator Access to CATI**
For a CATI Interviewer	**No Survey Access** and **Is CATI Interviewer**
For a Web Survey Designer	**Editor** and **Has No CATI Access**

> **What is the difference between a CATI Interviewer and a Senior CATI Interviewer?**
>
> While most of the access levels are self-explanatory – separating management of the system, from using the system – these two levels are not quite so obvious. A CATI Interviewer is the lowest form of access for CATI. These people can do little more than request the next person to call for a particular CATI Job. They cannot browse contacts. By default they cannot filter contacts either.
>
> Senior Interviewers are given more flexibility. This means that in addition to just getting the next contact, they can see a browse of prospective contacts, use filters, and choose anyone from that list to call.

Setting User Filters

The filtering system within WSC's CATI module is very powerful. It allows an interviewer to restrict who will be served up when the **Next Contact** button is pressed, and who will be shown in the browse of contacts to call under the **Contacts** tab. A filter can be based upon respondent tags, quotas and time zones. An example of a filter is as follows:

[Female, 18 to 29] [INCOME $50,000-$69,999] [AU-NSW (GMT+10)]

Some of the most common frequently asked questions about filters are as follows:

1. *How can I restrict an interviewer so that they will always use a particular filter (e.g. they must call women who are 18-29)?*
2. *Basic interviewers have no access to filtering by default. Is it possible to give them access to a limited number of filters?*
3. *Is there a quick way to customize what filters interviewers can see for a job en masse?*

The answers to all these questions can be found in WSC's User Filter system. This system allows you to set filter access on interviewers of all types on a job-by-job basis.

Allowing Respondent Tags to be used in Filters

Respondent tags are generally used for two purposes:

1. To categorize a respondent in some way – for example, whether a respondent's profession is "White Collar" or "Blue Collar"
2. To store a piece of specific information on a person – like their address

The first type of tag is something you would like to be able to filter on, since we may want to work with different categories of respondent. The second type of tag, however, would be useless in a filter, since every respondent would have a different value – for 1000 respondents, you would have 1000 addresses to choose from for the filter. This clearly would not make sense.

To distinguish which tags you want to be able to filter on, you have to add these tags into the "Tag Rules" as follows:

1. Choose the **User Filters** tab from under **MY CATI**

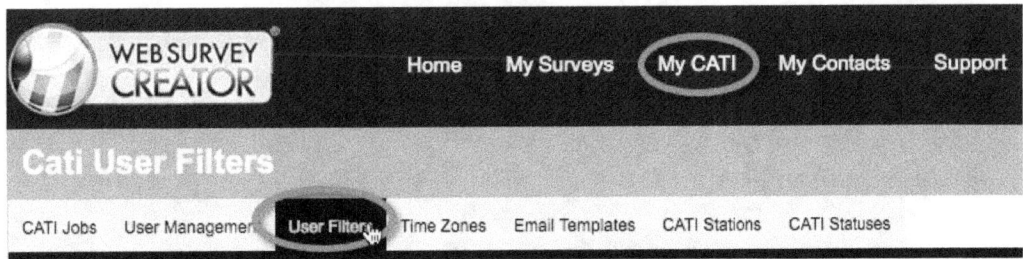

2. Click the **Tag Rules** submenu

Research Panel Integration

3. Enter each tag and value

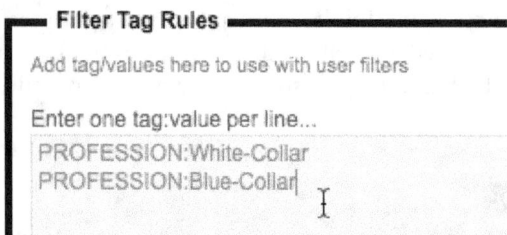

4. Press the **Update Tag Rules** button

Once tag rules have been set up, they can be used when creating user filters.

Creating User Filters

The steps to setting up user filters are as follows:

1. Choose the **User Filters** tab from under **MY CATI**

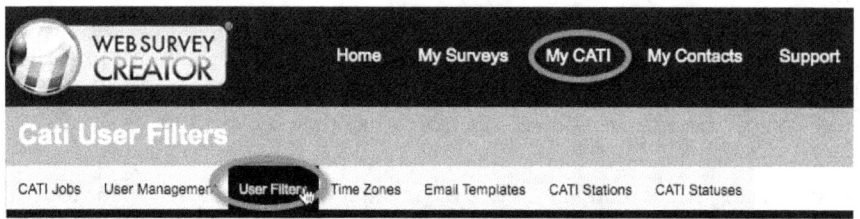

2. Click the **New CATI filter** toolbar button under the **User Filters** submenu.

3. Choose the interviewers to set filters for

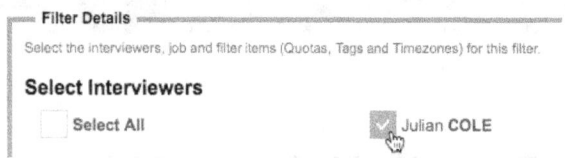

4. Choose a CATI job to apply filters to

5. Choose the rules for each filter element.

Filter Rules

Quotas:

	Default Behaviour	Selectable	Included	Excluded	Hidden
Female, 18 to 29			✓		
Female, 30 to 45	✓				
Female, 46 to 60	✓				
Male, 18 to 29	✓				
Male, 30 to 45	✓				
Male, 46 to 60	✓				

Respondent Tags:

	Default Behaviour	Selectable	Included	Excluded	Hidden
PROFESSION : White-Collar	✓				
PROFESSION : Blue-Collar	✓				

Time Zones:

	Default Behaviour	Selectable	Included	Excluded	Hidden
AU-NSW (GMT+11)	✓				
US-CA (GMT-8)	✓				
AU-QLD (GMT+10)	✓				
US-CO (GMT-7)	✓				
AU-WA (GMT+8)	✓				
US-TX (GMT-6)	✓				
US-OH (GMT-5)	✓				

6. Click the **Save Filter** button

Filter Rule Settings

When setting a filter rule, you have the following choices on an individual filter element:

Default Behaviour	This option basically says "provide filter capabilities based on a person's access level". So, for CATI interviewers, this means don't provide this filter (since by default they can not use filters). For Senior CATI interviewers and above however, filters are visible (i.e. selectable) by default.
Selectable	This filter will be available in the filter window for use. This choice only really needs to be set for CATI interviewers – every other level of user will be able to select a filter element by default anyway.
Included	This filter element will always be used in every filter – so only respondents that have this filter element will be shown. Mandatory filter elements are denoted by a lock symbol in the CATI filter bar. 
Excluded	This filter element will always be used in every filter as an "exclusion" – so only respondents that do not have this filter element will be shown. Mandatory filter element exclusions are denoted by a lock symbol in the CATI filter bar, and a line through the element description.
Hidden	Filter element will not be visible, or available for use.

Setting Time Zone Rules

Time zones are a key element of the CATI system, because there are likely to be times when the current time for the interviewer and the respondent is different due to their location.

Statements such as "I'm happy for someone to call me at 2pm" from a respondent really mean "I'm happy for someone to call me at 2pm my time". The actual call may need to be made at 4pm by an interviewer.

Failure to respect time zone differences can lead to a number of problems:

- Appointment times may be wrong
- A person may be called before or after a reasonable hour (it may be 9am for an interviewer, but 6am for a respondent!)
- A respondent may be missed (for example, it is after business hours for the respondent when they are called)

When is an appropriate time to call someone?

It is common sense to say that calling someone at 2am in the morning is unacceptable. The exact rules, however, need to be quantified in CATI through the **Time Zones** tab.

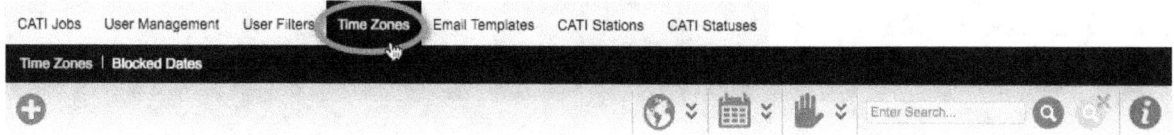

By default, a global time zone rule exists:

Time Zone	Mon	Tue	Wed	Thu	Fri	Sat	Sun	Start Time	Stop Time
Applies To All Time Zones	Yes	Yes	Yes	Yes	Yes	No	No	09:00 AM	12:00 PM
Applies To All Time Zones	Yes	Yes	Yes	Yes	Yes	Yes	No	01:00 PM	05:00 PM

This rule says:

1. On Monday to Friday, people can be called between 9:00am and 12:00pm then from 1:00pm to 5:00pm
2. On Saturday, people can be called between 9:00am and 12:00pm

Because this applies to all time zones, it will apply to everyone. The rule will be applied taking a respondent's current time in their location into account.

Setting specific rules for a time zone

To set a specific time zone, click the **Add Time Zone** toolbar button.

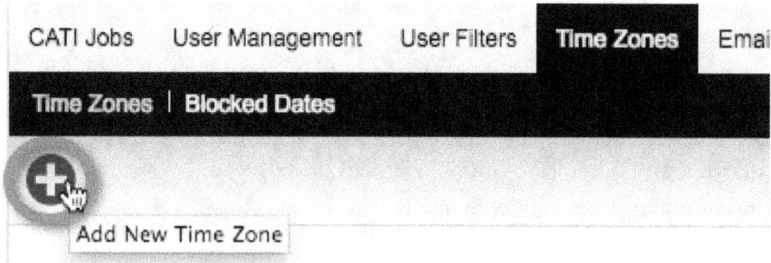

The time zone details can be entered into the **Time Zone** window.

158   Research Panel Integration

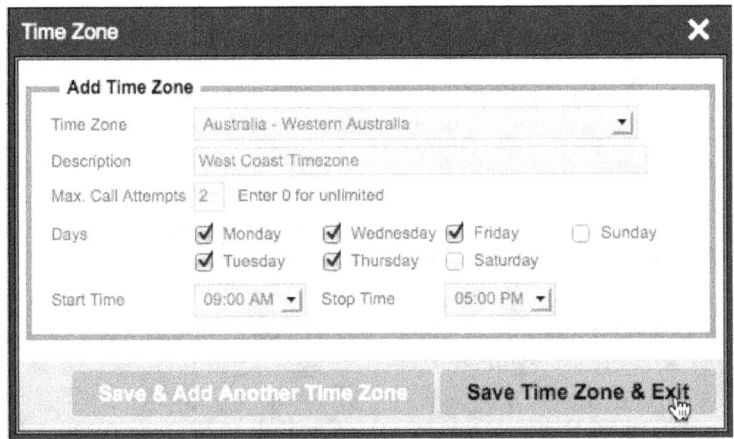

Note that when you add details for a specific time zone, it **replaces** the default time zone details. The default is then ignored and only time zone rules for the specific time zone will be considered.

Setting up CATI Stations

Each CATI workstation that is used a call center needs to be set up through the **CATI Stations** tab.

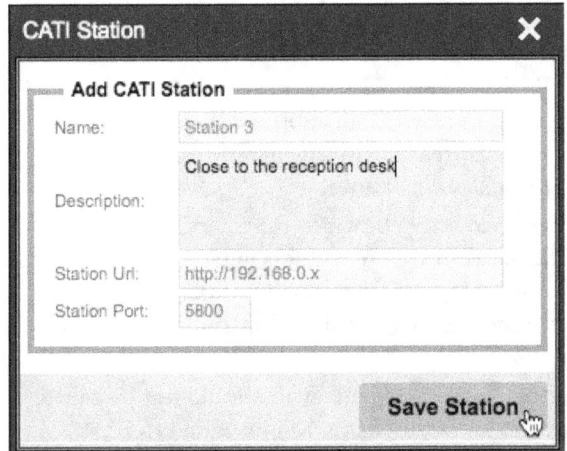

The **Station URL** and **Station Port** are used to identify the workstation for the purposes of viewing the screen by a supervisor. See the next section about setting up interviewer screen viewing for full details about what to enter for each CATI station.

Setting up CATI Statuses

CATI statuses can be set up to allow you to configure your CATI system to work with your preferred workflow. The CATI system will log everything that occurs for a particular respondent using the CATI statuses that have been set up. Statuses are added to a respondent's call log in one of two ways:

1. System statuses are added automatically by the system at appropriate times (for example, an "Opened" system status is added every time an interviewer opens a respondent to make a call)
2. Interviewers can add statuses to the call log that indicate what they have done for the respondent – for example, if there is no answer, a "No Answer" status can be added for a respondent.

Research Panel Integration 159

System Statuses

System statuses cannot be changed or deleted – they are used by the system to manage automated areas of the CATI process. Below is the list of the system statuses and details about when they are used.

OPENED	Every time an interviewer chooses a respondent, their details are shown onscreen, and they are immediately given an "Opened" status in their log. This can be used to see which interviewers have opened a particular respondent, and when.
CONTACTUPDATED	If an interviewer chooses to update the details that have been entered for a respondent, the fact they updated the details is tracked through the "Contact Updated" flag.
SKIPPED	Sometimes an interviewer may press "Next Contact" and get the next respondent, and for some reason they want to skip this respondent and move onto the next one. The system allows respondents to be skipped, but the fact they were skipped is tracked by giving them a "skipped" transaction in their log. By default, a "skipped" person will not appear in the interviewer's list of calls for 1 hour (they will still be visible to other interviewers).
APPOINTMENTCANCELLED	If an appointment was created, and subsequently cancelled, this transaction is generated to show when the cancellation was made, and by whom.
APPOINTMENTUPDATED	If an appointment was created, and subsequently changed to a new time and date, this transaction is generated to show when the update was made, and by whom.
APPOINTMENTDELAYED	Upcoming appointments are shown to the interviewer who needs to make the call just before the appointment is due. If the interviewer requests a delay of 15 minutes for the appointment, the appointment time will be shifted, and this transaction will be created.
CONTACTLIMITREACHED	This is a final status for respondents who should not be called again. There are two ways this status will be added to a respondent: 1. One of the other statuses has reached it's limit (for example, number of "no answers" has reached the maximum of 3). 2. The overall contact limit – total number of times a person can be contacted, regardless of the status – has been reached. We will see how these settings are set in the next section.
NOTATTEMPTED	If an interviewer opens a respondent, then immediately closes them, they are flagged as "Not Attempted". This is different from skipping, since the person remains in the queue of people to call. An interviewer may do this when they need to take a toilet break, for example. When they return, they are happy for the respondent to still be in the list of people for them to call.

LINKCLICKED	If an Email has been sent to a respondent, and they have clicked on the survey link, a "Link Clicked" status will appear in the person's log. This will make it easy for an interviewer to see that a person has at least started the survey.
SURVEYSTARTED	Once a respondent begins their survey online (either from an Email sent by an interviewer, or possibly from a separate invitation that has been sent to them) the "Survey Started" status is added to their log.
CONTACTREOPENED	If a contact has been closed by the system due to something other than a successful completion of a survey (for example, if CONTACTLIMITREACHED has occurred) there is the ability to reopen contacts so they can be called again. When they are reopened, a transaction is created with this status.
QUOTAOUT	If a person completes the survey on the Web, and they exceed the required quota for the survey, they will be flagged as a quota out.
SCREENOUT	If a person completes the survey on the Web, and they are not an appropriate type of for the survey, they will be flagged as a screen out.
COMPLETE	If a person successfully completes a survey on the Web, they will be flagged as a Complete.
TESTCONTACT	If an interviewer invokes a test run of the interview, a copy of a live contact is made for the test. The copied contact will have this transaction added to their log.
TESTMODESTARTED	This transaction is placed on a live contact that has been copied for a test of the process.

Custom Status Categories

All other CATI statuses can be set up to meet your requirements for your CATI workflow. The number and type of statuses is completely up to you. These statuses fall into the following categories:

Incomplete	Statuses in this category all relate to things that have occurred without the call being completed (for example, "no answer")
Hard Refusal	If a respondent makes it clear they do not want to participate this is a "Hard Refusal". For example, if they say "I don't want to do it – don't call again". Statuses in this category will remove the respondent from the call list.
Soft Refusal	A soft refusal is not as emphatic at hard refusals – for example "I don't feel like doing this at the moment". Statuses in this category will delay calling back of the respondent based upon the delay set up in the individual status.
Appointment	Appointments can be set up to organise a call to a respondent at a later stage. Any statuses set up within the Appointment category will allow an appointment to be set.
Email	All statuses set up under the Email category will allow an interviewer to select any of the Email templates that have been set up to send to respondents.
Supervisor	Statuses under the supervisor category will cause a call to be flagged as requiring supervisor assistance. These calls are easy for a supervisor to find and deal with.
Final	Statuses that are final will close a respondent down – they will no longer be in the call list.

Setting up a Custom Status

The steps to set up a custom status are as follows:

1. Click the **CATI Statuses tab** under **My CATI**

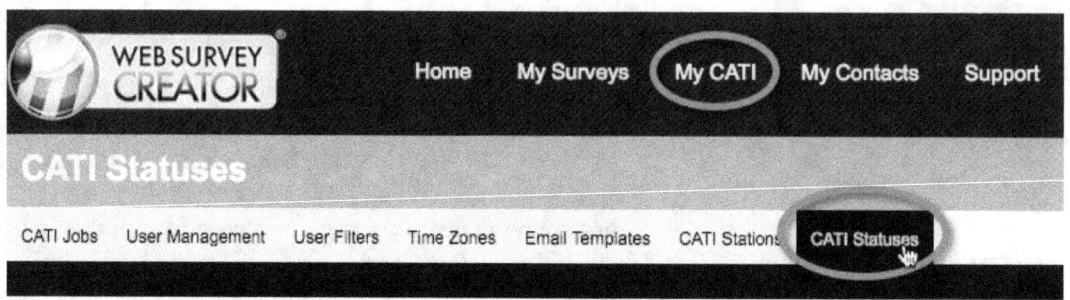

2. Click **Add New Status** on the toolbar

3. Enter the details for the status, and press the **Save Status button**. Descriptions for the details that can be entered are shown below.

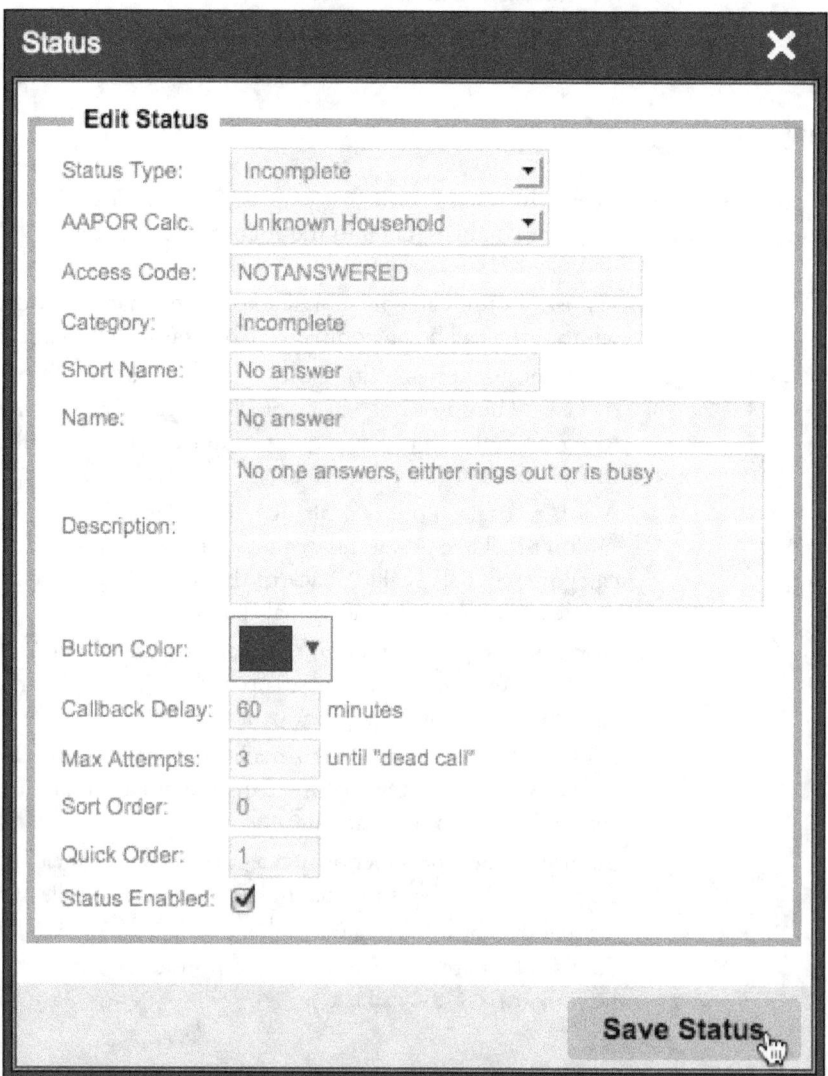

162   Research Panel Integration

The most important aspect to setting up a status is understanding what each of the settings in the status details is used for. The table below describes these settings:

Status Type	The type of status defines what effect choosing this status will have on a respondent. For example, if the status type is "Final", when this status is chosen, a respondent is removed from the pool of people who may be called.
AAPOR Calc.	Outcome rates can be calculated following the formulas worked out by the American Association for Public Opinion Research (AAPOR) if statuses are placed into the correct calculation categories. For further information, see http://www.aapor.org/Response_Rates_An_Overview1.htm
Access Code	This code will be shown in the log for this status.
Category	You can categorise statuses however you like - these categories can then be used in filters.
Short Name	This is a short name for the status that can be used in areas where there is no space to show the full name
Name	This is the full name of the status
Description	This description is shown in the browse of statuses. It can help explain what the status is used for.
Button Color	When this status is used in a call log, it can be given a specific colour so that it can be distinguished easily from other statuses. For example, all final statuses may be set to red to indicate that they terminate all calls to the respondent.
Callback Delay	You may optionally choose to take a respondent out of the calling pool when this status is chosen. Entering a positive number of minutes in this field will indicate how long they will be excluded from the pool. An example would be setting a 60 minute delay when a person is called and there is no answer. The next time the person would appear as a contact for someone to call would be a minimum of 60 minutes after the no answer status was set on the respondent.
Max Attempts	If a non-zero amount is entered for this field, this will be the maximum number of times this status can be used on a respondent before they are immediately given a status **CONTACTLIMITREACHED** (and they are permanently excluded from the calling pool). An example would be setting this value to 3 for a "No Answer" status. This would mean that if a person is called 3 times with a result that there is no answer, their status would be changed as soon as the third "No Answer" status is added.
Sort Order	This is a numeric that can be optionally entered to affect what order this status is shown in listings, relative to other statuses.

Quick Order	The quick order sets the ordinal position for the status in the "Quick Menu" that appears when a contact is closed. Only the most used statuses would ever be set up with a quick order. 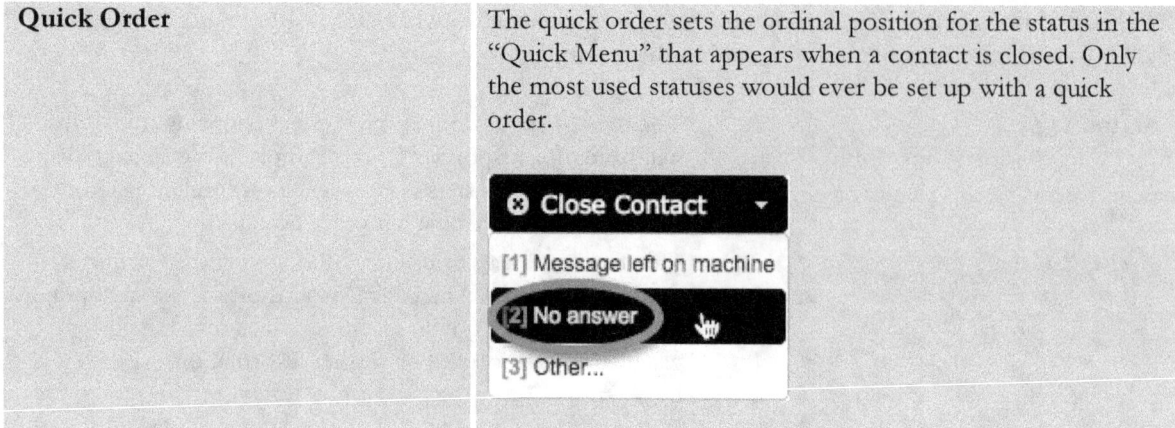

Setting up Interviewer Screen Viewing

It is important for supervisors to be able to verify the performance of interviewers. Key to this process is the ability to view an interviewer's screen. The way this needs to operate can be represented as follows:

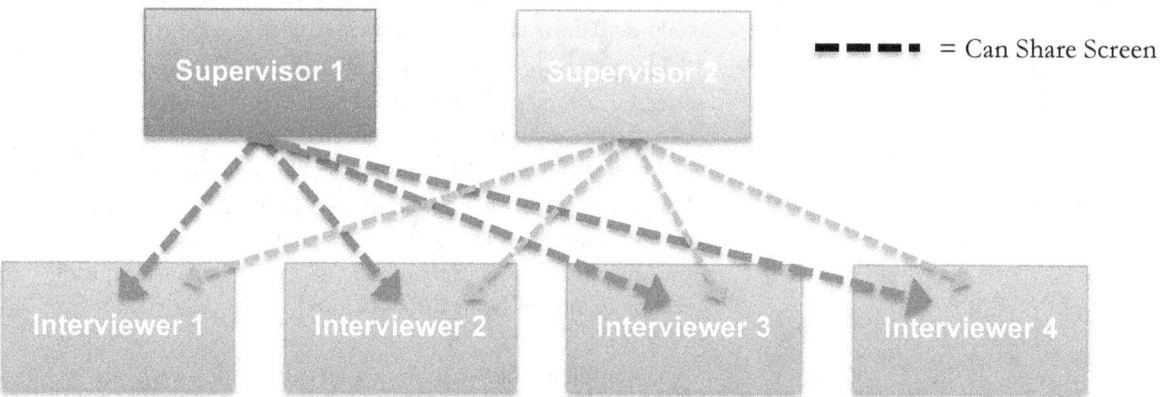

In reality, the screen sharing relates to viewing the screen on a workstation. In order to see an interviewer's screen, the supervisor needs to know which computer (workstation) an interviewer is using. This is why whenever an interviewer goes into a CATI job, they are asked to choose their workstation.

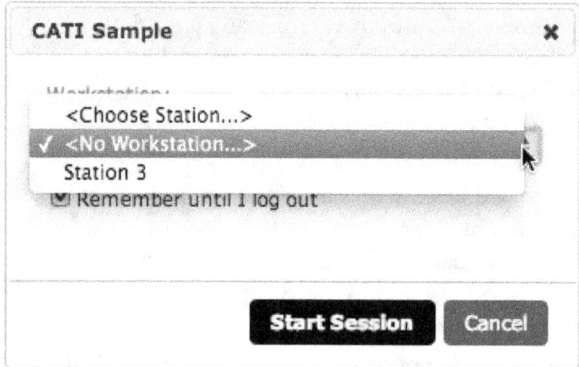

This means that workstations need to be set up. The exact details to be entered for each workstation are discussed in the next section.

Installing Screen Viewer Software on a Workstation

Each workstation that will be used for screen viewing must be set up. We support the UltraVNC screen sharing tool – it can be installed free of charge on as many workstations as you need.

> UltraVNC is a great balance of performance and cost. It is free, yet provides everything needed for screen sharing. Note that is can only be installed on Windows computers.

The steps in setting up workstations are as follows:

1. Run the VNC installation file. There are two different installations - ensure you run the appropriate version for your workstation.

    Installation for 64-bit Windows
    http://www.websurveycreator.com/resources/UltraVNC_1_1_9_X64_Setup.exe

    Installation for 32-bit Windows
    http://www.websurveycreator.com/resources/UltraVNC_1_1_9_X86_Setup.exe

2. Enter the installation directory. In most cases the default directory is fine. Click **NEXT**

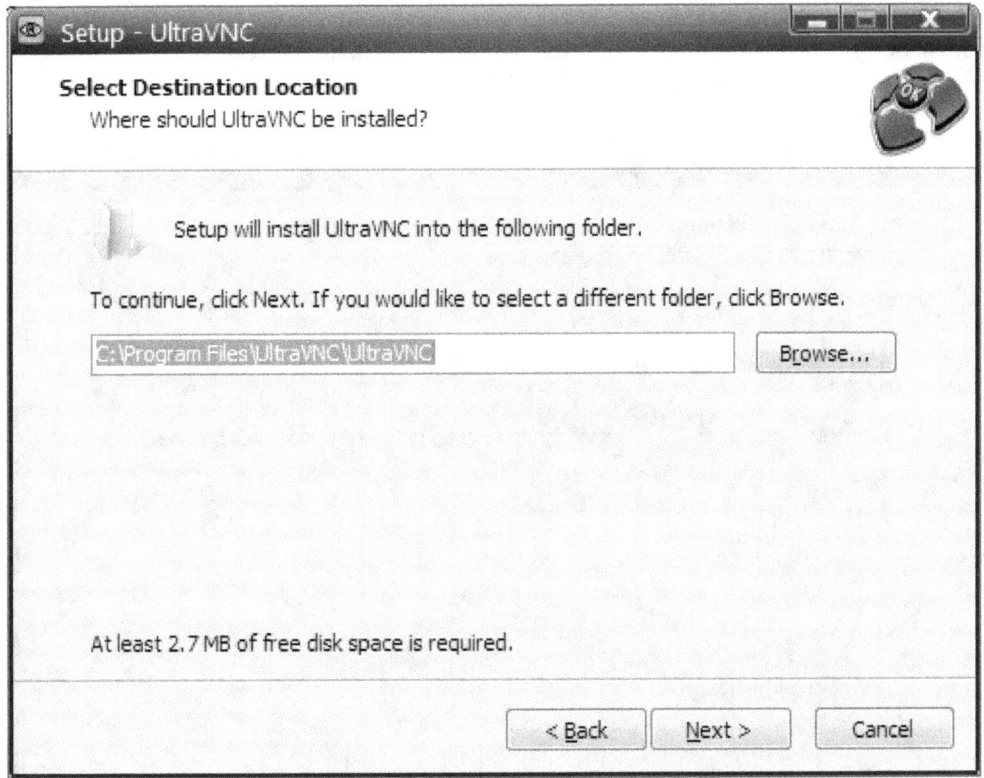

Research Panel Integration

3. When asked for which components to install, select "UltraVNC Server Silent". Click **NEXT**

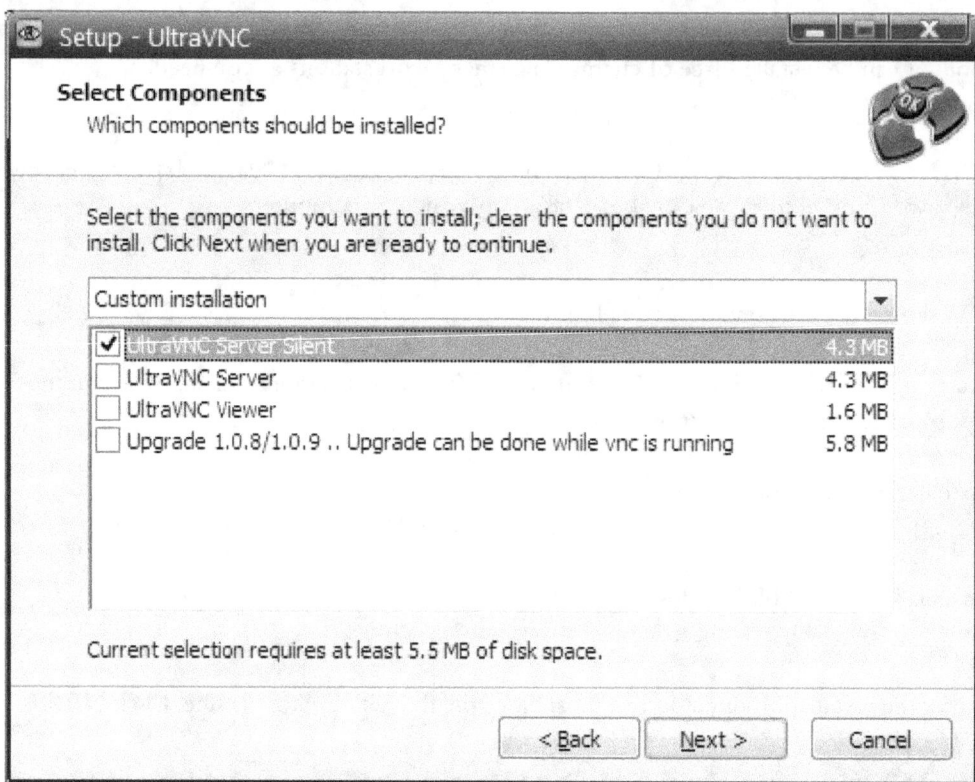

4. Enter the Start Menu shortcut folder. In most cases the default directory is fine. These shortcuts can be removed at a later stage. Click **NEXT**

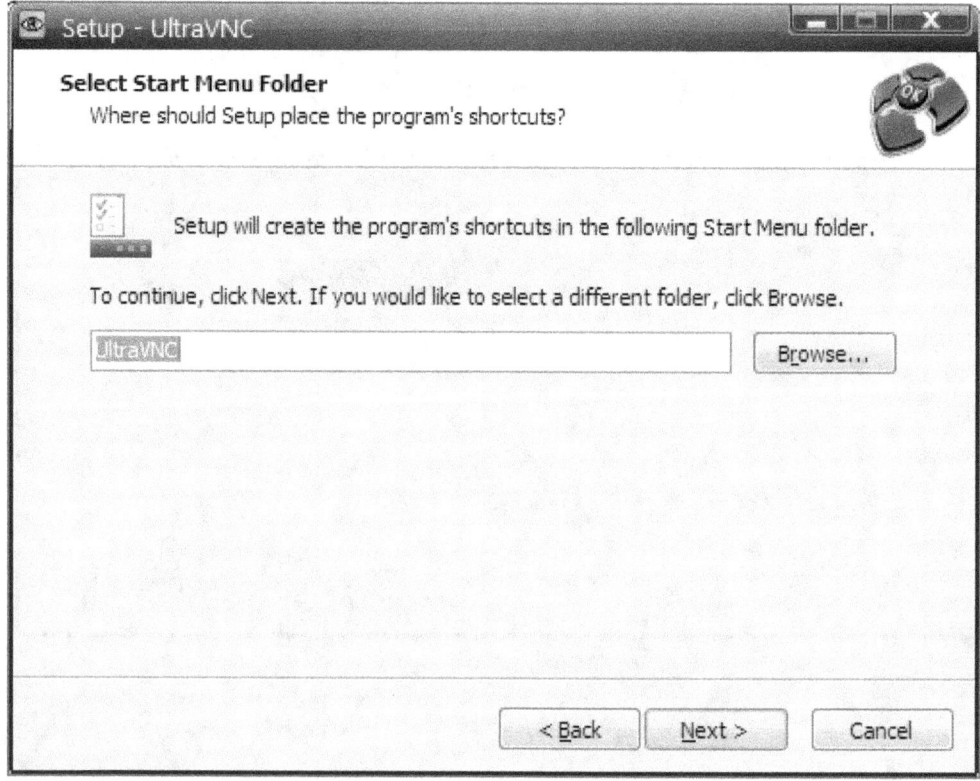

5. You can choose to either install the software as a program that can be run, or as a service (which is run in the background). Ticking the system service checkbox, and installing it as a service, means the software will run every time the machine is rebooted. Click **NEXT**

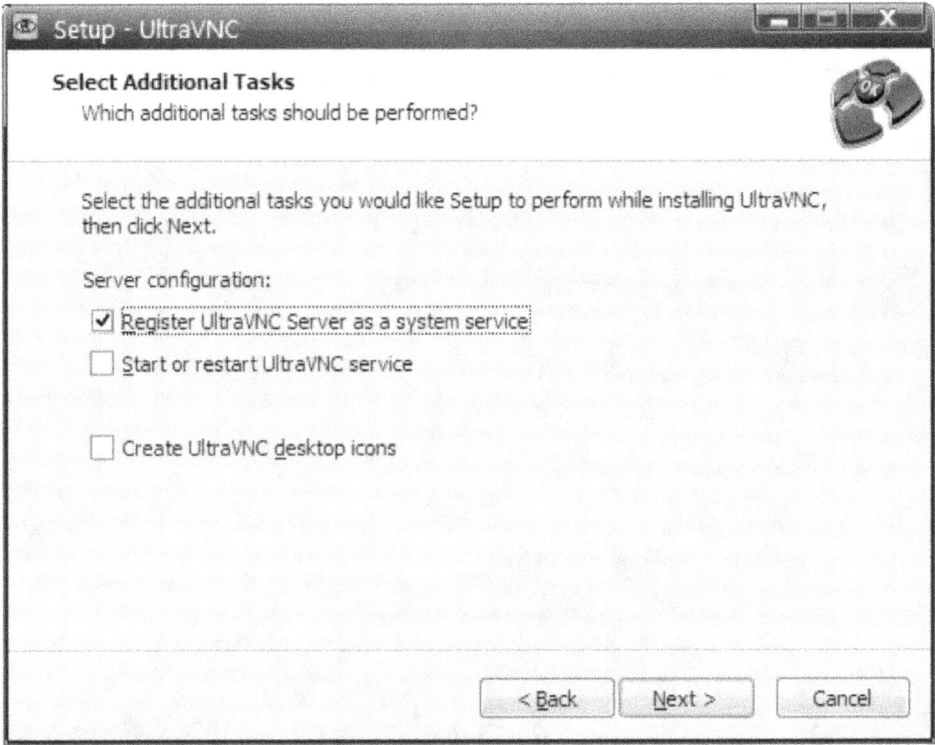

6. Click **INSTALL**
7. Click on the Start Menu, locate and run "**UltraVNC settings**"
8. Enter the following settings
    a. In the Network tab
        i. Tick **Enable incoming port**
        ii. Tick **Enable Java port**
        iii. Customise the **RFB Port** and **Http Port** if required however the standard ports will be fine in most installations. Ensure that your firewall has allowed traffic through these ports
    b. In the Input/File Transfer tab
        i. Tick **Disabled Viewer inputs**
    c. In the Misc/logging tab
        i. Tick **Disable Tray icon**
9. In the Task Bar you will find the UltraVNC icon. Right click and select Admin Properties
10. Enter the following settings
    a. In the Incoming Connections
        i. Tick **Accept Socket Connections**
        ii. Tick **Enable JavaViewer (Http Connect)**
        iii. Untick **Allow Loopback Connections**
    b. In Authentication
        i. Enter a VNC Password and a View-Only Password. **Note that these will be asked every time a workstation is viewed. Only Supervisors should be aware of the password you choose.**
    c. In File Transfer
        i. Untick **Enabled**
        ii. Untick **User impersonation**
    d. In Keyboard & Mouse
        i. Tick Disable Viewers inputs
    e. In Misc.
        i. Tick Disable **TrayIcon**

Research Panel Integration

        ii. Tick **Forbid the user to close down WinVNC**

11. Click **OK**

The next step is to find the workstation's IP address. To do this:

1. Click on the Start Menu and select **RUN**

2. In the Open field type in "**CMD**" and click **OK**

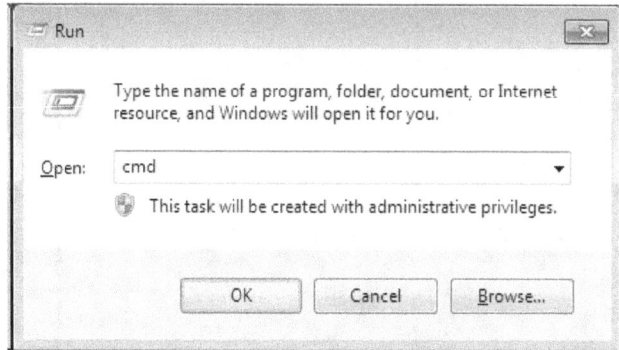

This will open a Command Prompt window

3. Type "**ipconfig**" and press **ENTER**

4. You will get a number of results. In most cases you will only have one active network connection so look for a reference to the IPv4 Address and note this down. This is your IP Address. In the example below the address is 192.168.0.139

Testing the connection to the CATI workstation

1. Log onto another workstation which sits on the same network as the CATI workstation and open a web browser
2. In the address bar type in the CATI workstation's IP address and Port number. In the previous example we would enter 192.168.0.139:5800. Press **ENTER.**
3. You may be asked to install JAVA if it is not already installed. If this is the then please following the instructions provided by your browser.
4. Once the page has loaded you will be asked for a password. Enter the View-Only Password that you entered in step 10b(i).

Setting up a Workstation for Screen Viewing

In the previous example, a workstation was set up that had an IP address of 192.168.0.139, and the default port of 5800 was used in the screen viewer software setup. The steps to set up this computer as a "Workstation" in WSC that supports screen viewing are as follows:

1. In WSC, click on **My CATI**, and go to the **CATI Stations tab**

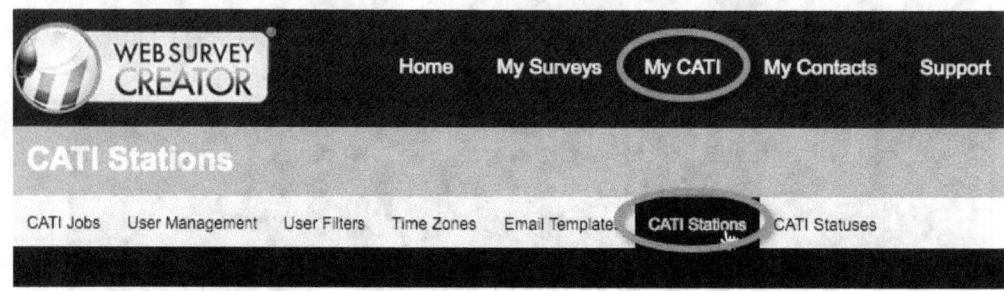

2. Click **Add New Station** on the toolbar

3. Enter the details for the Workstation. The key details that need to be entered are the IP Address for the Station URL and the Station Port.

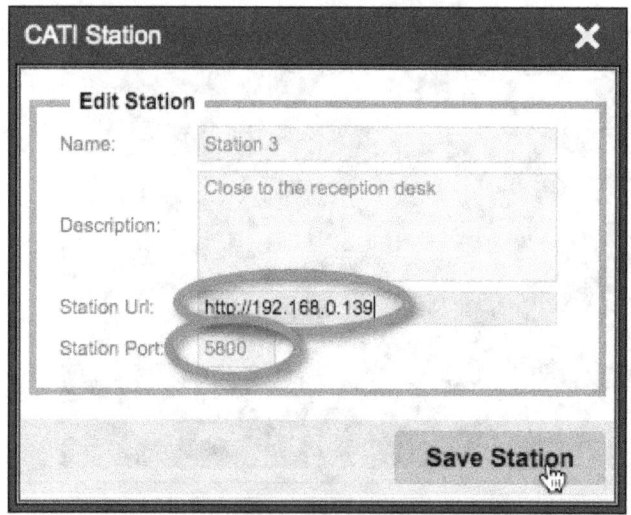

Viewing a Workstation through WSC

A supervisor can view a Workstation at any time through the following steps:

1. In WSC, click on **My CATI**, and go to the **CATI Stations tab**

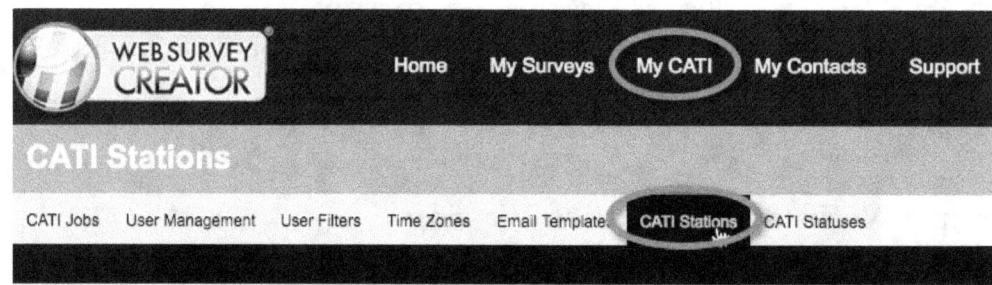

2. Click on the **Active** link in the CATI station list to view the interviewer that is currently using a particular workstation.

Name	Description	Last Interviewer	Status	Call 1
Station 1	Near Window	Daniel **Beeston**		
Station 2	Near Door	Julian **Cole**		
Station 3	In Office	Bun Rathana **Lim**	Active	
test	asdf			

3. You may be asked to install JAVA if it is not already installed. If this is the then please following the instructions provided by your browser.

4. Once the page has loaded you will be asked for a password. Enter the View-Only Password that you entered in step 10, b, i.

5. The Workstation screen will be shown

The CATI Interviewer Module

The people who make the calls for CATI – the interviewers – use a module outside of the main Web Survey Creator application. This means that they can have a login that is restricted to them performing their job as an interviewer, and also makes training simpler because they are presented with an interface that only includes features they need to be able to perform their jobs as interviewers.

The CATI module is available on the "cati subdomain" related to the Web Survey Creator site. For example, the main Web Survey Creator site, and associated subdomain Web Addresses in the following format ("mywscsite" would be replaced by the actual domain used for WSC):

Main WSC Site	http://www.mywscsite.com
CATI Site	http://cati.mywscsite.com

Key Features of the Interviewer Module

Before looking at an example workflow for an Interviewer, it is useful to understand the key features available through the site.

Simple Site Login

When an interviewer goes to the CATI site, they are required to enter a login. Usually they will be set up with a login that will only allow them to access the CATI site, with no access to the main site.

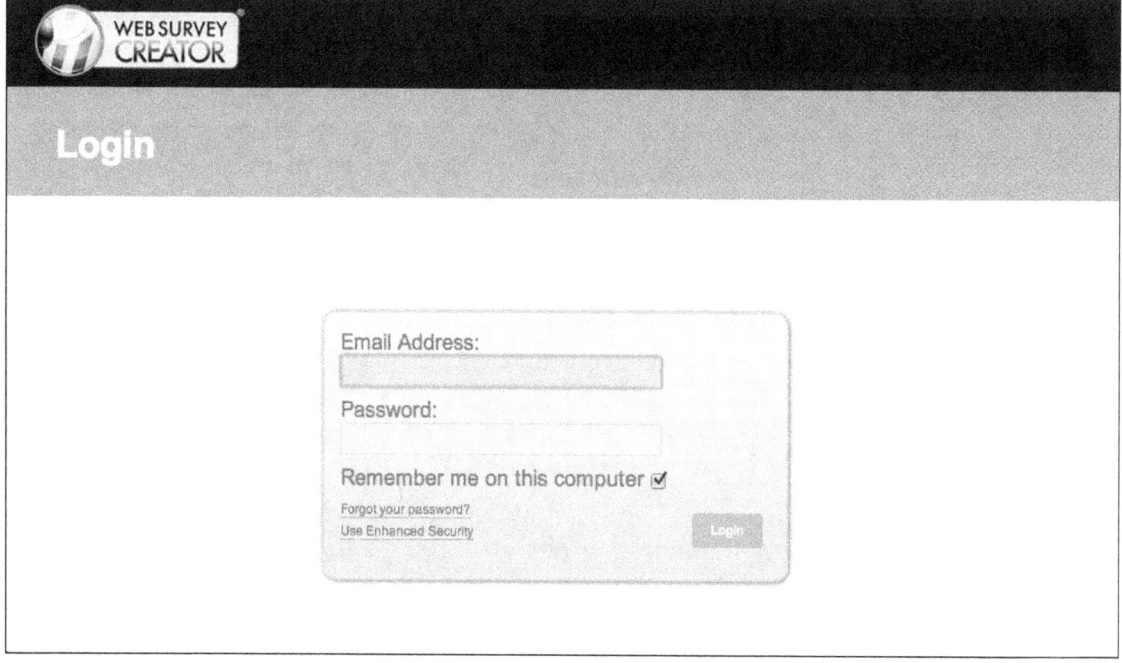

Quick Job Access

Each CATI job that the interviewer can access is shown once they log in on the **Jobs tab**. Key features of this tab are:

- The ability to enter a search to find a specific job
- Job ordering by any column
- The ability to choose how many jobs to show on a single page

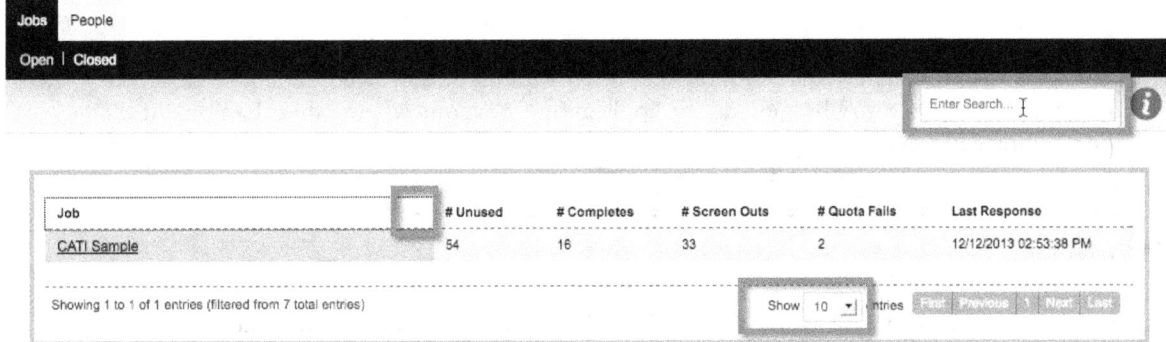

Quick Person Access

All the people (respondents) who are in currently live CATI jobs can be accessed from the **People tab**. The fast searching available in this tab is designed to make looking up a particular person quick and easy. This is particularly useful when a person calls in and you need to look them up without knowing what job they may currently be in.

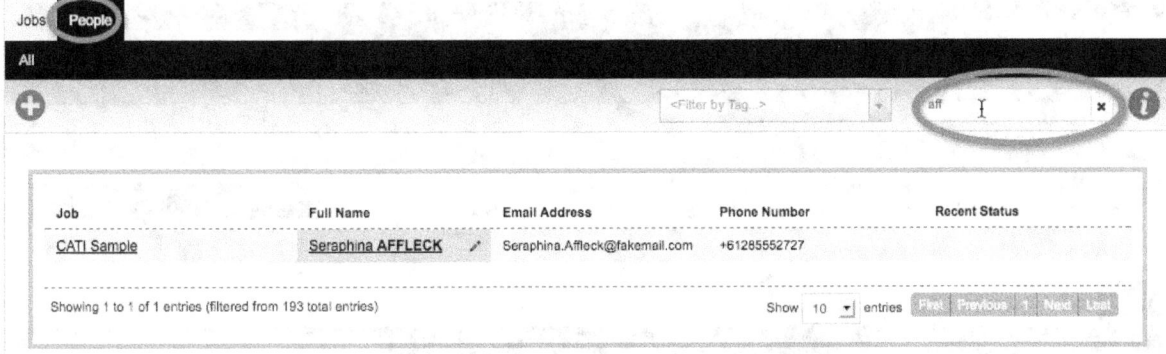

Workstation tracking

When an interviewer starts a job, the workstation they are using can be chosen. This allows an administrator to track who is working where, and once the interviewer is logged into a workstation their screen can be watched by an administrator.

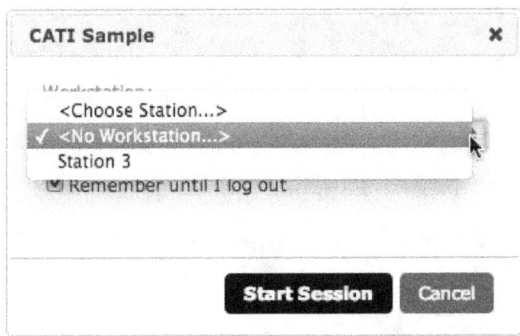

Administrators have the option of choosing **<No Workstation...>**. This allows an administrator to enter the CATI interviewer application, and use it without being forced to choose an actual workstation (since they may be running the application from somewhere other than one of the predefined workstation computers)

CATI Home

The interface for the main CATI screen – the CATI Home tab - is shown below. The key interface elements are:

1. Statistics for the current CATI session
2. Quick access to **End Session** button, and the ability to immediately start calling people with the **Next Contact** button
3. Access to a list of **Contacts** and **Quotas** from the tab selection bar
4. A listing of upcoming appointments
5. A complete listing of everything that has occurred in the current session

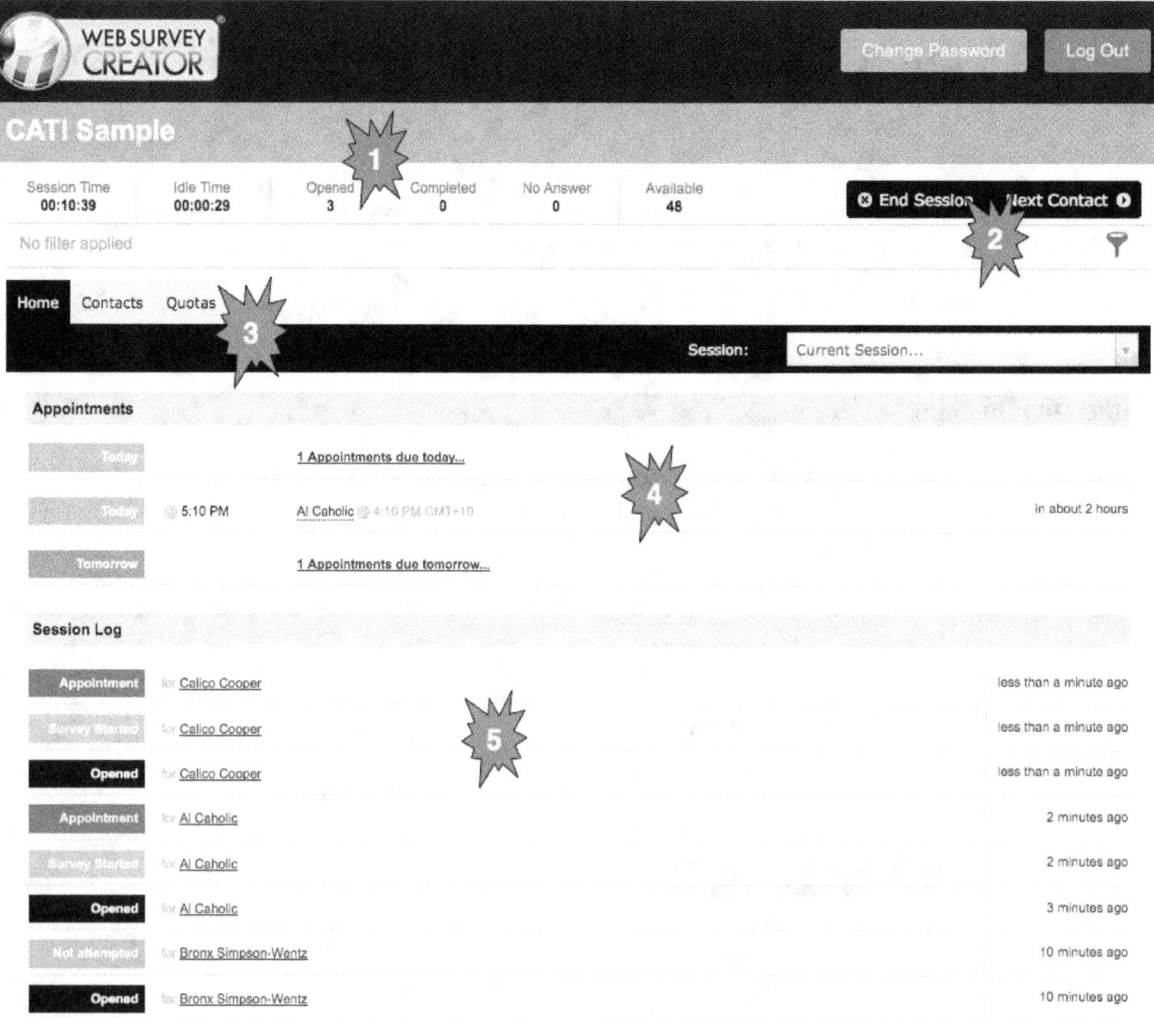

174 Research Panel Integration

Advanced Filtering Capability

For interviewers with the appropriate level of access, the respondents that will be called can be filtered on through the filtering system.

A filter can be based upon any combination of:

- Respondent Tags
- Quotas
- Time zones

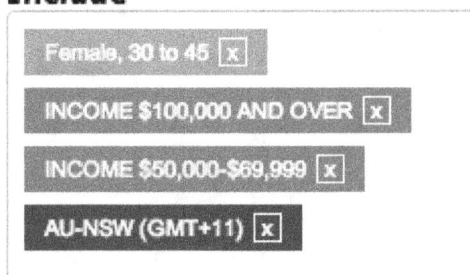

The filters that are chosen are shown on the main CATI window.

By default filtering can only be changed by Senior CATI interviewers and above. Administrators can lock in base filters for particular interviewers and jobs – thus ensuring interviewers focus on specific respondents. Base filters have a lock symbol next to them to indicate that they can not be removed by the interviewer.

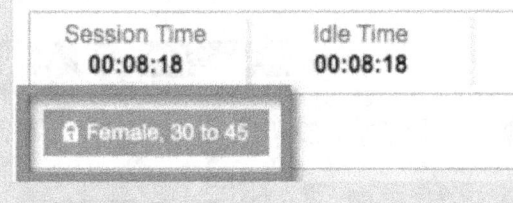

Research Panel Integration 175

Upcoming Contacts Browse

Senior CATI interviewers and above can view a list of the upcoming contacts in the call list by going to the **Contacts tab**. They can call a specific person on the list by pressing the appropriate **Contact button**, rather than pressing **Next Contact** and accepting whatever person the system wishes to serve up next.

Quota Statistics

The current status of all quotas can be viewed under the **Quota tab**. This makes it easy to see which quotas are filling more quickly than others, and may be used when deciding what filters to use (eg. So that quotas that are more empty can be focused on).

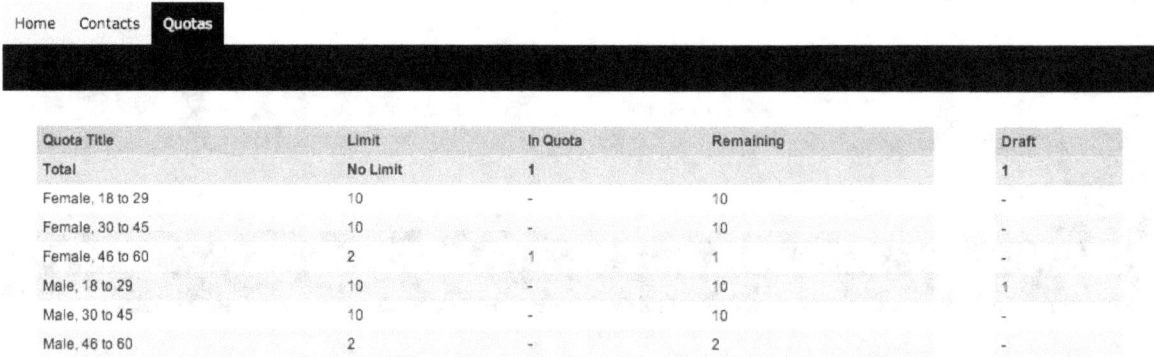

Respondent "Quick View"

At any time during the interview process, full details for the respondent can be viewed by simply clicking on their name in the **Call Details Bar**.

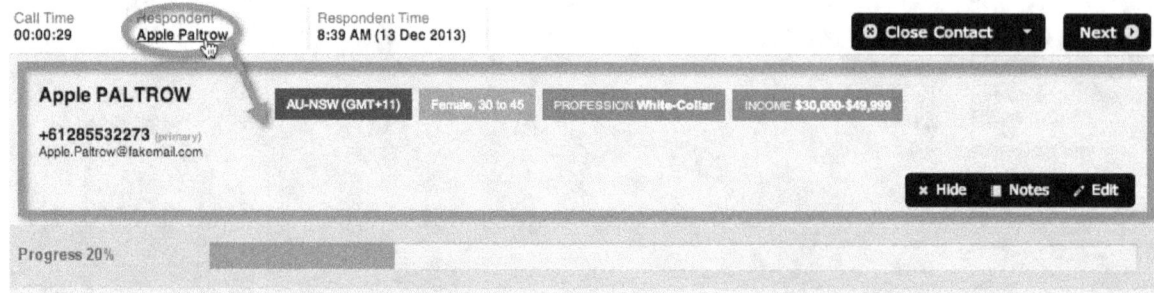

Powerful Survey System

The survey system that powers the interviewer in the CATI module is the same system that is used for WSC Web Surveys. It has a number of features that are specifically designed to make the interview process easy and efficient:

1. All choice questions have hotkeys associated with them, allowing you to simply press a number on your keypad to answer a question
2. Additional CATI-Only text can be used throughout the survey to provide scripting that is not visible when a person on the Web does the survey.

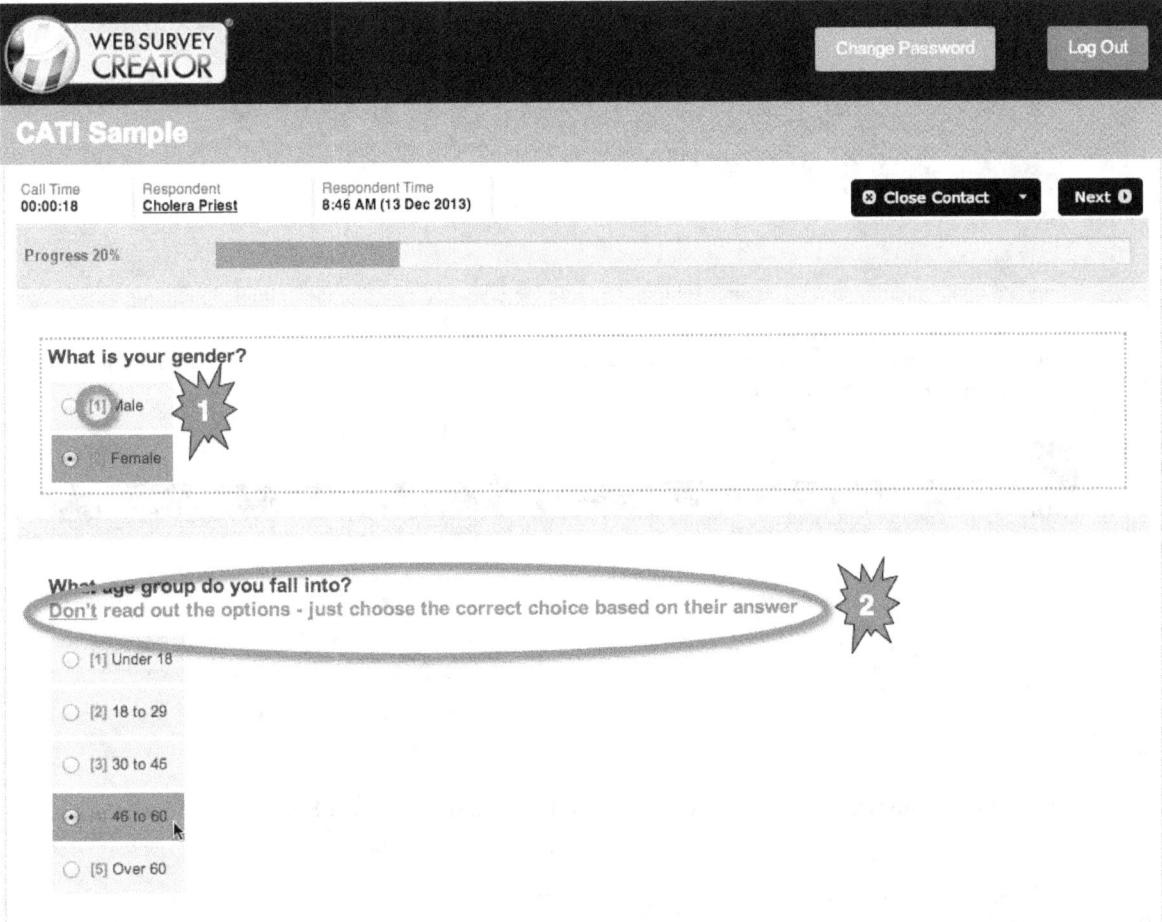

The entire interview process is designed so that it can be performed with a keyboard – that includes using your arrow keys to move between questions and pages, and pressing the tab key to move from one question to the next.

The Mixed-Mode Workflow

The easiest way to understand how to run mixed-mode processes in WSC is to see examples of common workflows. Regardless of the workflow, the first steps to using the Interviewer module are as follows:

1. Go to the WSC CATI site.

2. Log in to the site with the login and password that has been provided.

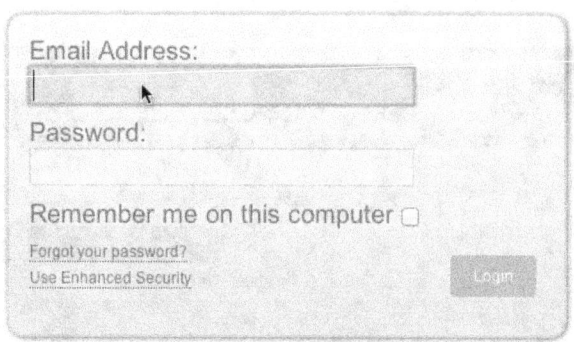

3. A list of the open CATI jobs will be shown. To begin a CATI process for a particular job, click on the job name in the browse.

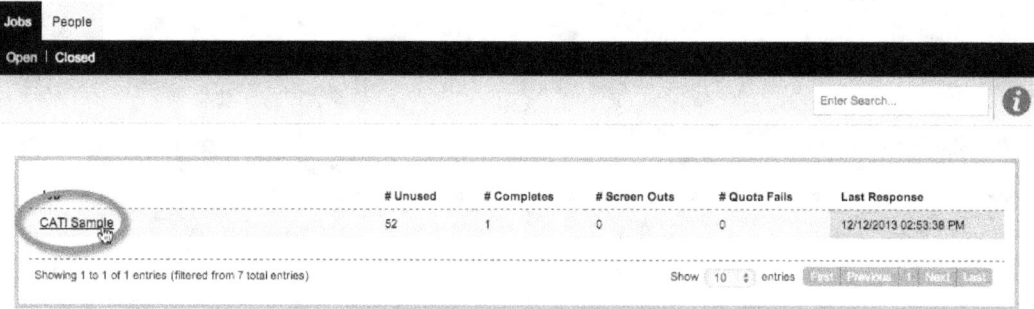

4. Next, choose the workstation call will be made from, and click **Start Session**.

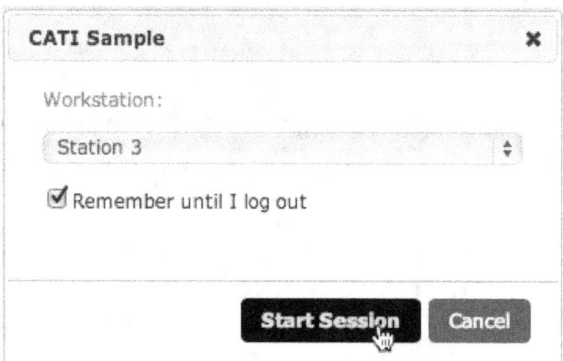

5. A **Session** is a block of time that the interviewer spends working in a particular job. Once they have started the session, the **CATI Home page** is shown. It is from this point that they begin one of the following workflows.

Once you are in a session, you are "on the clock". There are two ways to exit a session – logging out of the CATI module (which will return you to the login screen) or ending the session, which will take you to the Jobs Browse.

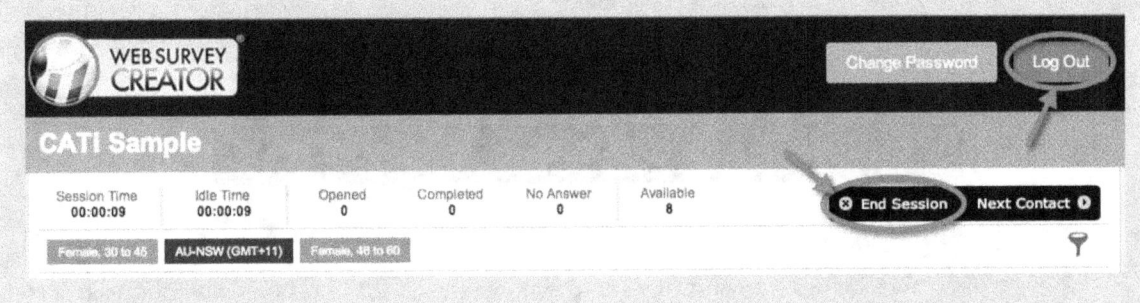

A Basic CATI Workflow

The simplest workflow for CATI is the standard workflow all CATI products deal with as follows:

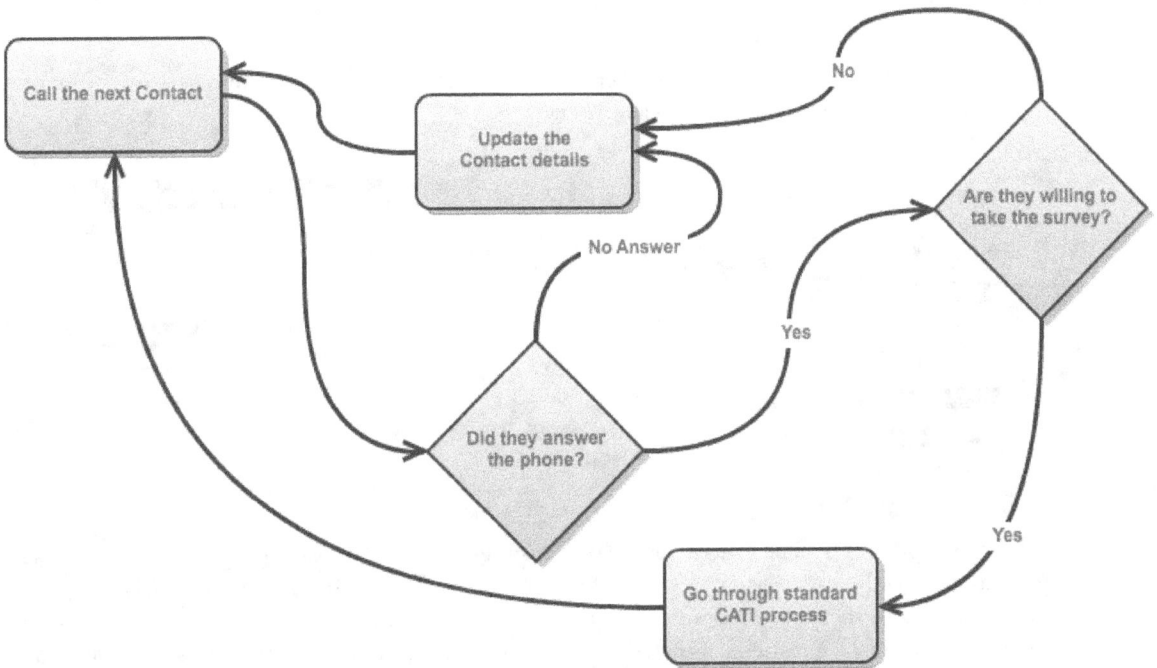

This process is handled by WSC in a straightforward manner. The key steps to the process are:

1. The interviewer commences the CATI process by clicking the **Next Contact** button.

2. The details of the contact are shown onscreen – including their telephone number. At this point the number can be called in one of a number of ways depending on the setup of the system:
   a. The number can be dialed manually on a phone; or
   b. If integrated with Skype, clicking on the number will begin the call; or
   c. If an automated dialer is being used, pressing the **Begin Call** button in step 3 would commence the dialing process

3. The interviewer clicks the **Begin Call** button to commence the call.

There are times when you want to simply test the CATI process, and not make a real call. If a job has been configured to allow test responses (this is a setting on the CATI distribution for the survey), there will be a down arrow next to the **Begin Call** button.

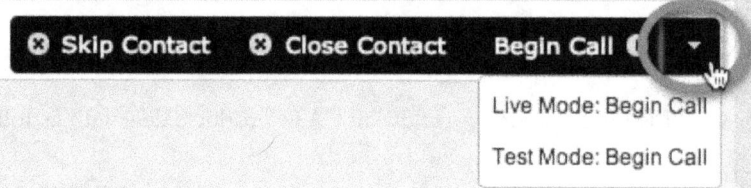

Choosing test mode will create a duplicate of the current contact, flag them as a test contact, and allow the interviewer to begin the call process.

Test respondents behave exactly like real respondents – they appear in reports, affect quotas etc. – because the only way to accurately test the system is to run the full standard process. The key difference with these respondents is they can be found and removed easily by an administrator when the testing is finished. In the respondents browse, filter test respondents (1), select them (2) and press the delete button (3). All test responses and response data will be removed.

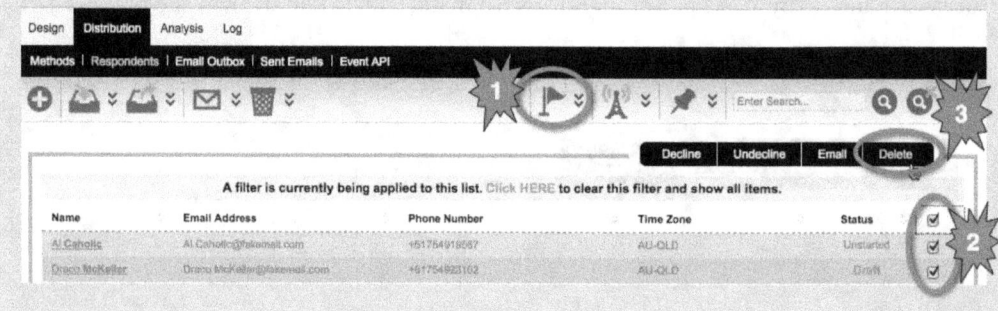

4. The introduction to read to the respondent as soon as they pick up the phone is read next.

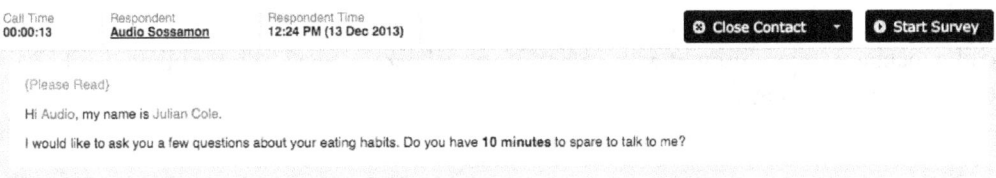

5. It is at this point that one of 2 things will happen:

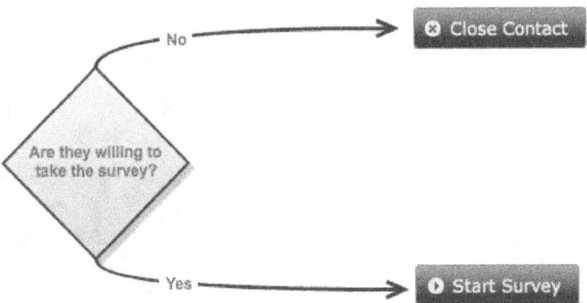

6. The next step depends upon the choice made in Step 5.

    a. If **Close Contact** is chosen, the interviewer will be able to choose from the list of predefined reasons for the ending of the call.

    b. If **Start Survey** is chosen, the survey will begin and can be completed for the respondent.

    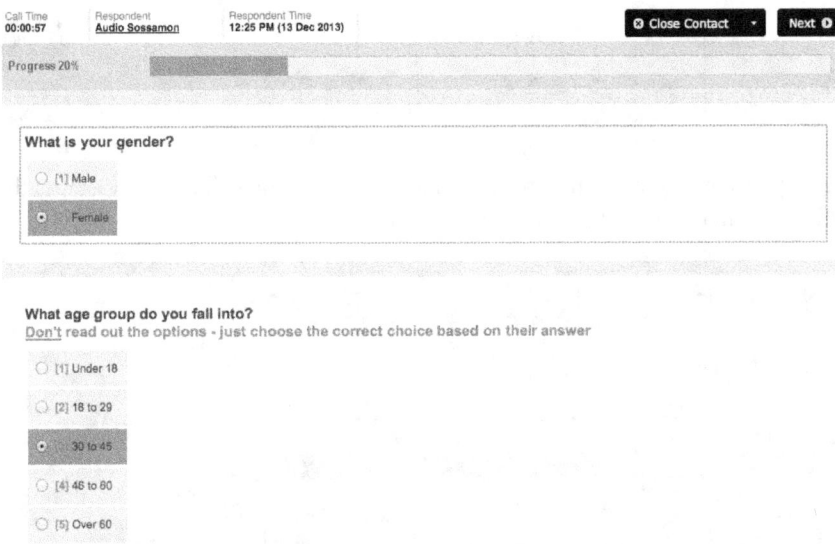

Making an Appointment

One variation of the standard CATI process is the need to call people back at a later time. This is achieved by making an appointment with details of the callback. The CATI workflow would be something like the following:

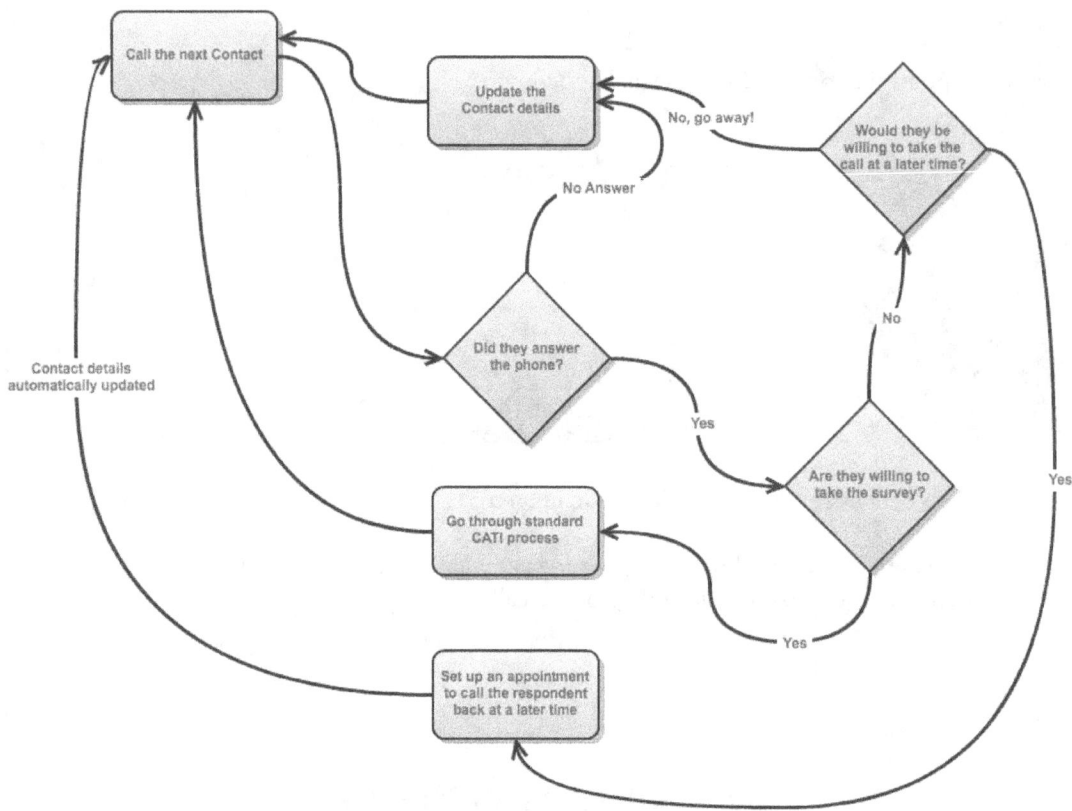

Setting up an appointment can be done through the following steps:

1. When the respondent indicates the can not take the call, the **Close Contact** button is pressed.

2. If the respondent indicates that they are happy to take the call at a later stage, the close status type for the call can be set to an appointment.

   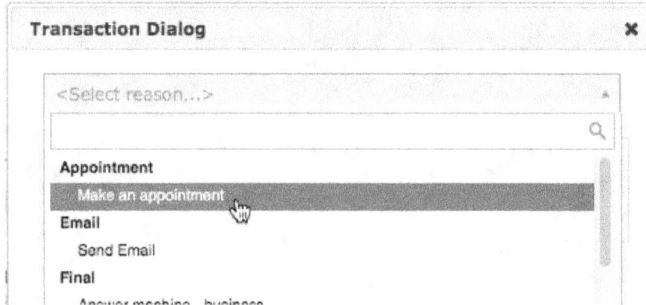

3. The details of the appointment can be set, including the time and date of the appointment, and optionally an interviewer who is the preferred person to do the callback.

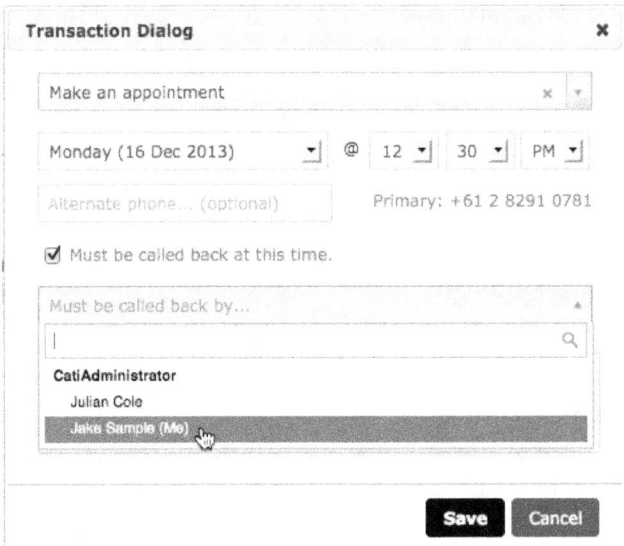

4. The call is closed, and the appointment will show on the list of appointments for the job.

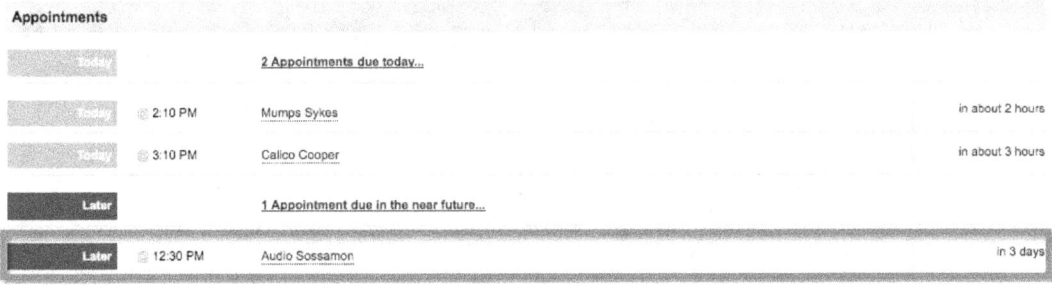

Appointments are managed automatically by the system to provide the best possible outcomes for the call. Key aspects of the appointment system are:

1. Outstanding appointments are shown within the main CATI window, with clear details about:

    a. When the appointment is for

    b. Who the appointment is with (including the appointment time in their time zone, if it is different to the interviewer's time zone)

    c. How long before the appointment is due

2. Appointments that are soft (e.g. "call around 10am") are given to an appropriate interviewer within a time period from 15 minutes before the set time to 15 minutes after.

3. Appointments that are "hard" (e.g. "call me at 10am") are given to an appropriate interviewer 5 minutes before the call time.

4. Appointments that are for a specific interviewer are highlighted for that interviewer when the call is within the next 30 minutes.

Sometimes, by the time an appointment is due, the person who needs to be called for the appointment is in a quota that is now full. What you do about such a person may differ from one case to the next. WSC still shows the appointment, and will process it as normal, however it is made clear that the person is in a quota that is now full. This makes it easy to see appointments with people in full quotas, so the appropriate action can be taken.

Sending a Link to a Survey via Email

Respondents who do not have time to talk on the telephone can be offered an option to complete the survey online. Let's consider the following workflow:

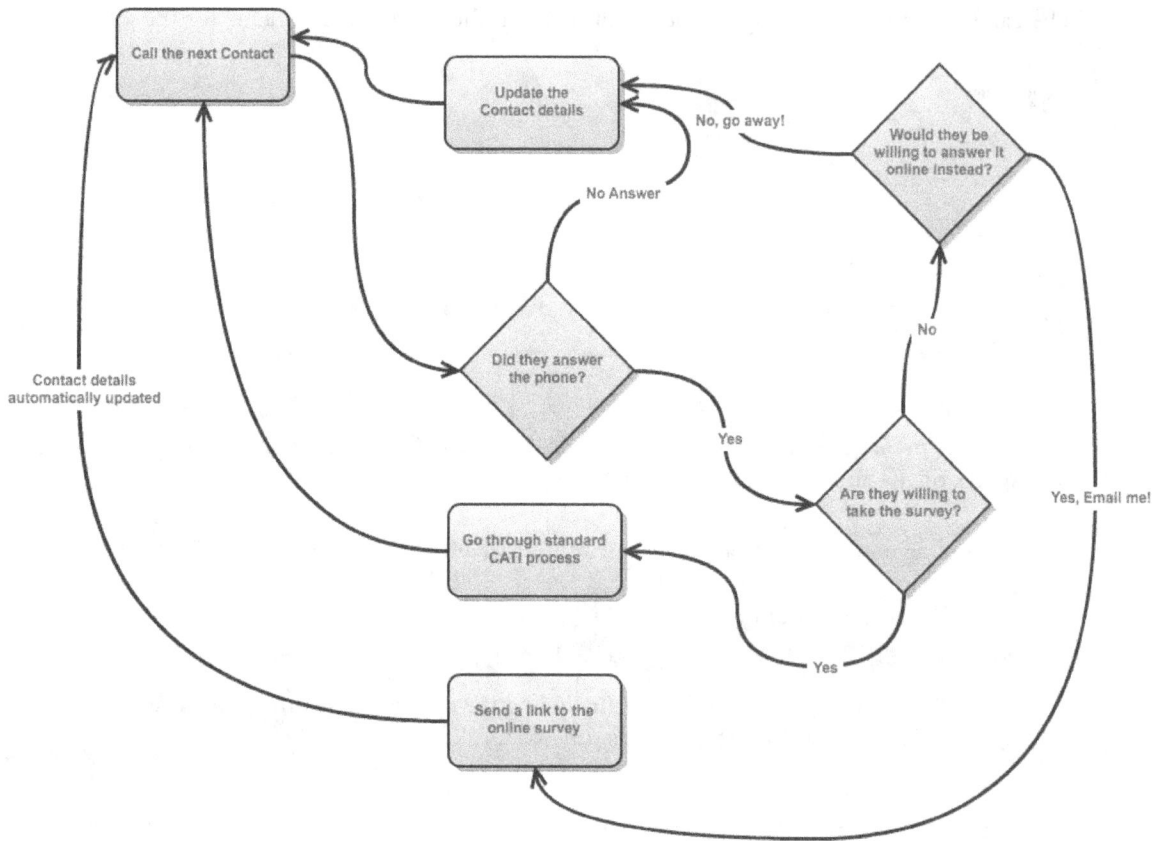

The key aspect of this workflow is the sending of the survey via Email, rather than doing the CATI process over the phone.

The steps for this process are as follows:

1. After reading the introduction to the survey, an interviewer is told by the respondent they do not want to do the survey.

184   Research Panel Integration

2. The interviewer closes the CATI process.

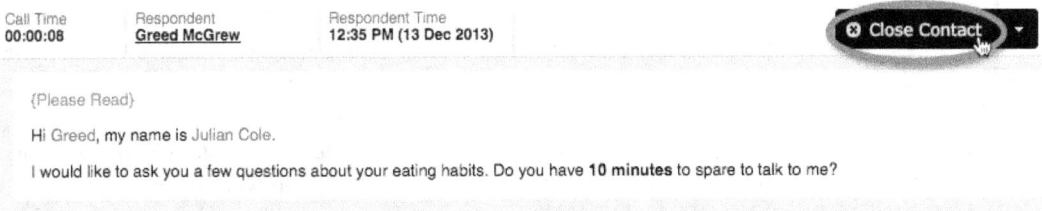

3. Choose "Email" as the reason for closing the call.

4. Choose an Email template to send (from the templates an admin would have set up previously)

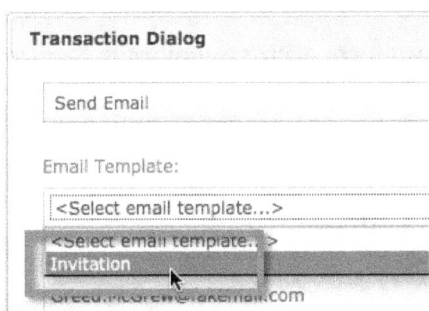

5. The invitation will be sent automatically, and the link that has been sent to the respondent is shown in the session log.

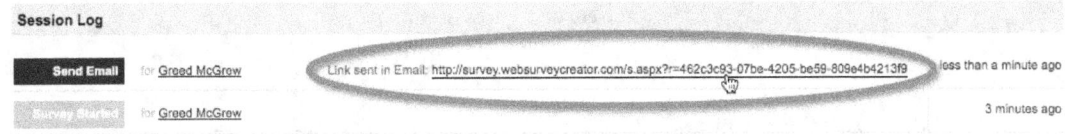

6. The interviewer can then move onto the next contact.

The Email status is similar to other statuses, in that a "delay" can be set on it before the respondent will appear on the call list again. This would make it possible, for example, to say not to call back for two days. After 2 days, the respondent would be on the call list again <u>only</u> if there response is still not completed.

The Introduction Text for the interviewer to read can be changed specifically when someone sent an Email is called again if you want to start with something like "You were recently sent an Email…" etc. This is achieved by only including a particular paragraph for people sent an Email.

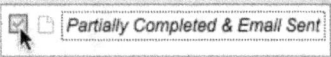

How does CATI find the "Next Contact"?

One of the most important aspects of the CATI system is how it manages people to call. For a CATI interviewer, the process is very simple – pressing the **Next Contact** button will give them the most appropriate person to call. This begs the question:

Who is the most appropriate person to call?

There are two aspects to the process of determining whom to call next:

1. A pool of "valid" respondents needs to be determined – not every respondent in the system should be included in this pool
2. From the pool of "valid" respondents, there needs to be some ordering applied so that the *most appropriate* person is served to an interviewer next

Getting the pool of "Valid" Respondents to Call

```
Valid Pool of Respondents =    Total Pool of Respondents
                             - People who have completed
                             - People who are completing online
                             - People in full quotas
                             - People who are closed (dead, wrong number etc.)
                             - People who were called recently
                             - People who have been called too much
                             - People awaiting an appointment
                             - People outside time zone rule limits (e.g. After hours)
```

Note that any filtering a CATI interviewer is using based upon respondent tags, quotas or time zones further restricts the pool of respondents.

Total Pool of Respondents

The total pool of respondents available within a CATI job is made up of every person that has ever been added to the job.

People who have completed

The respondents that have completed responses for the job – either completed through the Web, or over the telephone with a CATI interviewer.

People who are completing online

Whenever a respondent clicks on a link to complete the survey on the Web a CATI status of **Link Clicked** is added to their CATI transaction history. This status by default has a delay of 1 day, meaning that they will not be included in the possible pool of respondents to call for 1 day after the click. This gives them an opportunity to complete their response (and not get interrupted by an interviewer trying to call them).

People in full quotas

Got enough men for a particular job? The quota would be full, and all men would be excluded from future calls. This assumes, of course, that sufficient data has been imported about respondents to know that they are men before even calling them.

People who are closed

There are a serious of "final" statuses a respondent can have, including that they are dead, there is a language issue, or there is a problem with the telephone number (wrong number, business fax line etc.) Respondents with a final status are never included in future calls.

People who were called recently

There are many reasons that a respondent may have been called recently, and no response was completed. For example, the call may have gone to an answering machine, or there may simply have been no answer. All statuses that relate to "non-final" non-contact have a delay period. So, for example, after there has been no answer, there could be a delay of 1 hour before the person will be available again in the general pool of people to call.

People who have been called too much

There are three general types of mechanism to avoid overcalling people:

Too many calls overall	This is an absolute limit of the number of attempts to make on contacting a person (e.g. never try and contact a person more than 10 times). Once the limit is reached, a person should not be contacted again.
Too many calls overall for a <u>particular status</u>	This is where a person has been called too much with the <u>same result</u> (e.g. No Answer) and should not be called again. For example, after 5 no answers, you may set the rules to change the status of a respondent to the final status of **Contact Limit Reached**. These people will never be included in the pool of respondents to call again.
Too many calls within a period of time	An example of this type of restriction is where you only want a person called a maximum of 2 times in a particular shift. Once the limit is reached, the next chance to call a person will be when a new time zone period begins. For example, you could separate Monday, Tuesday, etc. as separate time zone periods, and limit the number of calls to 2 in each. Once 2 calls are made on Monday, a person will be excluded from the pool of people to call until Tuesday – when there will be another 2 opportunities to try and speak to them.

People Awaiting Appointments

If a person has an appointment attached to them, they will not be in the general pool of respondents until their appointment is due. Once they are in the pool, they will be the top person to call – so **Next Contact** will open them before anyone else in the pool.

There are two general rules that have to be considered for appointments:

1. Is the appointment at a specific time, or "around" a time (i.e. the respondent is more flexible about when they are called)
2. Does a specific interviewer need to call back, or can anyone in the job call back?

The basic rules that are used for appointments are:

- People with appointments **"around" a time** will become available in the pool of respondents **15 minutes** before the appointment time
- People with appointments at a **specific time** will become available in the pool of respondents **5 minutes** before the appointment time
- If an appointment is for a particular interviewer, they will be given the first opportunity to take the appointment, however after a period of time the appointment is given to the general pool of interviewers. When an appointment is for a particular interviewer:
    - People with appointments **"around" a time** will become available in the pool of respondents for <u>all interviewers from **15 minutes** after</u> the appointment time
    - People with appointments at a **specific time** will become available in the pool of respondents for <u>all interviewers from **5 minutes** after</u> the appointment time

The matrix of these possibilities, and how they are dealt with in the system, is shown below.

	Specific Time	**Rough Time**
Specific Interviewer	Appointment available from 5 minutes <u>before</u> appointment time <u>to the interviewer only</u>. Failure to take call will open the appointment <u>to all interviewers</u> 5 minutes <u>after</u> the appointment time.	Appointment available from 15 minutes <u>before</u> appointment time <u>to the interviewer only</u>. Failure to take call will open the appointment <u>to all interviewers</u> 15 minutes <u>after</u> the appointment time.
Any Interviewer	Appointment available from 5 minutes <u>before</u> appointment time <u>to all interviewers</u>.	Appointment available from 15 minutes <u>before</u> appointment time <u>to all interviewers</u>.

People outside time zone rule limits

Time zone rules indicate what times are valid for people within that time zone. Generally this is something simple, like indicating they can only be called between 9am and 5pm.

Ordering the pool of "Valid" Respondents

Once the pool of valid respondents has been determined, the only thing left is to determine the order that they are provided to interviewers. This order takes into account how full quotas are, together with a random element to ensure there is some mix quotas (not just the least complete quota) in the list of respondents to call.

Mixed Mode Appendix: Listing of Time Zone Codes

When setting up import data with the appropriate Time Zone, you must use a valid Time Zone code. Here is a complete list of all accepted time zone codes.

Country	Region	Code
Afghanistan	Afghanistan	AF
Åland Islands	Åland Islands	AX
Albania	Albania	AL
Algeria	Algeria	DZ
American Samoa	American Samoa	AS
Andorra	Andorra	AD
Angola	Angola	AO
Anguilla	Anguilla	AI
Antigua and Barbuda	Antigua and Barbuda	AG
Argentina	Buenos Aires	AR-BA
Argentina	Catamarca	AR-CT
Argentina	Chaco	AR-CC
Argentina	Chubut	AR-CH
Argentina	Ciudad de Buenos Aires	AR-DF
Argentina	Córdoba	AR-CB
Argentina	Corrientes	AR-CN
Argentina	Entre Rios	AR-ER
Argentina	Formosa	AR-FM
Argentina	Jujuy	AR-JY
Argentina	La Pampa	AR-LP
Argentina	La Rioja	AR-LR
Argentina	Mendoza	AR-MZ
Argentina	Misiones	AR-MN
Argentina	Neuquén	AR-NQ
Argentina	Rio Negro	AR-RN
Argentina	Salta	AR-SA
Argentina	San Juan	AR-SJ
Argentina	San Luis	AR-SL
Argentina	Santa Cruz	AR-SC
Argentina	Santa Fe	AR-SF
Argentina	Santiago del Estero	AR-SE
Argentina	Tierra del Fuego	AR-TF
Argentina	Tucumán	AR-TM
Armenia	Armenia	AM
Aruba	Aruba	AW
Australia	Australian Capital Territory	AU-ACT
Australia	Broken Hill	AU3
Australia	Lord Howe Island	AU1

Country	Region	Code
Australia	New South Wales	AU-NSW
Australia	Northern Territory	AU-NT
Australia	Queensland	AU-QLD
Australia	South Australia	AU-SA
Australia	Tasmania	AU-TAS
Australia	Victoria	AU-VIC
Australia	Western Australia	AU-WA
Australia	Western Australia (Exception)	AU-WA1
Austria	Austria	AT
Azerbaijan	Azerbaijan	AZ
Bahamas	Bahamas	BS
Bahrain	Bahrain	BH
Bangladesh	Bangladesh	BD
Barbados	Barbados	BB
Belarus	Belarus	BY
Belgium	Belgium	BE
Belize	Belize	BZ
Benin	Benin	BJ
Bermuda	Bermuda	BM
Bhutan	Bhutan	BT
Bolivia	Bolivia	BO
Bonaire, Sint Eustatius and Saba	Bonaire, Sint Eustatius and Saba	BQ
Bosnia and Herzegovina	Bosnia and Herzegovina	BA
Botswana	Botswana	BW
Brazil	Acre	BR-AC
Brazil	Alagoas	BR-AL
Brazil	Amapa	BR-AP
Brazil	Amazonas	BR-AM
Brazil	Bahia	BR-BA
Brazil	Ceara	BR-CE
Brazil	Distrito Federal	BR-DF
Brazil	Espirito Santo	BR-ES
Brazil	Fernando de Noronha	BR-FN
Brazil	Goias	BR-GO
Brazil	Maranhao	BR-MA
Brazil	Mato Grosso	BR-MT
Brazil	Mato Grosso (Araguaia region)	BR-MT1
Brazil	Mato Grosso do Sul	BR-MS
Brazil	Minas Gerais	BR-MG
Brazil	Para (eastern)	BR-PA1
Brazil	Para (western)	BR-PA2
Brazil	Paraiba	BR-PB
Brazil	Parana	BR-PR

Country	Region	Code
Brazil	Pernambuco	BR-PE
Brazil	Piaui	BR-PI
Brazil	Rio de Janeiro	BR-RJ
Brazil	Rio Grande do Norte	BR-RN
Brazil	Rio Grande do Sul	BR-RS
Brazil	Rondonia	BR-RO
Brazil	Roraima	BR-RR
Brazil	Santa Catarina	BR-SC
Brazil	Sao Paulo	BR-SP
Brazil	Sergipe	BR-SE
Brazil	Tocantins	BR-TO
Brunei Darussalam	Brunei Darussalam	BN
Bulgaria	Bulgaria	BG
Burkina Faso	Burkina Faso	BF
Burundi	Burundi	BI
Cambodia	Cambodia	KH
Cameroon	Cameroon	CM
Canada	Alberta	CA-AB
Canada	British Columbia	CA-BC
Canada	British Columbia (exception 1)	CA-BC1
Canada	British Columbia (exception 2)	CA-BC2
Canada	Labrador	CA2
Canada	Labrador (exception)	CA2A
Canada	Manitoba	CA-MB
Canada	New Brunswick	CA-NB
Canada	Newfoundland	CA-NF
Canada	Northwest Territories	CA-NT
Canada	Nova Scotia	CA-NS
Canada	Nunavut - Southampton Island	CA-NT2A
Canada	Nunavut (Central)	CA-NT2B
Canada	Nunavut (Eastern)	CA-NT2
Canada	Nunavut (Mountain)	CA-NT2C
Canada	Ontario	CA-ON
Canada	Ontario (western)	CA-ON1
Canada	Prince Edward Island	CA-PE
Canada	Quebec	CA-QC
Canada	Quebec (far east)	CA-QC1
Canada	Saskatchewan	CA-SK
Canada	Saskatchewan (exceptions - east)	CA-SK2
Canada	Saskatchewan (exceptions - west)	CA-SK1
Canada	Yukon	CA-YT
Cape Verde	Cape Verde	CV
Cayman Islands	Cayman Islands	KY

Country	Region	Code
Central African Republic	Central African Republic	CF
Chad	Chad	TD
Chile	Chile	CL
Chile - Easter Island	Chile - Easter Island	CL2
China	China	CN
Christmas Island (Indian Ocean)	Christmas Island (Indian Ocean)	CX
Cocos (Keeling) Islands	Cocos (Keeling) Islands	CC
Colombia	Colombia	CO
Comoros	Comoros	KM
Congo	Congo	CG
Congo, Democratic Republic of	(Eastern)	CD2
Congo, Democratic Republic of	(Western)	CD
Cook Islands	Cook Islands	CK
Costa Rica	Costa Rica	CR
Cote D'Ivoire	Cote D'Ivoire	CI
Croatia	Croatia	HR
Cuba	Cuba	CU
Curaçao	Curaçao	CW
Cyprus	Cyprus	CY
Czech Republic	Czech Republic	CZ
Denmark	Denmark	DK
Djibouti	Djibouti	DJ
Dominica	Dominica	DM
Dominican Republic	Dominican Republic	DO
Ecuador	Ecuador	EC
Ecuador - Galapagos Islands	Ecuador - Galapagos Islands	EC2
Egypt	Egypt	EG
El Salvador	El Salvador	SV
Equatorial Guinea	Equatorial Guinea	GQ
Eritrea	Eritrea	ER
Estonia	Estonia	EE
Ethiopia	Ethiopia	ET
Falkland Islands (Malvinas)	Falkland Islands (Malvinas)	FK
Faroe Islands	Faroe Islands	FO
Fiji	Fiji	FJ
Finland	Finland	FI
France	France	FR
French Guiana	French Guiana	GF
French Polynesia	Austral Islands	PF2A
French Polynesia	Gambier Islands	PF3
French Polynesia	Marquesas Islands	PF1
French Polynesia	Society Islands (including Tahiti)	PF
French Polynesia	Tuamotu Archipelago	PF2B

Country	Region	Code
Gabon	Gabon	GA
Gambia	Gambia	GM
Georgia	Georgia	GE
Germany	Germany	DE
Ghana	Ghana	GH
Gibraltar	Gibraltar	GI
Greece	Greece	GR
Greenland	Danmarkshavn	GL4
Greenland	Greenland	GL
Greenland	Ittoqqortoormiit	GL3
Greenland	Pituffik	GL2
Grenada	Grenada	GD
Guadeloupe	Guadeloupe	GP
Guam	Guam	GU
Guatemala	Guatemala	GT
Guernsey	Guernsey	GG
Guinea	Guinea	GN
Guinea-Bissau	Guinea-Bissau	GW
Guyana	Guyana	GY
Haiti	Haiti	HT
Holy See	Holy See	VA
Honduras	Honduras	HN
Hong Kong	Hong Kong	HK
Hungary	Hungary	HU
Iceland	Iceland	IS
India	India	IN
Indonesia	(Central)	ID2
Indonesia	(Eastern)	ID3
Indonesia	(Western)	ID
Iran, Islamic Republic of	Iran, Islamic Republic of	IR
Iraq	Iraq	IQ
Ireland	Ireland	IE
Isle of Man	Isle of Man	IM
Israel	Israel	IL
Italy	Italy	IT
Jamaica	Jamaica	JM
Japan	Japan	JP
Jersey	Jersey	JE
Johnston Atoll (U.S.)	Johnston Atoll (U.S.)	UM1
Jordan	Jordan	JO
Kazakhstan	(Eastern)	KZ
Kazakhstan	(Western)	KZ1
Kenya	Kenya	KE

Country	Region	Code
Kiribati	Gilbert Islands	KI
Kiribati	Line Islands	KI2
Kiribati	Phoenix Islands	KI3
Korea, Democratic People's Republic of	Korea, Democratic People's Republic of	KP
Korea, Republic of	Korea, Republic of	KR
Kuwait	Kuwait	KW
Kyrgyzstan	Kyrgyzstan	KG
Lao People's Democratic Republic	Lao People's Democratic Republic	LA
Latvia	Latvia	LV
Lebanon	Lebanon	LB
Lesotho	Lesotho	LS
Liberia	Liberia	LR
Libya	Libya	LY
Liechtenstein	Liechtenstein	LI
Lithuania	Lithuania	LT
Luxembourg	Luxembourg	LU
Macao	Macao	MO
Macedonia, The Former Yugoslav Republic Of	Macedonia, The Former Yugoslav Republic Of	MK
Madagascar	Madagascar	MG
Malawi	Malawi	MW
Malaysia	Malaysia	MY
Maldives	Maldives	MV
Mali	Mali	ML
Malta	Malta	MT
Marshall Islands	Marshall Islands	MH
Martinique	Martinique	MQ
Mauritania	Mauritania	MR
Mauritius	Mauritius	MU
Mayotte	Mayotte	YT
Mexico	Aguascalientes	MX-AGU
Mexico	Baja California	MX-BCN
Mexico	Baja California (Border Region)	MX-BCN1
Mexico	Baja California Sur	MX-BCS
Mexico	Campeche	MX-CAM
Mexico	Chiapas	MX-CHP
Mexico	Chihuahua	MX-CHH
Mexico	Chihuahua (Border Region)	MX-CHH1
Mexico	Coahuila	MX-COA
Mexico	Coahuila (Border Region)	MX-COA1
Mexico	Colima	MX-COL
Mexico	Distrito Federal	MX-DIF

Country	Region	Code
Mexico	Durango	MX-DUR
Mexico	Guanajuato	MX-GUA
Mexico	Guerrero	MX-GRO
Mexico	Hidalgo	MX-HID
Mexico	Jalisco	MX-JAL
Mexico	Mexico State	MX-MEX
Mexico	Michoacán	MX-MIC
Mexico	Morelos	MX-MOR
Mexico	Nayarit	MX-NAY
Mexico	Nayarit (Exception)	MX-NAY1
Mexico	Nuevo León	MX-NLE
Mexico	Nuevo León (Border Region)	MX-NLE1
Mexico	Oaxaca	MX-OAX
Mexico	Puebla	MX-PUE
Mexico	Querétaro	MX-QUE
Mexico	Quintana Roo	MX-ROO
Mexico	San Luis Potosí	MX-SLP
Mexico	Sinaloa	MX-SIN
Mexico	Sonora	MX-SON
Mexico	Tabasco	MX-TAB
Mexico	Tamaulipas	MX-TAM
Mexico	Tamaulipas (Border Region)	MX-TAM1
Mexico	Tlaxcala	MX-TLA
Mexico	Veracruz	MX-VER
Mexico	Yucatan	MX-YUC
Mexico	Zacatecas	MX-ZAC
Micronesia, Federated States Of	Kosrae, Pohnpei	FM
Micronesia, Federated States Of	Yap, Chuuk	FM1
Midway Islands (U.S.)	Midway Islands (U.S.)	UM2
Moldova, Republic of	Moldova, Republic of	MD
Monaco	Monaco	MC
Mongolia	(Central and Eastern)	MN
Mongolia	(Western)	MN1
Montenegro	Montenegro	ME
Montserrat	Montserrat	MS
Morocco	Morocco	MA
Mozambique	Mozambique	MZ
Myanmar	Myanmar	MM
Namibia	Namibia	NA
Nauru	Nauru	NR
Nepal	Nepal	NP
Netherlands	Netherlands	NL
New Caledonia	New Caledonia	NC

Country	Region	Code
New Zealand	New Zealand	NZ
New Zealand - Chatham Islands	New Zealand - Chatham Islands	NZ2
Nicaragua	Nicaragua	NI
Niger	Niger	NE
Nigeria	Nigeria	NG
Niue	Niue	NU
Norfolk Island	Norfolk Island	NF
Northern Mariana Islands	Northern Mariana Islands	MP
Norway	Norway	NO
Oman	Oman	OM
Pakistan	Pakistan	PK
Palau	Palau	PW
Palestinian Territory	Gaza Strip	PS1
Palestinian Territory	West Bank	PS
Panama	Panama	PA
Papua New Guinea	Papua New Guinea	PG
Paraguay	Paraguay	PY
Peru	Peru	PE
Philippines	Philippines	PH
Pitcairn	Pitcairn	PN
Poland	Poland	PL
Portugal	Azores	PT2
Portugal	Madeira Islands	PT1
Portugal	Portugal	PT
Puerto Rico	Puerto Rico	PR
Qatar	Qatar	QA
Reunion	Reunion	RE
Romania	Romania	RO
Russia	Adygea	RU-AD
Russia	Altai Republic	RU-AL
Russia	Altaskiy Kray	RU-ALT
Russia	Amur	RU-AMU
Russia	Arkhangel'	RU-ARK
Russia	Astrakhan'	RU-AST
Russia	Bashkortostan	RU-BA
Russia	Belgorod	RU-BEL
Russia	Bryansk	RU-BRY
Russia	Buryatia	RU-BU
Russia	Chechnya	RU-CE
Russia	Chelyabinsk	RU-CHE
Russia	Chukot	RU-CHU
Russia	Chuvashia	RU-CU
Russia	Dagestan	RU-DA

Country	Region	Code
Russia	Ingushetia	RU-IN
Russia	Irkutsk	RU-IRK
Russia	Ivanovo	RU-IVA
Russia	Jewish Autonomous Oblast'	RU-YEV
Russia	Kabardino-Balkaria	RU-KB
Russia	Kaliningrad	RU-KGD
Russia	Kalmykia	RU-KL
Russia	Kaluga	RU-KLU
Russia	Kamchatka	RU-KAM
Russia	Karachay-Cherkessia	RU-KC
Russia	Karelia	RU-KR
Russia	Kemerovo	RU-KEM
Russia	Khabarovsk	RU-KHA
Russia	Khakassia	RU-KK
Russia	Khanty-Mansi	RU-KHM
Russia	Kirov	RU-KIR
Russia	Komi	RU-KO
Russia	Kostroma	RU-KOS
Russia	Krasnodar	RU-KDA
Russia	Krasnoyarsk	RU-KYA
Russia	Kurgan	RU-KGN
Russia	Kursk	RU-KRS
Russia	Leningradskaya Oblast'	RU-LEN
Russia	Lipetsk	RU-LIP
Russia	Magadan	RU-MAG
Russia	Mari El	RU-ME
Russia	Mordovia	RU-MO
Russia	Moscow City	RU-MOW
Russia	Moskva	RU-MOS
Russia	Murmansk	RU-MUR
Russia	Nenets	RU-NEN
Russia	Nizhniy Novgorod	RU-NIZ
Russia	North Ossetia-Alania	RU-SE
Russia	Novgorod	RU-NGR
Russia	Novosibirsk	RU-NVS
Russia	Omsk	RU-OMS
Russia	Orel	RU-ORL
Russia	Orenburg	RU-ORE
Russia	Penza	RU-PNZ
Russia	Perm	RU-PER
Russia	Primorskiy	RU-PRI
Russia	Pskov	RU-PSK
Russia	Rostov	RU-ROS

Country	Region	Code
Russia	Ryazan'	RU-RYA
Russia	Sakha (Central)	RU-SA2
Russia	Sakha (Eastern)	RU-SA3
Russia	Sakha (Western)	RU-SA
Russia	Sakhalin	RU-SAK
Russia	Sakhalin (Kuril Islands)	RU-SAK2
Russia	Samara	RU-SAM
Russia	Saratov	RU-SAR
Russia	Smolensk	RU-SMO
Russia	St. Petersburg City	RU-SPE
Russia	Stavropol	RU-STA
Russia	Sverdlovsk	RU-SVE
Russia	Tambov	RU-TAM
Russia	Tatarstan	RU-TA
Russia	Tomsk	RU-TOM
Russia	Tula	RU-TUL
Russia	Tuva	RU-TY
Russia	Tver'	RU-TVE
Russia	Tyumen'	RU-TYU
Russia	Udmurtia	RU-UD
Russia	Ul'yanovsk	RU-ULY
Russia	Vladimir	RU-VLA
Russia	Volgograd	RU-VGG
Russia	Vologda	RU-VLG
Russia	Voronezh	RU-VOR
Russia	Yamalo-Nenets	RU-YAN
Russia	Yaroslavl'	RU-YAR
Russia	Zabaykalsky	RU-ZAB
Rwanda	Rwanda	RW
Saint Barthelemy	Saint Barthelemy	BL
Saint Helena, Ascension and Tristan da Cunha	Saint Helena, Ascension and Tristan da Cunha	SH
Saint Kitts and Nevis	Saint Kitts and Nevis	KN
Saint Lucia	Saint Lucia	LC
Saint Martin	Saint Martin	MF
Saint Pierre and Miquelon	Saint Pierre and Miquelon	PM
Saint Vincent and The Grenadines	Saint Vincent and The Grenadines	VC
Samoa	Samoa	WS
San Marino	San Marino	SM
Sao Tome and Principe	Sao Tome and Principe	ST
Saudi Arabia	Saudi Arabia	SA
Senegal	Senegal	SN
Serbia	Serbia	RS

Country	Region	Code
Seychelles	Seychelles	SC
Sierra Leone	Sierra Leone	SL
Singapore	Singapore	SG
Sint Maarten (Dutch part)	Sint Maarten (Dutch part)	SX
Slovakia	Slovakia	SK
Slovenia	Slovenia	SI
Solomon Islands	Solomon Islands	SB
Somalia	Somalia	SO
South Africa	South Africa	ZA
South Sudan, Republic of	South Sudan, Republic of	SS
Spain	Canary Islands	ES2
Spain	Mainland, Baleares, Melilla, Ceuta	ES
Sri Lanka	Sri Lanka	LK
Sudan	Sudan	SD
Suriname	Suriname	SR
Svalbard and Jan Mayen	Svalbard and Jan Mayen	SJ
Swaziland	Swaziland	SZ
Sweden	Sweden	SE
Switzerland	Switzerland	CH
Syrian Arab Republic	Syrian Arab Republic	SY
Taiwan	Taiwan	TW
Tajikistan	Tajikistan	TJ
Tanzania, United Republic of	Tanzania, United Republic of	TZ
Thailand	Thailand	TH
Timor-Leste	Timor-Leste	TL
Togo	Togo	TG
Tokelau	Tokelau	TK
Tonga	Tonga	TO
Trinidad and Tobago	Trinidad and Tobago	TT
Tunisia	Tunisia	TN
Turkey	Turkey	TR
Turkmenistan	Turkmenistan	TM
Turks and Caicos Islands	Turks and Caicos Islands	TC
Tuvalu	Tuvalu	TV
Uganda	Uganda	UG
Ukraine	Ukraine	UA
United Arab Emirates	United Arab Emirates	AE
United Kingdom	United Kingdom	GB
United States	Alabama	US-AL
United States	Alaska	US-AK
United States	Alaska (Aleutian Islands)	US-AK1
United States	Arizona	US-AZ
United States	Arizona (Navajo Reservation)	US-AZ1

Country	Region	Code
United States	Arkansas	US-AR
United States	California	US-CA
United States	Colorado	US-CO
United States	Connecticut	US-CT
United States	Delaware	US-DE
United States	District of Columbia	US-DC
United States	Florida	US-FL
United States	Florida (far west)	US-FL1
United States	Georgia	US-GA
United States	Hawaii	US-HI
United States	Idaho (northern)	US-ID1
United States	Idaho (southern)	US-ID
United States	Illinois	US-IL
United States	Indiana	US-IN
United States	Indiana (far west)	US-IN1
United States	Iowa	US-IA
United States	Kansas	US-KS
United States	Kansas (exception)	US-KS1
United States	Kentucky (eastern)	US-KY
United States	Kentucky (western)	US-KY1
United States	Louisiana	US-LA
United States	Maine	US-ME
United States	Maryland	US-MD
United States	Massachusetts	US-MA
United States	Michigan	US-MI
United States	Michigan (exception)	US-MI1
United States	Minnesota	US-MN
United States	Mississippi	US-MS
United States	Missouri	US-MO
United States	Montana	US-MT
United States	Nebraska	US-NE
United States	Nebraska (western)	US-NE1
United States	Nevada	US-NV
United States	Nevada (exception)	US-NV1
United States	New Hampshire	US-NH
United States	New Jersey	US-NJ
United States	New Mexico	US-NM
United States	New York	US-NY
United States	North Carolina	US-NC
United States	North Dakota	US-ND
United States	North Dakota (western)	US-ND1
United States	Ohio	US-OH
United States	Oklahoma	US-OK

Country	Region	Code
United States	Oregon	US-OR
United States	Oregon (exception)	US-OR1
United States	Pennsylvania	US-PA
United States	Rhode Island	US-RI
United States	South Carolina	US-SC
United States	South Dakota (eastern)	US-SD
United States	South Dakota (western)	US-SD1
United States	Tennessee (eastern)	US-TN1
United States	Tennessee (western)	US-TN
United States	Texas	US-TX
United States	Texas (far west)	US-TX1
United States	Utah	US-UT
United States	Vermont	US-VT
United States	Virginia	US-VA
United States	Washington	US-WA
United States	West Virginia	US-WV
United States	Wisconsin	US-WI
United States	Wyoming	US-WY
Uruguay	Uruguay	UY
Uzbekistan	Uzbekistan	UZ
Vanuatu	Vanuatu	VU
Venezuela	Venezuela	VE
Viet Nam	Viet Nam	VN
Virgin Islands (British)	Virgin Islands (British)	VG
Virgin Islands (U.S.)	Virgin Islands (U.S.)	VI
Wake Island (U.S.)	Wake Island (U.S.)	UM3
Wallis and Futuna	Wallis and Futuna	WF
Western Sahara	Western Sahara	EH
Yemen	Yemen	YE
Zambia	Zambia	ZM
Zimbabwe	Zimbabwe	ZW

Research Panel Integration

Respondents for Web Surveys often come from Research Panels. These panels can be used to find people who fit the required demographics for the survey.

Web Survey Creator can work generically with any standard panel, or can fully integrate with a panel if it uses the popular Contact Profiler panel software.

Overview of Research Panels

Research Panels provide a good source of survey respondents with specific attributes such as certain ages, genders and locations.

These panels must track how their members are used, so that:

1. the members can be rewarded for their effort
2. and fees can be paid to the panel provider for their use in a survey

For this tracking to be possible, there has to be communication between the survey and the panel provider's software.

A panel member who completes a survey must be flagged with an identifier that is chosen by the panel provider so that they can be matched up to their panel.

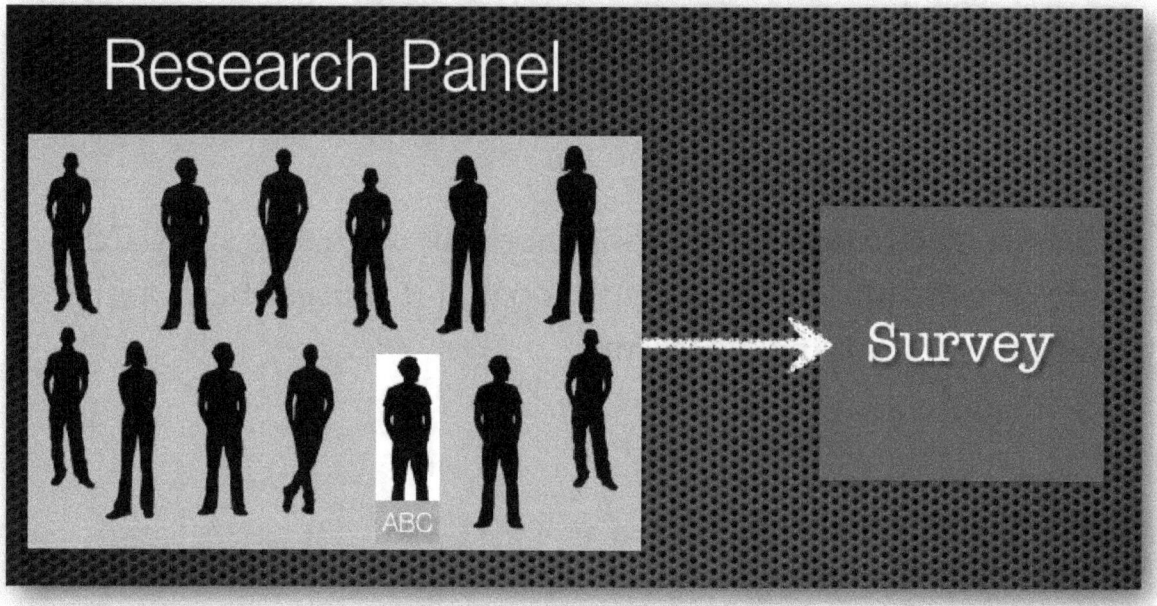

This means that there needs to be a mechanism for this data to be passed into the survey.

Upon completion of the survey, the panel provider needs to be told how the panel member went in the survey – things such as:

1. Did they complete the survey?
2. Were they screened out because they were an unsuitable respondent?
3. Were they quota-ed out because we already had enough responses from their type of respondent?

The panel provider, based upon this information, can determine rewards and fees.

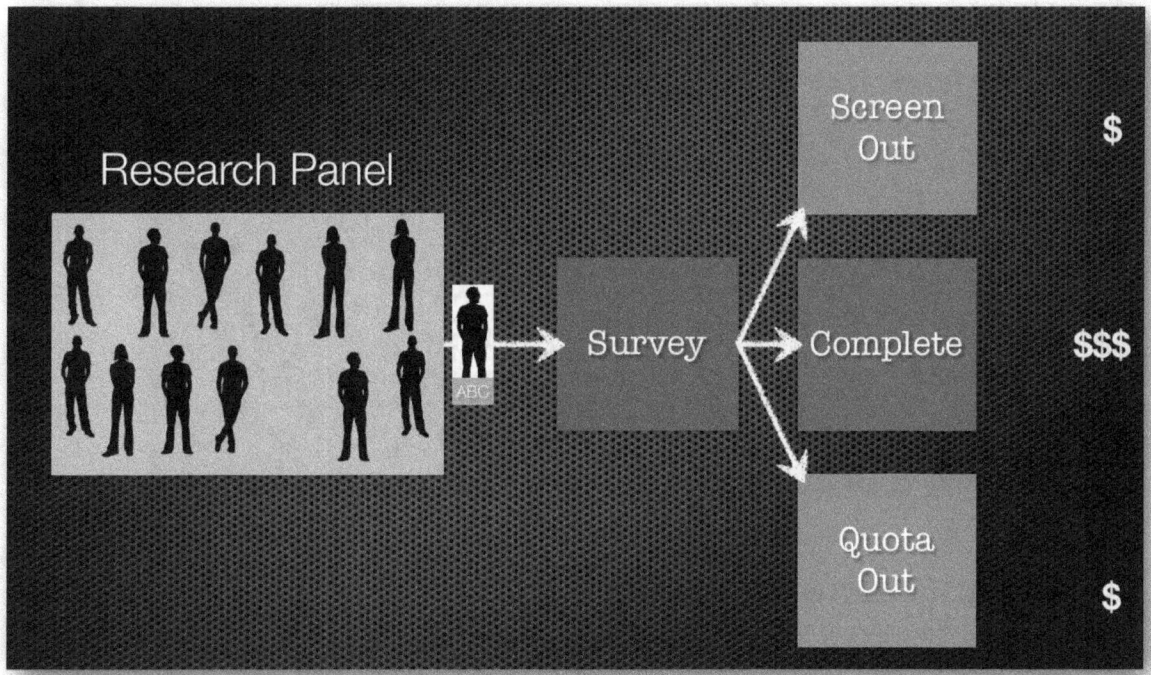

Using a Research Panel

Setting a respondent's unique code

OK, so let's start by looking at how we can use an identifier provided by a panel provider.

Our starting point is to use a standard anonymous survey distribution.

For example, I could have a survey link that looks as follows:

`http://survey.websurveycreator.com/s/myresearchsurvey`

A unique ID can be set for each respondent who completes the survey, by simply passing the ID to the survey link as follows:

`http://survey.websurveycreator.com/s.aspx?s=f4ef1799-2413-4514-b5ef-9ff20e1de322&usr={Unique Code}`

The passing of a unique code to each respondent would be handled by the panel management system, since it would be sending out the invitations.

Therefore, the links sent to three different respondents could look something like the following:

`http://survey.websurveycreator.com/s.aspx?s=f4ef1799-2413-4514-b5ef-9ff20e1de322&usr=1000`

`http://survey.websurveycreator.com/s.aspx?s=f4ef1799-2413-4514-b5ef-9ff20e1de322&usr=1001`

`http://survey.websurveycreator.com/s.aspx?s=f4ef1799-2413-4514-b5ef-9ff20e1de322&usr=ABC`

Codes can be any combination of letters and numbers up to 50 characters long.

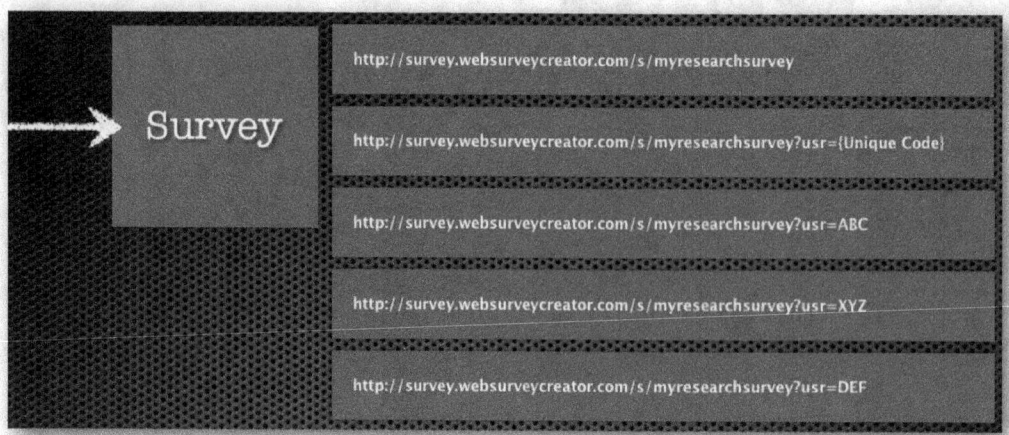

Passing back the Survey Result

Once a respondent completes a survey, the panel management system will need to be notified about the respondent's completion status.

This is achieved by redirecting back to the panel management system at the conclusion of the survey.

In general, two pieces of information are provided as part of the redirect:

1. The respondent's identifier
2. A code indicating the status of the respondent's response

The identifier is simply a passing back of the unique code that was given to Web Survey Creator when the respondent commenced the survey.

The code to indicate status will generally be one of three possibilities – a code indicating:

1. a complete
2. a screen out; or
3. a quota out

An example of a redirect URL could look as follows:

`http://www.mypanel.com/surveycompleted.aspx?id=ABC&success=Complete`

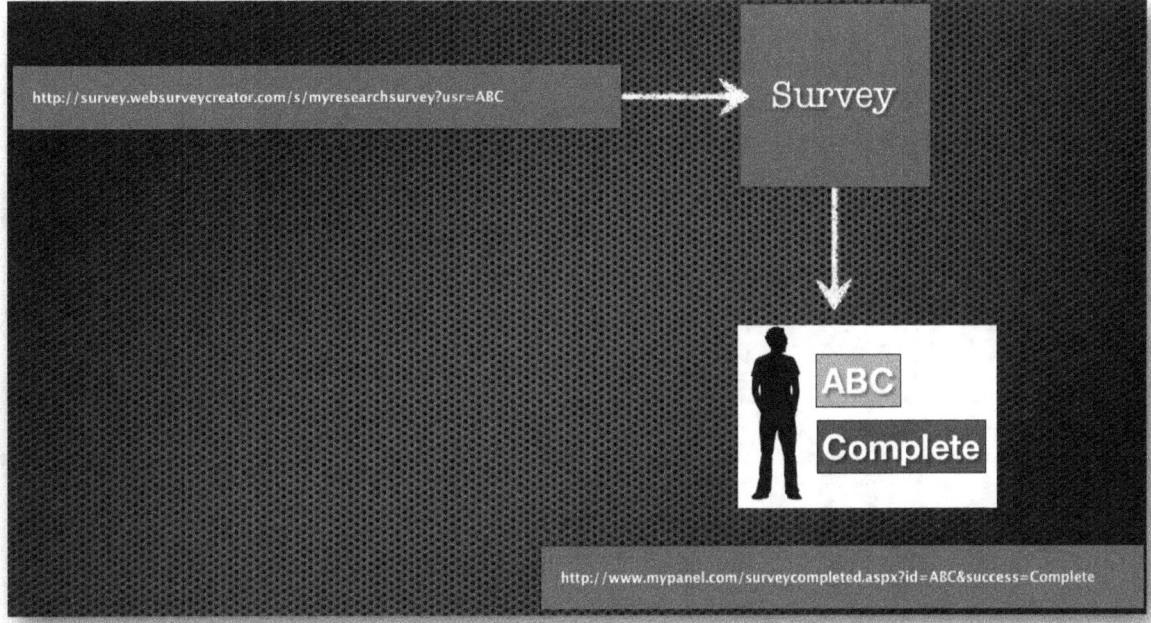

The different URLs needed are set up on the different Terminate Pages throughout the survey. For more information on Terminate Pages, see the discussion in an earlier chapter of this book.

Panel Example: SurveyVillage

Let's consider a real-life example, using the Australian "SurveyVillage" panel.

When we set up our redirection URLs, we make sure we pass the code that was sent through to the survey, together with the necessary "ActionCode".

SurveyVillage provides the format of the URL.

We simply place a Recall Code into the URL so that the respondent is identified with the same code that was passed through when the respondent commenced the survey.

The URLs for Completes, Screen-outs and Quota-outs are shown here.

Completes

```
http://www.surveyvillage.com/WebJobFinish.aspx?SurveyCode=x520afgv5r
t2umlqwja8&ContactId=RECALLCODE&ActionCode=q2yf4
```

Screen Outs

```
http://www.surveyvillage.com/WebJobFinish.aspx?SurveyCode=x520afgv5r
t2umlqwja8&ContactId=RECALLCODE&ActionCode=xry64
```

Quota Outs

```
http://www.surveyvillage.com/WebJobFinish.aspx?SurveyCode=x520afgv5r
t2umlqwja8&ContactId=RECALLCODE&ActionCode=q5jd8
```

You will notice that the only difference in the URLS is the "Action Code".

All we need to do in Web Survey Creator is place the re-directions at the appropriate place in the survey structure.

Completes will get to the end of the survey. We will therefore change the redirect that appears on the Survey Complete terminate page that appears at the end of our survey.

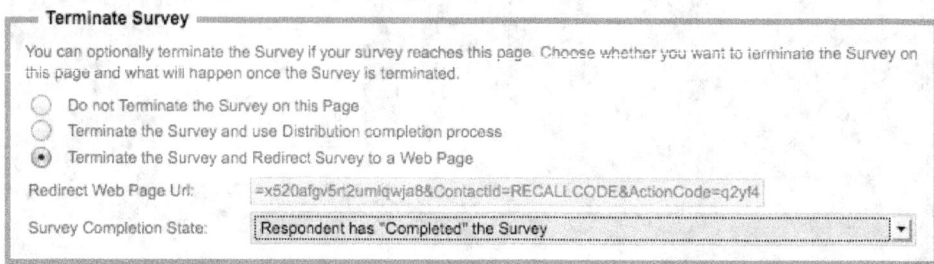

Screen Outs will occur for people who end up on the Screen Out terminate page. We therefore need to adjust the redirect on this page.

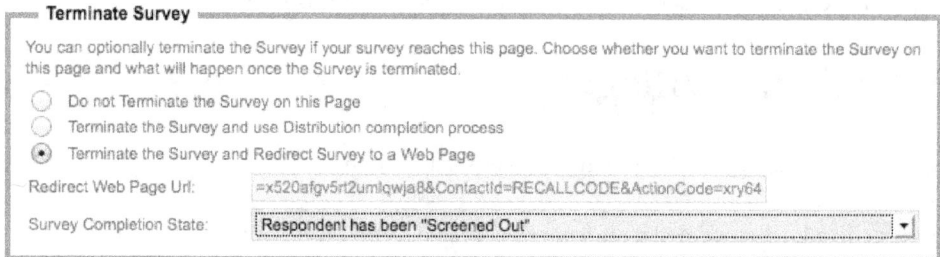

Quota Outs will occur for people who end up on the Quota Out page. We therefore need to adjust the redirect on this page.

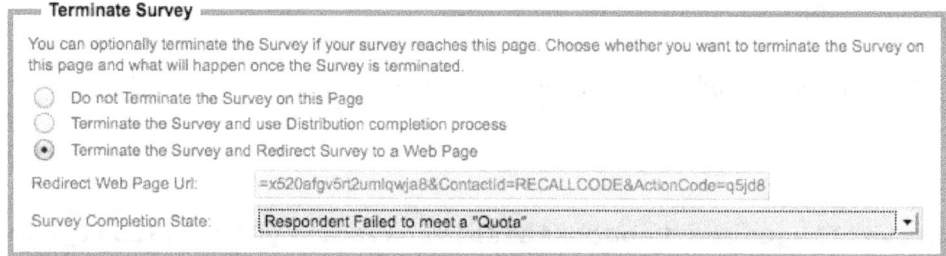

OK, great! Our survey is now ready to be used with the SurveyVillage panel.

Integration of Web Surveys with Contact Profiler

What is Contact Profiler?

Contact Profiler (CP) is a Web Application that can be used to manage respondent panels. It has been developed in close co-operation with the team that developed Web Survey Creator.

This means that:

- A level of integration is possible that simplifies many of the tasks described in the previous chapter
- Additional capabilities are available - including updating panel data with responses from the integrated survey.

Why use Integration?

The steps described earlier in this chapter are pretty straightforward and will work with any panel, so why worry about closer integration? There are a number of benefits:

1. Integration hides the technical aspects of the process completely, making it easier to understand
2. The easier the setup, the less chance there will be any mistakes. We're dealing with URLs and codes - a mis-typed letter can cause havoc
3. It's quicker to set up!
4. Features like updating of panel profile information are only available through true integration

Who can use Integration?

Contact Profiler integration is available to organizations who use both CP and WSC themselves. They are therefore the owners of the panel, and creators of the Web Surveys. External consumers of a research panel (who don't actually own the panel) would need to be set up using the general integration described in the previous chapter.

Web Survey Integration Overview

Users of Web Survey Creator can integrate surveys with Contact Profiler using the method described in the previous chapter. There is, however, a much quicker and simpler way of integrating.

Let's consider an example:

> "Beach Burger" is a fast growing burger chain that wants to determine whether it's new healthier menu and advertising campaign is working in it's key demographic of 18-39 year olds.
>
> A quick survey has been created in WSC for sending out to panel members in a research panel that is run in Contact Profiler.

Integration Checklist

It is important to understand how integration is achieved between WSC and CP. Part of this understanding relates to ensuring that your Web Surveys are set up correctly for integration. A checklist of things to consider is listed below.

Mandatory Checklist

The to do items in the checklist below <u>must</u> be completed for integration to be possible. Without them, you will be unable to set up integration.

To Do ITEM	Details
Create a Survey in Web Survey Creator	Integration is achieved by going into Contact Profiler and choosing a survey to integrate to. You therefore need to actually create a survey in Web Survey Creator first!
Create a Survey Complete Terminate Page	Integration supports completes, screen-outs and quota-outs. A single survey complete terminate page must exist in the survey at a minimum. Other pages are optional

As we can see, the list of mandatory items is minimal. If these are set up, we can provide the most basic form of integration as follows:

- Contact Profiler will be able to invite people to the survey
- People who complete the survey will be tracked, and Contact Profiler will be "informed" of their completion.

Optional Checklist

While the following to do items are not mandatory, they allow significantly more functionality to be achieved in the integration process.

To Do ITEM	Details
Create a Screen Out Terminate Page	A single Screen Out terminate page can be created to track people that are unsuitable for the survey and therefore need to be "kicked".
Create a Quota Out Terminate Page	A single Quota Out terminate page can be created to track people that are suitable for the survey, but are not needed because there is already enough of that type of respondent in the system. These people are therefore "kicked" as well.
Add Access Codes to Questions that match Profile Attribute Codes in CP	The most advanced feature of the integration is the updating of panel data with responses to the survey. This is achieved by matching the Access Code in WSC with the Profile Attribute Short Code in CP. Questions must also be of a compatible type, and have the same number of choices with the correct values for each choice.

These optional items significantly extend the capabilities available through integration. In particular, the linkage between a survey and profile attributes makes it easy to keep profile data up to date, without any additional effort by panel members.

Overview of the Integration Process

Before looking at specifics, let's review the basic process that is used to integrate a Web Survey with Contact Profiler. The steps for this integration are as follows:

In Web Survey Creator

1. Create a Survey in Web Survey Creator

   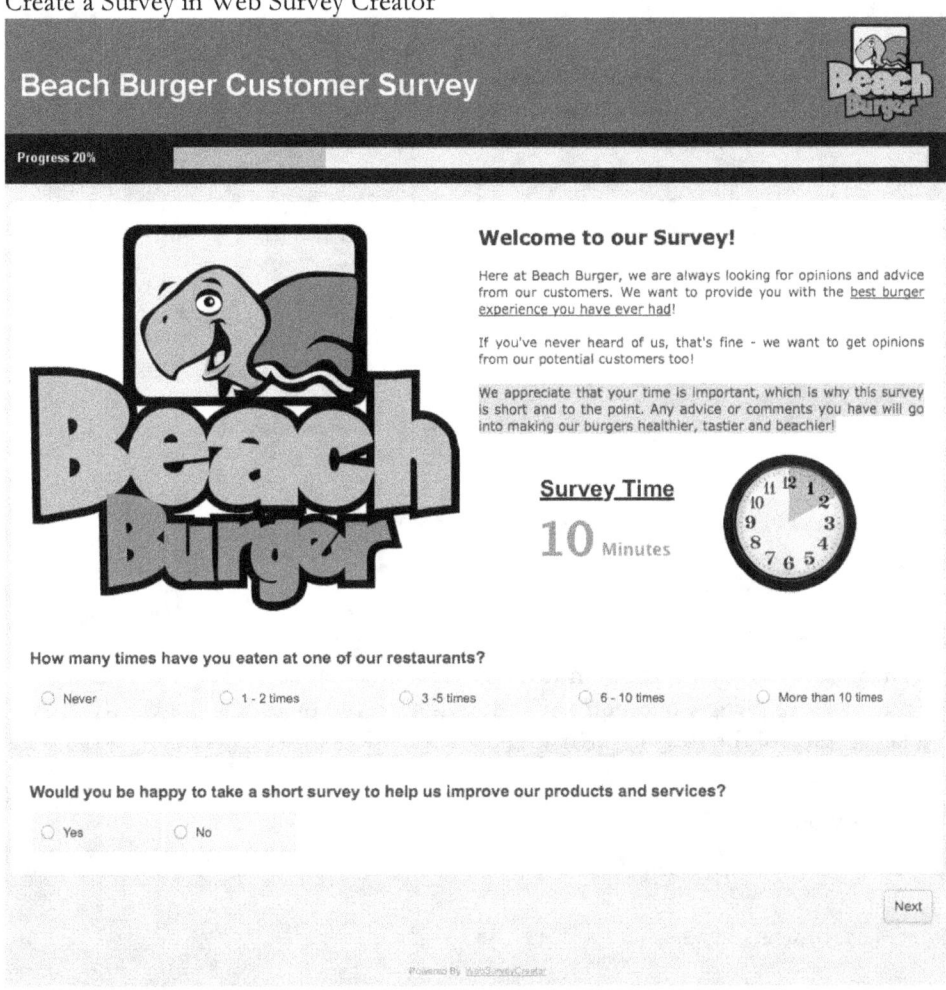

2. Ensure *at a minimum* that the survey has a "Survey Completed" terminate page (this is the page that successful respondents will see before they submit)

   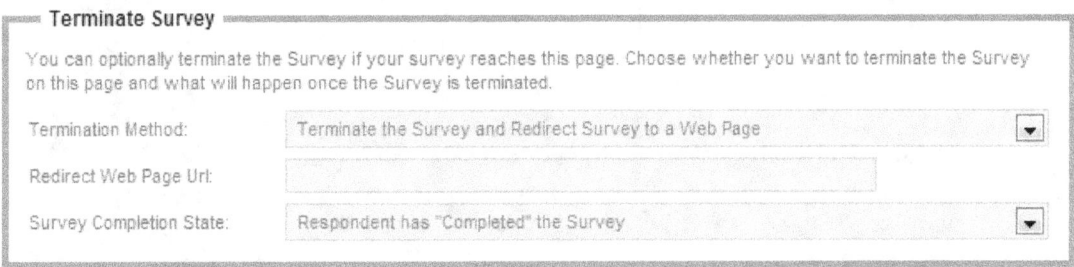

3. Optionally include Screen-Out and Quota-Out terminate pages.

4. Optionally use Unique Access Codes that match the short codes used for profile attributes in Contact Profiler.

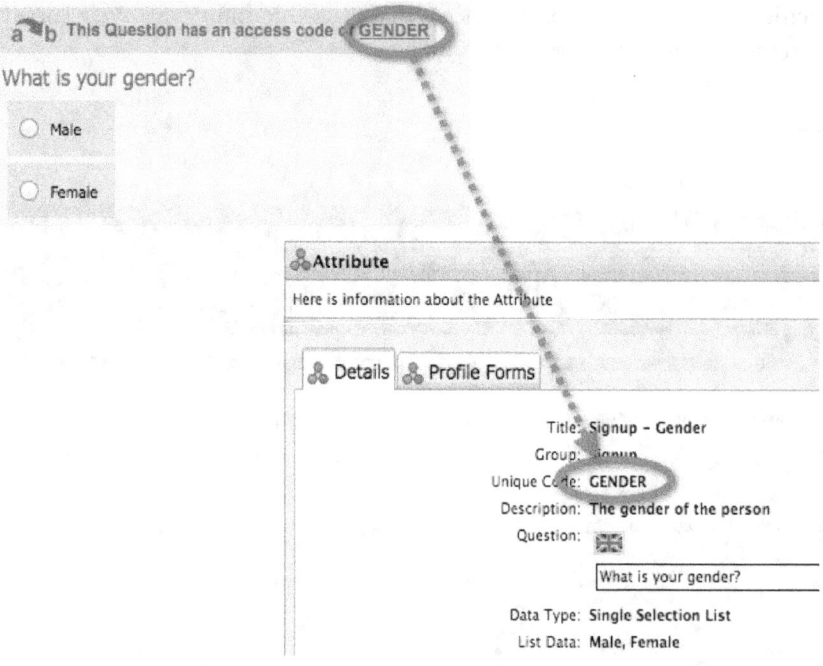

What if a Matrix Question is used in WSC?

Contact Profiler does not directly support matrix questions, but they can be set up in Web Survey Creator. So how can this integration work? The issue is that each row of the matrix needs to be integrated to a single question in CP. This is achieved by adding the UNIQUE CODE as a tag on each of the rows in the matrix in WSC:

To integrate to this, CP simply needs a question with the same choices in it as the matrix, and a code of "GOODVALUE".

212   Research Panel Integration

In Contact Profiler

1. Create a Web Survey Job in Contact Profiler, and enter the basic job details (name etc.)

   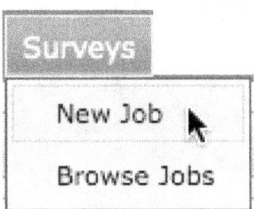

2. Go to the Content Tab for the Job

3. Enter the credits to be received by Panel Members for Completes, Screen-outs and/or Quota-outs.

   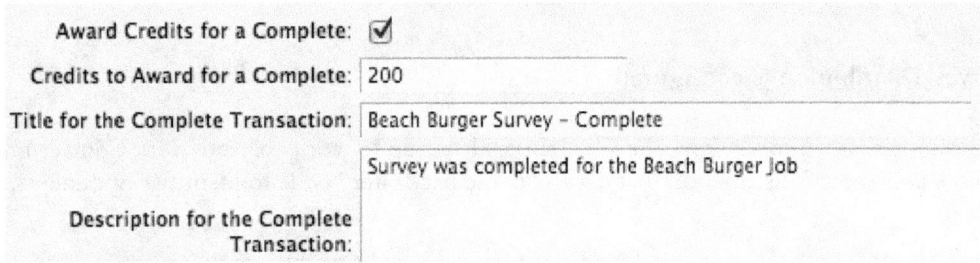

4. Click **Save and Next**

5. Click the **Link to WSC Survey** button

6. The Survey and Distribution must then be chosen to link to.

   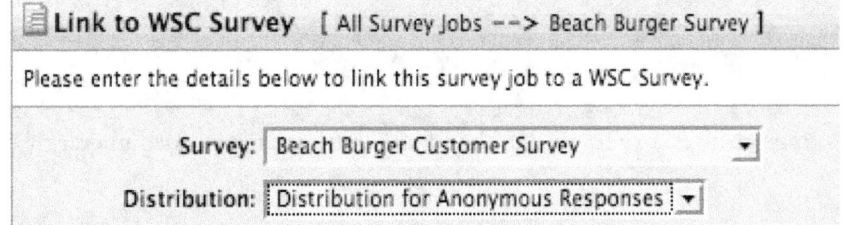

7. If the survey has questions with the same code as attributes in Contact Profiler, they can be connected.

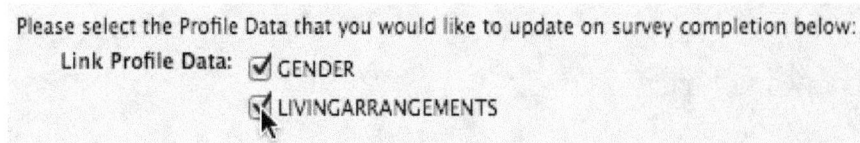

8. On the **Content** tab, click the test button to test that the Web Survey is working.

Hey, what just happened?

Integration is so quick and easy that you may wonder whether it did anything at all. While it is not crucial for the use of integration, it is handy to know what the automatic integration actually does behind the scenes.

The Survey Distribution is configured

The distribution that is chosen from the WSC survey is set up to work correctly with Contact Profiler. This is an "anonymous" distribution that uses a "come back later" code to identify respondents.

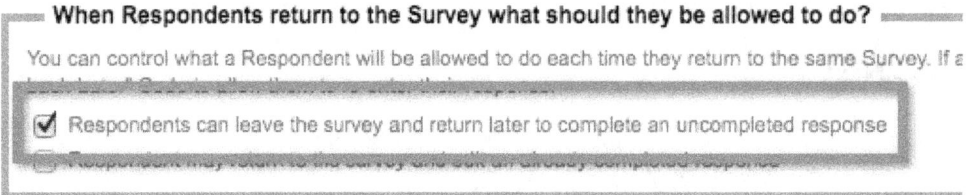

Contact Profiler will pass this code to the survey, and it will be used to send back complete, screen out and quota out codes to Contact Profiler when the survey is complete.

Contact Profiler knows the Survey Link

The content for the Web Survey Job is updated with the link to the Web Survey distribution for the WSC Web Job.

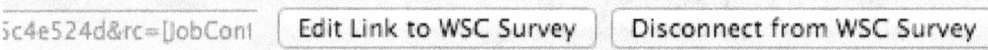

Note that if this needs to be changed or removed in the future, buttons are provided to quickly change the integration settings.

Changing the integration settings after a job has gone live could cause confusing results and is not recommended.

Web Survey Creator knows how to terminate

When a Web Survey Job is set up in Contact Profiler with Complete, Screen out and Quota Out completion details, the redirections appear on the Job Details screen:

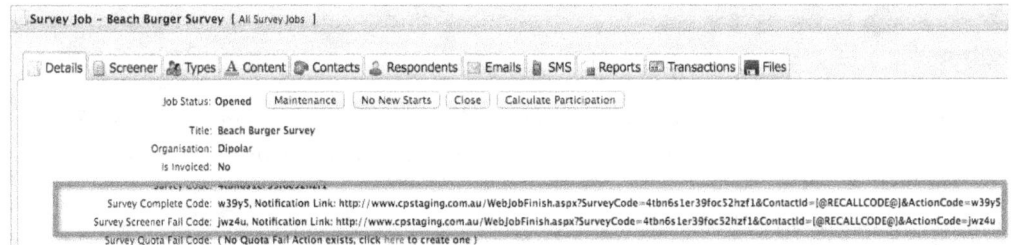

These redirections are required in the Web Survey to indicate which of the endings has occurred for a respondent. The integration takes care of this for us. For example, on the Survey Complete terminate page, the correct URL to redirect to for a complete is added for us:

Profile Data is updated

This is the only completely hidden aspect of the integration. Once the survey is complete, profile data is updated in the background.

If a linked question has no data entered in the Survey, the profile update is skipped for that question (i.e.. it doesn't remove the existing data). This ensures that existing profile data is not removed just because in a particular survey, the respondent fails to give an answer.

Integrating with Contact Profiler Screeners

What are Respondent Screeners?

Research Panels can be great at finding the people we need for our Web Surveys. One issue though, is that people can only be found based upon the information the panel has on them - things like age, gender, location and maybe a few general attributes.

So, what if we need to find 18-39 year old women who have eaten at Beach Burger in the last month? The age and gender can be searched on - what they ate in the last month cannot. These people need to be *screened* to determine if they are the people we are looking for.

A Screener is a short survey used to determine whether a panel member fits the specific needs of a project. It asks questions about the respondent that the panel data does not include.

Screeners in Contact Profiler

Contact Profiler has its own screener system that can be used to screen panel members for a project.

While this system is quite capable, it lacks a number of benefits that Web Survey Creator provides. Web Survey Creator surveys have the following benefits over the in-built screeners in Contact Profiler:

1. Support for responses on mobile devices
2. Much more flexible and "sexier" survey formatting
3. More question types
4. More powerful flow control
5. Data piping and other advanced features
6. Scripting

Screeners must work with other parts of a project's workflow in Contact Profiler. Of particular importance is the analysis performed at the end of a screener to determine whether a respondent "passes" the screener rules and is therefore suitable to participate in the project.

> Screener pass rules must be run by Contact Profiler to determine if a respondent is suitable for a project. An externally managed screening process through Web Survey Creator must integrate with this rule system.

The Contact Profiler Workflow

The basic Contact Profiler workflow remains the same, regardless of whether screeners are managed internally or externally. The basic steps in the workflow for a project using screeners always begins as follows:

1. Load people from the panel that are as close to our target audience as possible (based on age, gender and other profile attributes)
2. Invite these people to a Web-based screener survey
3. Based on responses to the screener, either "fail" them or move them into a new respondent type for people who have passed the screener
4. Continue with the project for the people who have passed the screener

Any changes to how the screener is run will only affect step 2. All other steps need to be run as normal in Contact Profiler.

How WSC fits in the standard Workflow

A number of aspects on the Contact Profiler workflow *require a Contact Profiler screener to exist*. For example, the rules for whether a respondent passes or fails are based upon screener questions.

So how can Web Survey Creator take over screening duties from the internal screener?

The answer is actually quite simple - an internal screener is generated automatically from the Web Survey Creator survey with the key questions that can then be used in screener pass rules.

There are a couple of extra steps, but they are all automatically handled by the integration (highlighted in **bold**):

Screening workflow USING CP only	SCREENING Workflow USING CP + WSC
	Create Screener in WSC
Create Screener in CP	**Generate Screening in CP from WSC Survey**
Invite Respondents to Screener	Invite Respondents to Screener
	WSC passes responses back to CP
Screener Pass/Fail Determined in CP	Screener Pass/Fail Determined in CP

In essence, the Contact Profiler workflow works exactly the same from Contact Profiler's perspective, regardless of how the screener is presented to respondents. This has been done on purpose - it means none of the power of Contact Profiler (like fully scripted pass rules) is lost when WSC-based screeners are used.

It truly is the "best of both worlds".

Screener Integration: Step-by-Step

OK, so let's have a look at an example screener integration process by considering an example:

> "Beach Burger" has decided they want to target a specific demographic for one of their surveys, focus groups and taste tests. They want to pre-screen these people to ensure they meet the following criteria:
>
> - Female
> - Aged 18 - 39
> - Has eaten at Beach Burger in the last month

There is only one way to get people who have eaten at Beach Burger in the last month - *we need to ask people in a screener.*

Creating the Screener in WSC

Our first step is to create a survey in WSC. This survey needs to include questions to confirm a person's gender and age (just to double check that the profile data is correct) and ask when the respondent has last eaten Beach Burger.

The screener includes the following questions:

When did the Respondent last eat?

This is the question that will determine whether a respondent has eaten at Beach Burger in the last month. If they have, they will be a valid respondent and therefore will pass the screener (assuming they also meet gender and age requirements). This question has been given the access code *LASTEATEN*.

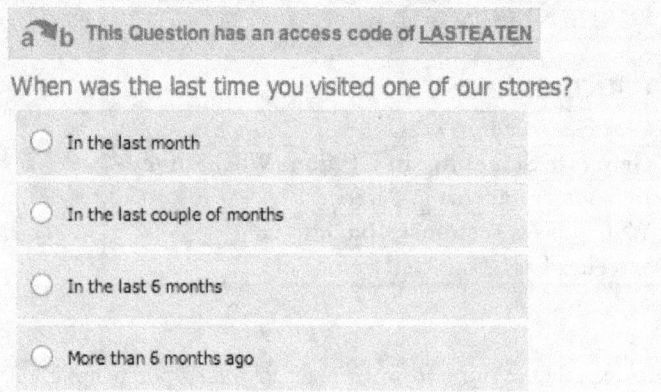

What is the Respondent's Gender?

A simple gender question with an access code of *GENDER* is asked to confirm that the respondents are female.

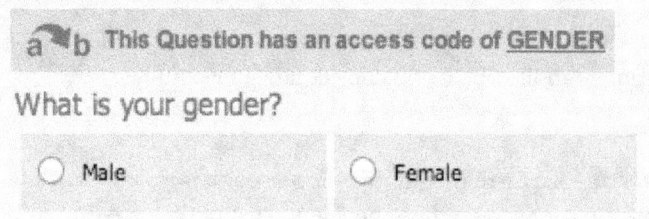

How old is the Respondent?

The possible age of the respondent is broken down into a number of age ranges. To pass the screener, respondents will need to be in the 18-39 year old age range. This question has the access code *AGE*.

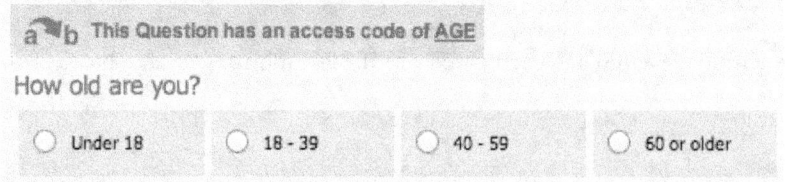

Linking the Screener to Contact Profiler

The steps for linking a Web Survey created in WSC to Contact Profiler as a screener are as follows:

1. Go to the Screener tab in the Contact Profiler job

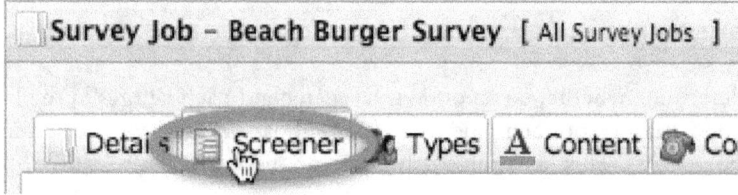

2. Click the **New WSC Screener** button

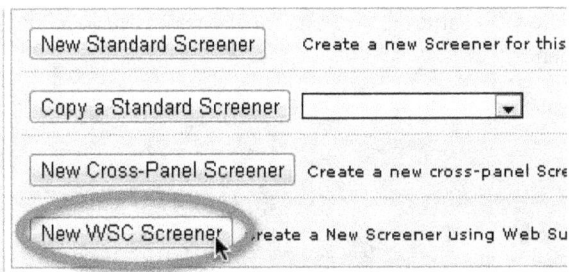

3. Choose the Survey, distribution and questions you want to include in the Screener

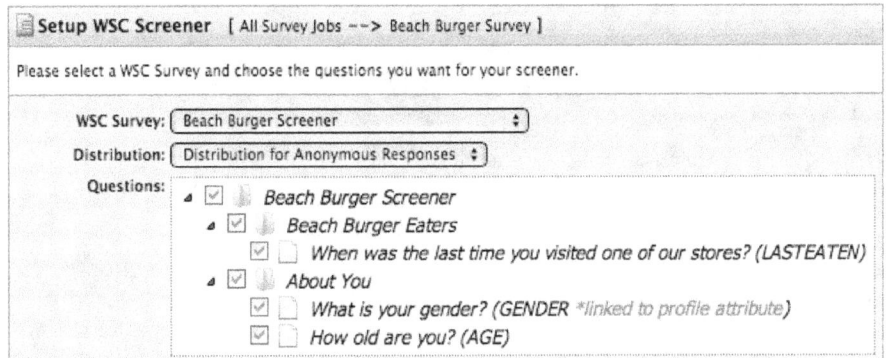

4. Click the **Create** button

The system will confirm you want to create the screener. Click the *OK* button

5. Further details for the screener must then be entered for the Screener, such as credits to receive for completing a survey. The WSC Survey URL is clearly visible on this screen for reference.

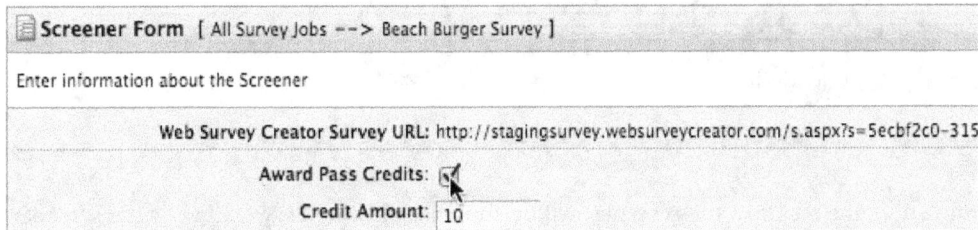

6. Once all the details have been entered, click the **Save** button

The screener is automatically generated from the WSC survey, and has the same appearance and capabilities as a standard Contact Profiler screener.

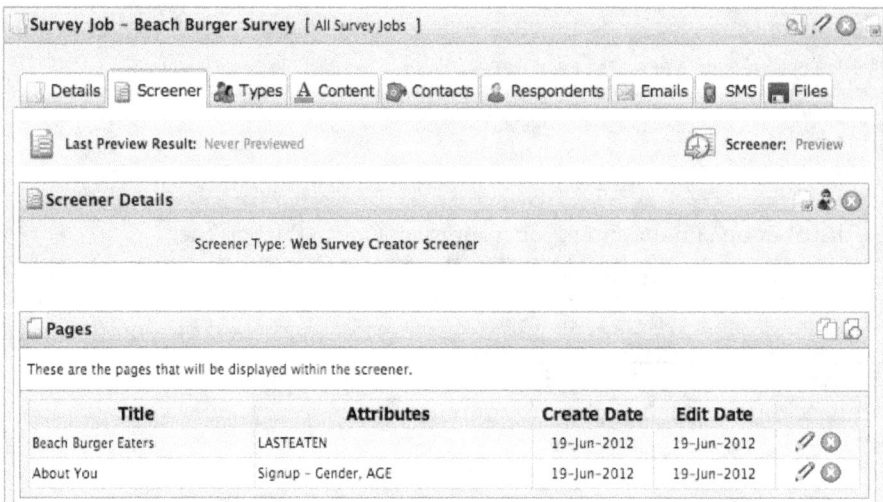

The screener can be tested by clicking the **Preview** link.

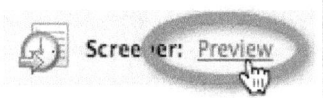

The screener is shown in a dialog, ready to be completed

Upon completion, the result of the screener will be shown - allowing easy testing of the screener pass/fail rules.

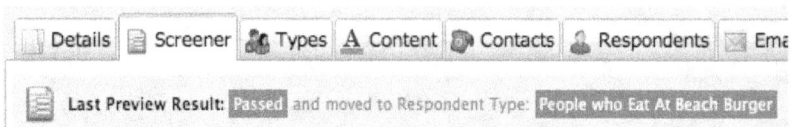

Product Testing

Product testing comes in many forms. In this chapter we will look at one example of product testing where we consider a series of car brands, and then ask specific questions about them.

This example brings together multiple advanced concepts, including page looping, data piping, flow control and choice linking.

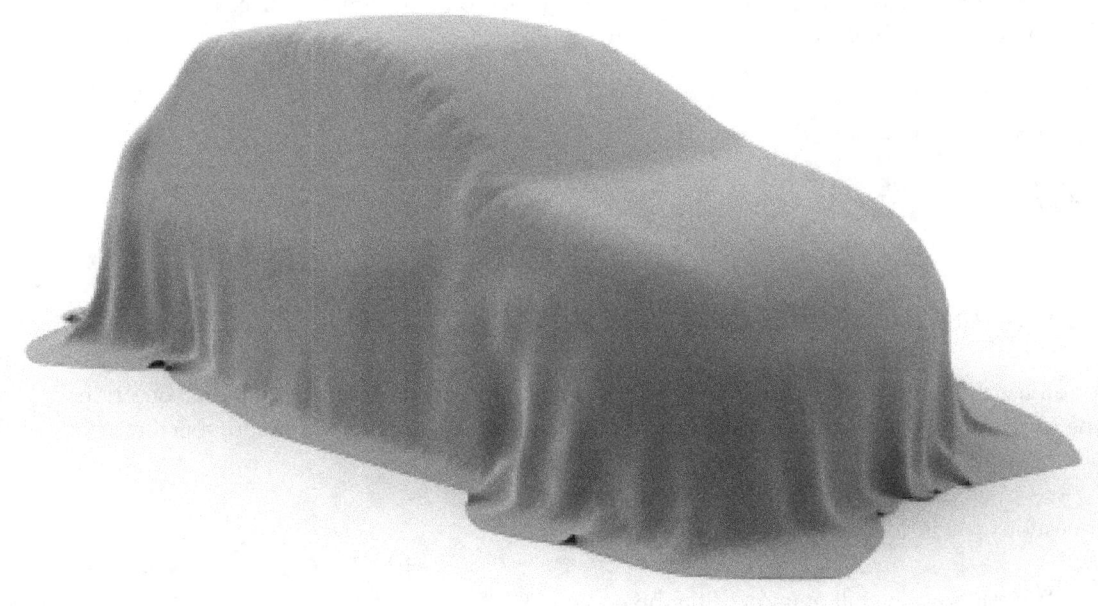

The Problem with Product Testing

Product testing can be a powerful way of finding out information about a large number of related products in a single survey.

One of the biggest issues with setting up such a survey *is* the large number of products. Let's consider an example:

> I want to product test 20 products. For each product I want 4 pages with 2 questions per page. So, what do I need to set up?
>
> **Pages:** 20 x 4 = 80 pages **Questions:** 20 x 4 x 2 = 160 questions

We can see from the example above that it doesn't take long before the setup becomes unwieldy - and it only gets worse if there is complex logic to be included as well.

Using Surveys to do Product Tests

When you create a survey for product tests, there are a number of standard processes you need to go through to set the survey up. These are briefly discussed in this section.

Note that a more detailed explanation of these processes - using the Web Survey Creator product - is the topic of the next section.

Base list of Products

A base list of the products we want to test will need to exist in our survey.

For our example, we will be using car brands as our "products". This "list" will be a question with each of the possible car brands as answers.

It is common for our base list to include a lot more information than simply a piece of text. For example, images can be used for brands:

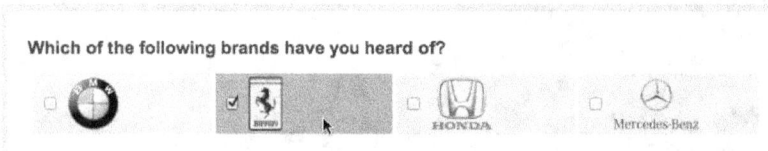

Questions for Each Product

Once you have determined that someone knows a brand, you can start asking additional questions relating to that brand. In our case, we are trying to get an overall opinion of a brand, together with specific views on products within the brand's range of cars.

Our questions will include:

1. What is your overall opinion of the brand?
2. Would you recommend this brand to your friends?
3. Have you ever owned a car from this brand?

4. Which of the following models have you owned?
5. How would you rate the car(s) you have owned from this brand?

We would want to ask these questions for each of the brands, and we would like to customize them by brand as well. How can all this be done? Through the use of advanced survey functionality!

Advanced Survey Functionality

All survey tools will allow you to ask a simple set of questions. Product testing, however, requires something much more powerful. We need:

- To be able to ask the same questions for each of the products
- To be able to refer to product-specific details - such as the product name - when we ask the questions
- To deal with advanced capabilities - like flow control - on a product-by-product basis

All of these things require advanced functionality as described below.

Page Looping

Let's consider the first question we want to ask:

What is your overall opinion of the brand?

We clearly need to ask this question for each of our brands. This question would be on it's own page.

What is your overall opinion of the brand?
○ Love it!   ○ Like it   ○ I have no opinion   ○ Don't like it   ○ Hate it!

This page would need to be "Looped" for each brand. "Looping" has two effects:

1. There will be a page for each brand asking this question
2. If someone does not chose a brand, the page relating to that brand would be automatically hidden

Flow Control

Flow Control refers to the flow of the survey. More specifically, it refers to the hiding of pages (and therefore questions) that are not needed for a particular survey.

The flow of pages that are looped for a product test will automatically be hidden when page loops are set up - but what about pages *within* the loop?

Let's consider an example. We have three questions in our list of questions as follows:

1. Have you ever owned a car from this brand?
2. Which of the following models have you owned?
3. How would you rate the car(s) you have owned from this brand?

If a respondent has never owned a car from a particular brand, there is no point rating the cars owned (since there won't be any!)

Product Testing 223

Flow control can be used to ensure invalid pages are not shown to a respondent.

Data Piping

All the questions we have are very generic. Data piping allows you to pipe answers from earlier in the survey into later survey content. For example, rather than:

What is your overall opinion of the brand?

we could have:

What is your overall opinion of BMW?

This would of course only appear in the BMW loop - the appropriate brand would be used in each of the loops. A more advanced use of data piping is the listing of models to choose from. Without data piping, the model question would have to be a generic question with a text answer.

Enter a list of models you have you owned from BMW

There is little we can do with a text list, and statistical analysis would be average at best. We will see in the next section that with data piping, we can pipe actual car models into this question, so it would look more like:

> Which of the following BWM models have you owned?
>
> - 1 Series
> - 3 Series
> - 5 Series
> - 7 Series

Choice Linking

Choice linking refers to showing a list of choices in a survey based upon a previous list.

In our example, the best use of choice linking would be to refer to the appropriate models for the question:

How would you rate the car(s) you have owned from this brand?

We could show this as a matrix, with each of the cars owned showing as a row - if I pick two models, for example, the matrix would have two rows.

How would you rate the car(s) you have owned from BMW?

	Very Good									Very Bad
	10	9	8	7	6	5	4	3	2	1
1 Series	○	○	○	○	○	○	○	○	○	○
3 Series	○	○	○	○	○	○	○	○	○	○

Product Testing Example

For the purposes of this section, we will consider an example that shows off all the key elements of a product test without getting too crazy (we'll test 4 brands - not 20!). Everything discussed can be used with real product tests of any size of course.

Our Products

In our example, our "products" will be Car Brands, and within those car brands we will be looking at four models. The car brands and models are listed below:

BRAND	Models
BMW	1 Series 3 Series 5 Series 7 Series
Ferrari	599 458 California F70
Honda	Civic Accord Odyssey NSX
Mercedes-Benz	A Class B Class C Class S Class

Product Questions

For each of the brands and models, we want to ask the following questions:

Page 1

1. What is your overall opinion of the brand?
2. Would you recommend this brand to your friends?
3. Have you ever owned a car from this brand?

Page 2

1. Which of the following models have you owned?

Page 3

1. How would you rate the car(s) you have owned from this brand?

Setting up the Product Test

We know what our products are, what models we have for each product, and what questions we are going to ask. The approach we will take will be as follows:

1. We will set up our list on products in our initial question
2. Three Pages (the **Looping Source** Pages) will be added
3. The **Product Questions** will be added to the pages
4. Flow control will be set up to ensure pages 2 and 3 are hidden for people that haven't owned a car of the particular brand
5. **Choice linking** will be used for the matrix on Page 3
6. We will use **Page Looping** to build all the pages needed to manage the Product Test
7. We will preview our product test!

Creating Our Example

We are going to build our example using Web Survey Creator. We will skip over many of the basics, as these are covered in our basic guide to Creating Web Surveys.

Our Initial Question

Setting up the initial question is very straightforward - we create a new survey, and then on the first page click **Add Content Here**.

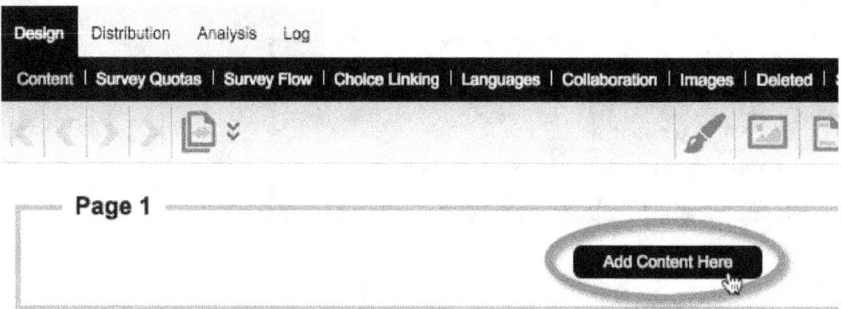

We will add a **Choice Question** with multiple values - since more than one brand can be selected.

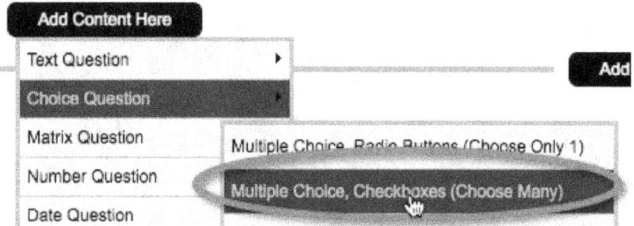

When entering our choices, we can take advantage of the quick entry of images by including the image details for each choice:

```
BMW|1|IMAGE:Car-BMW.png;;50
Ferrari|2|IMAGE:Car-Ferrari.png;;50
Honda|3|IMAGE:Car-Honda.png;;50
Mercedes-Benz|4|IMAGE:Car-Mercedes.png;;50
```

The format of an entry in the choice list is as follows:

```
Choice Text   |   Choice Value   |   IMAGE:abc.png ; width ; height
```

For our choices, we don't need either a value or an image width. By only entering the image height, we are telling the system to automatically make the width proportional to the height.

Just for looks, we are also going to show the choices on one row, and use 75% width.

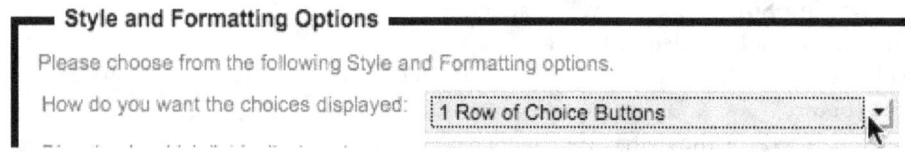

When we add the question, it looks as follows:

Which of the following brands have you every heard of?

Looping Source Pages

A "Looping Source Page" is simply a page that, when we come to creating our page loops, will be used as one of the pages that will be duplicated for each loop.

At this point, these pages are added just like any other page. We can add all three pages in one go from the **Pages** toolbar button.

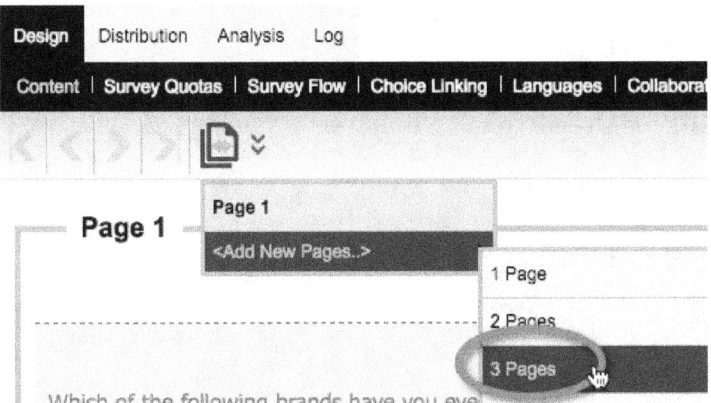

Product Questions

Our questions about the products need to be added to each of the pages in the order described earlier in this section. Adding questions is a basic procedure covered in our previous manual, so what we want to look at here are the things that are different when creating questions in preparation for our loops.

Data Piping the Brand Name

Our first question is as follows:

What is your overall opinion of the brand?

As we have discussed, we want this to be more specific to the brand we are looking at - for example:

What is your overall opinion of BMW?

This is achieved through **Data Piping**. As with any data piping, we have to start by adding a **Question Access Code** to our product question. We will give this question a code of **CARBRAND**:

Question Access Code (Optional) [Used for Data Piping, SPSS, etc]: CARBRAND

OK, so how do we use this piping? Under normal circumstances, our question would appear as follows:

What is your overall opinion of [@CARBRAND@]?

The question is, will this work? While your first instinct may be that this would be right, you need to consider how we are going to end up using this question - it will be copied 4 times - once for each of the page loops.

Data piping must be thought of differently when it is used on a page that will be copied for page looping. It must show something different for each loop.

A Data Pipe must be used that directly refers to the choice that relates to the current loop. To achieve this you must use the following syntax:

What is your overall opinion of [@CARBRAND:N@]?

When this is copied by creating a page loop, the four pages that will be generated will have the following data pipes:

What is your overall opinion of [@CARBRAND:1@]?

What is your overall opinion of [@CARBRAND:2@]?

What is your overall opinion of [@CARBRAND:3@]?

What is your overall opinion of [@CARBRAND:4@]?

These data pipes will be converted to:

What is your overall opinion of BMW?

What is your overall opinion of Ferrari?

What is your overall opinion of Honda?

What is your overall opinion of Mercedes-Benz?

Data Piping the Models for a Brand

For each brand that is chosen, a list of models needs to be shown. We need to pipe these details into the possible answers for the question:

Which of the following models have you owned?

This raises two questions:

1. Where are the models going to be stored for each of the brands?
2. How are we going to pipe these models into the question about models owned?

Let's consider the issue of storage of the models first. The answer to storing the models for a brand, and anything else that may be applicable for the brand, is to use **Choice Tags**.

These tags can contain any text data you wish. Tags have a simple structure:

`TAGNAME: Value`

Setting up tags on choices can be done by:

1. Editing the question with our choices by pressing the *Edit button*.

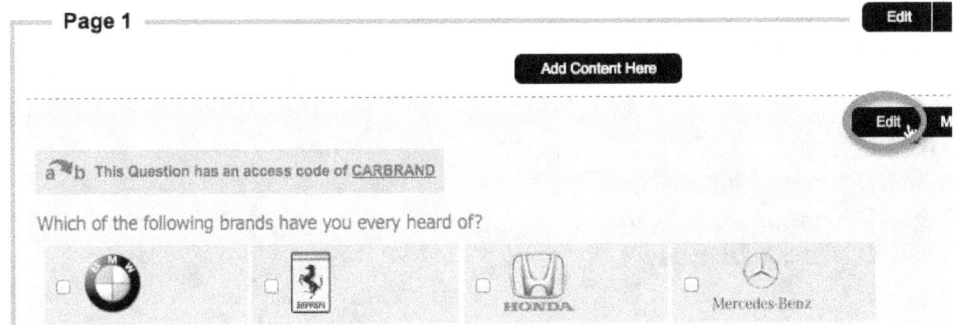

2. Editing a choice for the question.

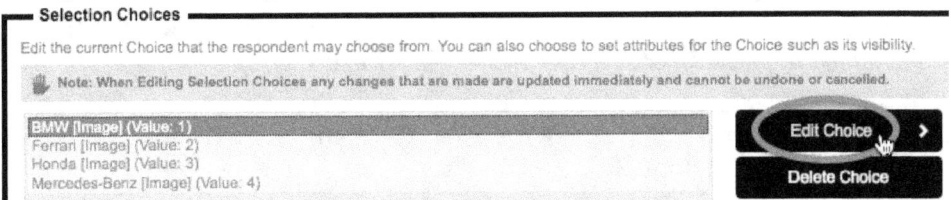

3. Enter new tags, one per line.

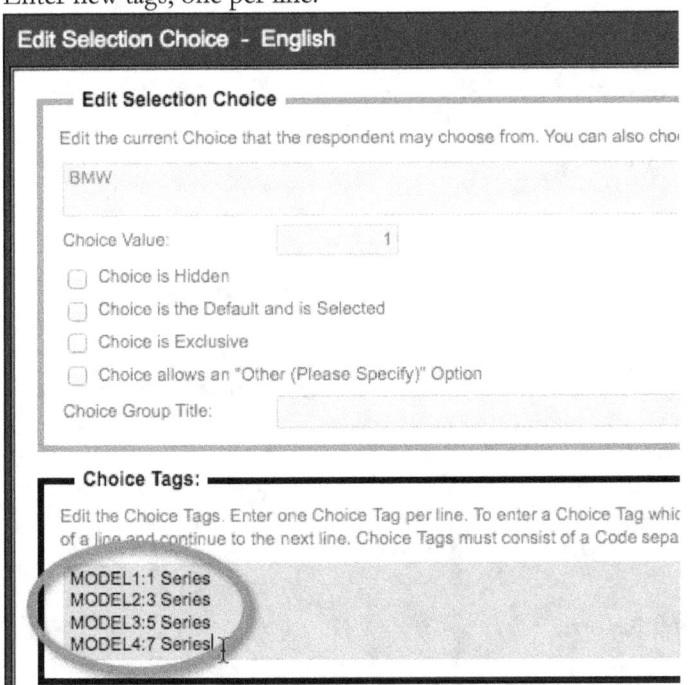

4. Saving the choice, and repeating for the other choices.

Note that tags can be added along with the other choice details when the choices are first added to - using the following format:

```
BMW|1|IMAGE:Car-BMW.png;;50|MODEL1:1 Series|MODEL2:3 Series|MODEL3:5 Series|MODEL4:7 Series
Ferrari|2|IMAGE:Car-Ferrari.png;;50|MODEL1:599|MODEL2:458|MODEL3:California|MODEL4:F70
Honda|3|IMAGE:Car-Honda.png;;50|MODEL1:Civic|MODEL2:Accord|MODEL3:Odyssey|MODEL4:NSX
Mercedes-Benz|4|IMAGE:Car-Mercedes.png;;50|MODEL1:A Class|MODEL2:B Class|MODEL3:C Class|MODEL4:S Class
```

Once we have added all our tags to our choices, they can be used through data piping.

We want to pipe into the values for the question:

Which of the following models have you owned?

We can do this by setting up the choices in this question as data-piped values:

```
[@CARBRAND:N|tag:MODEL1@]
[@CARBRAND:N|tag:MODEL2@]
[@CARBRAND:N|tag:MODEL3@]
[@CARBRAND:N|tag:MODEL4@]
```

These codes tell the system which choice to use for the data pipe, and the tag to show from that choice. The question would look as follows in the designer:

Which of the following models of [@CARBRAND:N@] have you owned?

☐ [@CARBRAND:N|tag:MODEL1@]   ☐ [@CARBRAND:N|tag:MODEL2@]   ☐ [@CAR

If a respondent chose BMW, the question would show in the survey as:

Which of the following models of BMW have you owned?

☐ 1 Series   ☐ 3 Series   ☐ 5 S

Flow Control

Flow control is used to hide pages based on answers in a survey. In our example, we have the following questions:

> **Page 1**
>
> ...Have you ever owned a car from this brand?
>
> **Page 2**
>
> Which of the following models have you owned?
>
> **Page 3**
>
> How would you rate the car(s) you have owned from this brand?

Clearly pages 2 and 3 need to be hidden if the respondent has never owned a car from the brand. Page 3 will also need to be hidden if the respondent owned none of the models listed on page 2.

Before we set up survey flow, there is one piece of "housekeeping" we will do to make the setup of flows easier.

> Flow Control and page looping both refer to pages as part of their setup. The time has come to name our pages to make them easier to distinguish.

Renaming pages is simply a matter of editing each page as follows:

1. We ensure we are on the page we want to name

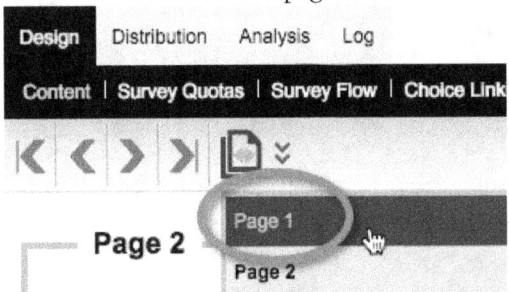

2. We click the *Edit button* to edit the page details

3. We enter the new name for the page, and save it

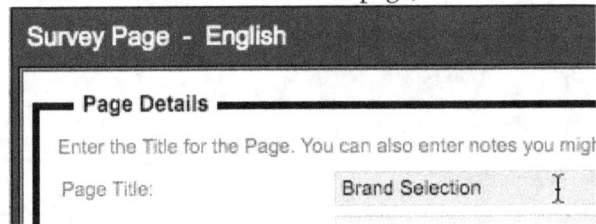

4. The new page name will be visible at the top of the page

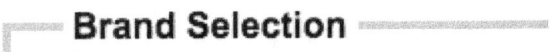

We will change all our page names as follows:

Page 1	Brand Selection
Page 2	Brand Opinion
Page 3	Models Owned
Page 4	Model Opinion

We are now ready to set up our flows. Flow control can all be set from the *Survey Flow* menu in Web Survey Creator.

We can to add each flow by:

Product Testing 231

1. Clicking on the **Survey Flow** menu

   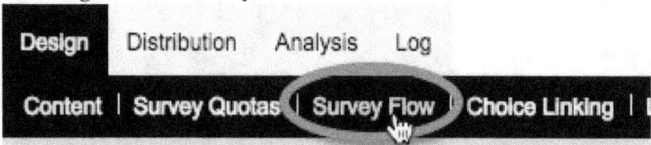

2. Clicking the **New Survey Flow** button on the toolbar

   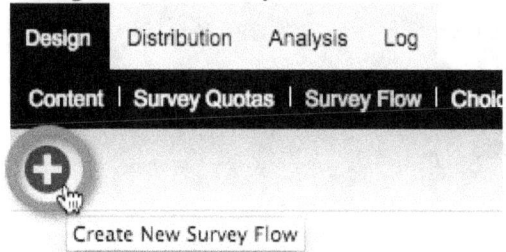

3. Choosing the pages we want to hide for the flow

   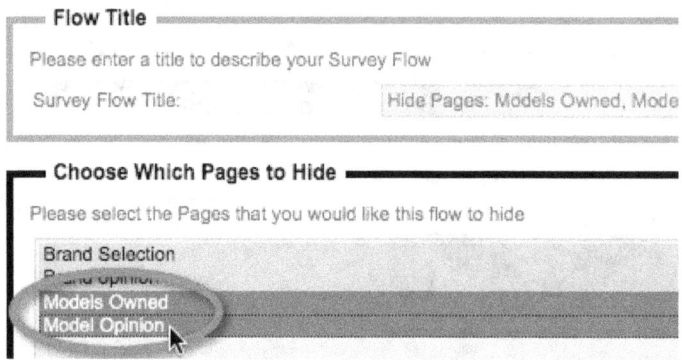

4. Choosing the rule to use to hide the pages chosen

   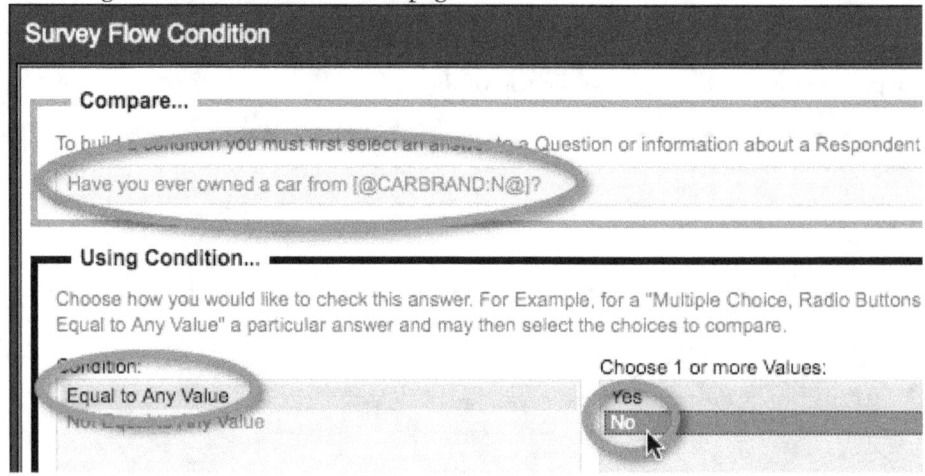

The flow relating to models can be created in the same way. The rule we would apply for hiding the "Model Opinion" page would be to check if none of the models were selected.

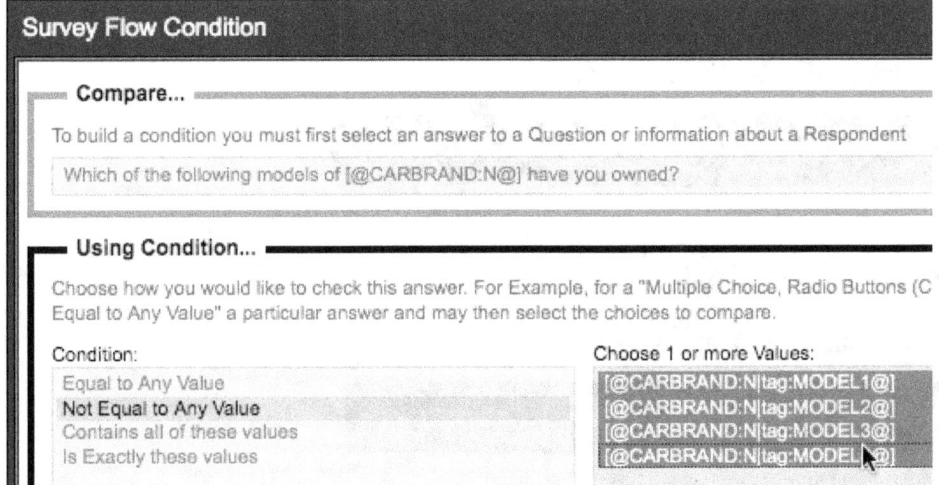

Choice Linking

Choice linking is used to only display appropriate choices in a question based on choices made earlier in the survey. The best way to understand this is to consider our example.

We have a question about models that can look as follows:

If we answer that we have owned a 1-Series and a 3-Series, it doesn't make sense for the next question to be:

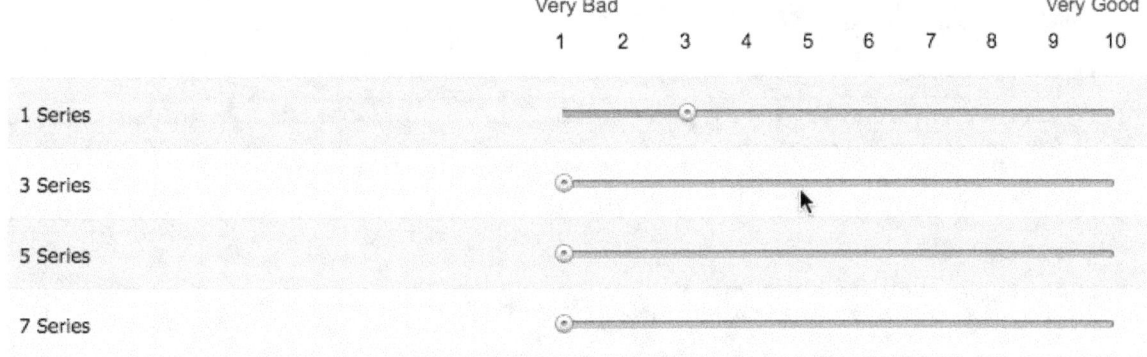

It doesn't make sense to ask about 5-Series and 7-Series models, because I have indicated I have never owned them. This is where **Choice Linking** is used - we only want to show rows in the matrix for the models that have actually been chosen.

We set up choice linking by:

1. Clicking on the **Choice Linking** menu

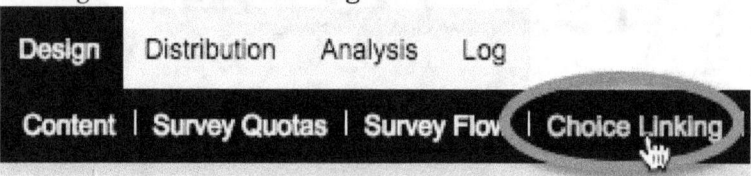

2. Clicking the **New Choice Link** button

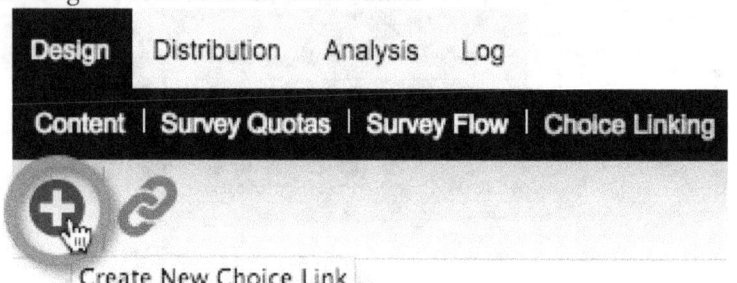

3. Set up the Choice Link

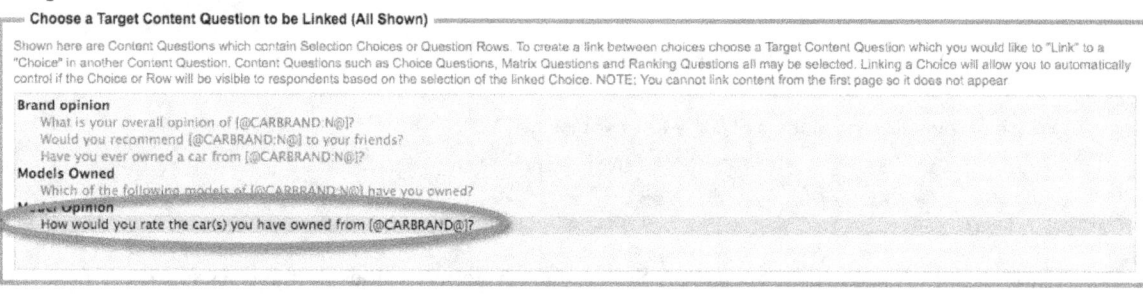

4. Accept the assistance to complete choice links for other choices

> The Source and Target selections you have made appear to be related or at least have the same number of options and you have selected the first option in each selection. Would you like to add all the options for the LINKED CHOICES as Choice Links?
>
> Click OK to Add all combinations of CHOICES OR Cancel to only add the single selection.
>
> Cancel   OK

We now have a four-page survey with all the content we need to create our Page Loops.

Building the Page Loops

Setting up Page Loops is all about preparation. Everything we have done so far in this section provides an indication of the sort of preparation that is necessary.

Setting up of Page Loops themselves is always the last thing you should do in your design. Page Looping is effectively a massive copy operation, so anything you have missed prior to building the loops will be missed in every single loop.
Check and double check your work!

Building Page Loops is a very straightforward process. To build them we:

1. Click on the **Page Loop** toolbar button and choose **Create Page Loop** from the drop-down menu

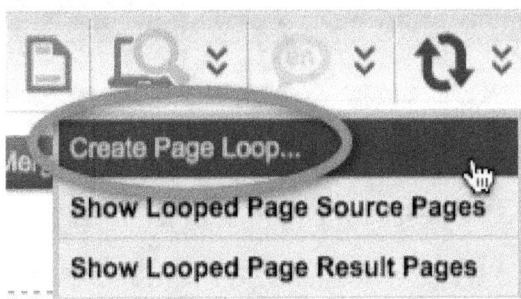

2. Choose the **Brand Question** as the basis for the loop, and the three brand pages for looping

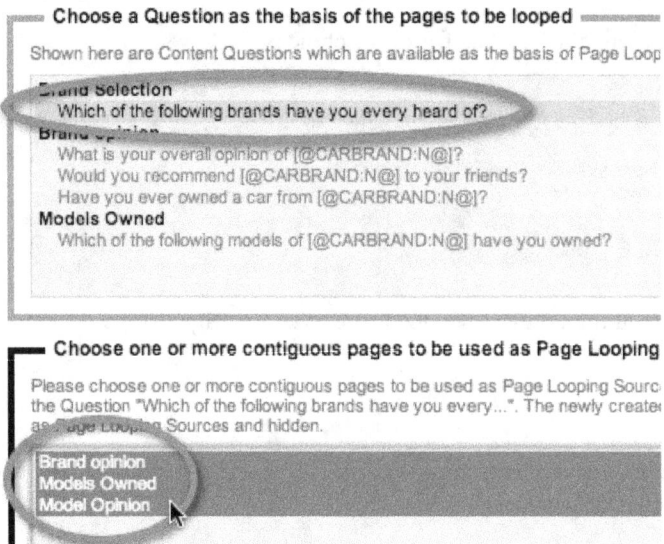

3. Click the **Create New Page Loop** button

4. We will be returned immediately to the **Design** tab - the looped pages will be created in the background. A warning message will show indicating that the looped pages are not yet created.

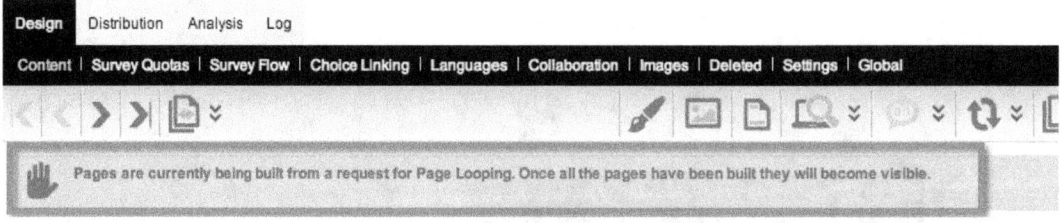

5. Once the process is completed, the warning will disappear, and we will be left with our looped pages in our design

Page Looping - What just happened?!

It is important to understand exactly what happens when we use page looping. Let's consider what happened to the four pages we had in our "pre-looped" survey.

Brand Selection Page

This page remained exactly as it was - it was not looped itself. Other pages were looped based on what the brand question on this page had as choices.

Original Opinion Pages

Our original pages are still in the survey. They formed the basis of all the looped pages. They are exactly like they always were, except:

- They are now flagged as "Looped Source" pages
- They are now hidden

These pages will never be shown to a respondent. They are kept in the survey mainly as a backup - if you ever need to delete your looped pages, and recreate them, you will want to recreate them from these original pages.

Looped Opinion Pages

Brand Opinion (BMW) [Loop Result]	Brand Opinion (Honda) [Loop Result]
Models Owned (BMW) [Loop Result]	Models Owned (Honda) [Loop Result]
Model Opinion (BMW) [Loop Result]	Model Opinion (Honda) [Loop Result]
Brand Opinion (Ferrari) [Loop Result]	Brand Opinion (Mercedes-Benz) [Loop Result]
Models Owned (Ferrari) [Loop Result]	Models Owned (Mercedes-Benz) [Loop Result]
Model Opinion (Ferrari) [Loop Result]	Model Opinion (Mercedes-Benz) [Loop Result]

These are the pages that have been created for each of the choices in the source question. They use the original name of the page as part of the page name (another good reason we named these pages properly) together with the value of each of the choices that the pages have been copied for.

What do I do with all these pages?

It's not hard to see that the number of pages shown in a survey can grow very quickly if page loops based on a large number of choices are set up. This can get unwieldy very quickly. Fortunately you can turn Loop Source Pages and Loop Result Pages off very easily from the **Page Loop** toolbar button.

If we turned off Page Loop Result Pages, our list of pages looks very familiar to the pre-looping design.

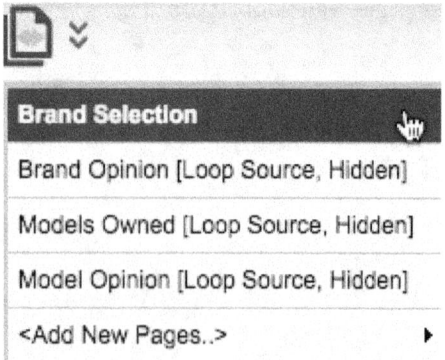

Note that you cannot do certain functions, like Page merging or moving, unless all pages are shown.

Page Looping DOs and DON'Ts

DO ensure you have set up all flows, piping and choice linking in the pages that will be included in the loop

DON'T modify loop result pages unless you have a specific reason for doing so. Any changes will ONLY be made on that one specific page

DON'T add or remove looped pages in a piecemeal fashion if you can avoid it.

DO delete all loop result pages and rebuild the entire page loop if there are changes to the source question (assuming there are no responses)

Introduction to Scripting

The most advanced Web Survey Creation tools available today can provide an amazing amount of functionality through a simple, non-technical interface.

There are times, however, when very specific "one-off" functionality is needed in a survey. This is when scripting is needed.

What is Scripting?

For the purposes of this manual, we will only be considering scripting from the point of view of creating Web Surveys. All scripting in Web Survey Creator is created in **JavaScript**.

> Scripting is simply a method of describing survey logic, or manipulating the survey interface, using an english-like "scripting language".

When you use a script, you "explain" to the software how something needs to be performed in a powerful language, rather than using a pre-defined interface (which is limited to only allowing you to do whatever the interface was originally designed for).

To Script or not to Script?

Scripting is great when there is no other way to achieve something. If there is another way, however, scripting adds complexity that would be good to avoid.

Scripting should only be used for functionality that is not possible through the standard survey design interface.

The good	The bad
Scripting is much more powerful than using a standard interface	You need to build the logic of the script yourself
Complex problems can be solved through scripting	You must understand the functions available and how to use them. You are responsible for ensuring the script is bug-free
All of the standard capabilities of JavaScript are available	There is a lot to learn to be able to benefit from all JavaScript has to offer

Let's consider a simple example. I have a choice question as follows:

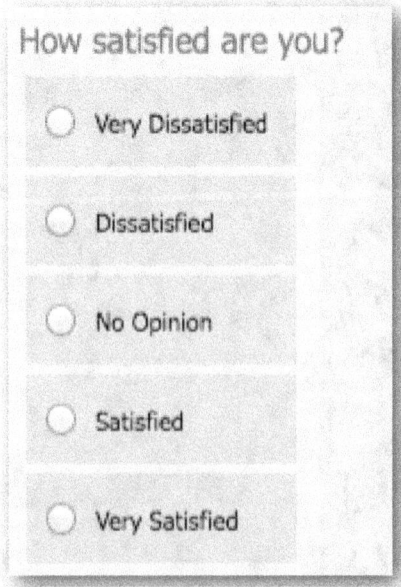

If I want this question to default to the answer "No Opinion", I can select this answer in script as follows:

```
var question = wscScripting.getQuestionByDataPipingCode('HOWSATISFIED');

if (question) {

    var choice = wscScripting.getChoiceByValue(question, 3);

    if (choice) {

        var isSelected = wscScripting.selectChoice(question, choice);   } }
```

While this will work, it's a pretty complex way to set the value of the question. The easy way to do this is simply to make the "No Opinion" value a default value in the question:

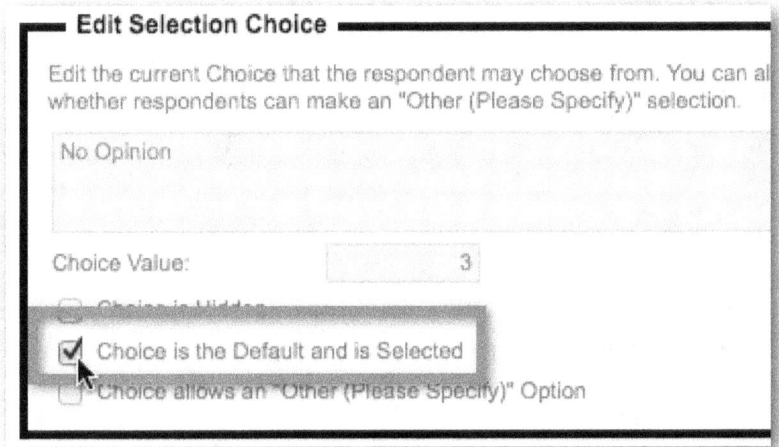

This is an example of a simple rule when it comes to scripting:

> Just because you can do something in scripting doesn't necessarily mean you should.
> Only use scripting to create functionality that is not available
> to you in a non-scripted way.

An Introduction to JavaScript

JavaScript is designed to add interactivity to Web pages. It is a lightweight programming language (also known as a "scripting language") that is embedded into Web pages.

Web Survey Creator was designed to use JavaScript for scripting for a number of reasons.

JavaScript is the most popular

JavaScript is the most popular scripting language on the Internet. This means that there are a large number of people who already know how to use it - if you don't, chances are you will easily be able to find someone who does.

This popularity is due in part to how easy it is to use JavaScript, so even if you don't know how to write in JavaScript yet, it won't take long to learn.

JavaScript works Everywhere

JavaScript works in all major browsers - for both PCs and mobile devices, including:

- Internet Explorer
- Firefox
- Chrome
- Safari
- Opera

This is important, because it means the scripts you write for your surveys will work everywhere.

JavaScript can react to Events

When adding a script to a survey, it is important to be able to control when a script is performed. For example, you may want to run a script as soon as a survey page is loaded.

JavaScript can react to events, so this sort of control is easy. Web Survey Creator allows you to choose when a script is run, including:

- When a Page is Loaded
- When Survey Quota Data is Loaded
- Testing visibility of Next or Submit buttons
- Before a Survey Page is Validated
- When Next or Submit buttons are pressed
- When Previous buttons are pressed

In addition to this, JavaScript can "hook in" to events like a radio button being pressed, or text being typed into a text field. This makes it possible to provide a high level of interactivity, as we will see later in this book.

JavaScript Basics

Before venturing into the world of Web Surveys, it is important to understand the fundamental concepts when using JavaScript.

The <script> tag

JavaScript is always contained within a <script> tag. Below is an example with a single line of JavaScript.

```
<script type="text/javascript">
document.getElementById("demo").innerHTML=Date();
</script>
```

Web Survey Creator includes the <script> tag automatically whenever you use script, so you will never need to put this tag in your own scripts.

JavaScript is Case Sensitive

Unlike some scripting languages, and HTML itself, JavaScript is <u>case sensitive</u>.

If you have written a piece of JavaScript and it looks right but is not working, the first thing to check is that you don't have the case wrong for any of the functions or variables.

Let's consider a simple piece of JavaScript that writes "Hello World" to the browser:

```
document.write("Hello World");
```

If this had been entered as follows, it simply wouldn't work:

```
document.Write("Hello World");
```

The only difference here is the capitalization of "Write".

```
document.Write("Hello World");
```

You can see how easy it would be to overlook this error. When using any JavaScript function - including the specialized functions that have been created for Web Survey Creator, always follow a simple rule...

> Always use the correct case for everything in your scripts!

JavaScript Code Essentials

JavaScript code is a sequence of JavaScript statements. They are executed in the order that they are written. It is best practice to end each statement with a semi-colon.

```
document.write("Hello World");
document.write("This is written with JavaScript!");
```

Inserting Comments

If an explanation is needed, comments can be added to a script by starting a line with //.

```
// Let's write something to the browser...
document.write("Hello World");
document.write("This is written with JavaScript!");
```

If you want to add multiple lines of comments, you can start with /* and end with */.

```
/*
Let's write something to the browser...
This will add multiple lines to the browser
*/
document.write("Hello World");
document.write("This is written with JavaScript!");
```

JavaScript Variables

JavaScript *variables* are used to hold values or expressions. A variable can have a short name, like *x*, or a more descriptive name, like *FavoriteColor*.

It is important to note that:

- Variable names are case sensitive (y and Y are two different variables)
- Variable names must begin with a letter, the $ character, or the underscore character
- Variables are declared with the *var* keyword.

```
var x;
var FavoriteColor;
```

After the declaration of a variable they are empty (they have no values yet). You can, however, assign values to the variables when you declare them:

```
var x = 100;
var FavoriteColor = "Red";
```

As we will see later when we start building scripts, variables can be manipulated in various ways. For example, you can do arithmetic operations with variables:

```
var y = x - 100;
var z = y + 100;
```

JavaScript Arithmetic Operators

Operator	Description	Example	Result
+	Addition	x=y+2	x=7 y=5
-	Subtraction	x=y-2	x=3 y=2
*	Multiplication	x=y*2	x=10 y=5
/	Division	x=y/2	x=2.5 y=5
%	Modulus (remainder)	x=y%2	x=1 y=5

Using the + Operator with Strings

When dealing with strings, the + operator can be used to join two or more strings. For example:

```
txt1="The weather looks";
txt2="pretty good today";
txt3=txt1+" "+txt2;
```

The result of this script is that the variable *txt3* will contain the text "The weather looks pretty good today".

JavaScript Comparison Operators

Let's assume we have a variable *x=5*.

Operator	Description	Example
==	is equal to	x==5 is true
===	is exactly equal to (value and type)	x===5 is true x==="5" is false
!=	is not equal	x!=8 is true
>	is greater than	x>8 is false
<	is less than	x<8 is true
>=	is greater than or equal to	x>=5 is true
<=	is less than or equal to	x<=4 is false

Comparison operators can be used in conditional statements to compare values and take action depending on the result.

We will see this in action when we start writing some scripts.

JavaScript Logical Operators

Let's assume we have a variable *x=6* and *y=3*.

Operator	Description	Example
&&	and	(x < 10 && y > 1) is true
||	or	(x==5 || y==5) is false
!	not	!(x==y) is true

The JavaScript Conditional Operator

JavaScript also contains a conditional operator that assigns a value to a variable based on some condition.

```
variablename=(condition)?value1:value2
```

For example:

```
var visitor="PRES";
var greeting=(visitor=="PRES")?"Dear President ":"Dear ";
document.write(greeting);
```

JavaScript Conditional Statements

Conditional statements are used to do different things in your script when different rules are met.

In JavaScript the following conditional statements can be used:

if statement - use this statement to execute some code only if a specified condition is true

Introduction to Scripting 247

if...else statement - use this statement to execute some code if the condition is true and another code if the condition is false

if...else if....else statement - use this statement to select one of many blocks of code to be executed

switch statement - use this statement to select one of many blocks of code to be executed

An example of a conditional statement is as follows:

```
var d = new Date()
var time = d.getHours()
if (time<10)
   {
   document.write("<b>Good morning</b>");
   }
else if (time>=10 && time<16)
   {
   document.write("<b>Good day</b>");
   }
else
   {
   document.write("<b>Hello World!</b>");
   }
```

The use of a *switch statement* can be a very efficient way to run the appropriate piece of code in your script.

This is how it works...

First we have a single expression n (most often a variable) that is evaluated once. The value of the expression is then compared with the values for each case in the structure. If there is a match, the block of code associated with that case is executed. Use break to prevent the code from running into the next case automatically.

```
//You will receive a different greeting based
//on what day it is. Note that Sunday=0,
//Monday=1, Tuesday=2, etc.

var d=new Date();
var theDay=d.getDay();
switch (theDay)
{
case 5:
  document.write("Finally Friday");
  break;
case 6:
  document.write("Super Saturday");
  break;
case 0:
  document.write("Sleepy Sunday");
  break;
default:
  document.write("I'm looking forward to this weekend!");
}
```

JavaScript Loops

Often when you write code, you want the same block of code to run over and over again in a row. Instead of adding several almost equal lines in a script we can use loops to perform a task like this.

In JavaScript, there are two different kind of loops:

for - loops through a block of code a specified number of times

while - loops through a block of code while a specified condition is true

The format of a *for loop* is as follows:

```
for (variable=startvalue;variable<=endvalue;variable=variable+increment)
{
code to be executed
}
```

Here is an example of a *for loop*:

```
var i=0;
for (i=0;i<=5;i++)
{
document.write("The number is " + i);
document.write("<br />");
}
```

A *while loop* has a simpler structure. The format of a *while loop* is as follows:

```
while (variable<=endvalue)
  {
  code to be executed
  }
```

Here is an example of a *while loop*:

```
var i=0;
while (i<=5)
  {
  document.write("The number is " + i);
  document.write("<br />");
  i++;
  }
```

A variation of the *while loop* is the *do...while loop*. This will execute the block of code <u>once</u>, and then repeat it for as long as the specified condition is true.

Introduction to Scripting

```
var i=0;
do
  {
  document.write("The number is " + i);
  document.write("<br />");
  i++;
  }
while (i<=5);
```

The *break statement* will break the loop and continue executing the code that follows after the loop (if any).

```
var i=0;
for (i=0;i<=10;i++)
  {
  if (i==3)
    {
    break;
    }
  document.write("The number is " + i);
  document.write("<br />");
  }
```

The *continue statement* will break the current loop and continue with the next value.

```
var i=0
for (i=0;i<=10;i++)
  {
  if (i==3)
    {
    continue;
    }
  document.write("The number is " + i);
  document.write("<br />");
  }
```

Adding Scripting in WSC

Web Survey Creator allows scripting to be added like any other survey content. If you know how to add a question, you know how to add scripting!

Scripting is an extremely powerful feature, and is designed to be used in the two highest versions of the software - the MR Premium and MR Ultimate editions.

MR Premium
Solo
Our Premium MR Plan

Single User

Unlimited Respondents

Unlimited Questions

10,000 Responses/Month *

30,000 Responses/Quarter *

120,000 Responses/Year *

MR Ultimate
Solo
The Ultimate MR Plan

Single User

Unlimited Respondents

Unlimited Questions

20,000 Responses/Month *

60,000 Responses/Quarter *

240,000 Responses/Year *

WSC Scripting Objects

Scripts written in WSC have access to two specialized objects. These objects allow you access to the questions that are exposed on the current page and additional help methods that can help you to perform various tasks.

1. args
2. wscScripting

args

args contains a single item isValid that can be used to set the status of an event. This is particularly relevant for confirming to the event engine that you wish to continue the current process. For example, you must set the value to true on Next or Previous Button events or those processes are halted and will not continue.

Property:	isValid
Return Value:	boolean - Is the current process Valid

Example:	var isOkay = true;
	if (isOkay) {
	    // All my changes allow me to continue
	    args.isValid = true;
	}

wscScripting

The wscScripting object provides access to all the custom methods that have been set up for use in your scripts. These methods will be discussed in detail throughout this book.

How to Use a Question in Scripting

Scripting in a survey inevitably will need access to the basic elements in any survey - the questions. Accessing a question from within a script requires that the question is set up correctly.

There is only one thing you need to do to a question to make it ready for scripting - give the question a **Question Access Code**.

There are a few simple rules when adding access codes:

1. Each code must be unique to a particular question
2. Codes can only be characters and numbers, with no spaces
3. Codes must be at least 2 characters in length
4. Codes are enforced as upper case

Accessing a question is a simple process once the access code is set. A call to *getQuestionByDataPipingCode* returns the question object in the script.

```
// Get the question to load the value from
var oFromTextQ = wscScripting.getQuestionByDataPipingCode('FROMQU');
```

How to add Scripting to a Survey

Adding a Scripting Question in Web Survey Creator is similar to adding any other content in the system. The steps are as follows:

1. Press the **Add Content Here** button in the Survey Designer to add new content.

2. Choose **JavaScript Script Question** as the type of content you wish to add from the **Add Content Here** button menu.

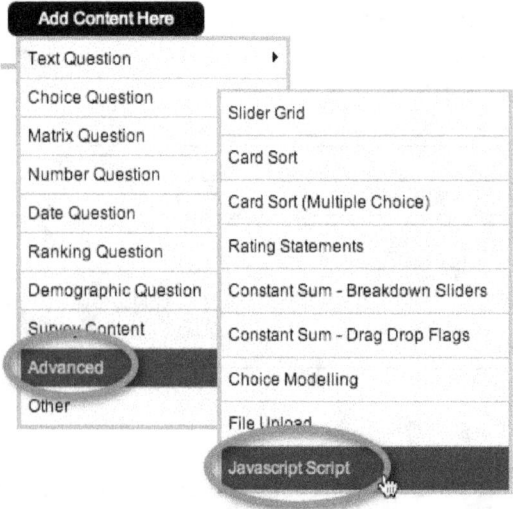

The content to be set consists of four parts:

1. **A description for the script** (straight text)
2. **Whether to show a container for the question**. You should show a container when you what to script something that shows on the survey page (as opposed to just scripting "behind the scenes" logic)

   ☐ Show a Content Container for this Javascript to use

3. **A choice for when the script will be executed**. We will see in later chapters the reasons for choosing different execution times.

   - ✓ Execute Javascript when Survey Page has Loaded
   - Execute Javascript when Survey Quota Data has been Loaded
   - Execute Javascript to Test Visibility of Next or Submit Buttons
   - **Execute Javascript before Survey Page is Validated**
   - Execute Javascript when Next or Submit Buttons are Pressed
   - Execute Javascript when Previous Button is Pressed
   - Execute Javascript to Test Randomization Parameters prior to Next Button

4. **The content of the script itself.** As previously mentioned, this is standard JavaScript without the <script> tag (or function references) - it is effectively the "guts" of the script we want to use. WSC will encapsulate it correctly on the page.

   ```
   Javascript to be Executed
   Enter the Javascript to be executed. This script will be executed at point selected.
   1  // Get the EMAIL question using it's data code
   2  var oQuestion1 = wscScripting.getQuestionByDataPipingCode('EMAIL');
   3  // Check if it is valid
   4
   5  // Mark it as initially false
   6  args.isValid = false;
   7
   8  if (oQuestion1) {
   ```

That's it! Once added, a script will be executed by WSC at the time you have chosen.

The hard part is ensuring you know how to write the script. That is the subject of the rest of this book. Happy scripting!

Scripting #101:
Dealing with Data

One of the most common uses of scripting is to perform some logic based upon responses entered into survey questions. This requires data to be "read" by a script.

It is also common to modify the data entered in a survey through scripting. This requires data to be "written" by a script. This chapter discusses how to "read" and "write" survey data through scripting.

Working with Data in Scripting

Loading and saving survey data with scripting is relatively simple. There are a couple of basic rules you must understand, however, before diving into scripting.

Rule #1: Script for each Question Type

The type of question determines how loading & saving must be implemented in script.

For example, a *text question* simply stores a piece of text, therefore the script to load and save values looks as follows:

```
// Get the question to load the value from
var oFromTextQ = wscScripting.getQuestionByDataPipingCode('FROMQU');
// Get the value from the question
var oGetValue = wscScripting.getValue(oFromTextQ);

// Get the question to write the value to
var oToTextQ = wscScripting.getQuestionByDataPipingCode('TOQU');
// Save the value to the question
wscScripting.setValue(oToTextQ, oGetValue);
```

The script above is very straightforward, since a text question has a single text value. Let's consider a *multi-selection choice question*, however. The answer to this type of question can be multiple choices.

In order to get the value from one multiple choice question and save it to a new multiple choice question, we would need to do more work than we had to do for the text question. We would need to loop through all the possible choices and work out which choices were selected. These choices would then need to be selected in the new question.

```
// Get the question to load the value from
var oFromTextQ = wscScripting.getQuestionByDataPipingCode('FROMQU');
// Get the value from the question
var oGetValue = wscScripting.getValue(oFromTextQ);

// Get the question to write the value to
var oToTextQ = wscScripting.getQuestionByDataPipingCode('TOQU');
// Save the value to the question
wscScripting.setValue(oToTextQ, oGetValue);

// Get the question to load the value from
var oFromMultiChoice = wscScripting.getQuestionByDataPipingCode('FROMQU');
// Get the question to write the value to
var oToMultiChoice = wscScripting.getQuestionByDataPipingCode('TOQU');

// Loop through the values in the question
for (i=1; i<=oToMultiChoice.choices.length; i++)
{
  // See if the value is selected in the from question
    var oSelected = wscScripting.isChoiceSelectedByValue(oFromMultiChoice, i);
    if (oSelected)
    {
     // The value was selected - make it selected in the to question
      wscScripting.selectChoiceByValue(oToMultiChoice, i);
    }
}
```

As we can see, it's a bit more complex for the more complex question types. The principles are the same however - you just have to methodically work through the correct way to deal with the data.

Rule #2: Data Location effects Script syntax

Dealing with question data through scripting has to work within the technical boundaries set by how JavaScript operates.

So what does this mean exactly?

JavaScript scripting runs on the browser. While technically speaking, JavaScript could access data from anywhere, speed and security considerations dictate that scripting can only get to data that is available on the current page.

Getting Data for Questions on the Current Page

If we are restricted to getting data from the current page, questions on the current page should be easy to get to, right?

Absolutely!

In fact, the previous examples all access data from questions on the current page. And regardless of the question type, getting the question is always the same:

```
// Get the question to load the value from
var oFromTextQ = wscScripting.getQuestionByDataPipingCode('FROMQU');
```

This is really easy. Unfortunately it's also relatively useless in real-world use, since you will almost always want to load data from a question that is <u>not</u> on the current page...

Getting Data for Questions on a Previous Page

If you are wishing to read up the data for a question, more often than not this question will appear on a *prior page of the survey*. The data for this question will not be available on the current page, because the question is not on the current page.

To access data for a question on a previous page, the script needs to explicitly indicate that the data will need to be loaded. If we look at our previous example, the script would need to change as follows if the question was on a prior page:

```
// Get the question to load the value from
var oFromTextQ = wscScripting.getQuestionByDataPipingCode('[@FROMQU#DATA#@]');
```

The code for the question takes the format of a data piping code if the question is on a different page. This tells the system that is has to load the data for this question onto this page because the script is going to need it.

Apart from the syntax for the code to access the question, everything else works exactly the same in the script.

Reading and Writing Data – the Basics

So far we have looked at script fragments to explain some basic scripting functionality. Now let's look in detail at *full scripts* for read and write data to and from questions with scripting.

For the purposes of these examples, we will use the simplest question type for scripting - text questions.

Writing Data to a Text Question

Let's look at all the steps needed to write data to a question in a survey - starting from the beginning.

Creating a Text Question

The creation of questions is covered earlier in this book, but the key steps are:

1. Press the **Add Content Here** button.

2. Choose a **Single Line Text** question.

    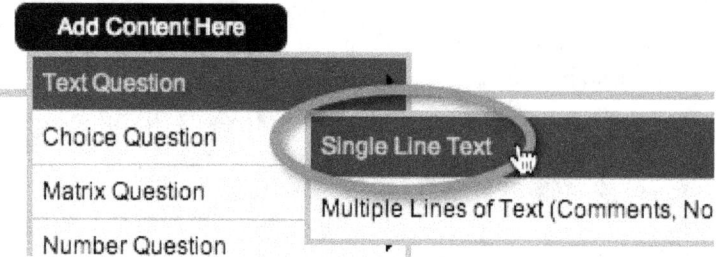

3. Enter a **Question Access Code** for the question. Note that this code is used in scripting - without it, this question can <u>not</u> be accessed in a script.

    Question Access Code (Optional) [Used for Data Piping, SPSS, etc]: CARBRAND

4. Enter the **Question Text**.

    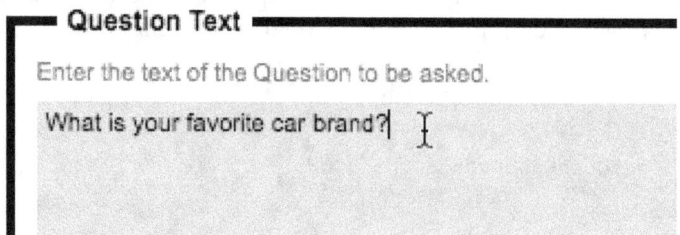

5. Press the *Save Content* button.

The question will be shown in the designer. The unique access code is displayed prominently above the question.

258 Scripting #101: Dealing with Data

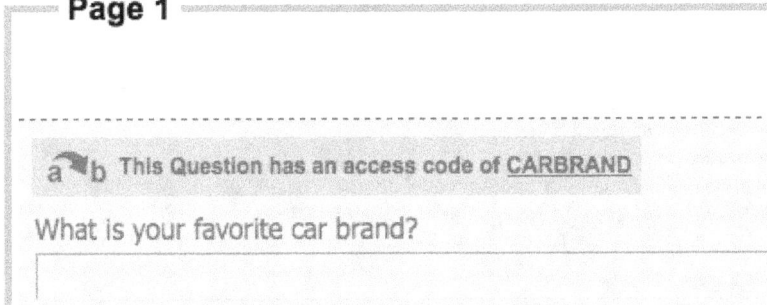

Writing Data to a Text Question

To write data to our text question, we need to add some scripting. Let's assume that we want to set the text question to "I don't know" when the page loads.

The steps to set up this script are as follows:

1. Press the **Add Content Here** button.

2. Choose a **Javascript Script Question**.

   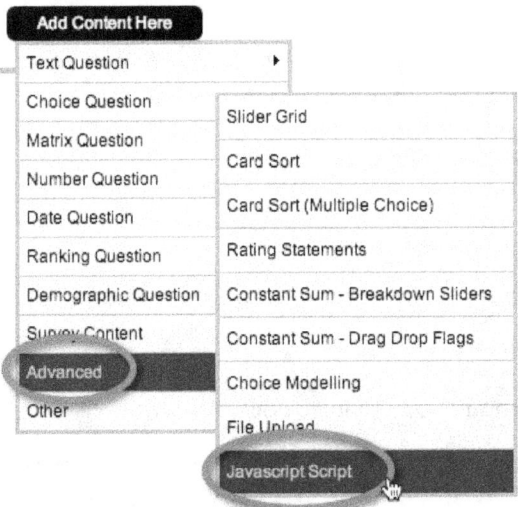

3. Enter a brief explanation of the script.

   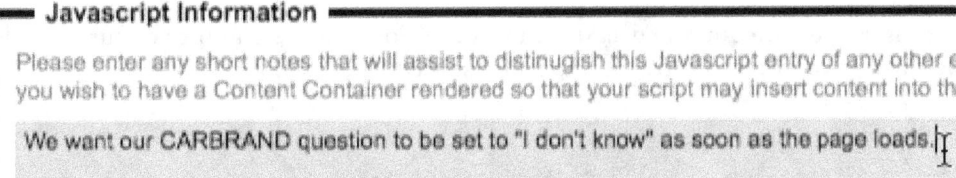

4. We don't want to create any custom interface on the survey page using the script, so we <u>don't</u> need a content container.

   ☐ Show a Content Container for this Javascript to use

5. Choose to execute the script when the page is loaded.

```
✓ Execute Javascript when Survey Page has Loaded
  Execute Javascript when Survey Quota Data has been Loaded
  Execute Javascript to Test Visibility of Next or Submit Buttons
  Execute Javascript before Survey Page is Validated
  Execute Javascript when Next or Submit Buttons are Pressed
  Execute Javascript when Previous Button is Pressed
  Execute Javascript to Test Randomization Parameters prior to Next Button
```

6. Enter the script.

```javascript
// Get the question
var oTextQuestion = wscScripting.getQuestionByDataPipingCode('CARBRAND');

if (oTextQuestion) // The question was loaded successfully
{

    // Set the question value. Note the use of \' in the text, since
    // using ' in a string is not directly allowed
    wscScripting.setValue(oTextQuestion, 'I don\'t know');

}

// Always return true unless you want to indicate a failure
// in the script
args.isValid = true;
```

7. Press the **Save Content** button.

Script Elements

The table below highlights fragments of the script that are important to learn and understand.

We want to...	Key script Fragment...
Load the question to use	wscScripting.getQuestionByDataPipingCode
Write to the question	wscScripting.setValue

Reading Data from a Text Question

Let's now consider how we can read data from a text question. For the purposes of our example, we will have a two-page survey, with each page containing a single text question:

We have already created the first question. The creation of the second question is exactly the same, except we give it a unique code of CARBRAND2.

What we now want to do is fill the second question with whatever the text is in the first question. This will mean that we have to *read* from CARBRAND and *write* to CARBRAND2.

The script to do this looks as follows:

```
// Get the question we want to load the data from
// It's on a different page, so note the syntax of the code
var oFromTextQuestion = wscScripting.getQuestionByDataPipingCode('[@CARBRAND#DATA#@]');

if (oFromTextQuestion ) // The question was loaded successfully
{

  // Get the value from the question
  var oGetValue = wscScripting.getValue(oFromTextQuestion);

  // Get the question we want to save the data to
  // It's on a this page, so note the syntax of the code
  var oToTextQuestion = wscScripting.getQuestionByDataPipingCode('CARBRAND2');

  if (oToTextQuestion ) // The question was loaded successfully
  {

    wscScripting.setValue(oToTextQuestion, oGetValue);

  }
}

// Always return true unless you want to indicate a failure
// in the script
args.isValid = true;
```

Script Elements

The table below highlights fragments of the script that are important to learn and understand.

We want to...	Key script Fragment...
Load a question from previous page	Must use [@CARBRAND#DATA#@] syntax
Read the value of a question	wscScripting.getValue

Data Scripting for Other Question Types

Scripting is all about taking what you already know, and making a couple of variations, or adding a small piece of additional functionality. This is why it is important to have a strong knowledge of the basics, and build from there.

We now know how the save data to and get data from a text question. All other questions will be a variation on this knowledge. Let's look at the other key question types you will want to access through scripting.

Choice Questions

Choice Questions are a little trickier than text questions. Rather than a flat piece of text, the "data" that must be saved or loaded in a script is a "choice" (or a number of choices if the question allows multiple selections). So this begs the question...

How do we manage choices in scripting?

To answer this question, let's consider an example.

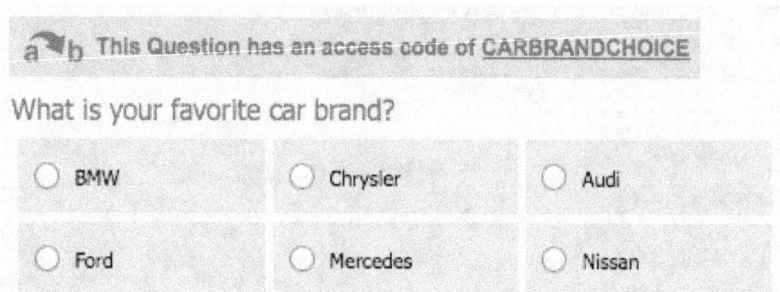

This is a choice question with a unique code of *CARBRANDCHOICE*. We already know how to get the question in script (just like we did with the text questions!) What we now need to understand is how to set the value of this type of question in script.

Attaching Values to Choices

There is one other thing that should be done when setting a choice question up to make scripting easier - allocating each choice a <u>numeric value</u>. This can be achieved by choosing to automatically apply values to the choices entered when the question is first added.

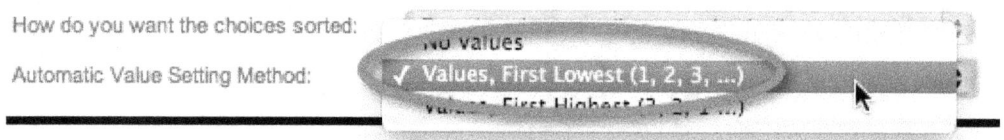

By doing this, our choices in this example question would be as follows:

Value	Description
1	BMW
2	Ford
3	Chrysler
4	Mercedes
5	Audi
6	Nissan

Choices with values can be managed directly in script by referring to those values. It is therefore best practice to do two things when creating any question that uses choices that you wish to manipulate in scripting:

1. Give each choice a numeric value
2. Make sure each of these values is <u>unique</u>

Writing Data to a Choice Question

Let's assume we want to set our sample question to "Audi". The script to achieve this would be as follows:

```
// Get the question
var oChoiceQuestion = wscScripting.getQuestionByDataPipingCode('CARBRANDCHOICE');

if (oChoiceQuestion ) // The question was loaded successfully
{

  // Audi has the value 5. Let's set the answer for the question to 5.
  var isSelected = wscScripting.selectChoiceByValue(oChoiceQuestion, 5);

}

// Always return true unless you want to indicate a failure
// in the script
args.isValid = true;
```

Script Elements

The table below highlights fragments of the script that are important to learn and understand.

We want to...	Key script Fragment...
Choose the choice to set the question to	wscScripting.selectChoiceByValue

Reading Data from a Choice Question

Reading data for a choice question is simply a matter of looping through each of the choices, and seeing if they are actually selected.

```
// Get the source question (we want to read from)
var oChoiceQuestion = wscScripting.getQuestionByDataPipingCode('[@CARBRANDCHOICE#DATA#@]');

if (oChoiceQuestion ) // The question was loaded successfully
{
  // Get the target question (we want to write to)
  var oChoiceQuestion2 = wscScripting.getQuestionByDataPipingCode('CARBRANDCHOICE2');

  if (oChoiceQuestion2 ) // The question was loaded successfully
  {
    for (i=1; i<=oChoiceQuestion.choices.length; i++) // Loop through the choice values
    {
      var oSelected = wscScripting.isChoiceSelectedByValue(oChoiceQuestion, i);

      if (oSelected) // What the item we are looking at selected?
      {
        // Yes it was - select the same choice in the target question
        wscScripting.selectChoiceByValue(oChoiceQuestion2, i);
      }
    }
  }
}

// Always return true unless you want to indicate a failure
// in the script
args.isValid = true;
```

Script Elements

The table below highlights fragments of the script that are important to learn and understand.

We want to...	Key script Fragment...
Create a loop to go through the choices	for (i=1; i<=oChoiceQuestion.choices.length; i++)
Test if a choice was selected	wscScripting.isChoiceSelectedByValue

How do Multi-Select Choice Questions Work?

Reading and writing to multi-select choice questions work in a similar way to single select questions, except that you have to manage the fact that multiple items can be selected.

In single select question, selecting a particular value <u>deselects other values automatically</u> because by definition there can be only one value. In multi-select questions, you need to manage the de-selection of values yourself.

In the previous example, if we were dealing with multi-select questions, we would have to modify the code as follows:

Instead of:

```
var oSelected = wscScripting.isChoiceSelectedByValue(oChoiceQuestion, i);

if (oSelected) // What the item we are looking at selected?
{
 // Yes it was - select the same choice in the target question
 wscScripting.selectChoiceByValue(oChoiceQuestion2, i);
}
```

We would need to deal with unselected values too:

```
var oSelected = wscScripting.isChoiceSelectedByValue(oChoiceQuestion, i);

if (oSelected) // What the item we are looking at selected?
{
 // Yes it was - select the same choice in the target question
 wscScripting.selectChoiceByValue(oChoiceQuestion2, i);
}
 else
{
 // No it wasn't - deselect the same choice in the target question
 wscScripting.deselectChoiceByValue(oChoiceQuestion2, i);
}
```

Script Elements

The table below highlights a fragment of the script that is important to learn and understand.

We want to...	Key script Fragment...
Deselect a choice that was not chosen	wscScripting.deselectChoiceByValue

Numeric Questions

When you are dealing with numeric questions, they are handled in exactly the same way as text questions. As you will note from the example below, you even put the numbers to place in the question in quotes ('), just like text values.

```
// Get the question
var oNumberQuestion = wscScripting.getQuestionByDataPipingCode('CARPRICE');

if (oNumberQuestion ) // The question was loaded successfully
{

  // Set the starting number for this question to $25000
  wscScripting.setValue(oNumberQuestion, '25000');

}

// Always return true unless you want to indicate a failure
// in the script
args.isValid = true;
```

> There are a number of question types that are effectively numeric questions, and therefore behave in the same way as shown above. These include star rating and slider questions.

Matrix Questions

Matrix Questions are one of the more complex question types, since each matrix row is a question by itself. We know how to get to a question in a script - using the *Unique Access Code*. The question is, how do we get to an individual row?

Getting to a Matrix Row

Each row of a matrix can be thought of as its own choice question. If we could get to a row, we could manipulate it in a similar way to a standard choice question.

Matrix rows do not have their own Access Codes, so there needs to be another way to uniquely identify a row. To identify and use a row, the key steps are as follows:

1. When creating rows in a matrix, each row you want to access needs to be given a tag with a value. For example, we will call the tag "ROW":

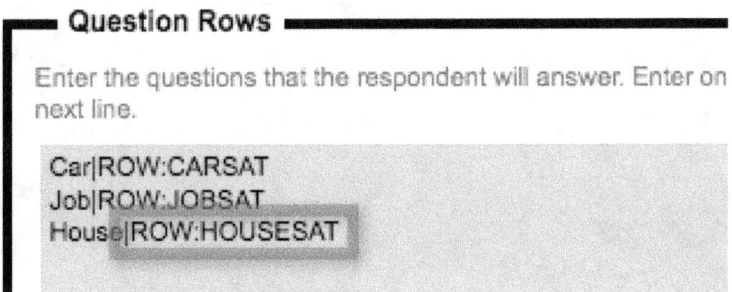

2. Get to the row in your script

```
var oMatrix = wscScripting.getQuestionByDataPipingCode('MYMATRIX');

if (oMatrix)
{
    var oRow = wscScripting.getRowByTagValue(oMatrix, 'ROW', 'JOBSAT');
}
```

Write to, or read from, a Matrix Row

Below is a code snippet showing how you can confirm if a value has been selected in a grid, and how to set a value for a row in a grid.

```
//Get the Job Satisfaction Row
var oRow = wscScripting.getRowByTagValue(oMatrix, 'ROW', 'JOBSAT');
// Are values 1 or 2 selected?
var isSelected = wscScripting.isAnyMatrixChoiceSelectedByValue(oMatrix, new Array(1,2), oRow)

// Is Value 3 selected
var isSelected2 = wscScripting.isMatrixChoiceSelectedByValue(oMatrix, 3, oRow )

// Select Value 4 in the Row
var isSelected3 = wscScripting.selectMatrixChoiceByValue(oMatrix, 4, oRow )
```

Script Elements

The table below highlights fragments of the script that are important to learn and understand.

We want to...	Key script Fragment...
Get the row to read from/write to	wscScripting.getRowByTagValue
Check if one of a number of values is selected	wscScripting.isAnyMatrixChoiceSelectedByValue
Check if a single value is selected	wscScripting.isMatrixChoiceSelectedByValue
Set the value for a matrix row	wscScripting.selectMatrixChoiceByValue

Scripting #101:
Validation of Responses

Web Survey Creator provides all the standard built-in validation capabilities that you would expect from a high-end MR Survey Tool. There's often a "one-off" validation, however, that needs to be scripted because it is so specific to the survey at hand.

In this chapter we look at how you can set up custom validation within your surveys using scripting.

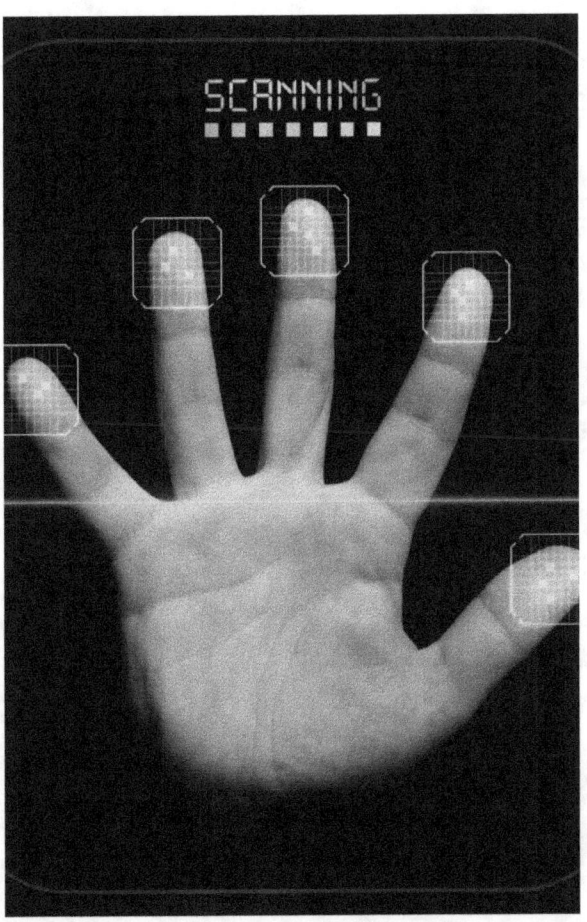

What does Validation do?

When considering the lifecycle of a typical question in a typical survey, it looks something like this:

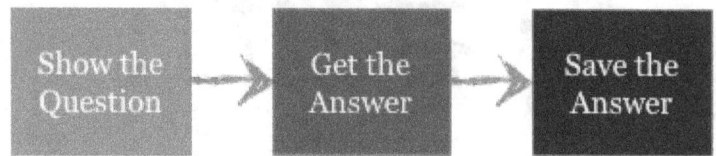

This is nice and simple, but doesn't deal with a key question:

What if the answer entered is invalid?

This is where validation comes in - we want to "validate" that a response is correct before saving it. The validation process therefore occurs just before we save the response:

Validation Example

One of the simplest examples of validation is *Mandatory checking*. This involves checking that an answer has actually been entered.

For example, a survey may ask for the name of the respondent. This could be used to identify who created a particular response. It is therefore important that the name is actually entered. Placing a mandatory validation on the name question will ensure that a respondent can not continue until a name is entered.

In Web Survey Creator, validations are run as soon as a respondent moves off a survey page (by pressing the *Next button* or *Submit button*).

If a validation fails, the survey does <u>not</u> advance, and a warning is provided for the question to explain why the validation failed.

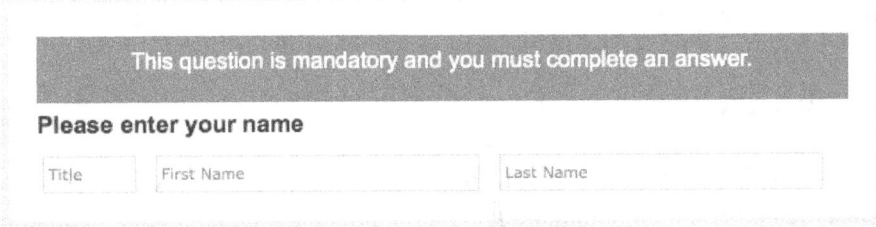

Validations Available without Scripting

Web Survey Creator has a series of standard validations for the various types of questions available in the software. Checking a box indicating that the validation should be tested, and setting the related details for the validation can set up these validations.

Validations all feature a validation message that is shown if the validation fails. Web Survey Creator has standard messages for all validations in more than 10 of the most common languages. These messages can be changed if required as part of the validation setup.

The standard validations available for different question types are shown below.

TEXT QUESTIONS		
Single & Multi-line	Mandatory	
	Format	Email address, text only, numeric only, URL, phone number, zip code, social security number
	Length	Minimum, maximum

CHOICE QUESTIONS		
Single Selection	Mandatory	
Multi Selection	Mandatory	
	No. of Selections	Minimum, maximum

NUMERIC QUESTIONS		
Numeric	Mandatory	
	Format	Integers, decimals, US currency, Euro currency, integer percentage, decimal percentage
	Range	Minimum, maximum

Most other question types simply have mandatory validations.

Validation using Scripting

Why is scripted validation needed?

The standard validations are often sufficient to ensure that the data entered into a survey is valid. For more advanced surveys, however, they do have a number of limitations:

- The "logic" they apply is quite rudimentary
- They don't allow validations between questions

Scripted validation is thus needed to take validations past these limitations.

How Does Scripted Validation Work?

All validations have two processes to complete:

1. Perform the *validation logic*
2. If the logic fails:
    a. Show a warning message; and
    b. Halt the progress of the survey

A scripted validation changes the first step. It replaces the simplified logic that can be created through a couple of clicks with a much broader, more capable logic that is created by using a script.

Scripted Validation Logic

Scripts can be set up to run at different times. A validation script must be set up to run *before the Survey Page is Validated*.

```
  Execute Javascript when Survey Page has Loaded
  Execute Javascript when Survey Quota Data has been Loaded
  Execute Javascript to Test Visibility of Next or Submit Buttons
✓ Execute Javascript before Survey Page is Validated
  Execute Javascript when Next or Submit Buttons are Pressed
  Execute Javascript when Previous Button is Pressed
```

This means that the script is run <u>after</u> the next or submit button is pressed, and <u>before</u> WSC moves to a new page (or completes the survey).

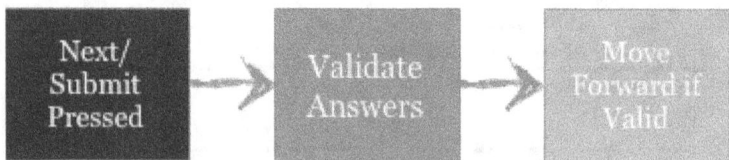

The contents of the validation script are completely up to you. All WSC cares about is:

1. Whether the validation is passed or failed.
2. If the validation failed, what validation error text should be shown?

If the validation is passed, the script must set:

```
args.isValid = true;
```

If the validation is failed, the script must set:

```
args.isValid = false;
```

Failure to validate will halt the survey on the current page. The script needs to tell WSC what validation text needs to be shown, and on which question:

```
wscScripting.setValidation(oQuestion, 'This is not valid!');
```

We will see how all this works together in the next section of this book.

What the Respondent Sees...

A respondent only sees the result of the second part of the validation process - the warning message, and the halted survey. Therefore, from the perspective of a survey respondent, a scripted validation will look exactly the same as a standard validation - it will appear in a box above the question that is being validated.

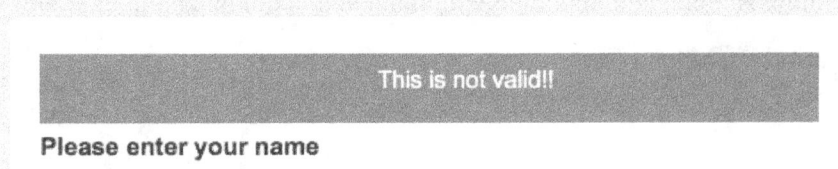

Scripted Validation Example

We want to survey people about air travel. This survey relates specifically to the last time they took a flight domestically in Australia. We are looking to achieve the following functionality in our survey:

Two of the key questions we need to ask are:

1. Which Australian destination did you fly FROM?
2. Which Australian destination did you fly TO?

We want to make sure that people enter valid data. Specifically, someone can't depart from and fly to the same destination.

The two questions look as follows:

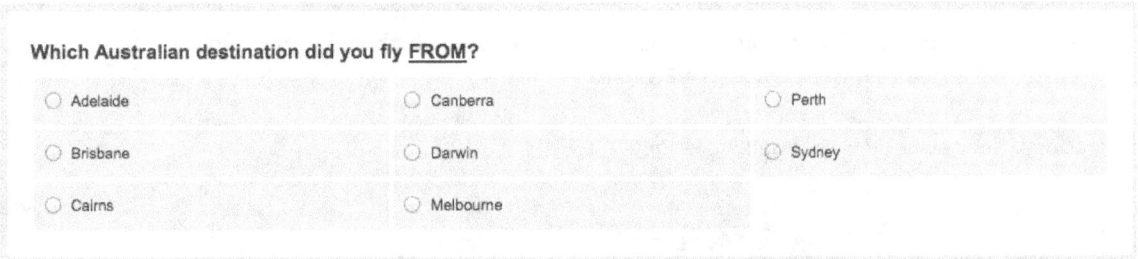

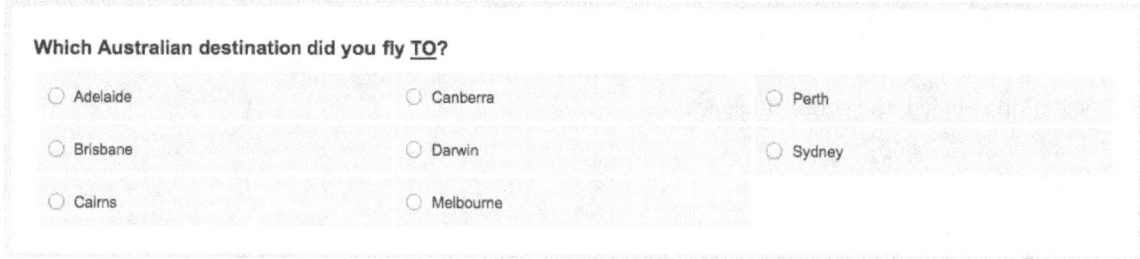

Preparing for our Validation Script

Before we focus on the content of our script, we need to prepare for it.

Giving questions unique access codes

We will give our questions the access codes:

DEPARTURECITY
ARRIVALCITY

We add them to the questions and they are visible in the designer so we can be sure they have been added:

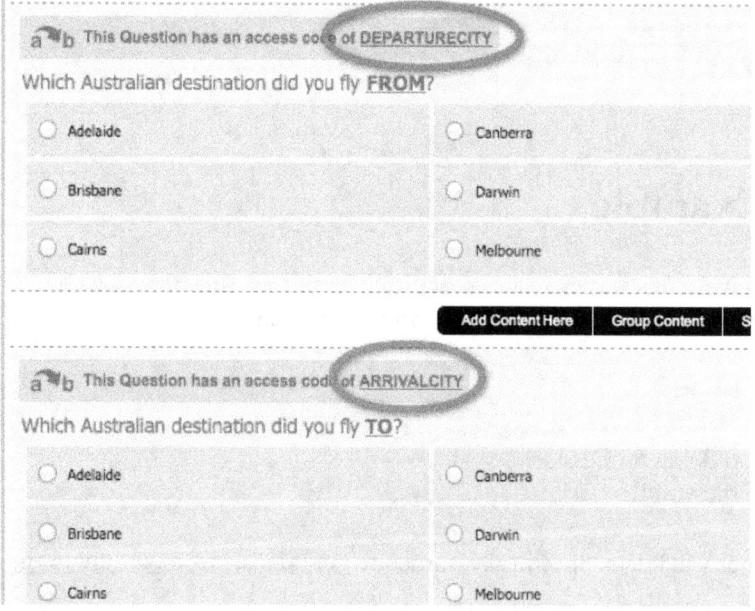

Making sure choices have values

The easiest way to access choices through scripting is to refer to each choice by it's numeric value. We will therefore make sure that our choices have values.

This is done when the choice are originally added:

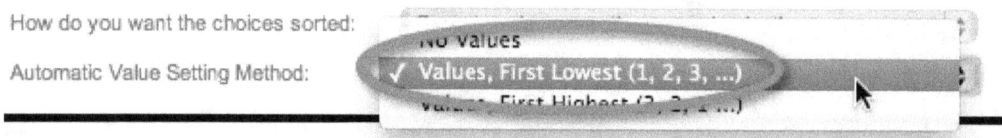

Writing the Script: Step-by-step

Our validation script uses things we have learned in the previous chapter about loading question data, together with the validation methodology from the previous section in this chapter. Let's work through the script a step at a time.

Choose when the script will run

When we create our script, we must make sure that it runs at the appropriate time. Specifically, it need to run the script *before the Survey Page is Validated*.

```
✓ Execute Javascript when Survey Page has Loaded
  Execute Javascript when Survey Quota Data has been Loaded
  Execute Javascript to Test Visibility of Next or Submit Buttons
  Execute Javascript before Survey Page is Validated
  Execute Javascript when Next or Submit Buttons are Pressed
  Execute Javascript when Previous Button is Pressed
  Execute Javascript to Test Randomization Parameters prior to Next Button
```

Get the Questions

Validations always require data to work with. Comparison of an answer to some set of rules clearly requires the loading of the questions by the script. In our example, we need to load two questions:

```
// Get our Questions
var oDep = wscScripting.getQuestionByDataPipingCode('DEPARTURECITY');
var oArr = wscScripting.getQuestionByDataPipingCode('ARRIVALCITY');
```

Test the Data

The testing of the question data is the key function of this script. We need to work out:

What is the best way to determine if the same choice has been made for both questions?

The wscScripting object allows us to test whether a certain value has been selected:

```
var oSelected = wscScripting.isChoiceSelectedByValue(
```

The easiest way to tell if two choice questions have the same choice selected is to loop through the choices one at a time. A standard loop would look as follows:

```
for (i=1; i<=oQuestion.choices.length; i++)
```

This loop who count from 1 up to the total number of choices for the question.

So, if we put all of the knowledge we have so far together, we could create a script to test the data as follows:

```
// Get our Questions
var oDep = wscScripting.getQuestionByDataPipingCode('DEPARTURECITY');
var oArr = wscScripting.getQuestionByDataPipingCode('ARRIVALCITY');

if (oDep && oArr)
 {
  // Loop through the choices...
  for (i=1; i<=oDep.choices.length; i++)
  {
   // Was this choice selected as the departure city?
   var oDepSelected = wscScripting.isChoiceSelectedByValue(oDep, i);
   // Was this choice selected as the arrival city?
   var oArrSelected = wscScripting.isChoiceSelectedByValue(oArr, i);

   if ( oDepSelected && oArrSelected) // Same selection! Invalid!
   {
     // Need to throw a validation error
   }
    else
   {
    // No error
   }
  }
 }
```

This is looking great - now we need to deal with the validation itself.

Stop the Survey

If the data is invalid, we need to stop on the current page of the survey rather than going to the next page, or submitting. This is achieved by ensuring that:

```
args.isValid = false;
```

This is quite different from most scripts we write. In fact, unless we want to indicate an error such as a validation failure, or scripts normally end in:

```
args.isValid = true;
```

Show the Validation Message

If the survey just stopped in its tracks with no warning, this would be very off-putting to a respondent. We need to ensure that the script will provide a visual warning for the validation so that the respondent knows what is going on.

This is achieved by attaching a validation message to one or more questions to indicate what the validation error is.

```
wscScripting.setValidation( oQuestion, 'Not Valid!');
```

Once a validation message has been attached to a question, it will remain attached to it until cleared. It is therefore important to ensure that any validation message that may have been previously added to a question is cleared if the question now passes validation.

```
wscScripting.clearValidation( oQuestion);
```

Putting it all together: The Final Script

We now have all the pieces to create the custom validation. Our final validation script would look as follows:

```
// Get our Questions
var oDep = wscScripting.getQuestionByDataPipingCode('DEPARTURECITY');
var oArr = wscScripting.getQuestionByDataPipingCode('ARRIVALCITY');
var bValid;

if (oDep && oArr)
 {
  // Loop through the choices...
  for (i=1; i<oDep.choices.length; i++)
  {
   // Was this choice selected as the departure city?
   var oDepSelected = wscScripting.isChoiceSelectedByValue(oDep, i);
   // Was this choice selected as the arrival city?
   var oArrSelected = wscScripting.isChoiceSelectedByValue(oArr, i);

   if ( oDepSelected && oArrSelected) // Same selection! Invalid!
   {
     // Need to throw a validation error
     wscScripting.setValidation(oArr, 'Invalid location choice!');
     bValid = false;
     break; // No need to continue looping - error found
   }
    else
   {
     // Clear the validation text
     wscScripting.clearValidation(oArr);
     bValid = true;
   }
  }
 }
args.isValid = bValid;
```

The interface that will be seen by a respondent when invalid data is entered will look as follows:

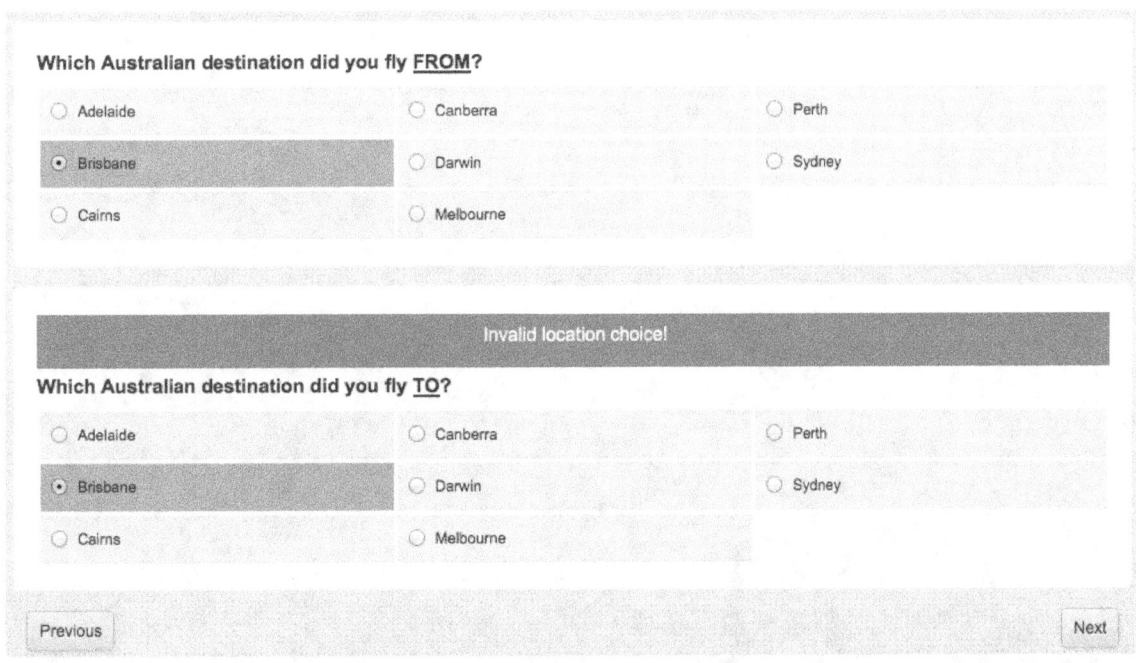

Scripting #101: Validation of Responses 275

Scripting #101:
Tweaking the Interface

JavaScript is a client-side scripting language, which makes it perfectly placed to control and manipulate what is shown in the browser.

This chapter looks at some examples of what you can do to the survey interface through scripting.

Overview of Interface "Tweaking"

Interface "tweaking" is definitely an advanced topic, particularly when it comes to playing with existing interface elements in a survey. Compared to the other uses of scripting we have discussed so far, interface "tweaking" is more complex, less structured, and more directly tied to your level of knowledge of HTML, CSS and JavaScript.

The scripts demonstrated in this chapter are merely a couple of examples of what is possible.

The most common things you can do to the interface using scripting fall under the following headings:

1. Create new content (e.g. HTML Content on a page)
2. Modifying Existing Content (e.g. modifying the layout of existing questions)
3. Creating interactive interface elements (e.g. reacting to a button click)

We will consider examples of each of these in this chapter.

Creating Content Using Scripting

The simplest form of interface "tweaking" is the adding of custom content to a survey page. All the script requires in these situations is a container on the page for the script to "hook" on to.

Using a Content Container

In order to use a content container on a page, there are two steps:

1. Tick the "Show Content Container" checkbox on the script settings.

    ☑ Show a Content Container for this Javascript to use

2. Access the container in the script. Note that the container for the current script is always accessed with the following code using {QuestionContainer}.

    ```
    var oContainer = wscScripting.getElementById('{QuestionContainer}');
    ```

Once we have the container in script, we can do anything we like with it. For example, we could place some simple HTML in it...

```
var oContainer = wscScripting.getElementById('{QuestionContainer}');

if (oContainer)
{
    // NOTE: when adding to innerHTML - put everything in a temp
    // variable first, as innerHTML will attempt
    // to complete missing tags for each line you add to it.
    var content = '';

    content += '<strong>Hello World!</strong> This is some HTML.';

    oContainer.innerHTML = content;
}

args.isValid = true;
```

This script will result in the following content being shown on the page:

Hello World! This is some HTML.

Modifying Existing Content

For the purposes of this discussion, let's look at a simple example of modifying existing content. For this example, we will start with the following question:

Modifying Question Layout

Questions shown in Web Survey Creator provide a number of layout options, including how wide to make the question, and whether to show values across the page. In this case we want to do something a little different - *we want to center the Yes and No options in the middle of the page*.

The choices in this question are in a table, so what we need to do in our script is "hook in" to that table and modify it so that it will be centered.

We have given the question a *unique code* of YESNO. The script (which will be run on page load) needed to get the table for this question, and make it centered, is as follows:

```
// Get our question object
var oVote = wscScripting.getQuestionByDataPipingCode('YESNO');

if (oVote) // If the question object is valid...
{
  // Get the table used for the question
  var oTable = wscScripting.getElementById(oVote.identity + '_table');

  if (oTable)
  {
    // Do something with the table
    // Change the left and right margins
    oTable.style.marginLeft = 'auto';
    oTable.style.marginRight = 'auto';

  }
}

args.isValid = true;
```

By using this script, we have changed the layout of the question so that it now looks as follows:

Hiding the Previous Button

Web Survey Creator gives you the option of hiding or showing previous buttons on your survey pages. This is a global setting, though. What if I want to show previous buttons on all but one page?

Fortunately all aspects of the interface are accessible to the script. Let's write a script that hides the previous button on a single page.

Once we understand how to get access to the previous button in script, this becomes a very simple script to write:

```
// Get the previous button
var oButton = wscScripting.getElementById('previousbutton');

if (oButton) // If the button object is valid...
{
  // Change the button style so the button is not shown
  oButton.style.display = 'none';
}

args.isValid = true;
```

The page now looks as follows (no previous button is shown):

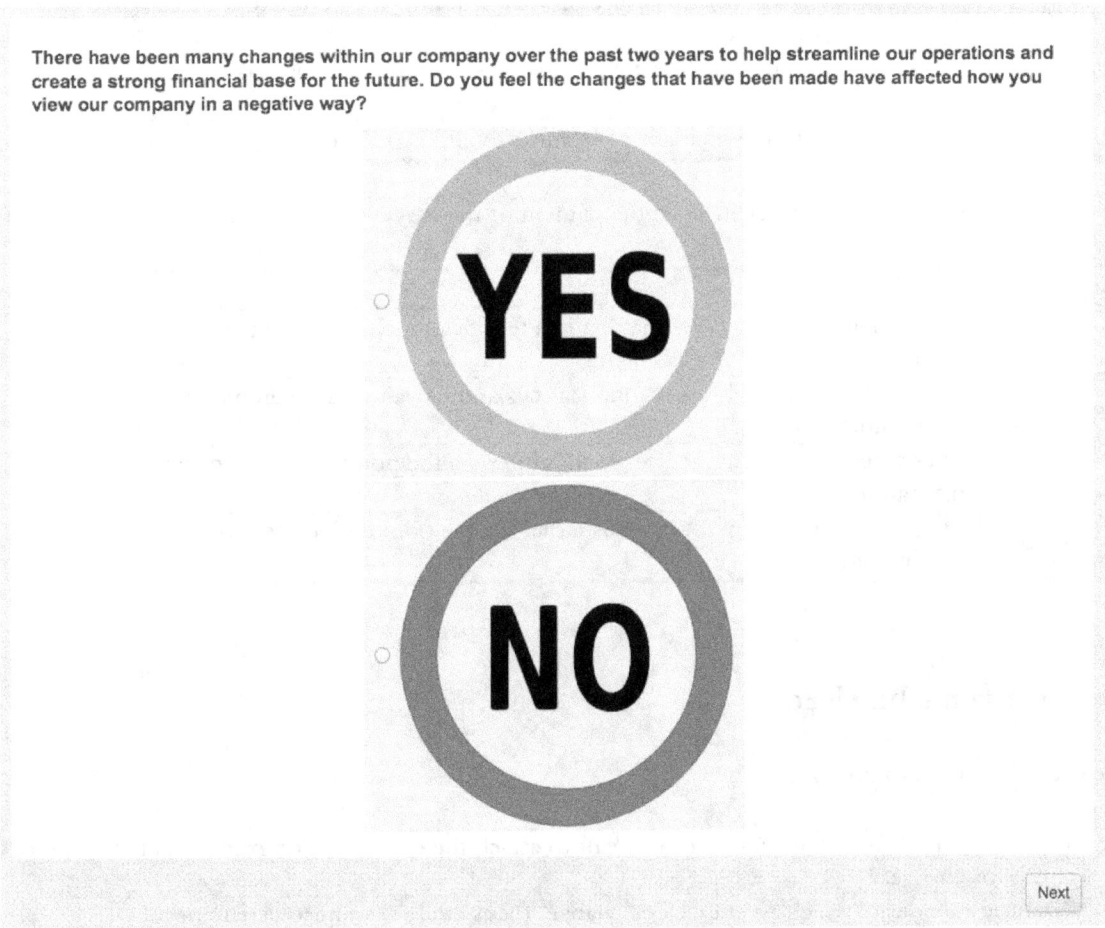

Dealing with UI Events

What Events can be Hooked into?

There are a number of events that can be hooked into through scripting. A list of the key events for input devices are shown below.

Device	Event	Details
Mouse	*click*	Fires when the pointing device button is clicked over an element. A click is defined as a mousedown and mouseup over the same screen location.
	dblclick	Fires when the pointing device button is double clicked over an element
	mousedown	Fires when the pointing device button is pressed over an element
	mouseup	Fires when the pointing device button is released over an element
	mouseover	Fires when the pointing device is moved onto an element
	mousemove	Fires when the pointing device is moved while it is over an element
	mouseout	Fires when the pointing device is moved away from an element
Keyboard	*keydown*	Fires before keypress, when a key on the keyboard is pressed.
	keypress	Fires after keydown, when a key on the keyboard is pressed.
	keyup	Fires when a key on the keyboard is released

There are other events that relate to changes in the content of the survey page as follows:

Event	Details
select	Fires when a user selects some text in a text field, including input and textarea
change	Fires when a control loses the input focus and its value has been modified since gaining focus
focus	Fires when an element receives focus either via the pointing device or by tab navigation
blur	Fires when an element loses focus either via the pointing device or by tabbing navigation

How can Events be Used?

To use events, we need to do three things:

1. We need to have an HTML interface element to attach the event to - for example, a text field to check for changes
2. We need to indicate which Event (select, change, focus etc.) we want to listen out for
3. We need to script what needs to happen when the event is fired

Getting an HTML Interface Element

The act of "getting" an interface element differs depending upon what type of question you are scripting for. For simple questions that have only one input control - like text, drop-down and numeric question, you can get to the HTML Interface Element relatively easily.

Getting a Simple Interface Element

Let's assume we have a drop-down list question with a unique code of DEPARTMENT.

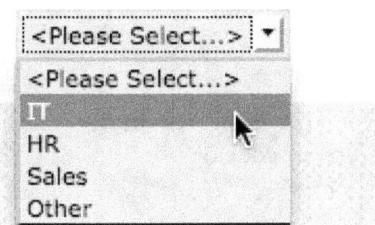

In the script below, we are loading the HTML Element for this question.

```
// Get the Question
var oQuestion = wscScripting.getQuestionByDataPipingCode('DEPARTMENT');

if (oQuestion)
{

  // Get the HTML Element for this Question
  var HTMLElementForQuestion = $('#' + oQuestion.identity);

}
```

Getting Question Choice Interface Elements

Attaching an event script to a choice question can be very useful. The trick, however, is to deal with the fact that a choice question is has multiple interface elements - each of the choices. Let's assume we have a drop-down list question with a unique code of DEPARTMENTCHOICE.

In the script below, we are loading the HTML Elements for each of the choices in this question.

```
// Get the Question
var oQ = wscScripting.getQuestionByDataPipingCode('DEPARTMENTCHOICE');

if (oQ)
{
  // Get the HTML Elements for each choice
  var ChoiceButtonIT    = $('#' + oQ.identity + '_' + oQ.choices[0].identity);
  var ChoiceButtonHR    = $('#' + oQ.identity + '_' + oQ.choices[1].identity);
  var ChoiceButtonSales = $('#' + oQ.identity + '_' + oQ.choices[2].identity);
  var ChoiceButtonOther = $('#' + oQ.identity + '_' + oQ.choices[3].identity);

}
```

Note that access to choices is zero-based. Therefore, to access the first choice, we actually get:

```
oQ.choices[0].identity
```

Complex Interface Elements

Getting an interface element to attach an event to can be "tricky" if you are dealing with more complex question types. Let's assume we have a constant sum question with a unique code of DEPARTMENTSUM.

How many hours a week do you spend dealing with people from these departments?

	Hours
IT	6
HR	10
Sales	15
Other	6
Total	**37 hours**

A Constant Sum question is effectively a matrix with one column ("hours" in our example), and a number of rows. If we wanted to attach an event to the "other" numeric element, we'd need to first get to the row. The easiest way to get a row is to search for a particular row tag and value:

```
// Get the Question
var oQ = wscScripting.getQuestionByDataPipingCode('DEPARTMENTSUM');

if (oQ)
{
    // Get the Row by looking for a specific tag with a specific value
    var rowObject = wscScripting.getRowByTagValue(constantSum, 'ROWTAG', 'OtherRow');

    if (rowObject)
    {
        // Get the HTML Element for the numeric input box
        // We need to refer to both the row, and the column (choice)
        var inputBox = $('#'+oQ.identity+'_'+rowObject.identity+'_'+oQ.choices[0].identity);

    }
}
```

Attaching an Event

Once we have an HTML element, attaching an event is quite trivial. The appropriate event is "bound" to the HTML element, and a function is run whenever that event occurs.

```
// Get the Question
var oQuestion = wscScripting.getQuestionByDataPipingCode('DEPARTMENT');

if (oQuestion)
{
    // Get the HTML Element for this Question
    var HTMLElementForQuestion = $('#' + oQuestion.identity);

    // Do something when the value changes
    $(HTMLElementForQuestion).bind('change',
                                   function()
                                   {
                                       // Script to run goes here
                                   });
}

args.isValid = true;
```

UI Event Example

Let's consider a complete example for one of the question types we have discussed earlier in this section.

Drop-down List with "Other"

Choice questions that are shown as radio button or check boxes include a text box for other in the question. Drop-down lists don't have this capability. We can add this using scripting, however. All we need is an "Other" text question that is hidden when Other is selected.

Before we set up our script, the questions would look as follows:

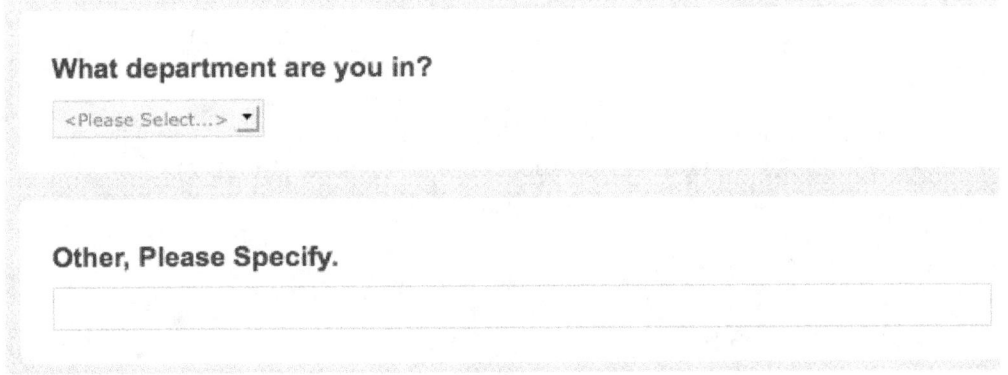

We only want the "Other Specify" question to show if "other" is selected - this is what the script needs to do for us. Our two questions have the following unique codes:

DEPARTMENT

OTHERDEPARTMENT

```javascript
// Get the Drop-down
var oDD = wscScripting.getQuestionByDataPipingCode('DEPARTMENT');
// Get the "Other" text question
var oOther = wscScripting.getQuestionByDataPipingCode('OTHERDEPARTMENT');

if (oDD && oOther)
{ // We want to only show the other question if the DD = 4 (Other)

  // Get the HTML Element for Drop Down List
  var HTMLElementForDD = $('#' + oDD.identity);
  // Get the HTML Element fof Other Specify box
  var HTMLElementForOther = $('#' + oOther.identity);

  // What Choice is currently selected?
  var aSelectedItem = wscScripting.getSelectedChoices(oDD);

  if (aSelectedItem)
  {
    if (aSelectedItem.value != 4) // Other is not selected
    {
      // Hide the other text question on the load
      $("#" + oOther.containerName).hide();
    }

  // Do something when the value of the Drop-Down changes
  $(HTMLElementForDD).bind('change',
        function() {

            var LocalHTMLElementForDD = $('#' + oDD.identity);
            var LocalHTMLElementForOther = $('#' + oOther.containerName);
            // Get the "Other" choice for testing
            var oChoice = wscScripting.getChoiceByValue(oDD, 4);

            if (LocalHTMLElementForDD.val() == oChoice.identity)
                { // They chose the other choice - show "Other"
                  LocalHTMLElementForOther.fadeIn('slow', function() {});
                }
                else
                { // They didn't choose the other choice
                  LocalHTMLElementForOther.fadeOut('slow', function() {});
                }

            });

}}

args.isValid = true;
```

Scripting #101:
Ordering of Pages & Choices

All surveys follow a particular "flow". At it's simplest, this is just going from one page to the next, and one choice to the next, in the order a survey was created.

Sometimes, however, survey flow needs to be managed in a very specific way that varies from respondent to respondent. This is when scripting needs to be used.

Page Ordering in the Designer

Before considering how page ordering may be managed through scripting, let's first consider how page ordering can be achieved without scripting.

Basic Page Order

Basic page ordering is determined by the order in which they have been added to a survey in the content manager.

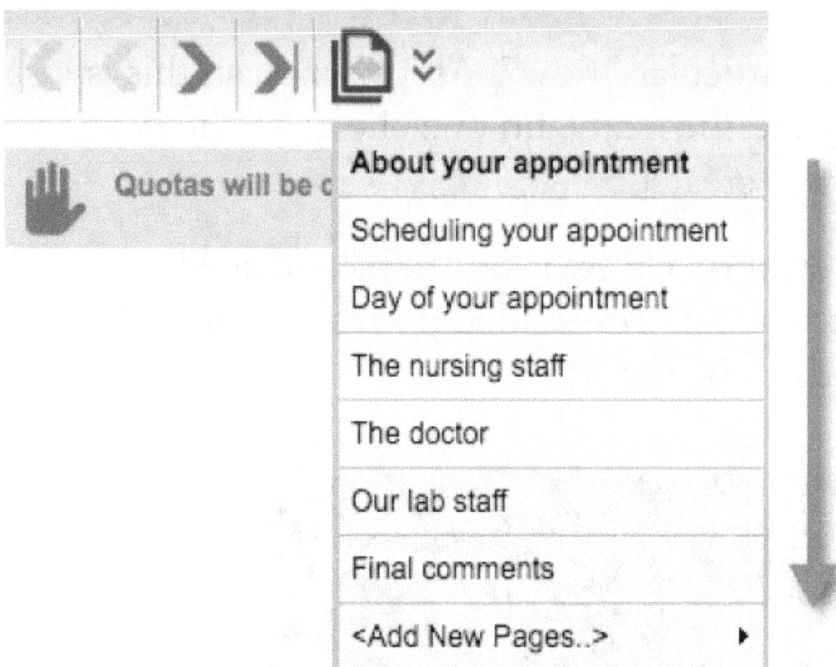

When new pages are added to a survey, they can be added before or after an existing page by pressing the appropriate button at the top or bottom of the existing page.

This is of course the way page ordering works, even on the most basic survey systems.

Randomization of Pages

If everyone sees pages in the same order, there can be some unforeseen effects on responses including:

1. Better quality responses for pages earlier in long surveys - later pages suffer from respondent fatigue
2. Responses later in a survey being affected by questions seen by the respondent earlier in a survey - they make react differently because of what they have previously seen

So, if ordering can change resulting data, how can we minimize these problems?

The only effective way to minimize how page ordering affects responses is to spread the possible ordering bias evenly. Specifically - page order needs to be randomized.

To use standard page randomization in Web Survey Creator, you need to:

1. Edit the first page you want to randomize

2. Check the randomization check box

   Randomization: ☑ Randomize this Page

3. If you want to group pages together in the random order, enter an optional Block Code

   Randomization Block Code: A

4. Save the page
5. Repeat for each subsequent page you wish to randomize.

Another way to randomize - A/B Testing

Users of A/B testing will distribute multiple samples of a test to see which single variable is most effective in increasing a response rate or other desired outcome. The test, in order to be effective, must reach an audience of a sufficient size that there is a reasonable chance of detecting a meaningful difference between the control and other tactics.

Web surveys are a great candidate to use A/B testing, since gaining access to a large audience is relatively easy. A simple example of an A/B test is shown below.

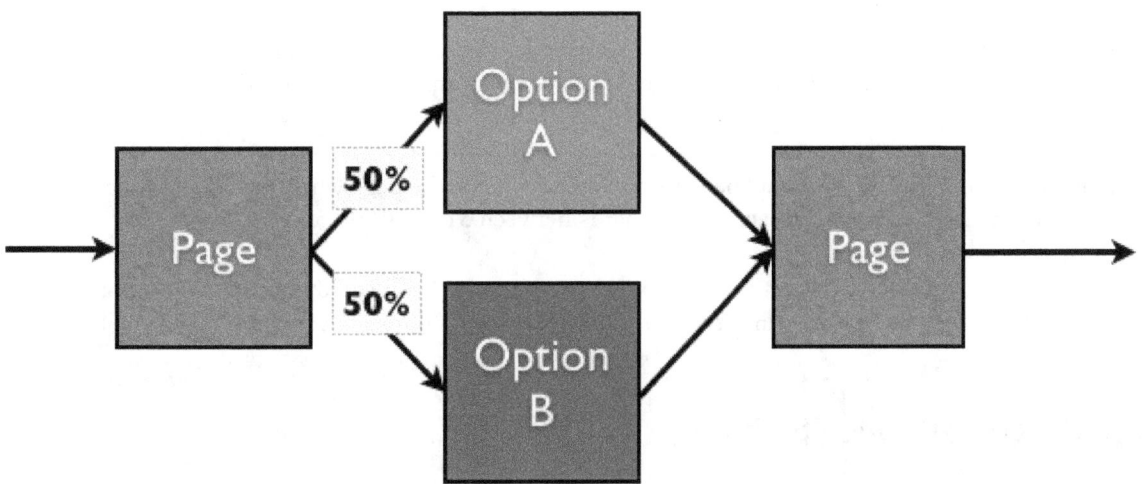

What we want is 50% of respondents to go to the page Option A, and 50% to go to the page Option B. Achieving this result is another example of randomization.

As soon as a respondent begins a response in Web Survey Creator, they are allocated a random number. This number can be used for various things - one of which is A/B testing. Setting up an A/B test is actually done through flow control. The true structure of a survey that has the A/B test above would be:

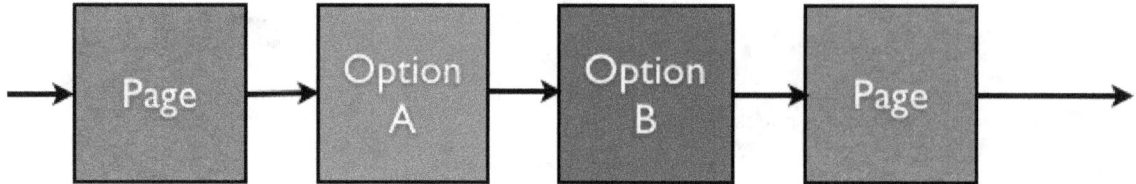

The create our A/B test, we want to hide the Option A page 50% of the time, and hide the Option B page 50% of the time.

Hiding the option A page would require the following flow:

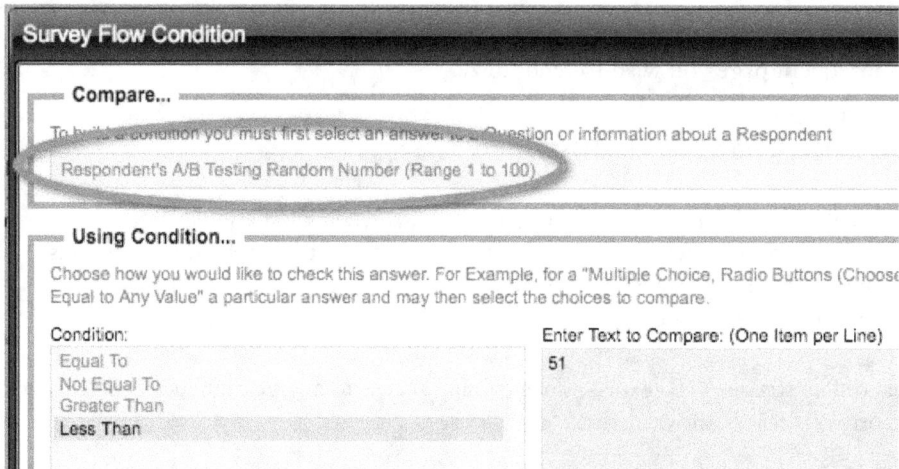

We use the A/B testing Random Number for the Respondent (which is always a number between 1 and 100) to do the flow. We want to hide the Option A page if the number is less than 51 (i.e. the number is between 1 and 50).

The hiding of the option B page would be the opposite test - hide the page when the A/B testing Random Number is greater than 50 (i.e. the number is between 51 and 100).

Of course this methodology wouldn't just apply to a two page test - you could have up to 100 options that are randomly chosen between, since the AB testing Random Number is equal to 1 of a possible 100 values.

Page Ordering through Scripting

Randomization is great for spreading the effects of bias due to page order. It does have one limitation though, that may cause issues in circumstances...

Randomization cannot be predicted - the order of pages a particular respondent will see is determined at the time they enter their response.

This is great in most circumstances, but what happens if I want to manipulate the order in a known way? To achieve this, we would need to modify the page order through scripting.

Let's consider an example...

We want to create a survey that includes two advertisements - each of their own page. The basic flow of the survey will be as follows:

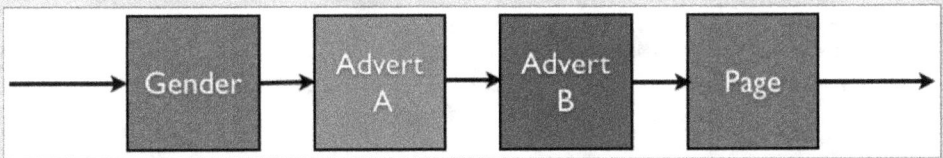

Our client wants us to show *Advert A* first for all <u>men</u> and *Advert B* first for all <u>women</u>. The order of the pages is therefore determined by the answer to a particular question, rather than being completely random.

What is needed for Page Order Scripting?

If you want to manage page order through scripting, there are a couple of things that need to be set up correctly as follows:

1. **Name your pages** so they can be referred to by name in the script. In our example, we will edit the page names and make them:

    a. Gender
    b. Advert A
    c. Advert B
    d. Next Page

2. **Make at least one page in the survey randomized** so the system knows to include data in pages to allow script to access page order. You will be able to move any pages in a survey, as long as at least one is randomized.

3. **(Optionally) place individual randomization block codes on pages** if you want to access them by block code (rather than page name).

4. **Add the reordering script** to a page that comes before the pages to be reordered (it will be run when the next button is pressed, and pages will be reordered before the survey moves forward).

Our Example: Ordering Pages based on Gender

In our previous example, we want to set up our page ordering so that men see the pages in this order:

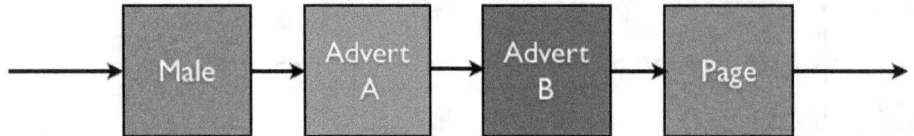

and women see pages in this order:

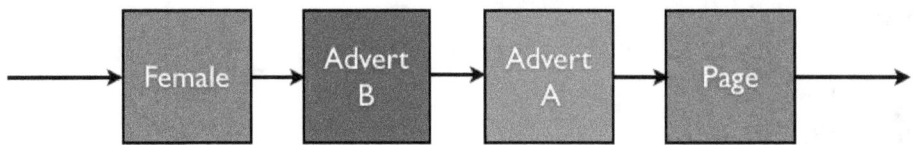

In order to achieve this, we do the following setup in our survey:

1. Name the pages of our survey "Gender", "Advert A", "Advert B" and "Next Page"

   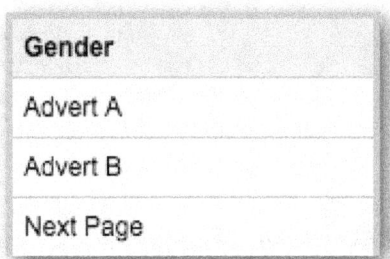

2. Add the access code "GENDER" to our gender question.

   Question Access Code (Optional) [Used for Data Piping, SPSS, etc]: GENDER

3. Set the advertisement pages to random, and give them both a block code of "ADVERTS". We are doing this so we can get to them in the script through their block code.

4. Create a **Randomization script**.

   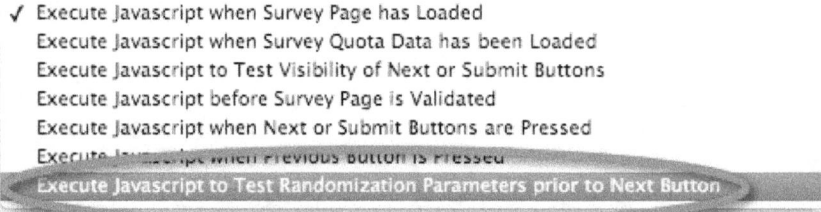

Web Survey Creator will provide all the data you need on a page for scripted changing of page orders as long as two things are true - at least one page is randomized in the survey AND a test randomization parameter script exists on the page. If either these things is false, no ordering is possible.

OK, everything is set up on our survey to allow us to manage the ordering of the pages. Let's go through the script we need to create.

The first thing we will need to do in the script is get to the value of the gender question:

```
// Did we pick a male or female?
var bMale = false;
var oGender = wscScripting.getQuestionByDataPipingCode('GENDER');
if (oGender != null) {
  var aSelected = wscScripting.getSelectedChoices(oGender);
  if (aSelected != null) {
    bMale = (aSelected[0].value == 1);
  }
}
```

We now know whether the respondent is male or not. The next step is to get the page items in an array for the survey, and work out where the advertisement pages are in this array.

```
// Get the page order
var aPages = wscScripting.getPageRandomizationItems();
if (aPages != null) {
  // Find the pages that are blocked as GENDER...
  // We need to changed their order dependant on the gender
  var nOrdinal = -1;
  for(var nPage = 0;nPage<aPages.length;nPage++) {
    if (aPages[nPage].blockCode == 'ADVERTS') {
      // this is the right block
      nOrdinal = nPage;
      break;
    }
  }
}
```

We want to...	Key script Fragment...
Get the pages for the survey	wscScripting.getPageRandomizationItems

Through this script, we have determined the position in the pages array that contains the first of our advertisements. We know that the page after this page will be the second advertisement.

> This example shows a clever use of **Block Codes** on pages. The two pages we want to swap around have been given the same block code:
>
> **ADVERTS**
>
> This means in our script we can just work through pages and look for the block code "ADVERTS". As soon as we find a page with this block code, we know we have found the *first of our two advertisement pages*. If we didn't use the block code, we'd have to check for both of our pages by name as we moved through the array of pages, because we wouldn't know which page was shown first.

All that is left to do is make sure the advertisements are in the correct order. The full code for the script (including the ordering) is shown below:

```
// Did we pick a male or female?
var bMale = false;
var oGender = wscScripting.getQuestionByDataPipingCode('GENDER');
if (oGender != null) {
  var aSelected = wscScripting.getSelectedChoices(oGender);
  if (aSelected != null) {
    bMale = (aSelected[0].value == 1);
  }
}
// Get the page order
var aPages = wscScripting.getPageRandomizationItems();
if (aPages != null) {
  // Find the pages that are blocked as GENDER...
  // We need to changed their order dependant on the gender
  var nOrdinal = -1;
  for(var nPage = 0;nPage<aPages.length;nPage++) {
    if (aPages[nPage].blockCode == 'ADVERTS') {
      // this is the right block
      nOrdinal = nPage;
      break;
    }
  }
  // Did we correctly find this page?
  if (nOrdinal > -1) {
    // if bMale then should be Advert A first
    // if !bMale then should be Advert B first
    // get them so we can flip them
    var oPage1 = aPages[nOrdinal];
    var oPage2 = aPages[nOrdinal + 1];
    // we might already have done this so check the title to be sure
    var sTitle = oPage1.title;
    if (bMale && sTitle == 'Advert B') {
      // Should be Advert A so flip them
      aPages[nOrdinal] = oPage2;
      aPages[nOrdinal + 1] = oPage1;
      // update them
      wscScripting.setPageRandomizationItems(aPages);
    }
    else if (!bMale && sTitle == 'Advert A') {
      // Should be Advert B so flip them
      aPages[nOrdinal] = oPage2;
      aPages[nOrdinal + 1] = oPage1;
      // update them
      wscScripting.setPageRandomizationItems(aPages);
    }
  }
}
args.isValid = true;
```

Note how we save down the page items at the end of the script once they are ordered in the way we want.

We want to...	Key script Fragment...
Save the pages in order back to the survey	wscScripting.setPageRandomizationItems

Page Ordering in a Nutshell

As can be seen from the previous example, a page ordering script has 3 distinct parts to it:

Step 1: Get the current page order

The script gets the current page objects into an array using *getPageRandomizationItems*.

```
// Get the page order
var aPages = wscScripting.getPageRandomizationItems();
```

Step 2: Alter the Page Order in the array from step 1

This is the heart of the script - you do whatever is needed to move pages around in the array. As we can see from the previous example, getting page objects from the array is easy:

```
var oPage1 = aPages[nOrdinal];
var oPage2 = aPages[nOrdinal + 1];
```

As is putting them back into the array:

```
aPages[nOrdinal] = oPage2;
aPages[nOrdinal + 1] = oPage1;
```

Step 3: Update the Page Ordering from the Array

Once you have finished manipulating the array, it can be used to update the page ordering for the survey.

```
wscScripting.setPageRandomizationItems(aPages);
```

Ordering Choices

Choice questions are one of the simplest, and most used question types in Web Survey Creator. An example of a choice question is shown below:

Standard Ordering of Choices

The vast majority of choice questions are ordered the same way as they appear in the content manager. It is also possible to choose other ordering options when adding or editing a choice question as follows:

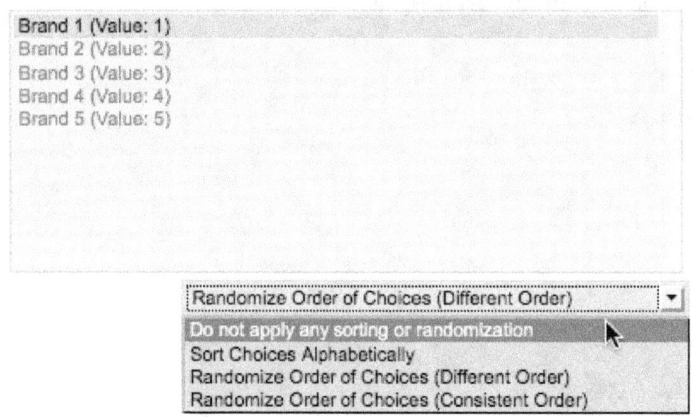

Here is what our example question might look like, if we chose to randomize the order of choices:

While alphabetical sorting and randomization can be very useful, sometimes you want to set up an exact order of choices. This is when scripting needs to be used to manage choices.

Setting up for Scripted Choice Ordering

All question types that have choices can have the ordering of those choice managed through scripting. For a question to be available in scripting, the following setup must be done:

1. **An access code must set up on the question** so that the question can be referred to in script.

2. **The choices must be randomized** by selecting one of the two randomization choices on the question.

   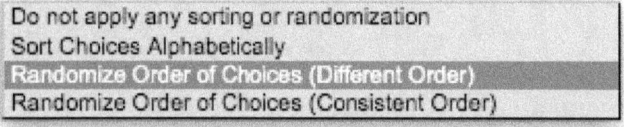

3. **Question must be made available for scripting** - if this is not ticked, the system will not put the appropriate data into the page for choice ordering to be modifiable.

> **Randomization Scripting**
> ☑ Force Question to be accessible from scripting when using Randomization Scripting
> If this Randomization Scripting is utilized choose whether this question is forced to be available.

Example: Scripted Choice Ordering

There are any number of reasons you may want to reorder choices. For the purposes of demonstration, we are going to use a contrived, but straight-forward example - we will take a randomized set of choices, and in script sort them alphabetically.

Choice Questions

Let's start with a question that is randomized and has the following values:

What is your favorite fruit?

○ Apple

○ Pear

○ Banana

○ Orange

○ Pineapple

To script this question so that the values are alphabetical, we first need to set the question up so it can be used with scripting:

1. **Set Access Code** on the question so it can be accessed through scripting

   Question Access Code (Optional) [Used for Data Piping, SPSS, etc]: SINGLE

2. **Use randomization** for the question choices

   Apple (Value: 1)
   Pear (Value: 2)
   Banana (Value: 3)
   Orange (Value: 4)
   Pineapple (Value: 5)

   How do you want the choices sorted: Randomize Order of Choices (Different Order)

3. Make the question **accessible to scripting**

We then need to write a script that does the re-ordering of the choices. The script needs to be set up as a test of randomization parameters (similar to the scripts that are used for page ordering):

- Execute Javascript when Survey Page has Loaded
- Execute Javascript when Survey Quota Data has been Loaded
- Execute Javascript to Test Visibility of Next or Submit Buttons
- Execute Javascript before Survey Page is Validated
- Execute Javascript when Next or Submit Buttons are Pressed
- Execute Javascript when Previous Button is Pressed
- **Execute Javascript to Test Randomization Parameters prior to Next Button**

The script to change the order of choice items in a question <u>must</u> be created on a page prior to the page containing the actual question. Trying to change the ordering on the same page as the question will not work - the script would be run too late.

The first thing we would need to do in our script is load the details for our question:

```
oQuestion = wscScripting.getQuestionByDataPipingCode('SINGLE');
if (oQuestion) {
  aRandom = wscScripting.getChoiceRandomizationItems(oQuestion, 0);
```

We want to...	Key script Fragment...
Get the choices for a question	wscScripting.getChoiceRandomizationItems

For the purposes of our demonstration, we are going to go through the choice objects, and set up the sort order so that the choices are in alphabetical order.

We achieve this by updating "sortorder" with the actual text of each of the choices, and then re-sorting the array.

```
// Get the title from the choice
for(var nChoice = 0;nChoice < oQuestion.choices.length;nChoice++) {
  var oChoice = oQuestion.choices[nChoice];
  var sText = oChoice.text;
  var sIdentity = oChoice.identity;
  for(var nRandom = 0;nRandom < aRandom.length;nRandom++) {
    if (aRandom[nRandom].identity.toLowerCase() == sIdentity) {
      aRandom[nRandom].sortOrder = sText.toLowerCase();
      break;
    }
  }
}
// Sort it
aRandom.sort(function(a,b) {
  if (a.sortOrder < b.sortOrder) { return -1 }
  if (b.sortOrder < a.sortOrder) { return 1 }
  if (b.sortOrder == a.sortOrder) { return 0 }
} );
```

Once we have re-sorted our array, we can save it back to the survey.

```
// Update the randoms for updating on next
bSuccess = wscScripting.setChoiceRandomizationItems(oQuestion, aRandom, 0);
```

We want to...	Key script Fragment...
Save the choices for a question back to the survey	wscScripting.setChoiceRandomizationItems

```
var oQuestion;
var aRandom;
var bSuccess;

// Single Selection List
oQuestion = wscScripting.getQuestionByDataPipingCode('SINGLE');
if (oQuestion) {
  aRandom = wscScripting.getChoiceRandomizationItems(oQuestion, 0);

  if (aRandom) {

    // Get the title from the choice
    for(var nChoice = 0;nChoice < oQuestion.choices.length;nChoice++) {
      var oChoice = oQuestion.choices[nChoice];
      var sText = oChoice.text;
      var sIdentity = oChoice.identity;
      for(var nRandom = 0;nRandom < aRandom.length;nRandom++) {
        if (aRandom[nRandom].identity.toLowerCase() == sIdentity) {
          aRandom[nRandom].sortOrder = sText.toLowerCase();
          break;
        }
      }
    }

    // Sort it
    aRandom.sort(function(a,b) {
      if (a.sortOrder < b.sortOrder) { return -1 }
      if (b.sortOrder < a.sortOrder) { return 1 }
      if (b.sortOrder == a.sortOrder) { return 0 }
    } );

    // Update the randoms for updating on next
    bSuccess = wscScripting.setChoiceRandomizationItems(oQuestion, aRandom, 0);
  }
}

args.isValid = true;
```

Once this script is run, the choices in the question will appear in alphabetical order as shown here:

What is your favorite fruit?

○ Apple

○ Banana

○ Orange

○ Pear

○ Pineapple

Single Range Matrix

Let's now consider another "choice" question - a single range matrix. For this example, let's use a matrix that looks as follows:

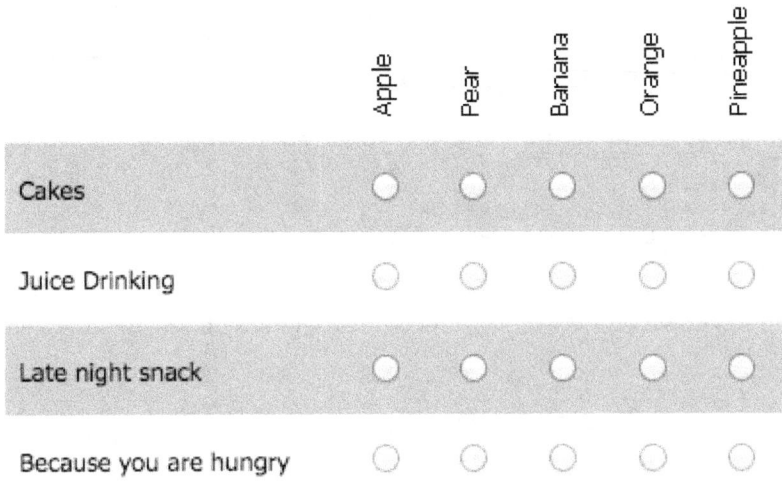

Setting up this question so that we can manipulate choice order (i.e. column order) is exactly like a standard choice question. We need to perform the same setup:

1. **Set Access Code** on the question so it can be accessed through scripting. In this case we will give the question a code of "MATRIXSINGLE"

2. **Use randomization** for the question choices

3. Make the question **accessible to scripting**

The script will *exactly* match the script for the simple choice question, with one simple change - the code to access the question:

```
// Single Matrix
oQuestion = wscScripting.getQuestionByDataPipingCode('MATRIXSINGLE');
```

Accessing and modifying the choices in questions work in a similar way, as can be seen by the scripts used for single choice questions, and single range matrixes - they are essentially identical. This is also true for other questions that have choices - such as ranking questions.

The full script for sorting the matrix rows into alphabetical order is shown here:

```
var oQuestion;
var aRandom;
var bSuccess;

// Single Matrix
oQuestion = wscScripting.getQuestionByDataPipingCode('MATRIXSINGLE');
if (oQuestion) {
  aRandom = wscScripting.getChoiceRandomizationItems(oQuestion, 0);
  if (aRandom) {

      // Get the title from the choice
    for(var nChoice = 0;nChoice < oQuestion.choices.length;nChoice++) {
      var oChoice = oQuestion.choices[nChoice];
      var sText = oChoice.text;
      var sIdentity = oChoice.identity;
      for(var nRandom = 0;nRandom < aRandom.length;nRandom++) {
        if (aRandom[nRandom].identity.toLowerCase() == sIdentity) {
          aRandom[nRandom].sortOrder = sText.toLowerCase();
          break;
        }
      }
    }
    // Just sort by the natural order rather than random
    aRandom.sort(function(a,b) {
      if (a.sortOrder < b.sortOrder) { return -1 }
      if (b.sortOrder < a.sortOrder) { return 1 }
      if (b.sortOrder == a.sortOrder) { return 0 }
    } );

    // Update the randoms for updating on next
    bSuccess = wscScripting.setChoiceRandomizationItems(oQuestion, aRandom, 0);
  }
}
args.isValid = true;
```

The columns will appear in alphabetical order:

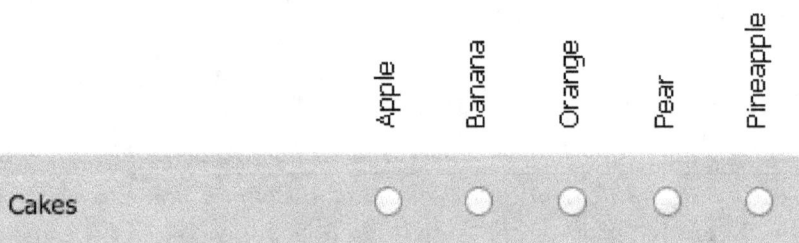

Choices are the same for all question types - but matrix questions also have **rows**. Managing rows is similar to choices - you just need to use the right functions that relate to rows...

We want to...	Key script Fragment...
Get the rows for a question	wscScripting.getRowRandomizationItems
Save the rows for a question back to the survey	wscScripting.setRowRandomizationItems

This is the script we use to sort rows:

```
var oQuestion;
var aRandom;
var bSuccess;

// Single Matrix
oQuestion = wscScripting.getQuestionByDataPipingCode('MATRIXSINGLE');
if (oQuestion) {

  aRandom = wscScripting.getRowRandomizationItems(oQuestion);
  if (aRandom) {
    // Get the title from the row
    for(var nRow = 0;nRow < oQuestion.rows.length;nRow++) {
      var oRow = oQuestion.rows[nRow];
      var sText = oRow.text;
      var sIdentity = oRow.identity;
      for(var nRandom = 0;nRandom < aRandom.length;nRandom++) {
        if (aRandom[nRandom].identity.toLowerCase() == sIdentity) {
          aRandom[nRandom].sortOrder = sText.toLowerCase();
          break;
        }
      }
    }


    // Sort it
    aRandom.sort(function(a,b) {
      if (a.sortOrder < b.sortOrder) { return -1 }
      if (b.sortOrder < a.sortOrder) { return 1 }
      if (b.sortOrder == a.sortOrder) { return 0 }
    } );

    // Update the randoms for updating on next
    bSuccess = wscScripting.setRowRandomizationItems(oQuestion, aRandom);
  }
}

args.isValid = true;
```

The question will then look as follows - with both rows and coumns in alphabetical order:

What is your favorite fruit for the following?

	Apple	Banana	Orange	Pear	Pineapple
Because you are hungry	○	○	○	○	○
Cakes	○	○	○	○	○
Juice Drinking	○	○	○	○	○
Late night snack	○	○	○	○	○

Dual Range Matrix

We have already seen how choices can be retrieved and saved for a single range matrix. We get the choices as follows:

```
aRandom = wscScripting.getChoiceRandomizationItems(oQuestion, 0);
```

And to save choices we do the following:

```
bSuccess = wscScripting.setChoiceRandomizationItems(oQuestion, aRandom, 0);
```

So how do we get to the second matrix in a dual range matrix?

The answer to this can be seen in the two lines above. If you are dealing with any question type <u>except</u> a dual range matrix, the "range" that will be dealt with is the first matrix - designated by a zero (0) in the function call:

```
wscScripting.getChoiceRandomizationItems(oQuestion, 0)

wscScripting.setChoiceRandomizationItems(oQuestion, aRandom, 0)
```

For a dual range matrix, if we want to load and save the choices from the second matrix, we enter one (1) in the function call:

```
wscScripting.getChoiceRandomizationItems(oQuestion, 1)

wscScripting.setChoiceRandomizationItems(oQuestion, aRandom, 1)
```

Scripting Reference

Web Survey Creator provides specific objects and methods for use in scripting.

This chapter is a reference guide for these objects and methods.

Scripting Objects

When a custom JavaScript is executed you will have access to two objects. These objects allow you access to the questions that are exposed on the current page and additional help methods that can help you to perform various tasks.

args

wscScripting

args

args contains a single item isValid that can be used to set the status of an event. This is particularly relevant for confirming to the event engine that you wish to continue the current process. For example, you must set the value to true on Next or Previous Button events or those processes halted and will not continue.

Property:	isValid
Return Value:	boolean - Is the current process Valid

Example:	var isOkay = true;
	
	if (isOkay) {
	
	    // All my changes allow me to continue
	    args.isValid = true;
	
	}

wscScripting

The following methods available in the wscScripting object. Some methods contain a method and an identical method post-fixed with the number 2. These methods are used where the question has two (2) choice ranges.

For example, Dual Range Matrix questions consist of a Primary Range and a Secondary Range.

In these circumstances the Secondary Range can be utilized by using the methods with a post-fix of 2. For example. getChoiceByValue2(question, value). In this document methods post-fixed with a number of 2 will be documented only in their primary method. Each method explanation will denote if the method has a second range capability.

A listing of the methods available for the wscScripting object are shown below. Detailed explanations are provided in the next section.

clearValidation(question)

derankChoice(question, choice)

deselectChoice(question, choice)

deselectChoice2(question, choice)

deselectChoiceByValue(question, value)

```
deselectChoiceByValue2(question, value)

getChoiceRandomizationItems(question, matrixnumber)

getRowRandomizationItems(question)

getPageRandomizationItems()

deselectMatrixChoice(question, choice, row)

disableQuestion(question)

enableQuestion(question)

getABTesting()

getBrowserData()

getChoiceByTagValue(question, tagName, value)

getChoiceByTagValue2(question, tagName, value)

getChoiceByValue(question, value)

getChoiceByValue2(question, value)

getDateStringFromDate(date)

getDirection()

getDisplayType()

getDistribution()

getElementById(id)

getEventData(name)

getLanguageId()

getQuestionByDataPipingCode(dataPipingCode)

getQuestionByIdentity(identity)

getQuotaByCode(code)

getQuotaByIdentity(identity)

getRecallCode()

getRowByTagValue(question, tagName, value)

getSelectedChoices(question)
```

```
getSelectedChoices2(question)
getSelectedMatrixChoices(question, row)
getSelectedMatrixChoices2(question, row)
getSelectedRanks(question)
getSubstringLeft(str, n)
getSubstringRight(str, n)
getTrimString(str)
getValidators(question)
getValue(question)
hideElement(element)
isAnyChoiceSelected(question, choices)
isAnyChoiceSelected2(question, choices)
isAnyChoiceSelectedByValue(question, values)
isAnyChoiceSelectedByValue2(question, values)
isAnyMatrixChoiceSelected(question, choices, row)
isAnyMatrixChoiceSelected2(question, choices, row)
isAnyMatrixChoiceSelectedByValue(question, values, row)
isAnyMatrixChoiceSelectedByValue2(question, values, row)
isChoiceSelected(question, choice)
isChoiceSelected2(question, choice)
isChoiceSelectedByValue(question, value)
isChoiceSelectedByValue2(question, value)
isMatrixChoiceSelected(question, choice, row)
isMatrixChoiceSelected2(question, choice, row)
isMatrixChoiceSelectedByValue(question, value, row)
isMatrixChoiceSelectedByValue2(question, value, row)
rankChoice(question, choice, rank)
```

```
selectChoice(question, choice)

selectChoice2(question, choice)

setChoiceRandomizationItems(question,choices,matrixnumber)

setRowRandomizationItems(question,rows)

setPageRandomizationItems(pages)

selectChoiceByValue(question, value)

selectChoiceByValue2(question, value)

selectMatrixChoice(question, choice, row)

selectMatrixChoice2(question, choice, row)

selectMatrixChoiceByValue(question, value, row)

selectMatrixChoiceByValue2(question, value, row)

setEventData(name, value)

setValidation(question, text)

setValue(question, value)

showElement(element)
```

Function Reference

Method: **clearValidation(question)**

Parameters: question object - object of the question
Return Value: Nil
Example:
```
var question = wscScripting.getQuestionByDataPipingCode('mydatapipingcode');
if (question) {
    wscScripting.clearValidation(question);
}
```

Method: **derankChoice(question, choice)**

Parameters: question object - object of the question
choice object - object of a choice
Return Value: Nil
Example:
```
var question = wscScripting.getQuestionByDataPipingCode('mydatapipingcode');
if (question) {
    var choice = wscScripting.getChoiceByValue(question, 1);
    if (choice) {

        wscScripting.derankChoice(question, choice);
    }
}
```

Method: **deselectChoice(question, choice)**
                                    second range
Parameters: question object - object of the question
choice object - object of a choice
Return Value: boolean - confirmation that the choice was deselected
Example:
```
var question = wscScripting.getQuestionByDataPipingCode('mydatapipingcode');
if (question) {
    var choice = wscScripting.getChoiceByValue(question, 1);
    if (choice) {

        var isUnselected = wscScripting.deselectChoice(question, choice);
    }
}
```

Method:	**deselectChoiceByValue(question, number)** second range
Parameters:	question object - object of the question number - value of the question choice to check
Return Value:	boolean - confirmation that the choice was deselected
| Example: | ```
var question = wscScripting.getQuestionByDataPipingCode('mydatapipingcode');
if (question) {

    var isUnselected = wscScripting.deselectChoiceByValue(question, 1);
}
``` |

Method:	**deselectMatrixChoice(question, choice, row)** second range
Parameters:	question object - object of the question choice object - object of a choice row object - object of a row
Return Value:	boolean - confirmation that the choice was deselected
| Example: | ```
var question = wscScripting.getQuestionByDataPipingCode('mydatapipingcode');
if (question) {
    var row = wscScripting.getRowByTagValue(question, 'bankcode', 'AMER');
    if (row) {

        var choice = wscScripting.getChoiceByValue(question, 1);
        if (choice) {

            var isUnselected = wscScripting.deselectMatrixChoice(question, choice, row);
        }
    }
}
``` |

Method:	**disableQuestion(question)** second range
Parameters:	question object - object of the question
Return Value:	boolean - confirmation that the choice was disabled
| Example: | ```
var question = wscScripting.getQuestionByDataPipingCode('mydatapipingcode');
if (question) {
    var isDisabled = wscScripting.disabledQuestion(question);
}
``` |

Method:	**enableQuestion(question)** second range
Parameters:	question object - object of the question
Return Value:	boolean - confirmation that the choice was enabled
| Example: | ```
var question = wscScripting.getQuestionByDataPipingCode('mydatapipingcode');
if (question) {
    var isDisabled = wscScripting.enabledQuestion(question);
}
``` |

Method:	**getABTesting()**
Parameters:	Nil
Return Value:	integer - Value (range 1..100) of for use by AB Testing
Example:	`var ABTest = wscScripting.getABTesting();`
	`if (ABTest <= 50) { // Split 50:50`
	`}`

Method:	**getBrowserData()**
Parameters:	Nil
Return Value:	object - Browser Object
	o.browser = Browser Name
	o.version = Browser Version
	o.OS = Operating System
Example:	`var browser = wscScripting.getBrowserData();`
	`if (browser.OS == 'Windows') { // The respondent is on a Windows computer`
	`}`

Method:	**getChoiceByTagValue(question, tagName, value)** second range
Parameters:	question object - object of the question
	string - name of the tag to search for
	string - value of the tag being searched
Return Value:	object or undefined
Example:	`var question = wscScripting.getQuestionByDataPipingCode('mydatapipingcode');`
	`if (question) {`
	`    var choice = wscScripting.getChoiceByTagValue(question, 'position', 'Manager');`
	`        if (choice) {`
	`            // I can do something with this choice`
	`        }`
	`}`

312 Scripting Reference

Method:	**getChoiceByValue(question, value)**
	second range
Parameters:	question object - object of the question
	number - value of the question choice to retrieve
Return Value:	object or undefined
| Example: | ```
var question = wscScripting.getQuestionByDataPipingCode('mydatapipingcode');
if (question) {

    var choice = wscScripting.getChoiceByValue(question, 1);
    if (choice) {

        // I can do something with this choice
    }
}
``` |

Method:	**getDateStringFromDate(date)**
Parameters:	Date = Value of Date type to be converted to a string in format usable by WSC
Return Value:	string = Newly created string in format of YYYY.MM.DD.HH.mm
| Example: | ```
var newDate = new Date();
var newString = wscScripting.getDateStringFromDate(newDate);

// newString contains today's date
// e.g. 2012.01.31.16.24
``` |

Method:	**getDirection()**
Parameters:	Nil
Return Value:	string containing:-
	ltr = Left to Right
	rtl = Right to Left e.g. Arabic
| Example: | ```
var direction = wscScripting.getLanguageId();

if (direction == 'rtl') {

    // This is a survey using a RTL language
}
``` |

Method:	**getDisplayType()**
Parameters:	Nil
Return Value:	string containing:-
	standard = Standard Display
	tablet = Tablet Computer e.g. iPad
	mobile = Mobile Phone / Cellular Phone e.g. iPhone
| Example: | ```
var display = wscScripting.getDisplayType();

if (display == 'tablet') {

    // This is a tablet based display
}
``` |

Method:	**getDistribution()**
Parameters:	Nil
Return Value:	object or undefined
Example:	`var object = wscScripting.getDistribution();`

```
if (object) {

    // I can do something with this object
}
```

Method:	**getElementById(id)**
Parameters:	string - Identity of an Html Element
Return Value:	object or undefined
Example:	`var object = wscScripting.getElementById('mycontrol');` `if (object) {`

```
        // I can do something with this element
}
```

Method:	**getEventData(name)**
Parameters:	string - Identity of an item of data temporarily stored for later use on the current page only
Return Value:	value or undefined
Example:	`var object = wscScripting.getEventData('myvalue');` `if (object) {`

```
        // I can do something with this value
        // Value contains the text 'Hello World!'
}
```

Method:	**getLanguageId()**
Parameters:	Nil
Return Value:	string - Two Character Language Code
Example:	`var language = wscScripting.getLanguageId();`

```
if (language == 'fr') {

        // This is a survey using French Language

}
```

Method:	**getQuestionByDataPipingCode(dataPipingCode)**
Parameters:	string - Data Piping Code of a Question - Must be a WSC Data Piping Code. If the question is not on the current page then you should use a Data Piping ShortCut to include the question on the current page
Return Value:	object or undefined
Example:	

```
// Using a data piping code
var object =
wscScripting.getQuestionByDataPipingCode('mydatapipingcode');
if (object) {

        // I can do something with this question
}

// Using a data piping symbol if the Question is not on the same page

// The data piping symbol with the code #data# is required to
// tell the system to have the question available
var object2 =
wscScripting.getQuestionByDataPipingCode('[@mydatapipingcode#data#@]');
if (object2) {

        // I can do something with this question
}
```

Method:	**getQuestionByIdentity(identity)**
Parameters:	string - Identity of a Question - Must be a WSC internal identity
Return Value:	object or undefined
Example:	

```
var object = wscScripting.getQuestionByIdentity('61ce3764-1288-
e111-8eae-0019b9c4ecf3');
if (object) {

        // I can do something with this question
}
```

Method:	**getQuotaByCode(code)**
Parameters:	string - Code of the Quota
Return Value:	quota object - object of the quota
Example:	`var oQuota = wscScripting.getQuotaByCode('GENDER');`

Method:	**getQuotaByIdentity(identity)**
Parameters:	string - Identity of a Quota - Must be a WSC internal identity
Return Value:	quota object - object of the quota
Example:	

```
var object = wscScripting.getQuotaByIdentity('61ce3764-1288-
e111-8eae-0019b9c4ecf3);
if (object) {

        // I can do something with this quota
}
```

Method:	**getRecallCode()**
Parameters:	Nil
Return Value:	string - Unique Code which identifies the response
Example:	`var recallCode = wscScripting.getRecallCode();`

Method:	**getRowByTagValue(question, tagName, value)**
Parameters:	question object - object of the question string - name of the tag to search for string - value of the tag being searched
Return Value:	object or undefined
| Example: | ```
var question = wscScripting.getQuestionByDataPipingCode('mydatapipingcode');
if (question) {

        var row = wscScripting.getRowByTagValue(question, 'bankcode', 'AMER');
        if (row) {

                // I can do something with this row
        }
}
``` |

Method:	**getSelectedChoices(question)** second range
Parameters:	question object - object of the question
Return Value:	array or undefined
| Example: | ```
var question = wscScripting.getQuestionByDataPipingCode('mydatapipingcode');
if (question) {

        var selectedChoices = wscScripting.getSelectedChoices(question);
        if (selectedChoices) {

                // I can do something with this array
        }
}
``` |

Method:	**getSelectedMatrixChoices(question, row)**
	second range
Parameters:	question object - object of the question
	row object - object of a row
Return Value:	array or undefined
| Example: | ```js
var question = wscScripting.getQuestionByDataPipingCode('mydatapipingcode');
if (question) {

    var row = wscScripting.getRowByTagValue(question, 'bankcode', 'AMER');
    if (row) {

        var selectedChoices = wscScripting.getSelectedMatrixChoices(question, row);
        if (selectedChoices) {

            // I can do something with this array
        }
    }
}
``` |

Method:	**getSelectedRanks(question)**
Parameters:	question object - object of the question
Return Value:	array or undefined
| Example: | ```js
var question = wscScripting.getQuestionByDataPipingCode('mydatapipingcode');
if (question) {

    var ranks = wscScripting.getSelectedRanks(question);

}
``` |

Method:	**getSubstringLeft(string, number)**
Parameters:	string = Base string from which a new string will be extracted
	number = Number of Characters from the Left side of the string to be extracted
Return Value:	string = Newly extracted string
| Example: | ```js
var newString = wscScripting.getSubstringLeft('Hello World!', 5);

// newString contains 'Hello'
``` |

Method:	**getSubstringRight(string, number)**
Parameters:	string = Base string from which a new string will be extracted
	number = Number of Characters from the Right side of the string to be extracted
Return Value:	string = Newly extracted string
| Example: | ```js
var newString = wscScripting.getSubstringLeft('Hello World!', 5);

// newString contains 'orld!'
``` |

Method:	**getTrimString(string)**
Parameters:	string = Base string from which a new string will be created with spaces at either end of the string removed
Return Value:	string = Newly created string

Example:	`var newString = wscScripting.getTrimString('   Hello World!   ');`
	
	`// newString contains 'Hello World!'`

Method:	**getValidators(question)**
Parameters:	question object - object of the question
Return Value:	array

Example:	`Var question = wscScripting.getQuestionByDataPipingCode('mydatapipingcode');`
	`if (question) {`
	
	`    var validators = wscScripting.getValidators(question);`
	`    if (validators) {`
	
	`        // I can do something with this array of validators`
	`    }`
	`}`

Method:	**getValue(question)**
Parameters:	question object - object of the question
Return Value:	value or undefined dependent on the question type value only suitable for SingleText, MultipleText, DemographicEmail, DemographicPhone, Number, Slider and DateTime Questions

Example:	`Var question = wscScripting.getQuestionByDataPipingCode('mydatapipingcode');`
	`if (question) {`
	
	`    var value = wscScripting.getValue(question);`
	`}`

Method:	**hideElement(string)**
Parameters:	string = id of an Html control to hide
Return Value:	boolean - confirmation that the control was hidden
Example:	`wscScripting.hideElement('mydiv');`

Method:	**isAnyQuestionChoiceSelected(question, choices)** second range
Parameters:	question object - object of the question array - array of choice objects to check
Return Value:	boolean - confirmation that the choice is selected
| Example: | ```js
var question = wscScripting.getQuestionByDataPipingCode('mydatapipingcode');
if (question && question.choices) {
    // Make an array of just 1 choice

    var arrayChoices = new Array();

    arrayChoices.push(question.choices[0]);

    var isSelected = wscScripting.isAnyQuestionChoiceSelected(question, arrayChoices);
}
``` |

Method:	**isAnyQuestionChoiceSelectedByValue(question, values)** second range
Parameters:	question object - object of the question array - array of number values to check
Return Value:	boolean - confirmation that the choice is selected
| Example: | ```js
var question = wscScripting.getQuestionByDataPipingCode('mydatapipingcode');
if (question && question.choices) {
    // Make an array of values

    var arrayChoices = new Array(1, 2, 3);

    var isSelected = wscScripting.isAnyQuestionChoiceSelectedByValue(question, arrayChoices);
}
``` |

Method:	**isAnyQuestionMatrixChoiceSelected(question, choices)**
	<div align="center">second range</div>
Parameters:	question object - object of the question
	array - array of choice objects to check
	row object - object of the row
Return Value:	boolean - confirmation that the choice is selected
Example:	

```
var question = wscScripting.getQuestionByDataPipingCode('mydatapipingcode');
if (question && question.choices) {
        var row = wscScripting.getRowByTagValue(question, 'bankcode', 'AMER');
        if (row) {

                // Make an array of just 1 choice

                var arrayChoices = new Array();

                arrayChoices.push(question.choices[0]);

                var isSelected = wscScripting.isAnyQuestionChoiceSelected(question, arrayChoices);

        }

}
```

Method:	**isAnyQuestionMatrixChoiceSelectedByValue(question, values, row)**
	<div align="center">second range</div>
Parameters:	question object - object of the question
	array - array of number values to check
	row object - object of the row
Return Value:	boolean - confirmation that the choice is selected
Example:	

```
var question = wscScripting.getQuestionByDataPipingCode('mydatapipingcode');
if (question && question.choices) {
        var row = wscScripting.getRowByTagValue(question, 'bankcode', 'AMER');
        if (row) {

                // Make an array of values

                var arrayChoices = new Array(1, 2, 3);

                var isSelected = wscScripting.isAnyQuestionMatrixChoiceSelectedByValue(question,

                                        arrayChoices, row);

        }

}
```

Method:	**isQuestionChoiceSelected(question, choice)** second range
Parameters:	question object - object of the question choice object - object of a choice
Return Value:	boolean - confirmation that the choice is selected
| Example: | ```
var question = wscScripting.getQuestionByDataPipingCode('mydatapipingcode');
if (question) {

    var choice = wscScripting.getChoiceByValue(question, 1);
    if (choice) {

        var isSelected = wscScripting.isQuestionChoiceSelected(question, choice);

    }
}
``` |

Method:	**isQuestionChoiceSelectedByValue(question, value)** second range
Parameters:	question object - object of the question number - value of the question choice to check
Return Value:	boolean - confirmation that the choice is selected
| Example: | ```
var question = wscScripting.getQuestionByDataPipingCode('mydatapipingcode');
if (question) {

    var isSelected = wscScripting.isQuestionChoiceSelectedByValue(question, 1);
}
``` |

Method:	**isQuestionMatrixChoiceSelected(question, choice, row)** second range
Parameters:	question object - object of the question choice object - object of a choice row object - object of the row
Return Value:	boolean - confirmation that the choice is selected
| Example: | ```
var question = wscScripting.getQuestionByDataPipingCode('mydatapipingcode');
if (question) {

    var choice = wscScripting.getChoiceByValue(question, 1);
    if (choice) {

        var row = wscScripting.getRowByTagValue(question, 'bankcode', 'AMER');
        if (row) {

            var isSelected = wscScripting.isQuestionMatrixChoiceSelected(question, choice, row);
        }

    }
}
``` |
```

Method: **isQuestionMatrixChoiceSelectedByValue(question, value, row)**
second range
Parameters: question object - object of the question
number - value of the question choice to check
row object - object of the row
Return Value: boolean - confirmation that the choice is selected
Example:
```
var question = wscScripting.getQuestionByDataPipingCode('mydatapipingcode');
if (question) {

	var row = wscScripting.getRowByTagValue(question, 'bankcode', 'AMER');
	if (row) {

		var isSelected = wscScripting.isQuestionChoiceSelectedByValue(question, 1, row);
	}
}
```

Method: **selectChoice(question, choice)**
second range
Parameters: question object - object of the question
choice object - object of a choice
Return Value: boolean - confirmation that the choice was selected
Example:
```
var question = wscScripting.getQuestionByDataPipingCode('mydatapipingcode');
if (question) {
	var choice = wscScripting.getChoiceByValue(question, 1);
	if (choice) {

		var isSelected = wscScripting.selectChoice(question, choice);
	}
}
```

Method: **selectChoiceByValue(question, number)**
second range
Parameters: question object - object of the question
number - value of the question choice to check
Return Value: boolean - confirmation that the choice was selected
Example:
```
var question = wscScripting.getQuestionByDataPipingCode('mydatapipingcode');
if (question) {

	var isSelected = wscScripting.selectChoiceByValue(question, 1);
}
```

Method:	**selectMatrixChoice(question, choice, row)** second range
Parameters:	question object - object of the question choice object - object of a choice row object - object of a row
Return Value:	boolean - confirmation that the choice was selected
| Example: | ```
var question = wscScripting.getQuestionByDataPipingCode('mydatapipingcode');
if (question) {
    var row = wscScripting.getRowByTagValue(question, 'bankcode', 'AMER');
    var choice = wscScripting.getChoiceByValue(question, 1);
    if (row && choice) {
        var isSelected = wscScripting.selectMatrixChoice(question, choice, row);
    }
}
``` |

Method:	**setEventData(name, value)**
Parameters:	string - Identity of an item of data temporarily stored for later use on the current page only object - Value of an item of data temporarily stored for later use on the current page only
Return Value:	boolean - confirmation that the value was correctly added
Example:	`wscScripting.setEventData('myvalue', 'Hello World!');`

Method:	**setValidation(question, text)**
Parameters:	question object - object of the question string - text of the validation message
Return Value:	Nil
| Example: | ```
var question = wscScripting.getQuestionByDataPipingCode('mydatapipingcode');
if (question) {
    wscScripting.setValidation(question, 'Something doesnt make sense!');
}
``` |

Method:	**setValue(question, value)**
Parameters:	question object - object of the question value - type dependent on question type value only suitable for SingleText, MultipleText, DemographicEmail, DemographicPhone, Number, Slider and DateTime Questions
Return Value:	Nil
| Example: | ```
var question = wscScripting.getQuestionByDataPipingCode('mydatapipingcode');
if (question) {
    wscScripting.setValue(question, 'Hello World!');
}
``` |

Scripting Reference 323
```

Method:	**showElement(string)**
Parameters:	string = id of an Html control to show
Return Value:	boolean - confirmation that the control was shown
Example:	wscScripting.showElement('mydiv');

Additional Objects

The following objects exist and have the properties as described with *type* and *name*.

Note: You do not have the ability to affect the rendering of a standard question by altering a property.

SurveyQuestion

string **addressType**

string **allRankedText**

array [surveychoice] **choices**

array [surveychoice] **choices2**

string **clearText**

string **containerName**

string **dataPipingCode**

number **defaultValue**

string **fieldWidth1**

string **fieldWidth2**

string **formatType**

string **gridHeadingFormat**

number **gridTotal**

string **identity**

number **increment**

number **interval**

boolean **isCommentsEnabledByDefault**

boolean **isHeadingTextVertical**

boolean **isLargeComments**

boolean **isLength**

boolean **isMandatory**

boolean **isPivot**

boolean **isQuestionOnPage**

boolean **isResetAllowed**

boolean **isSpecify**

string **javascriptBodyName**

string **listDirection**

string **listType**

number **maxIncrement**

number **maxValue**

number **minValue**

string **noneRankedText**

number **numberGrids**

string **popupType**

string **primaryRangeTitle**

string **questionNumber**

string **rankedText**

number **repeatRows**

string **resetText**

string **rowHeight1**

string **rowHeight2**

array [surveyrow] **rows**

number **scaleIncrement**

string **secondaryRangeTitle**

string **text**

string **textPosition**

string **type**

string **unRankedText**

SurveyChoice

number **grid**

string **identity**

string **imageHeight**

string **imageToolTip**

string **imageUrl**

string **imageWidth**

boolean **isComments**

boolean **isDefault**

boolean **isExclusive**

boolean **isPegged**

string **labelText**

string **numberPostText**

string **numberPreText**

array [surveychoicetag] **tags**

string **text**

number **value**

SurveyChoiceTag

string **identity**

string **name**

string **text**

SurveyRow

string **identity**

string **imageHeight**

string **imageToolTip**

string **imageUrl**

string **imageWidth**

array [surveyrowtag] **tags**

string **text**

SurveyHierarchicalListItem

string **identity**

string **description**

string parent **Identity**

SurveyRowTag

string **identity**

string **name**

string **text**

SurveyQuota

string **code**

string **identity**

bool **isPriority**

int **numberLimit**

int **numberAllowed**

int **numberResponded**

int **numberOverflow**

string **title**

SurveyDistribution

string **identity**

array [surveydistributiontag] **tags**

string **title**

SurveyDistributionTag

string **identity**

string **name**

string **text**

Browser

string **browser**

string **OS**

string **version**